New Exodus in Hebrews

Bong Chur Shin

WIPF & STOCK · Eugene, Oregon

Wipf and Stock Publishers
199 W 8th Ave, Suite 3
Eugene, OR 97401

New Exodus in Hebrews
By Shin, Bong Chur
Copyright©2016 Apostolos
ISBN 13: 978-1-5326-6986-6
Publication date 9/23/2018
Previously published by Apostolos, 2016

Acknowledgements

To God be all the glory for his grace and blessing upon me during my research work for the PhD degree in Wales.

I would like to thank, first of all, Dr. Tom Holland, who has helped and encouraged me to develop this research. I would also like to thank Dr. Eryl Davies, the recently retired principal of the Evangelical Theological College of Wales. My appreciation is to be extended to Professor D. P. Davies for his guidance and kindness.

I also greatly appreciate the kind support of the members of the Gasil Presbyterian Church. In addition, I thank my brother, elder Won-min Shin and my friend Dr Ki hyung Kim, Mrs. Nan hee Do, Mrs. Eun hwa Shin and Mrs. Ock sook Lee.

Finally, I wish to express my deepest awareness of my debt to my wife, Jung-Hee, who has dedicated her life for my work, to my daughter Hanna and my son Isaac, who have been very patient and given me energy to finish this study.

Sola Deo Gloria

Abbreviations

AB	Anchor Bible
ABD	The Anchor Bible Dictionary, Edited by D. N. Freedman. 6 Vols. (Garden City, NY: Doubleday, 1992)
BibSac	Bibliotheca Sacra
BNTC	Black's New Testament Commentary
BT	The Banner of Truth
CBQ	Catholic Biblical Quarterly
CGTC	Cambridge Greek Testament Commentary
CQR	Church Quarterly Review
CTJ	Calvin Theological Journal
EIATS	Ecumenical Institute for Advanced Theological Studies
EQ	Evangelical Quarterly
ERT	Evangelical Review of Theology
ExpT	Expository Times
GTJ	Grace Theological Journal
HTR	Harvard Theological Review
ICC	International Critical Commentary
Int	Interpretation
JBL	Journal of Biblical Literature
JETS	Journal of Evangelical Theological Society
JSNT	Journal of the Study of the New Testament
JSOT	Journal of the Study of the Old Testament
JTS	Journal of Theological Studies
NAC	The New American Commentary

Neot	*Neotestamentica*
NICNT	*The New International Commentary on the New Testament*
NICOT	*The New International Commentary on the Old Testament*
NIGC	*New International Greek Commentary*
NovT	*Novum Testamentum*
NovTSup	*Novum Testamentum, Supplements*
NTC	*New Testament Commentary*
NTS	*New Testament Studies*
OC	*One in Christ*
RevExp	*Review & Expositor*
RTJ	*Reformed Theological Journal*
RTR	*Reformed Theological Review*
SBET	*Scottish Bulletin of Evangelical Theology*
SBL	*Society of Biblical Literature*
SBLMS	*Society of Biblical Literature Monograph Series*
SBT	*Studies in Biblical Theology*
SJT	*Scottish Journal of Theology*
SNTSMS	*Society for New Testament Studies Monograph Series*
TDNT	*Theological Dictionary of the New Testament*
TDOT	*Theological Dictionary of the Old Testament*
Th.T	*Theology Today*
TrinJ	*Trinity Journal*
Tynb	*Tyndale Bulletin*
VoxEv	*Vox Evangelica*
VT	*Vetus Testamentum*

VTSup	*Vetus Testamentum, Supplements*
WBC	*World Biblical Commentary*
WTJ	*Westminster Theological Journal*
ZAW	*Zeitschrift für die Alttestamentliche Wissenschaft*

Abstract

This study examines the new exodus expectations raised by the Old Testament prophets in Second Temple Judaism. It has been lately accepted that these expectations resulted in the aspirations of intertestamental Judaism which were known to, and utilized by, the writers and the first readers of the New Testament documents. With this in mind, I shall examine the Epistle to the Hebrews to see in what ways (if any) such expectations are present in the text. My conclusions demonstrate that the epistle is indeed constructed around these expectations, which I shall summarize as follows:

The epistle is built around the theme of deliverance, as promised by the prophets. The author to the Hebrews first demonstrates what such deliverance means in corporate terms and then proceeds to explain it has been fulfilled in the life and death of Christ.

The writer shows his readers that, as believers in Christ, they have a journey to endure before arriving at the goal of their salvation. This journey theme is related to that of deliverance, as I shall demonstrate by contrasting Israel's experience in the wilderness with that of the church.

The Jews in exile in Babylon were promised that they would return from the exile led by a son of David who would establish a new covenant—another theme picked up by the writer of Hebrews.

There was widespread expectation of a Messiah who would be both a king and priest as promised in the prophetic writings as part of the new exodus motif. This book explores the ministry of this priestly king and his key role in the salvation of the covenant community.

The theme of Holy Spirit is also examined. The Spirit is closely related to the new exodus. This study shows that the Spirit witnesses to his people, enabling them to obey and to live in unity and fellowship during their eschatological pilgrimage.

Contents

Acknowledgements 3

Abstract 7

Chapter 1: Introduction 12

    Introduction 12

    Summary of the New Exodus Theme in Biblical and Extra-Biblical Literature 12

        The Old Testament 14

        The Dead Sea Scrolls 15

        The Apocrypha and the Pseudepigrapha 16

        Rabbinic Writings 17

        Josephus 18

        The New Testament 18

    The Current State of New Exodus Studies in New Testament Theology 21

        New Exodus in the Gospels 21

    The Significance of the Paschal Setting in the Exodus 26

        Greco-Roman Tradition 27

        Aqedah Tradition 27

        Passover Tradition 28

    The Current State of Paschal Studies in New Testament Theology 30

Chapter 2: Summary of Earlier Scholars' Appreciation of the Presence of New Exodus Expectations in Hebrews 33

    Introduction 33

    Survey 33

    Analysis 59

Chapter 3: The Deliverance Theme 61

    Introduction 61

    Some Views of Deliverance 63

        In Hellenism 63

Gnosticism 65

Deliverance in the Old Testament 67

Deliverance in the Synoptics and the Epistles 75

Deliverance in the Epistle to the Hebrews 83

What is Deliverance in Hebrews? 83

The Deliverance of God's People Through Christ's Death 89

Deliverance from the Power of Death 95

The Corporate Nature of Deliverance 100

Conclusion 102

Excursus: The Meaning of the Paschal Lamb Implied to the Firstborn in the Passover. 103

Chapter 4: The Pilgrimage Theme 115

Introduction 115

Pilgrimage and Passover 116

Pilgrimage as an Essential Element of Israel's Obligation 116

Pilgrimage in the Psalms and Prophets 119

Pilgrimage in the Intertestamental Literature 125

Pilgrimage in Gospels and the Epistles 126

The Gospels 126

The Epistles 130

Pilgrimage in Hebrews 132

Impending Danger, but with Purpose: Heb 3–4 133

Pilgrimage in the Passover Setting 134

Pilgrimage in the Face of Impending Danger 137

Pilgrimage with Purpose 142

Summing Up 144

The Goal of Pilgrimage: Heb 12 151

Conclusion 160

Chapter 5: The New Covenant Theme 161

Introduction 161

The New Covenant and its Context 162

    The Day of Atonement Setting 162

    The Passover Setting..164

    The Nature of the New Covenant in the Passover Setting..............167

    The New Covenant Theme in the Old Testament 170

    The New Covenant in the Intertestamental Literature....................177

The New Covenant Theme in the Gospels and the Epistles 178

    The Gospels 178

    The Epistles...181

The New Covenant Theme in Hebrews 186

    Διαθήκη in the New Exodus Setting 186

    The Term "μεσίτης" in the New Covenant.......................................192

    Corporate Concept in the New Covenant 197

Conclusion 200

    Excursus: The Term "Perfection" (τελείωσις) in the Paschal Setting 201

Chapter 6: The Priestly King Theme 208

Introduction 208

Some Views of the Priestly King Theme...210

    Philo's Understanding of the Priesthood..210

    The Levitical Priesthood 212

    6.2.3 The Priesthood in Qumran 213

    The Priestly King Resulting in Deliverance 215

The Priestly King Theme in the Old Testament 218

    Genesis 218

    Psalms..219

    Chronicles...221

    Ezekiel 221

    The Priestly King Theme in the Gospels and Acts and the Epistles 224

        The Synoptic Gospels 225

        Acts 227

        John 227

        Romans 228

        Timothy 228

        Peter 229

    The Priestly King Theme in Hebrews 230

        Priestly King Relating to Deliverance 230

        Christ's Priestly Kingship in Eschatology 238

    Conclusion 250

Chapter 7: The Holy Spirit Theme 251

    Introduction 251

    Some Views Relating to the Spirit 254

        Persian Influences 255

        Philo 256

    The Holy Spirit Related to Redemption in the Passover 257

    The Spirit Theme in the Old Testament 259

        The Spirit Theme in the Intertestamental Literature 262

        The Spirit Theme in the Gospels, Acts and the Epistles 263

    The Spirit Theme in Hebrews 272

        The Spirit and Deliverance 272

        The Spirit in Eschatology 277

        The Spirit and His Corporative Presence 279

    Conclusion 281

Chapter 8: Conclusion 282

Bibliography 286

Chapter 1: Introduction

Introduction

During the exodus, the Jews experienced deliverance from bondage in Egypt and consequently, the exodus may be viewed as Israel's founding moment. Not only did it shape the national identity and character of the nation, but the later prophets of the Babylonian exile used it as the paradigm for the deliverance they announced.[1] The return of Israel from the Babylonian exile in the Old Testament was therefore portrayed as a new exodus.[2]

Not only so, but the writings of the intertestamental period were also influenced by this paradigm, so that a new exodus theme is found extensively throughout Jewish literature. It ought not to be surprising then, that this same paradigm of new exodus was picked up and utilized by the mainly Jewish New Testament writers.

In the New Testament the events of the exodus are treated as parables of Christian experience.[3] Jesus's death is referred to as his "exodus";[4] and he is the true Passover, sacrificed for his people[5] as "a lamb without blemish and without spot."[6] Christ is seen as the eschatological saviour from the power of the darkness. Thus the redemptive work of Christ is understood to by the New Testament authors to be another new exodus.

Summary of the New Exodus Theme in Biblical and Extra-Biblical Literature

Since the actual term "new exodus" was not used in Jewish literature, my assertion that it is present as a theme may at first seem controversial. Some

---

[1] M. Fishbane, *Biblical Interpretation in Ancient Israel* (New York: Oxford University Press, 1985), 356–68.

[2] R. E. Nixon, *The Exodus in the New Testament* (London: SPCK, 1963), 63. cf. Isa 41:17; 42:9; 43:16–21; 52:12.

[3] Jude draws practical lessons for his fellow-believers from the fact that "Jesus, having saved a people out of the land of Egypt, afterward destroyed them that believed not" (1:5). Paul tells the Corinthians that the record of Israel's rebellion and punishment in the wilderness has been preserved "for our admonition", lest we should imitate their disobedience and be overtaken by comparable judgment (1 Cor 10:6).

[4] Luke 9:31 (ἔξοδον).

[5] 1 Cor 5:7b (the same idea underlies the passion narrative of the Fourth Gospel).

[6] 1 Pet 1:19.

scholars regard it as a label for a Mosaic typology. Manek relates Moses to Jesus, identifying the "two men" in Luke 24:4 with Moses and Elijah.[7] Manek sees that as Moses led Israel from Egypt to the promised land, so Jesus leads the new Israel from the earthly Jerusalem to a heavenly Jerusalem.[8] Similarly, Moessner[9] and Evans[10] see it as a replay of the narrative patterns of the exodus described in Deuteronomy. Moessner points out that Luke's account of Jesus's mountain transfiguration is paralleled with the Deuteronomic account of Moses being called to mediate the voice of God on the mountain (Deut 18:15–19), thus effecting a new exodus for a renewed people of God.[11] According to Moessner, the pattern in Luke 9 provides a preview which controls the central section of Luke. Watts challenges the claims of Moessner and Evans by saying that Luke begins the new exodus with John the Baptist's ministry in the wilderness—a parallel with Isa 40:3–5.[12] Thus Watts sees the term as a description of a post-Exilic constellation of hopes developed from Isa 40–55.[13] Whilst he does not relate it to the exodus accounts directly, he uses Isaiah's exodus typology to depict Israel's deliverance from exile. Watts concludes that Isaiah's new exodus theme is the basis for Mark's Gospel.

However, the new exodus theme is foundational to the whole of the Scriptures. Isaiah's "prophetic transformation of the past Exodus" reads the Torah as a reference to the return from captivity. The prophets announced that a new and final redemption from slavery will take place, and the New Testament claims that this redemption takes place in Jesus.

Therefore, I shall summarize the new exodus expectations derived from the Old Testament, intertestamental literature, and rabbinic literature as well as those found in the New Testament itself, to see if there are reasonable grounds

---

[7] J. Manek, "The New Exodus in the Book of Luke," *NovT* (1957), 8–23 [12].

[8] Manek, "The New Exodus in the Book of Luke," 18.

[9] D. P. Moessner, "Luke 9:1–50: Luke's Preview of the Journey of the Prophet Like Moses of Deuteronomy," *JBL* 102/4 (1983): 575–605

[10] C. F. Evans, "The Central Section of Saint Luke's Gospel," in *Studies in the Gospels: Essays in Memory of R. H. Lightfoot,* ed. D. E. Nineham (Oxford: Blackwell, 1955): 37–53. Evans points out that Luke's transfiguration account (Luke 9:28–36) launches Luke into a prolonged Deuteronomic Mosaic typology. Jesus is depicted as accomplishing a new exodus, leading Israel towards the Promised Land.

[11] Moessner, "Luke 9:1–50", 588–9.

[12] R. E. Watts, *Isaiah's New Exodus in Mark* (Grand Rapids: Baker, 1997), 82–4.

[13] Watts, *Isaiah's New Exodus in Mark,* 76–82.

for supposing that it might have been a significant influence on the thinking of the early church. I shall then evaluate the current state of these studies on the new exodus theme in the New Testament before specifically appraising the studies written on the influence of the Passover. Finally, I shall examine the studies that have considered the description of the death of Christ as Passover sacrifice.

The Old Testament

The exodus of Israel from Egypt was *the* great act of redemption within the Old Testament. Even so, the exodus event became the basis of expectation for God's future redemptive acts. In particular, when the Israelites of the northern kingdom were in exile in Assyria, and Jews of the southern kingdom were in exile in Babylon, the paradigm served to provide them with the hope of a new exodus. For this reason, the model of new exodus which they expected was from the first based on that of the exodus from Egypt.

The composer of Psalm 98 reflects on the many times when God had saved Israel. The first stanza of the Psalm is reminiscent of the exodus, the wars won under Joshua, the times God delivered Israel from foreign oppressors during the period of the judges, the deliverance from the Philistines under David, and so on, down to the time when God brought the remnant safely back from Babylon.[14]

Isaiah speaks of a new beginning—a new exodus more glorious than the old exodus from Egypt. The first exodus is the prototype for the eschatological exodus. The new exodus brings liberty to the captives,[15] and is led by a Davidic prince.[16] According to Isaiah, the eschatological king once again comes down to meet with his people. He comes awesomely and terribly,[17] but condescendingly; graciously tabernacling in the midst of his people.[18] The Lord

---

[14] T. Longman III, *How to Read the Psalms* (Leicester: IVP, 1988), 161.

[15] Isa 11:11; 48:20-21; 52:1-12; 61:1; Ezek 37:24.

[16] Isa 11:1; 55:3-4; Jer 33:14-17.

[17] Isa 29:6; 30:27-33; 50:3; 64:1-3; cf. Joel 3:16; Zech 9:14.

[18] Isa 4:6; 7:14; cf. Ezek 37:27-28.

enters into a new covenant with the eschatological pilgrims.[19] At last, the new exodus will conclude with the possession of the land.[20]

Jeremiah prophesied that the evidence of membership of the covenant community was to be the circumcised heart.[21] The promise concerning the new covenant, given during the time of Israel's deportation, is seen by the New Testament writers as being fulfilled in the person and work of Jesus the Christ and extends to the consummation of all things.[22]

Ezekiel predicted that God would give his people life as the gift of salvation.[23] The event by which Israel was given back its life was the return, which began with Cyrus's decree in 538 BC. This allowed those in Babylon who wanted to return to go back to their homeland, symbolically giving new life to "dead" Israel.

Micah points out that the wonders performed during the exodus would be repeated.[24] Zechariah along with others signified that the Davidic prince would build a new temple for the Lord and cleanse the sin of the people.[25] Hosea concludes that the second exodus would culminate in the marriage of Yahweh to his people.[26]

The Dead Sea Scrolls

The Qumran community waited for victory by a Messiah who would stand alongside the Davidic Messiah. A coming Messiah would fulfill the Isaianic prophecies and be called "the branch of David":

> [… just as it is written in the book of] Isaiah the prophet, "And [the thickets of the forest] shall be cut down (1) [with an axe, and Lebanon with its majestic trees w]ill fall. (2) A shoot shall come out from the stump of Jesse [and a branch shall grow out of his roots" (Isa 10:34–11:1). This is the] Branch of David. (3) Then [all forces of Belial] shall

---

[19] Isa 55:3; 61:8; cf. Jer 31:31–34.
[20] Isa 49:8, 9; cf. Hos 2:15.
[21] Jer 31:31–34.
[22] Jer 31:31ff; Ezek 37:26ff; cf. Luke 22:20; 2 Cor 3:6; Heb 8:8; 9:15; 10:15–18; 12:24.
[23] Ezek 37:1–14.
[24] Mic 7:15.
[25] Zech 3:9; 13:1; cf. Isa 53; Ezek 16:62–63.
[26] Hosea 2:16, 19; cf. Isa 54:1–8; 61:10.

> be judged, [and the king of the Kittim shall stand for judgment] and the Leader of the nation—the Bra[nch of David]—will have him put to death. (4) [Then all Israel shall come out with timbrel]s and dancers, (5) and the [High] Priest shall order [them to cleanse their bodies from the guilty blood of the c]orpse[s of] the Kittim.[27]

God reveals the time when the Temple will be built and tells of what the descendant of David would carry out about the community's expectation:

> He will not [abandon Zion], to make His name dwell there, the Tent of Meeting ... [to the end] of time, for look, a son is born to Jesse of Perez son of Ju[dah ... he will choose] the rock of Zion and drive out from there all the Amorites from Jeru[salem ...] to build the temple for the Lord, God of Israel, gold and silver [...] cedar and pine shall he bring from Lebanon to build it; and his younger son [shall build the temple ... and Zadok] shall serve as priest....[28]

The Damascus Document has a reference to the future spirit-empowered ministry of the Messiah: "... the Holy Spirit [sett]led upon His Messiah".[29]

Taken together, the Qumran community anticipated that the prophecies of the exilic period would yet be fulfilled in the raising up of a Davidic Messiah who would accomplish all that the prophets had foretold.[30]

The Apocrypha and the Pseudepigrapha

Cohn-Sherbok[31] has pointed out the various stages of messianic anticipation in Ben Sira 36.1–22—the destruction of Israel's enemies, the sanctification of God's name by elevating the Jewish nation, the performance of miracles, the ingathering of the exiles, the glorification of Jerusalem and the Temple, reward for the righteous and punishment for the wicked, and the fulfillment of prophetic expectations.

---

[27] 4Q285 Frag. 5.
[28] 4Q522 Frag. 1 Col 2. (p. 422; Wise & Michael)
[29] 4Q286–287.
[30] T. S. Holland, *The Paschal—New Exodus Motif in Paul's Letter to the Romans with Special Reference to its Christological Significance* (PhD diss., University of Wales, 1996), 11.
[31] D. Cohn-Sherbok, *The Jewish Messiah* (Edinburgh: T&T Clark, 1997), 23.

In Baruch, the author prophesies that God will bring about the return of the exiles to the land of their fathers once they have turned from their evil ways.[32] Furthermore, he describes how Jerusalem is to be renewed.

The Book of Jubilees not only refers to the new exodus theme, but also to messianic ideas similar to what is found in the Apocrypha. The Israelites will be punished because of the nation's sinfulness, but this will be followed by repentance, and only then Israel will be redeemed. The Lord will build his sanctuary in their midst and dwell among them:

And I will build my sanctuary in their midst, and I will dwell with them, and I will be their God and they shall be my people in truth and righteousness.[33]

The Testament of Judah also contains a vivid description of messianic redemption:[34]

A shoot will come forth from the stock of Judah and the rod of righteousness will be in his hand to judge and save all those who call upon him. Those who died in grief will arise and awake to everlasting life. The hungry will be satisfied, the poor made rich, and the weak become strong.

Rabbinic Writings

After the Second Temple had been destroyed by the Romans, the Jewish people were again driven out of their homeland. During their trials they desired a kingly figure who, drawing on messianic ideas found in Scripture, would deliver them from exile and rebuild their holy city. The Rabbinic writings repeatedly mention the exodus as a model of final redemption.[35] They taught that God would himself act on behalf of Israel. Thus in the midrash, the rabbis maintain that:

> There are four shinings forth: the first was in Egypt, as it is written (Psalm 80:1), "Give ear, O Shepherd of Israel, thou that lead Joseph like a flock, thou that art enthroned upon the cherubim, shine forth"; the second was at the time of the giving of the Law, as it is written

---

[32] Baruch 2:24–35.
[33] Jubilees 1.18
[34] Testament of the Twelve Patriarchs 25.3–4.
[35] Cohn-Sherbok, *Messiah*, 53.

(Deuteronomy 33:2), "He shone forth from Mount Paran"; the third will take place in the days of Gog and Magog, as it is written (Psalm 94:1), "Thou God to whom vengeance belongeth, shine forth"; the fourth will be in the days of the Messiah (ben David) as it is written (Psalm 50:2), "Out of Zion, the perfection of beauty, shall God shine forth."

Furthermore, Ben-Sira prays for a repetition of the signs and wonders of the exodus in a final redemption established on exodus lines. Joshua ben Hananiah assumes that the final redemption would happen on the night of Passover.[36]

Josephus

Josephus introduced the presence of the new exodus theme by telling the Theudas narrative in Antiquities. Theudas, a charlatan, told a great part of the people that he was a prophet, promising that the Jordan would divide once again.[37] The repetition of the miracle of Jericho on the walls of Jerusalem was predicted by another prophet.[38] Josephus also tells how the weaver Jonathan foretold of miracles in the wilderness.[39] He repeatedly tells how the messianic pretenders called their followers to the desert,[40] the location that popular opinion associated with the coming of eschatological salvation. This practice was founded on the historical fact that the Jews came from the wilderness following their exodus, to claim their inheritance.

The New Testament

The New Testament declares Jesus to be the promised Son of David; this is evidence of new exodus expectations. Simeon was convinced that he would not die before seeing the promised Messiah.[41] Matthew in the genealogy of Jesus Christ demonstrated him to be the offspring of David.[42] John the Baptist

---

[36] L. Goppelt, *Typos: The Typological Interpretation of the Old Testament in the New*, trans. D. H. Madvig (Grand Rapids, MI: Eerdmans, 1982), 34.
[37] Josephus, Ant. 20.5.1.
[38] Ibid., Ant. 20.8.6.
[39] Ibid.
[40] Ibid.
[41] Luke 2:26.
[42] Matthew clearly has an exodus structure, but it is not Moses who brings this deliverance about, but the son of David.

identified himself—as did the Qumranians—as a voice in the wilderness preparing the way of the Lord. Jesus himself asserted that the kingdom of heaven was at hand.[43]

Therefore, the fact that the New Testament declares Jesus to be the promised son of David must not be missed. The Messiah who was to be the promised descendant of David would have an everlasting throne.[44] The identification of Jesus with the promises relating to the Davidic deliverer is crucial to appreciate how the early church understood the person and work of its saviour.[45] The Son of David Christology represents the earliest Christology which emerges alongside the Son of Man description.

Both Jesus and the Baptist began their missions by citing Isa 40:3–5 and Isa 61:1–2.[46] Holland points out that by citing these words they were announcing that the final salvation had at last broken into human history.[47]

In Mark 13 Jesus appears himself to be a priestly king. There he seems to follow the idea which Ezekiel had outlined in Ezek 45:18–25. That is, Jesus is depicted as the priestly king for redemption.

In Luke 1:32–33, the author mentioned the characteristics of the Messiah:

> He will be great, and will be called the Son of the Most High, and the Lord God will give to him the throne of his ancestor David. He will reign over the house of Jacob forever, and of his kingdom there will be no end (Luke 1:32–33).

In Acts 2:17 the outpouring of the Spirit is linked to the arrival of the eschatological age as described in Joel 2:28. The outpouring of the Spirit at Pentecost is a decisive sign of the eschatological events which proceed the day of the Lord as the mark of the new exodus. Pao links the Pentecost event in Acts 2 to the Sinai tradition of the giving of the Law to emphasize the

---

[43] C. F. Pfeiffer, *The Dead Sea Scrolls and the Bible* (Grand Rapids: Baker, 1969), 128.
[44] Its Old Testament basis is in such passages as 2 Sam 7:16; Ps 89:3, 19; Isa 11:1, 10; Jer 23:5; 30:9; Ezek 34:23; 37:24.
[45] W. Kramer, *Christ, Lord, Son of God* (London: SCM Press, 1966), 241. The title 'Son of David' affected the primitive Christology of Acts.
[46] Cf. Isa 40:3–5 in Luke 3:4–6; Matt 3:3; Mark 1:2–3. Isa 61:1–2 in Luke 4:18–19. Isaiah predicted the eschatological salvation.
[47] Holland, *Paschal,* 14.

importance of the event as the dawn of a new era which brings about the reconstitution of the people of God.[48]

The pilgrimage theme is also widely acknowledged in the New Testament.[49] This pilgrimage is emphasized by reminders of Jesus's final journey to Jerusalem, which becomes the dominant image of discipleship for the eschatological salvation. In Acts 7 Stephen's speech recounts the exodus journeying with Moses in order to present the essential heritage of the church as well as justifying its existence during one of the most critical stages of the community's early history.

In Mark 14:24 Jesus described the wine in the cup as his blood of the διαθήκης. It seems that Jesus conceived of his messianic work, fulfilled in his death, from the point of view of the fulfillment of the eschatological διαθήκης based on both Exod 24:8 and Jer 31:31.

To sum up, a new exodus theme is basic for all Scripture. Watts points out that Isaiah's exodus typology is used for depicting Israel's deliverance from exile, because he does not see the importance of the first exodus. Rather the new exodus results from merger of both the exodus from Egypt and the exodus from Babylon.[50] The former focuses on the paschal sacrifice to interpret the death of Jesus for deliverance; the latter introduces the promises of the prophets of a new covenant to produce a new exodus paradigm. It has been pointed out, therefore, that new exodus themes throughout the New Testament are "eschatological redemption,[51] the new Covenant,[52] outpouring of the Spirit,[53] pilgrimage,[54] [and] the priestly kingship."[55]

---

[48] D. W. Pao, *Acts and the Isaianic new exodus* (Grand Rapids: Baker, 2000), 131.

[49] F. V. Filson, "The Journey Motif in Luke-Acts," in *Apostolic History and the Gospel: Biblical and Historical Essays Presented to F. F. Bruce on the 60th Birthday*, ed. W. W. Gasque and R. P. Martin (Exeter: Paternoster, 1970), 68–77.

[50] T. Holland, *Contours of Pauline Theology: A Radical New Survey of the Influences on Paul's Biblical Writings* (Fearn: Christian Focus, 2004), 153–4.

[51] Mark 10:45; Rom 3:23–25; Heb 9.

[52] 2 Cor 3:6; 5:17; 6:16–18; Heb 8:8–13.

[53] Rom 8:9–27; Gal 4:6–7; 2 Cor 3:16–17; 4:6–7; Eph 1:13–14.

[54] Gal 5:18, 25; 2 Cor 5:1–5; Eph 6:13–17; Phil 3:12–14; Heb 3:7–4:11; 12:1–3, 18–28.

[55] Mark 12:35–40; Acts 5:31–32; John 17, passim; Rom 8:34–35; 1 Pet 3:21–22.

The Current State of New Exodus Studies in New Testament Theology

There is a growing interest in the new exodus motif. The following discussion examines how the New Testament is being read in the light of new exodus.

New Exodus in the Gospels

Matthew

Johnston examined the Old Testament background of Matt 2–4. He understood that in Matthew Israel's redemptive history is repeated in the person who represents the new Israel, the Messiah Jesus.[56] In Micah's promises, the one who would restore Israel's dominion was a new David. This is described by Isaiah, Jeremiah, Hosea, and Ezekiel as a new exodus. Johnston focused on Israel's saviour, but he failed to explore the death of Christ in the light of the Passover which was the clear setting of Jesus himself provided for its significance (Matt 26:17–19, 26–29).

Dennison saw that the transition from slavery to freedom performed in the Old Testament must be linked with the transition from death to life spoken in the New Testament.[57] He regarded Isa 53 as referring to vicarious suffering that would be the ransom-price of the people of God in the new exodus. He associated the innocent victim with Jesus, and understood that the new covenant was sealed by a fellowship Supper.[58] However, Dennison failed to observe the presence of references which reflect the promises of the Davidic prince being fulfilled in Jesus.

Mark

Piper identified the first exodus as a key to understanding both the Old and New Testaments.[59] He pointed out that both Isaiah and Hosea had used the exodus to interpret their own situation. According to him, Jesus is the second Moses, "not primarily as Lawgiver, but as the leader of his people to the

---

[56] E. D. Johnston, "The Old Testament Background of Matthew 2–4," *Mishkan* 6/7 (1987), 20–26 [26].

[57] J. T. Dennison, "The Exodus and the People of God," *The Banner of Truth* 171 (1977), 6.

[58] Ibid., 7. According to Dennison, the new covenant at Calvary is accompanied by darkness (Matt 27:45), quaking of the earth (Matt 27:51,54) and the "loud voice" of Jesus who bears the curse of the law as and for the Israel of God (Matt 27:50).

[59] O. Piper, "Unchanging Promises: Exodus in the New Testament," *Int* 11 (1957), 3–22 [3].

promised goal".[60] Jesus's journeys into Phoenicia and Caesarea Philippi echo Israel's wanderings and Piper believes that "the fact that of all Jesus's visits to Jerusalem only the last one is mentioned in Mark, and that it is described as the entry of a conqueror" shows that it is regarded as the goal of this new exodus migration.

Piper conducted an extensive survey of the new exodus theme in the New Testament, but he did not identify the creativity of the early church in linking the new exodus promises of the eighth century prophets, with all of their theological motifs, to the Egyptian Exodus model of salvation.

Watts sees the introduction to the Gospel of Mark as being programmatic for the understanding of Mark's Gospel as a whole.[61] According to him, John the Baptist is Malachi's Elijah who prepares the way for Yahweh's long-delayed Isaianic new exodus coming. Watts pays more attention to the contribution of Isaiah and the prophetic expectation of a new exodus. He understands the two themes to be intersected in Mark's account of the events of Jesus's arrival and death in Jerusalem.[62] The weaknesses of Watts's proposal are: first, Isaiah's new exodus theme is basic not only to Mark; it is seen in all writers of the New Testament. The New Testament repeatedly claims that a new and final redemption from slavery will take place in Jesus. Secondly, Watts does not pay adequate attention to the paschal theme itself, thus omitting the cultic interplay between the two exoduses made by the New Testament writers.

Luke

Manek[63] interpreted the gospel of Luke in the light of the new exodus theme. He linked the departure of Jesus from Jerusalem with the departure of the Jews from Egypt, both bringing judgment on those who did not believe. He pointed out that the forty days that Jesus spent with the disciples after his resurrection

---

[60] Ibid., 18–19. According to Piper, Mark 10:45 reflects Moses's offer in Exod 32:32, and the words of the Institution, "chosen for their close resemblance with Exodus 24:8", present the new covenant in an Exodus setting.

[61] Watts, *Mark*, 113.

[62] Ibid., 223–39. According to Watts, the two themes are (1) a positive schema whereby Jesus's identity and ministry is presented in terms of Isaiah's new exodus; and (2) a negative schema by which Jesus's rejection by the nation's leaders and his action in the Temple are cast in terms of the prophet Malachi's warning; a warning which itself concerned the delay of the Isaianic new exodus.

[63] J. Manek, "Luke", 8.

was echoed in the forty years spent in the wilderness by the Israelites before entering into their inheritance. However, Manek saw Moses as the antitype of Jesus, so he missed the promises of the Davidic prince at the beginning of the gospel. He also failed to see that Luke expanded the exodus typology to include the Babylonian exodus with its Davidic leader.

Garrett understood that for Luke the exodus from Egypt serves as a theological paradigm.[64] She argued that Luke regarded the death, resurrection, and ascension of Jesus as an "exodus" because in these events Jesus, "the one who is stronger," led the people out of bondage to Satan. She saw Jesus's explanation of his exorcisms as a conquering of "the strong one" by "one who is stronger" in Luke 11:21–22 as an echo of Isa 53:12. However, she failed to see the death of Christ in the light of the Passover and the promises of Davidic prince being fulfilled in Jesus.

John

Boismard understood that the theme of the sending of the Christ by God is derived from the Old Testament (prophetic and wisdom tradition).[65] He argues that John's Gospel attempts to show that Jesus is the new Moses predicted in Deut 18:18. According to Boismard, John styles Jesus as "the prophet" who was designed to evoke images of Moses. He went on to say that the first three of Jesus's signs were performed so that the people might recognize the "envoy" from God.[66] He also noted that Jesus died on the very day of Passover, but he did not see the paschal significance of Jesus's death.

Glasson pointed out that the messianic time was modelled upon the exodus and its sequel.[67] According to him, the coming deliverance was to be a repetition of the deliverance from Egypt, and thus there would be a second deliverer (the Messiah) comparable to the first (Moses). In other words, the mission of Moses was a shadow of that of Christ.[68] Glasson interpreted John's

---

[64] S. R. Garrett, "Exodus from Bondage: Luke 9:31 and Acts 12:1–24," *CBQ* 52 (1990), 656–680 [659]. According to her, the exodus is a pointed allusion to Jesus's death and exaltation, conceptualized as a deliverance of "the people who sat in darkness" from bondage to Satan, the prince of darkness and ruler of this world.

[65] M. E. Boismard, *Moses and Jesus: An Essay in Johannine Christology* (Minneapolis; Fortress, 1993), 1–22.

[66] Ibid., 42.

[67] T. F. Glasson, *Moses in the Fourth Gospel* (London: SCM Press, 1963), 16.

[68] That is, the leading up of him with his people out of the sea was a shadow of Christ's ascent from the grave: the covenant with Israel a shadow of the eternal covenant.

Gospel in the light of the Egyptian Exodus. He did not appreciate the major contribution of the prophets to the new exodus and so, like many others, restricted his understanding largely to the Egyptian Exodus.

New Exodus in Acts

Strauss points out that the exodus image of Jesus (Luke 9:31) as a "prophet like Moses" (Acts 3:22; 7:37) may be seen as a reflection of Isaiah's portrait of eschatological salvation. According to Strauss, Isaiah is the major source for Luke's Christological construct. Therefore, the Isaianic new exodus serves as a way of integrating royal and prophetic traditions in the context of a drama of deliverance.[69] Strauss was concerned with the importance of the Davidic promise tradition. Then he explored how Luke conceives the Davidic promises to be fulfilled in Jesus in the narrative of Acts.[70] He pointed out that Jesus pours out salvation blessings upon his people, in his exalted status.[71] However, Strauss failed to examine the significance of the Passover because of his main concern, which is that Jesus fulfilled the Davidic promises.

Pao[72] points out that the entire Isaianic new exodus programme provides the structural framework for the narrative of Acts. He traces the importance of Isa 40:1–11 as a hermeneutical lens, arguing that the new exodus themes are found in the prologue of Isa 40–55, which brings a reversal to the judgment of Isa 6:9–10 by announcing the good news of salvation. What is significant is that Luke reverses the Isaianic reversal, so that the narrative begins with the proclamation of the salvation of God in Luke 3:6 and closes with judgment on the Jews who reject the message in Acts 28:26.[73] It reminds the readers to consider the themes that Luke develops in harmony with Isaiah. He does not relate it to the exodus accounts directly, but he uses Isaiah's exodus image for

---

[69] M. L. Strauss, *The Davidic Messiah in Luke-Acts: The Promise and its fulfilment in Lukan Christology* (Sheffield: Sheffield Academic Press, 1995), 285.

[70] Ibid., 131–2. It is suggested that the early chapters of Luke's gospel introduce and define Jesus programmatically as the one who will fulfil the Old Testament promises made to David.

[71] Ibid., 253. According to Strauss, through Jesus's death, resurrection, and exaltation, he has been vindicated and enthroned as the Davidic messiah, the king of Israel. Furthermore, all who repent receive forgiveness of sins and the gift of the Holy Spirit.

[72] Pao, *Acts*, 250.

[73] Ibid., 105–9.

illustrating Israel's deliverance from exile. Pao concludes that Isaiah's new exodus theme is basic for Acts.

New Exodus in the Epistles and Revelation

Goppelt identified Christ's death with the slaughter of the Passover lambs in 1 Cor 5:6–8.[74] In doing so, he pointed out that, like the sacrifice of a Passover lamb, Christ's death means a change that brings salvation, deliverance from death, release from slavery, and the beginning of something new. However, he did not observe that the deliverance from the kingdom of darkness is the fulfillment of the second exodus promises predicted by the prophets. He also failed to notice that the promise of the Davidic prince is fulfilled in Christ.

Stott understood that the nature of the death of Jesus was as a sacrifice for sin and that sin may be forgiven and put away by this unique sacrifice.[75] According to him, the term ἐξαγοράσῃ (redeem) in Gal 4:5 is used of the rescue of the Israelites from their Egyptian slavery in Acts 7:34. Christ gave himself as a sacrifice for our sins to deliver us from the present evil age. However, Stott saw the death of Jesus not in the light of the Passover, but in terms of the Day of Atonement. He also missed the second exodus promises foretold by the prophets.

Keesmaat examined Paul's use of the Old Testament tradition in Rom 8:14–30 in the light of exodus as the major formative event, which had held a central place within Israelite historical consciousness.[76] Israel knew that God had acted for them in the past, so they could be sure that God would act similarly for them in the future. According to Keesmaat, the prophetic books anticipate God's restoration of Israel in terms of a new exodus event. She also pointed out that the Passover was the central Israelite ritual which grounded Israelite identity in the exodus event. She pointed out that Jer 31:8–9 provided the matrix for the leading of God's people in the context of a new Passover, claiming that there was a verbal link between Ephraim as first-born and Jesus as first-born in Rom 8:29. She summed up that the exodus motif was a

---

[74] Goppelt, *Typos*, 149.

[75] J. R. W. Stott, *Only One Way: The Message of Galatians* (London: IVP, 1968), 17.

[76] S. C. Keesmaat, "Exodus and The Intertextual Transformation of Tradition in Romans 8.14–30" *JSNT* 54 (1994), 29–56 [35].

recollection of the past which guided Israel's actions in the present and provided hope for their future.[77]

Casey pointed out that Deut 26:8–9 is a key for John, the writer of Revelation.[78] Casey saw that the exodus involved God's redemption of Israel, his judgment upon her oppressors, and his granting of an inheritance to the nation. He regarded Jesus as a new and great paschal lamb, Christ as fulfilling the prediction concerning the Davidic prince. However, he seemed to only glance at the death of Christ in the light of the Passover, and noted only a limited presence of the Passover theme in other parts of the New Testament.

Holland pointed out that the Christ hymn in Col 1:15–20 has an introduction in vv. 12–14.[79] The introduction was based on the new exodus promises of being delivered from the kingdom over which Satan rules and being brought into the kingdom of light of which Christ is the Lord. According to Holland,[80] Christ's status is not limited merely to representing his family in his work of redemption; he represents the whole of creation. Christ's title as first-born was understood not ontologically but soteriologically. Therefore, Holland saw that Jesus died in the context of the Passover as King of the Jews. He also understood the promises of the Davidic prince foretold by prophets to be fulfilled in Jesus.

The Significance of the Paschal Setting in the Exodus

It has been argued that the contemporary context for New Testament teaching on sacrifice is both Greco-Roman and Jewish, for on one hand Christianity originated in the Jewish faith, whilst on the other hand it was preached and practised in a world where Greek culture and Roman power reigned supreme. Therefore, I will next deal with the theme of sacrifice in the first century.

---

[77] Ibid., 36.
[78] J. Casey, "The Exodus Theme in the Book of Revelation against the Background of the New Testament," *Concilium* 189 (1987), 34–43 [34].
[79] Holland, Paschal, 190.
[80] Ibid., 192.

Greco-Roman Tradition

Hengel pays attention to the theme of the dying hero, giving his life for the city and his friends.[81] He understands that the hero dying for his people in Greece and Rome is often spoken of in sacrificial terms.[82] He establishes that the statement "the Messiah died for us" is pre-Pauline and traces it back to the circle of Hellenists in Jerusalem.[83] Therefore, Hengel relates his view to the Maccabean heroes, who gained an everlasting name by dying, not just for their people, but for their God and his laws.[84] He also proposed that John 15:13 and Rom 5:7 should be interpreted in the light of this tradition. He believed that it came into Judaism from Greco-Roman traditions in the intertestamental period. Barrett[85] also related the death of Jesus to the death of the Maccabean martyrs because the Maccabean martyr prayed that his death would be an expiation for the nation's sins.

Aqedah Tradition

As this was closely linked to the offering of Isaac, the prototype of all martyrs, it links into an extensive rabbinical theological structure of atonement. Vermes pointed out that Pseudo-Jonathan understood the whole of Gen 22 as a test of Isaac's fidelity and Abraham's faithfulness.[86] According to him, the targumic tradition about Isaac's role in the sacrifice was already implicit in three works of the first century CE, that is, the *Jewish Antiquities of Josephus*,[87] *4 Maccabees*[88] and Pseudo Philo's *Liber Antiquitatum*.[89] Vermes noted that the atoning efficacy of all the sacrifices in which the lamb was immolated was thought to depend on the power of the sacrifice of Isaac.

---

[81] M. Hengel, *Atonement: The Origins of the Doctrine in the New Testament* (London: SCM, 1981), 6–14.
[82] Ibid.
[83] Ibid., 49–51. According to Hengel, the glorification or even the superhuman transfiguration of the martyr is completely alien to the Old Testament.
[84] 1 Macc 2:50–51, 64; 6:44; 2 Macc 13:14.
[85] C. K. Barrett, *A Commentary on the Epistle to the Romans* (London: SPCK, 1957), 217–8.
[86] G. Vermes, "Redemption & Genesis xxii: The Binding of Isaac and the Sacrifice of Jesus," in *Scripture and Tradition in Judaism Haggadic Studies* (Leiden: Brill, 1961), 197.
[87] Josephus explained that the offering of Isaac was not only a test for Abraham, but also insisted on Isaac's merit and on his voluntary self-surrender.
[88] In 4 Maccabees, Isaac is expressed as the proto-martyr, and in several other passages there is an allusion to the power of the blood of the martyrs, though with no explicit reference to Isaac.
[89] In *Liber Antiquitatum*, the willingness of Isaac for sacrifice is stressed. Furthermore, Isaac's sacrifice is related to other sacrifices offered to God for the sins of men.

Passover Tradition

Vermes's claim has been challenged by Davies and Chilton in saying that "our discussion of all the relevant passages in this source allows us the confident assertion that there is no evidence of the Aqedah to be found."[90] Holland has, furthermore, argued that Chilton and Davies have not made a correct assessment, for he believes that the Passover with the death of the lamb was the most dominant model for the New Testament writers in their interpretation of the significance of the death of Christ.[91]

Wellhausen,[92] however, posited a new picture of the origin and development of the Passover to support his dating of the Pentateuchal sources. He pointed out that the Passover and the Feast of Unleavened Bread were unrelated prior to about 620 BCE. Gray[93] sought to isolate various ancient features of the Passover by focusing on its customs, accepting the validity of Wellhausen's general approach. De Vaux[94] understood that the Passover began as the springtime sacrifice of a young animal, not necessarily the firstborn, by nomadic or semi-nomadic shepherds in order to guarantee the prosperity of the flock.

Van Seters[95] rejected Wellhausen's approach, and said that the Passover, as reflected in the earliest source D, was a one-day festival in the spring at a local sanctuary. After the slaughter of an animal from the flock or herd, there was a meal, eaten at night without unleavened bread. About a century and a half later, with the destruction of the temple, it was no longer possible to celebrate the Passover. He went on to say that as a result the Feast of Unleavened Bread was instituted by J as a substitute. He concluded that with the restoration of the temple after the exile, the revived Passover celebration was combined with the Feast of Unleavened Bread.

---

[90] B. D. Chilton and P. Davies, "The Aqedah: A Revised Tradition History," *CBQ* 40(1978), 514–46 [528].
[91] Holland, *Paschal*, 120.
[92] J. Wellhausen, *Prolegomena to the History of Israel* (Edinburgh: Black, 1985), 83–120.
[93] G. B. Gray, *Sacrifice in the Old Testament: Its Theory and Practice* (Oxford: Clarendon, 1925), 338.
[94] R. de Vaux, *Ancient Israel: Its Life and Institutions* (London: Darton, Longman & Todd, 1965), 485.
[95] J. Van Seters, "The Place of the Yahwist in the History of Passover and Massot," *ZAW* 95 (1983): 167–82 [169–170].

However, Haran[96] demonstrated, contra Wellhausen, that J knew of both feasts; there is no reason to delete the term *pesah* (Passover) in Exod 34:25. McConville[97] also pointed out that it is not necessary to remove, as Van Seters suggested, all references to unleavened bread in Deut 16. Rather, given the unanimity of the biblical tradition, there are surely good grounds for believing that both feasts were united from their birth.[98]

With regard to the Old Testament, all the Pentateuchal sources link the Passover with the Israelite exodus. The exodus from Egypt is clearly presented within the Old Testament as one of the most important events in the history of God's relationship with Israel—with the expression "out of Egypt" used with reference to the exodus approximately 135 times. The central character in the Passover was the sacrifice, and this is a description that was applied to Christ by New Testament writers.

Head[99] saw that Mark's narrative of the last supper had a clear allusion to sacrificial categories. The institutional words of Jesus in Mark 14:24, "This is my blood of the covenant, which is poured out for many," clearly echo Exod 24:8. He pointed out that the vicarious nature of the sacrifice is presented in words which are again reminiscent of Isa 53:12. What is more important is the fact that the meal is a Passover supper.[100] Jesus appropriates the content of the paschal lamb imagery, in order to speak of the redemptive power of God in making his covenant operative. Jeremias said that, "his death is the vicarious death of the suffering servant, which atones for the sins of the 'many'…, which ushers in the beginning of the final salvation and which effects the new covenant with God."[101] Head argued that Luke clearly presents the last supper (22:14-22) as a Passover meal. It seems that Jesus is expressed as the paschal

---

[96] M. Haran, "The Passover Sacrifice," *Studies in the Religion of Ancient Israel*, VTSup 22 (Leiden: Brill, 1972): 96-101.

[97] J. G. McConville, *Law and Theology in Deuteronomy* (Sheffield: JSOT, 1984), 115.

[98] The two events are linked together in Exod 12:1-13:16; 23:15; 34:18; Num 9:1; 33:3; Deut 16:1, 3, 6. cf. only in Lev 23:5-6 is there no mention of the exodus.

[99] P. M. Head, "The Self-Offering and Death of Christ as a Sacrifice in the Gospels and the Acts of the Apostles," in *Sacrifice in the Bible*, ed. R. T. Beckwith and M. J. Selman (Grand Rapids: Paternoster, 1995), 113.

[100] On the Passover viewed as a sacrifice, see Exod 12:27; 34:25; Num 9:7, 13; Josephus, Ant 2.312; 3.248; War 6.423; Exod Rab 15.35a, b; Philo, Vit.Mos.II.224.

[101] J. Jeremias, *The Eucharistic Words of Jesus* (London: SCM, 1966), 231.

lamb.[102] Smalley pointed out that "if Jesus is represented as dying on the day of the preparation of the Passover, then his death coincides with the slaughter of the sacrificial Passover lambs; and this is theologically suitable in a Gospel which uniquely designates Jesus 'the Lamb of God.'"[103]

It has been posited that Passover sacrifice inaugurated deliverance from bondage, and was observed in commemoration of that deliverance. Jesus fulfils the Passover sacrifice, delivering us from judgment and bondage by his blood. The link with the Passover is made explicit in 1 Cor 5:6–8, where Paul directly compares Jesus to the sacrificial Passover lamb.

To sum up, even though the Passover is undoubtedly the best known of all the Jewish festivals, its origin is debated. The Passover was instituted in association with the exodus, and the death of Christ is also itself called an "exodus." The death of Christ can be understood as a Passover sacrifice.

Thus we see by reviewing the scholarship that some have failed to appreciate the death of Christ in the light of the Passover and the deliverance from the kingdom of darkness to be the fulfillment of the second exodus promises made through the prophets. Others have also failed to notice the promises of the Davidic prince being fulfilled in Jesus.

The Current State of Paschal Studies in New Testament Theology

The beginning of Israel's national life started with the original Passover. Stott regards the Passover story (Exod 11–13) as a self-disclosure of the God of Israel.[104] He points out, therefore, that the death of Christ is identified with the fulfillment of the Passover, likewise, the emergence of his new and redeemed community the new exodus.

Goppelt points out that "both the relationship of the Last Supper to the Passover Feast and the saying about the cup are reminiscent of the founding of the former people of God through the deliverance from Egypt and the covenant on Sinai."[105]

---

[102] Ibid., 117

[103] S. S. Smalley, *John: Evangelist and Interpreter* (Exeter: Paternoster, 1978), 20.

[104] J. Stott, *The Cross of Christ* (London: IVP, 1986), 139.

[105] Goppelt, *Typos,* 110.

Howard sees the Passover theme as a major key to John's thought, focusing on the lamb.[106] He examines the Passover/exodus theme in 1 Corinthians; Christ was regarded as our Passover (5:6), the redeemer (7:22), and the heavenly manna (10:1-6), and in 11:23 the Lord's Supper was developed.[107] Howard understood, furthermore, that the Day of Atonement had been linked with the Passover in Ezek 45:21-25, although he did not develop this point.

Gerlach noted that Paul's first letter to Corinth shows that the Passover theme was valued, and it had been linked with the death of Christ by the early church.[108] In 1 Cor 5:6-8 the ritual is not explained; which means that the Corinthians already knew something about the custom.

Jeremias pointed out that the Jews in the New Testament were familiar with the Passover theme.[109] In Luke 2:41-51 Jesus visits the temple during the Passover pilgrimage. Furthermore, Christ was sacrificed as the paschal lamb and reference is made to the unleavened dough in 1 Cor 5:6. It means that "to be in Christ is to be already in the fulfilled Passover."[110]

Selman argued that two major aspects of Israelite sacrifice in the Old Testament were the various atonement sacrifices and the Passover.[111] Holland pointed out that there is a link between atonement and Passover in the New Testament.[112] The death of Jesus is understood as an atonement in the Passover setting because of Old Testament associations as well as explicit New Testament statements and the timing of his death.[113] It has a semantic source with clear new exodus links.

It seems that all the important events of the past in Israel were absorbed into paschal events. The participation in the events assured the individual and the nation of receiving the salvific effects of the Pesach. Furthermore, the

---

[106] J. M. Howard, "Passover and Eucharist in the Fourth Gospel," *SJT* 20 (1967), 329-37 [329].

[107] J. M. Howard, "Christ our Passover: A Study of the Passover-Exodus Theme in 1 Cor," *EQ* 41 (1969), 97-108 [97].

[108] K. Gerlach, *The Antenicene Pascha: A Rhetorical History* (Leuven: Peeters, 1998), 32

[109] J. Jeremias, "Πάσχα," [pascha] in *TDNT* V, 896-904

[110] Ibid., 902.

[111] M. J. Selman, "Sacrifice in the Ancient Near East," in *Sacrifice in the Bible*, ed. R. T. Beckwith and M. J. Selman (Grand Rapids: Paternoster, 1995), 101.

[112] Holland, *Paschal*, 69.

[113] M. Dibelius, *Jesus*, trans. by C. B. Hedrick and F. C. Grant (London: SCM, 1963), 85.

eschatological end event was expected to be a paschal event. Passover, therefore, was an important theme within the soteriological development of the early church.

Chapter 2: Summary of Earlier Scholars' Appreciation of the Presence of New Exodus Expectations in Hebrews

Introduction

This chapter investigates earlier scholars' theories on the presence of new exodus expectations in the letter to the Hebrews. After a detailed analysis of this work, I shall link relevant points with characteristics of the new exodus motif so as to explore the extent that the new exodus motif is used in Hebrews.

Survey

F. F. Bruce, *The Epistle to the Hebrews* (Grand Rapids: Eerdmans, 1964)

Bruce pointed out that the typological parallel between the historical exodus and the redemptive work of Christ is fundamental in Hebrews.[114] According to him, this typology was familiar both to the writer of Hebrews and his readers. He thought that the judgment of the wilderness days, which took place when the Israelites rejected Moses, was parallel to the loss which occurred in rejecting Christ in terms of a new exodus. Bruce compared the action of the Israelites when they turned back in their hearts to Egypt to a relapsed believer who turns from following Jesus the Messiah back to Judaism.[115]

Bruce also linked Christ's role to that of Moses. The author of Hebrews designates Jesus as "the Apostle and high priest of our confession."[116] Concerning this phrase, Bruce comments that the combining of these two roles in one person was not common in the Old Testament. It appears only in a few outstanding characters, such as Moses.[117] When Moses as the spokesman of God was challenged by members of his own family, his faithfulness was vindicated by God in Num 12:7. Moses was acknowledged by God as chief steward over his household. According to Bruce,[118] the "house" of Num 12:7, in

---

[114] F. F. Bruce, *The Epistle to the Hebrews* (Grand Rapids: Eerdmans, 1964), 62.
[115] Ibid., 67.
[116] Heb 3:1: τὸν ἀπόστολον καὶ ἀρχιερέα τῆς ὁμολογίας ἡμῶν
[117] Bruce, *Hebrews*, 56. In fact, Aaron was high priest of Israel, but Moses was Israel's true advocate with God (cf. Exod 32:11; Num 14:13).
[118] Ibid.

which Moses served so faithfully, is not the tent of meeting but the people of Israel, the family of God.

The author of Hebrews compares the old covenant instituted at Mt Sinai to the new covenant whose inauguration Jeremiah foretold. The old covenant made provision for the removal of external pollution by means of animal sacrifices, but these things could never remove sin; under the new covenant Jesus, by yielding up his life to God as an effective sacrifice, cleanses the conscience from guilt. The new covenant is established on: (1) "I will put my laws into their mind"; (2) "all shall know me"; (3) "their sins will I remember no more".[119] Bruce points out that the old covenant involved divine promises, but not promises like these.[120] The new covenant foretold by Jeremiah is set in contrast with the covenant which Yahweh made with the people of Israel when he delivered them from the land of Egypt. The fulfillment of such promises gives a new meaning to the old covenant words: "I will be to them a God, and they shall be to me a people." Therefore, the new order into which Christ brings his people is to the old Levitical order what substance is to shadow.

Bruce understands Heb 9 in the light of the Day of Atonement.[121] In Heb 9, the author of Hebrews has in mind the particular sanctuary which is the wilderness tent described in detail in the book of Exodus. Therefore, just as on the Day of Atonement it was necessary for the sacrificial blood first to be shed in the court and then to be brought into the holy of holies, so Christ carried his own blood into the heavenly sanctuary. He offered up his life to God as a sacrifice for his people's sin. Heb 9:12 shows that Christ entered into the heavenly sanctuary once for all, to be enthroned there in perpetuity, because the redemption procured by him is perfect in nature and eternal in effect. Here redemption represents the Greek word λύτρωσιν which is derived from the root λυτρον ("ransom"). According to Bruce, Christ completed in reality what Aaron and his successors performed in type by presenting its blood in the holy of holies.[122]

---

[119] Heb 8:10–13.
[120] Bruce, *Hebrews*, 176.
[121] Ibid., 182.
[122] Bruce, *Hebrews*, 201.

The author of Hebrews quotes from Ps 40:6–8 in Heb 10:5–7. Here Bruce finds a prophetic utterance which the author recognizes as appropriate to the Son of God at the time of his incarnation.[123] The title of Ps 40:6–8 marks it as Davidic.[124] Bruce pointed out that the words of the Psalm could not refer to David since David did not offer sacrifices.[125] Bruce also understood that they should be recognized as referring to "great David's greater Son."[126] Christ is expressed as the Son of God and firstborn because he existed before all creation and because all creation is his heritage. The title "firstborn" may be traced back to Ps 89:27, where God says "I will also appoint him my firstborn" of David and in general of the Davidic kingship.[127]

Bruce identified the exodus as a key to understanding the letter to the Hebrews. He noticed the correspondence between the death of Jesus and the annual sacrifice on the Day of Atonement, although he did not link the Day of Atonement to the Passover. Therefore, Bruce did not see that Jesus was presented as the antitype of the paschal lamb.

R. Williamson, *Philo and the Epistle to the Hebrews* (Leiden: Brill, 1970)

Williamson delivered a detailed study on Hebrews in which he concluded that the differences between Philo and the writer of Hebrews were striking and fundamental, both in outlook and exegetical method. It is a full-scale attack on the theory that the Epistle to the Hebrews reflects the influence of Philo of Alexandria. Williamson pointed out that the two writers "belonged...to entirely different schools of O.T. exegesis".[128]

In Philo's eyes, according to Williamson, Moses was the "guardian" and "leader" of the nation.[129] Philo saw Moses as very near to God and claimed that he was a living reality within the religious experience of the Jewish people as he understood it and shared in it. Williamson asked if Moses was human or divine

---

[123] Ibid., 232.
[124] Cf. In Masoretic and Septuagint texts alike.
[125] Bruce, *Hebrews*, 232.
[126] Ibid.
[127] Ibid., 15. Cf. Christ is called the "firstborn" in Rom 8:29 and Col 1:15, 18.
[128] R. Williamson, *Philo and the Epistle to the Hebrews* (Leiden: Brill, 1970), 25.
[129] See Philo's work, *On the Virtues* 42, for "the leader of the nation," and *On Rewards and Punishments* 77, for "the guardian and ruler of the nations". In *Moses* I 243, Philo calls Moses the "leader of the Hebrews."

in Philo's understanding, given that the appraisal of Moses in Philo's works is so elevated.

Williamson claimed that Jesus is called the ἀρχηγὸν ("author") of the salvation of many sons in Heb 2:10, and the ἀρχηγὸν and τελειωτὴν of the faith of the Christian community in Heb 12:2, but nowhere in Hebrews is he called the ἡγεμών ("leader") of the people of God. Williamson commented that in Hebrews Jesus is presented as the Messiah who has offered his own life as a real sacrifice for sin—by which he has succeeded in making purification for sins.

Williamson understood the purpose of the words of Heb 3:1, "consider Jesus, the apostle and high priest of our confession," to be contrasting the high priest of the Christian confession with the high priest of the Old Testament. He went on to say that the author of Hebrews insists that Jesus was πιστόν ("faithful") to him who appointed Him. Williamson saw a comparison between the faithfulness of Jesus and that of Moses in saying that Moses was faithful in God's house in Num 12:7. He concluded that the author of Hebrews understands the story of Moses in the light of Christ.[130]

Williamson also understood that, for the writer of Hebrews, life is a pilgrimage which begins on earth and has heaven for its goal. The pilgrimage terminates in the heavenly city.[131] He went on to say that there is no suggestion in Hebrews that the Christian pilgrimage is a pilgrimage of the soul out of the body—an idea stemming from the Philonic disparagement of the body and sense-perception.[132]

Williamson concluded that there is certainly no evidence that the author of Hebrews borrowed from Philonic thought. He identified Moses as the type of Jesus, but missed the Davidic emphasis nor did he pay sufficient attention to the paschal theme itself.

---

[130] Williamson, "*The Hebrews*", 468.

[131] Ibid., 490.

[132] For Philo life is a pilgrimage in which the mind of man seeks to escape from the body, which in language influenced by Philo, Williamson calls "the soul prison-house." See Philo, On the migration of Abraham, 9.

G. W. Buchanan, *To the Hebrews* (Garden City, NY: Doubleday, 1972)

Buchanan pointed out that the first twelve chapters of Hebrews, which seem to have been independent of chapter 13, are a homiletic midrash on Psalm 110.[133] He went on to say that chapter 13 is a text prepared for a different group from that for which the homily in the first twelve chapters was written. Its purpose seems to be to give the homily the appearance of a letter to allow its admission into the canon.[134]

According to Buchanan, the exodus of the Hebrews from Egypt was a type which the recipients of the document called "to the Hebrews" were familiar with.[135] Even though both were placed in situations where the achievement seemed incredible, they received the good news that the promise given to Abraham could be fulfilled in them.[136] Thus the author urged his readers to learn from the exodus generation so that they might be different from it and thus experience God's salvation.

Buchanan claimed that there was obviously a strong Jewish and Christian conviction that the devil was in command of death.[137] Death was closely related to sin; it was sin that caused death. Buchanan argued that Jesus' sacrifice was considered enough to cancel all sins. In other words, Jesus incapacitated death through his death.

Buchanan considered that Heb 3–4 contained a well-reasoned comparison of the office and work of Moses with the office and work of Jesus.[138] The good news given to Israel through Moses had again been renewed through Jesus. Jesus, through his sacrificial offering of himself, prepared a new way whereby the new Israel could be recipient of a new covenant and the fulfillment of the

---

[133] G. W. Buchanan, *To the Hebrews* (Garden City, NY: Doubleday, 1972), xxi–xxii

[134] Ibid., 227–33, 268.

[135] Ibid., 251.

[136] Furthermore, in both cases, success depended on the faith of the covenanters and their ability to hold fast to their confession and never give up hope that God would fulfil his promises and give the children of Abraham the land promised to Abraham. Both were tempted to doubt God's ability to fulfil his promises. Of the exodus generation, only Caleb and Joshua were confident and refused to give up hope.

[137] Ibid., 34. According to the Wisdom of Solomon, "God did not make death" (1.13). "Death entered the world by means of the envy of the devil" (2:24). Paul also said of all the rules, authorities, and powers that God would put under Jesus's feet, that "the last enemy incapacitated is death" (1 Cor 15:26). Paul held that the sin of Adam caused death, so that death ruled from Adam to Moses (Rom 5:12–21).

[138] Ibid., 60.

old promise which had never been achieved. Buchanan saw that, like Moses before God, Jesus had done all that was necessary to make the fulfillment of the promises available.

Buchanan pointed out that the Levitical priesthood was a type for which Jesus, who did not belong to his order, was the antitype.[139] Buchanan saw, however, that Jesus's purpose was the same as that of the Levitical priesthood. Jesus, as the perfect priest, entered the holy of holies, pouring out his own blood to cleanse, sanctify, and perfect himself and the people (7:26–27; 9:14, 23, 26; 10:14). Buchanan concluded that Jesus was a superior antitype for their inferior type.

It was also widely accepted that Jesus was from the family of David and that the Messiah should also be a son of David, but the author of Hebrews made no mention of that. He admitted the Judaic origin of Jesus, partly because of tradition, partly because of scriptural prophecy (Gen 49:9–10), and partly because of the Jewish tradition that Melchizedek was from Jerusalem, but he never mentioned the son of David as the Messiah nor Jesus as the son of David. He used messianic prophecies that had usually been applied to the son of David and applied them to Jesus, but without calling Jesus the son of David.[140]

Buchanan restricts his understanding largely to the Egyptian Exodus. Thus he identified Moses as the type of Jesus. But in a sense, Buchanan seems to have understood the creativity of the early church in linking the new exodus promises of the eighth century prophets in seeing Jesus as the son of David.

G. Vos, The Teaching of the Epistle to the Hebrews (Phillipsburg, NJ: The Presbyterian & Reformed Publishing Company, 1975)

Vos pointed to a comparison between the first covenant (διαθήκη), which was the Sinaitic, and the second which was instituted by Christ.[141] This distinction was due to the fact that the author of Hebrews wished to establish the new

---

[139] Ibid., 122.

[140] Ibid., 123.

[141] G. Vos, *The Teaching of the Epistle to the Hebrews* (Phillipsburg, NJ: The Presbyterian & Reformed Publishing Company, 1975), 49. The first is referred to as the διαθήκη made with the fathers (Heb 8:9; 9:1–22), the second is called a new διαθήκη (Heb 8.8; a better διαθηκη in Heb 8.6; an eternal διαθήκη in Heb 13:20).

covenant upon the promise to Moses. The former begins with Moses and the latter with Christ. That is, the dividing point between the old διαθήκη and the new is the death of Christ. The death makes the thing effectual. Therefore, Vos pointed out that the new covenant has arrived when there is forgiveness of sins, and this is because of the death of Christ.

Vos argued that the eschatological state of the people of God is observed in the epistle as a cult organization, and that the epistle distinguishes two ages, namely this age and the age to come, linked to two covenants.[142] The old covenant pertains to this present world, whereas the new covenant is linked to the future eschatological world. According to Vos, although covenant and world are not exactly co-extensive, the two terms, the new covenant and the new world are co-extensive. That is, believers are eschatological creatures. The author of Hebrews states that they have tasted the power of the age to come in Heb 6:5. The author shows them that the eschatology is present for the most part, only certain features of it being reserved for the future. Therefore, believers were intensively interested in eschatology.

The Epistle to the Hebrews stands alone among the New Testament books in calling Christ a priest. Vos points out that Heb 5:1 gives us a statement of what a priest does.[143] He acts for man in things pertaining to God, and he brings both gifts and sacrifices for sins. In connection with these gifts, therefore, the priesthood is necessary because of the fact of sin, which has resulted in God being inaccessible to man. Man in himself is unclean; therefore, he needs a priest to bring these gifts in his stead. Vos pointed out that Christ as a high priest is able to sympathize with our weaknesses.[144]

With regard to the essence of the office of priest, he brings men near to God. The priest himself must approach God first. That is, the priest brings men to God representatively, through himself.[145] It is plain that to satisfy these requirements there must be a close identification between the priest and his followers. They must follow him in his nature. All of this may be embodied in the term identification.

---

[142] Ibid., 50.
[143] Ibid., 99.
[144] Ibid., 102.
[145] Ibid., 94.

Vos analyzed the rationale of the sacrificial act of Christ.[146] Heb 9:28 tells us, according to Vos, that Christ was offered up to bear (ἀνενεγκεῖν) the sins of many. Vos pointed out that here the ritual and the forensic formulas meet together. It is here clearly stated that Christ removes sin. He takes it upon himself. Vos went on to say that the verb ἀνενεγκεῖν is literally taken from the LXX of Isa 53, which is a purely vicarious interpretation.

Vos regarded shadowing in Hebrews as shadowing down from heaven to earth, not shadowing forward from Old Testament to New Testament. According to him, the New Testament is an actual substance of the heavenly reality come down from heaven, the very image. His premise for Hebrews is limited to the Egyptian Exodus, although he did use the prophecies of the prophets. Thus he missed the Davidic emphasis in the epistle, and he missed the paschal theme itself.

P. E. Hughes, A Commentary on the Epistle to the Hebrews (Grand Rapids: Eerdmans, 1977)

Hughes noted the relationship between the New Testament and Old Testament that in the New Testament Christ is the realization of the promises, prophecies, and figures which form the heart of the Old Testament.[147] He pointed out that the Mosaic system was a shadow of the good things which were on their way but not yet realized.[148] Under the old order Moses was prominent as the apostle; but in the new order the office of apostleship is combined in the one person of Christ. According to Hughes, Moses was a notable type of Christ in his role as deliverer, who led the chosen people from the bondage of Egypt to the borders of the promised land.[149] According to Hughes, Christ is the true focal point of the Mosaic typology.[150]

Hughes saw that the death of Christ was essential if he was to lead many sons to glory.[151] By his death, Christ not only destroyed him who had the power of death—the devil—but also liberated his people from the fear of death and its

---

[146] Ibid., 119.
[147] P. E. Hughes, *A Commentary on the Epistle to the Hebrews* (Grand Rapids: Eerdmans, 1977), 37.
[148] Ibid., 136.
[149] Ibid., 493.
[150] Ibid., 136.
[151] Ibid., 99.

bondage. In other words, the sons are those who are redeemed, not in their own right, but by virtue of their union with Christ. Hughes saw Christ on the cross as the spotless Lamb of God in the place of the sinner.[152] The restoration of man in Christ points to the restoration of the whole created order and the achievement of the will and purpose of the Creator. Therefore, Hughes regarded "leading many sons to glory" as the joyful liberation and reintegration of the cosmos.[153]

Hughes noted that the quotation from Ps 8 in Heb 2 is applied to Christ, and treated it as messianic.[154] Ps 8 relates to the whole of mankind, but it finds its true focus in him who is the Son of Man. The author of Hebrews points out that the intention and achievement of his incarnation was to restore to fallen man to his previous dignity. In union with Christ man can become man as God meant and made him to be. Commenting on Heb 2:5, Hughes pointed out that the coming age of the Messiah was the time when the messianic promises and prophecies would find their fulfillment.[155] He went on to say that this age is still future insofar as its ultimate consummation is yet to be manifested. But it is also now present, in that the Messiah has come in the person of the incarnate Son, and by his coming has inaugurated the era of fulfillment. He concluded that the promise of an everlasting kingship concerns one who belongs to the line of David.

The author of Hebrews sees a typological relationship between the wilderness table and the heavenly sanctuary in Heb 9 with reference in particular to what took place on the Day of Atonement when the high priest, after offering a sacrifice for the people, passed into the inner shrine of God's presence. According to Lev 16:14, on the great annual Day of Atonement the culminating moment of propitiation and reconciliation came when the high priest, on entering the holy of holies, sprinkled the blood of atonement on the mercy seat. However, the author of Hebrews insists on the imperfection and

---

[152] Ibid., 100. Hughes linked Heb 2: 10 to 1 Pet 1:18; 3:18.

[153] Ibid., 100.

[154] Ibid., 84. It was not regarded by the Jews as one of the specifically messianic psalms. However, in Matt 21:16 Jesus quotes from this Psalm in justification of the messianic acclamation accorded him by the children in the temple. Paul also teaches that the Psalmist's saying that God has put all things in subjection under man's feet finds its fulfilment in Christ in 1 Cor 15:27 and Eph 1:22.

[155] Ibid., 80–86.

transitoriness of the earthly sanctuary. Hughes understood that the Day of Atonement and its ceremonies were fulfilled in the perfect high-priestly work of Christ.[156] Thus, Hughes commented that this ritual was shadowed in Christ, the perfect high priest, who offered the perfect sacrifice for the forgiveness and the removal of their sins forever.[157]

The author of Hebrews sees that the message of Scripture is the voice of the Holy Spirit in Heb 3:7–11.[158] This means that Scripture is not a dead letter of a bygone period but is fully existential in its significance, so that what was spoken or written in the wilderness situation centuries before continued to have a dynamic application to the people of God in his own day. The Holy Spirit is also said to indicate certain truth in connection with the tabernacle, whose pattern of construction and scheme of worship were revealed to Moses by God (Heb 9:8–9).[159] Therefore Hughes understood that the Holy Spirit is admonishing the readers through the passages of Scripture.[160]

The period of forty years in the wilderness was not a glorious episode in the history of Israel. In Heb 3:7–11 (quoted from Ps 95) reference is made to one disgraceful instance of their hard-hearted perversity: namely, the rebellion which took place on the day of testing. To put God to the test in this way was evidence of unbelief. It meant that although they had seen his works for forty years, they had not known or learned his ways. Therefore, Hughes found a logical connection between the words in verse 7 ("therefore, as the Holy Spirit says") and those found in verse 12 ("take care, brothers ..."). It means that the Holy Spirit has said these things to admonish us in our days.[161] It is noticeable that the author of Hebrews addresses his readers as *brothers*, indicating that he does not despair of there being true faith among them.

Hughes explored the degree to which Christology has influenced the presentation of Moses. He sought to account for all the allusions to Moses in the text and through them to account for the writer's Christology. He

---

[156] Ibid., 313–4.
[157] Ibid., 320.
[158] Ibid., 141. Furthermore, the Holy Spirit and Yahweh are one. It is implied by the equation of what the Holy Spirit says with what the Lord says.
[159] Ibid., 321.
[160] Ibid., 141.
[161] Ibid., 145.

examined the correspondences between Christ and Moses to see how the writer's perception of Christ, and of the relationship of the Christian movement to Judaism, had shaped his understanding of Moses. He concluded that there was a correspondence between Moses and Christ in almost every book of the New Testament in which Moses was mentioned. However, Hughes gives no suggestion that the author of Hebrews shared the creativity of the early church in linking the new exodus promises of the eighth century prophets. As a result, Hughes failed to see that the epistle expanded the exodus typology to include the Babylonian Exodus with its Davidic leader. Furthermore, he did not to pay sufficient attention to the paschal theme itself.

W. G. Johnsson, "The Pilgrimage Motif in the Book of Hebrews," *JBL* Vol. 97/2 (1978), 239–51

Johnsson attempts to clarify the idea of pilgrimage in the book of Hebrews. He argues that Hebrews is shown to conform to the structure of pilgrimage.[162] According to Johnsson, the data in Hebrews which relates to the idea of pilgrimage is located in the parentheses of the document. In chapters 3–4, the important point is the idea of movement toward a goal. It was necessary for the people of Israel to struggle to occupy the promised land. Here the leading motif is one of rest. The final verses of chapter 11 support ideas implied in Heb 3:6b–4:11. The key expression in Heb 11:39–40 was "did not receive what was promised." That is, the Israelites were explicitly seen to be those who were on a pilgrimage. Even though Heb 12 does not appear to contain data which either directly or indirectly relates to the issue of pilgrimage, according to Johnsson, there is a link reference to the wilderness experience of Israel.[163] Furthermore, Heb 13:12–14 indicates the foreignness of the Christians in the world and their hardships at the hands of the world. This means that Hebrews includes substantial data relative to movement and expectation.

Johnsson considered that Partin's analysis about the religious structure of pilgrimage was incontestable.[164] However, Johnsson pointed out that the

---

[162] W. G. Johnsson, "The Pilgrimage Motif in the Book of Hebrews," *JBL* Vol. 97/2 (1978), 239–51 [239].

[163] Ibid., 241. "You have come to Mount Zion," rather than the earthly Sinai (Heb 12:18–24, 26).

[164] H. B. Partin, The Muslim Pilgrimage: Journey to the Center (PhD. diss., University of Chicago, 1967). He finds four essential elements: (1) Pilgrimage entails a separation, a leaving home. (2) It involves a journey to a

pilgrimage motif in Hebrews displays features other than those developed in Partin's model.

First of all is the figure of Jesus.[165] As Moses led the people of God under the old covenant, so Jesus is the leader of the new people of God, whom he has purged from sin with his own blood. His death broke down the barriers between man and God. Thus, a significant idea of Hebrews is the complete efficacy of the blood of Christ to deal with man's sin. Secondly, Johnsson pointed out that in Hebrews the Christian community is viewed as a cultic community on the move. They are "holy," "sanctified," "perfected," "purified"[166]—the people of God—and they are on the move toward the sacred place of heaven. Thirdly, Johnsson saw that the chief concern of Hebrews is unfaithfulness. Christians may drift away or neglect the great salvation already received.[167] As pilgrims, God's people are ever on the move, and although great privileges are theirs, the possibility of failure to attain the goal is ever-present. The great need is for faithfulness. Thus, the idea of the cultic community gives rise to the idea of defilement-purification, while the cultic community on the march recalls the conflict between unbelief-faithfulness present in Israel's wilderness journey.

Johnsson linked the figure of Jesus to the idea of pilgrimage in Hebrews. However, he also saw Jesus as a priestly king about to bring deliverance, and recognized the outworking of the phenomenological model of pilgrimage in Exod 19 and Heb 12. Therefore, he identified Moses as the type of Jesus, but missed the Davidic emphasis and paid insufficient attention to the paschal theme itself.

---

sacred place. (3) It is made for a fixed purpose, such as purification or forgiveness of sins. (4) It involves hardship.

[165] Jesus is depicted as the pioneer or pathfinder (Heb 2:10; 12:2) and the forerunner (6:20).

[166] Heb 1:3; 2:11; 3:1; 5:14; 7:11, 19; 9:13–14, 22; 10:1–2, 10, 14, 29; 11:40; 12:2, 23–24; 13:21; 13:24.

[167] Heb 2:1–4; 3:6–4:11; 6:4–6; 10:26–31; 12:16,17; 12:3–15.

J. Swetnam, Jesus and Isaac: A Study of the Epistle to the Hebrews in the Light of the Aqedah (Rome: Biblical Institute, 1981)

Swetnam discussed the Aqedah not only as it existed in Gen 22 but also as it existed in Jewish tradition.[168] According to Swetnam, the dating of the sacrifice of Isaac was the day of Passover in Jubilees, and the same date is linked to each major event in the lives of the patriarchs with a major Jewish festival. Therefore, he examined some relevant sections of the epistle in the light of this study. The first two are treated in considerable detail (Heb 11:17–19; Heb 2:5–18) and the others quite briefly (Heb 5:7–10; 6:13–15; 9:23).

Swetnam pointed out that Heb 11:17–19 is a reference to the sacrifice of Isaac.[169] He argued that the "seed" promised to Abraham is regarded not merely as his numerous offspring through Isaac but as "spiritual 'seed' composed of all those who, like Abraham, have faith when they are tested in God's power to raise from the dead."[170] Thus ὅθεν αὐτὸν καὶ ἐν παραβολῇ ἐκομίσατο ("whence also in a foreshadowing did he receive him") mean that Abraham's offering was a foreshadowing of another offering, and that Abraham's receiving was a foreshadowing of another receiving from the dead. Swetnam related the one in Hebrews who is preeminently offered and preeminently raised from the dead to Jesus (for the offering cf. 7:27; 9:14, 28; 10:12; for the resurrection 13:20).

Swetnam proposed a number of factors which seem to come together in the Aqedah as the background of Heb 2:5–18.[171] That is, the death, resurrection, and exaltation of Jesus are a natural fulfillment of the foreshadowing of the Aqedah. There is also the aspect of expiation, which in the Jewish tradition of the Aqedah is associated with the death of martyrs and the relation of Ps 8 to the Aqedah in the Jewish tradition.

---

[168] J. Swetnam, *Jesus and Isaac: A Study of the Epistle to the Hebrews in the Light of the Aqedah* (Rome: Biblical Institute, 1981), 189. Swetnam rejected the view of P. R. Davies and B. D. Chilton: "The Aqedah: A Revised Tradition History," *CBQ* 40 (1978): 514-46. According to Davies and Chilton, Aqedah is "a haggadic presentation of the vicariously atoning sacrifice of Isaac." Therefore, Swetnam said, "this narrow definition rules out the use of the term in Christian tradition."

[169] Ibid., 122. According to Swetnam, 1) Abraham intends to sacrifice Isaac and tries to do so, and 2) he receives Isaac ἐν παραβολῇ as a result of his faith in God's ability to raise the dead.

[170] Ibid., 128.

[171] Ibid., 155-77.

According to Swetnam, the fear of death in Hebrews is to be linked with the Sinai dispensation.[172] He went on to say that this dispensation is inadequate and imperfect (7:18; 8:7, 13) because it cannot remove sin (9:9; 10:2, 4, 11), but at the same time God punishes sin, involuntary and deliberate. God's judgment is fearful (10:30–31) and it lies in store for everyone. Thus it has been seen how the Mosaic law could make men pass their whole life in fear of death, in particular because of a reverential fear for God and his revelation in the Mosaic law.

Heb 6:13–15 presents God swearing to Abraham after Isaac has been restored to him (citation of Gen 22:17 in Heb 6:14). Swetnam pointed out that the purpose of the presentation is to give to the recipients of the letter as pilgrims an example of faith and patience (6:12).[173] Thus the recipients should be ready to exercise faith and patience in order to receive what they hope for. He went on to say that Abraham's comportment at the Aqedah is here chosen as the most impressive and most important example of the ancestors, which is in accord with the central position taken in chapter 11 of the Aqedah.

Swetnam understood that the Aqedah was in the mind of the author of Hebrews when he was writing of Abraham and Isaac and also at other moments less immediately obvious. However, the picture of the Aqedah—while not treated insignificantly—requires further investigation. What is important is that the meaning and significance of Christ's death was not as a martyr but the Saviour from the bondage of Satan. It was also set in the context of Old Testament concepts of redemptive history. Swetnam also argued that the Epistle to the Hebrews was built around the type of the Egyptian Exodus. As a result, he missed the echoes from the prophets in the letter.

---

[172] Ibid., 171.
[173] Ibid., 184.

R. Brown, *The Message of Hebrews* (Leicester: IVP, 1982)

R. Brown pointed out that the letter to Hebrews gathers all its principal ideas around two immense themes, revelation and redemption; in other words, the word of God and the work of Christ. Both these major aspects of Christian preaching are dexterously interwoven in the author's arrangement of his message.[174]

Concerning the latter Brown saw the Levitical scapegoat as the type of Jesus. Thus, in God's redemptive purpose sin has been carried away by Christ in the same way as the Levitical scapegoat bore the iniquities of the Israelite people into the wilderness.[175] He went on to say that there is also another picture here, extracted from prophetic literature. The author has placed Heb 9:28 in parallel to the famous Servant Song passage from Isaiah where it says that "he bore the sin of many."[176] Almost identical terminology is used here in Hebrews and in Isa 53:12. Therefore, Brown linked Jesus with the offering on the Day of Atonement and the servant in Isaiah.

Brown argued that the author of Hebrews used the sad historical event of the wilderness wanderings as a parable or type of Christian pilgrimage and its attendant perils.[177] He supposed that if the Christian believers were influenced by the teaching of the Dead Sea Scrolls, then the author's choice of the "Israel in the wilderness" theme would have even greater significance for the first readers of this letter. The Qumran sect consisted of people who had deliberately withdrawn themselves from everyday Judean life in order to re-enact the exodus events. They used the forty years in the wilderness as a model or pattern of life to prepare themselves for eventual re-entry into a Jerusalem purged of a corrupt temple and its false leadership.

The New Testament makes it clear that the coming of Jesus was the beginning of the end for the devil. Hebrews adds to this indisputable statement that

---

[174] R. Brown, *The Message of Hebrews* (Leicester: IVP, 1982), 17. According to him, the word of God certainly dominates the opening and closing chapters (1–6 and 11–13), whilst the work of Christ is given priority of place in the four chapters (7–10) which comprise the highly important central section of the letter.

[175] Symbolically the high priest had to lay both his hands on the scapegoat as he confessed the sins of the congregation: "and he shall put them upon the head of the goat, and send him away." As was the case for these Hebrew people, our guilt is "taken away," and our sin is purged.

[176] Ibid., 173.

[177] Ibid., 82.

Christ has triumphed over the devil's power, and the author makes this point in three ways. He is convinced that Christ's victory for us began with the incarnation, was revealed in his sinlessness, and achieved by the atonement. Therefore, Brown regarded Christ as our liberator. Heb 2:14–18 vividly portrays helpless humanity as the terrified victim of a triple enemy: sin, death, and the devil. The author insists that, as our perfect pioneer, Christ had to meet these evil powers and malevolent influences.

Brown in his book focused on the presentation of the work of Christ for expiating the sins of the people by his death. In other words, he explored the significance of the Levitical system for the perfecting of believers and found the earthly sanctuary and old covenant to be limited. Therefore, he failed to see that it expanded the exodus typology to include the Babylonian Exodus with its Davidic leader. There is no suggestion that he has seen the creativity of the early church in linking the new exodus promises of the eighth century prophets. Brown examined the role of the high priest on the Day of Atonement, but did not relate it to the Passover. That is, Brown saw the Levitical scapegoat as the type of Jesus.

E. Käsemann, *The Wandering People of God (Minneapolis, MN: Augsburg, 1984)*

Käsemann argued that Hebrews was directly influenced by a type of pre-Christian Gnosticism.[178] He saw the myth of the perfected redeemer as the pattern which unites themes of pilgrimage, cult, and priesthood. So the journey on which Christians follow their Lord is that of a pilgrimage, the goal of which is the attainment of "rest", that is, mystical union with God. The redeemer, like the high priest before him, needs himself to be perfected or redeemed in order to lead others to this beatific state.[179]

Fundamental to Käsemann's views of Hebrews is his belief that its Christology is built on the gnostic myth of the heavenly man.[180] He adduces late Jewish and heretical Christian parallels to show that in Hebrews a heavenly son takes on human form to suffer and die in order to release his followers from bondage to

---

[178] E. Käsemann, *The Wandering people of God* (Minneapolis, MN: Augsburg, 1984), 87.
[179] Ibid., 91.
[180] Ibid., 17.

the evil powers and death, and then ascends once again to the world of light, where he is crowned with glory and honour. Käsemann viewed the motifs of the son as creator and the enthronement "on the right hand of the majesty on high" (Heb 1:2) as gnostic. The use of Ps 8 is also said to be pressed into a gnostic framework: the heavenly redeemer is himself redeemed, and the son become as the redeemer. According to Käsemann, therefore, the son in Hebrews was now seen to be the gnostic anthropos or *urmensch*, while the "enlightened" are those who advance toward the same stage of "perfection" in knowledge which the son has already achieved.[181]

Käsemann saw "the wandering people of God" as the leading motif of Hebrews. For him "men have εὐαγγελίον on earth only as ἐπαγγελία," and "the only proper form of existence in time for those who receive revelation is pilgrimage."[182] Apart from chapters 3–4, Käsemann sees the gnostic pilgrimage of souls in such passages as Heb 10:19–25, and accordingly lists verbs of movement in Hebrews. He claims that "way" (ὁδός) is a gnostic technical term for such a journey.[183]

According to Käsemann, the concept of ἐπαγγελία in Hebrews is eschatological.[184] That is, the concept oscillates between the act of promise and completion, between the already fulfilled and yet to be fulfilled reality of the promise. By means of tension, the attitude of faith can be described as wandering.

Käsemann saw the main influence behind Hebrews as a pre-Christian Gnosticism which, centering on a myth of the perfected redeemer, conceived of salvation as a journey from the enslaving realm of the material to the heavenly realm of light. However, the main difficulty of Käsemann's approach is the lack of evidence for either a "proto-gnosticism" or "Gnosticism" earlier than the second century. Käsemann found it difficult to admit that these systems arose out of Christianity. However, it is reasonable to see pilgrimage and wandering in Hebrews as rooted in the Old Testament rather in any proto-gnostic traditions.

---

[181] Ibid., 97–117.
[182] Ibid., 19.
[183] Ibid., 37.
[184] Ibid.

W. Lane, Hebrews, WBC (Dallas: Word, 1991)

W. Lane pointed out that typological interpretation in Hebrews acts as a key function in the developing argument. Lane pointed out that the figure of Moses, as the mediator of Israel's covenant and cult, is of central importance in Hebrews. However, Lane saw that the ineffective sacrifices of the old covenant have been superseded by the sufficient sacrifice of Jesus,[185] and that Hebrews develops the parallel between Moses as the mediator of the Old Testament and Jesus as the mediator of the New. The allusion to Num 12:7[186] in Heb 3:2–5 suggests that the demonstration of Jesus's superiority to Moses in Heb 3:1–6 is already anticipated in the opening sentence of the passage. Lane seems to understand that Jesus was prefigured in Moses. In doing so, Jesus Christ is expressed as the sole mediator of salvation.

Lane understood that the conception of Christian life as pilgrimage to the city of God is constituted in Heb 3:7–4:13.[187] Lane held that the purpose of Hebrews was to exhort the tired and weary members of a house church to respond with courage and vitality to the prospect of renewed suffering in view of the gifts and resources God had generously given them.[188] Attention is focused upon the wilderness experience of Israel, who failed to enter God's promised land because of unbelief and disobedience. According to Lane, pilgrimage is characteristic of the obedient people of God under both the old and the new covenant, and it cannot be in vain, since God has prepared for them a land.

The allusion to Ps 110:4 in Heb 6:20 is transitional, leading to describing Jesus as a high priest "like Melchizedek" in Heb 7:1–28.[189] The writer points out that Melchizedek met Abraham, refreshed him, and then retreated into the shadows of history (Heb 7:1–10). The verses of Heb 7:11–28 shows that the superiority of the priest "like Melchizedek." Lane understood that the basis of the exposition was an exegesis of Gen 14:17–20 in the light of the interpretation

---

[185] Ibid., 210.

[186] Ibid., 77. Num 12:7 tells us that the testimony to Moses was used to prove that Moses had been granted a higher rank and privilege than the ministering angels.

[187] Ibid., 95.

[188] W. Lane, *Hebrews 1–8*, WBC (Dallas: Word Books, 1991), xcviii–ci.

[189] Heb 7:1–10 shows interpretation of Gen 14:17–20, and Heb 7:11–28 directs attention to the significance of each phrase in Ps 110:4.

implied in Ps 110:4.[190] Therefore Melchizedek is not regarded as a type to be fulfilled, but as a witness to the higher priesthood the writer finds foreshadowed in the Old Testament. Melchizedek serves as a precedent for a superior priesthood ordained by God apart from law. There is a comparison between the Levitical high priesthood and the unique priesthood of Christ in Heb 7. Thus, Lane concluded the new concept of the priesthood of Christ implicit in the oracle of Ps 110:4.

Two weakness of the Levitical arrangement are shown on the basis of Scripture in Heb 8:1–5.[191] The writer assumes that the new covenant required a new mediator. So the ministry of the new heavenly high priest, enthroned at God's right hand, is mentioned with the new covenant in vv. 6–13. Lane saw that Jesus's death on the cross was a covenant sacrifice, and Jesus inaugurated the new covenant of Jer 31:31–34. Jesus's entrance into the heavenly sanctuary guarantees God's acceptance of his sacrifice and the actualization of the provisions of the superior covenant he mediated. Lane saw that the central new aspects of the new covenant are: (1) the pledge the presence of the law in the hearts of believers as the gift of God, and (2) the manner of presenting Torah, not newness of content.[192] Lane understood that the treatment of the two covenants in Heb 8:7–8a show the eschatological point of view of the writer.[193] In other words, God was at work in the old covenant, and God's action in Jesus also occurred within the context of divine intervention in the life of Israel. The writer of Hebrews traced a line of continuity from the event of God's speaking at Sinai to the event of God's speaking at that moment.

Lane saw that the superior achievement of Christ's sacrifice in Heb 9:11–14 is considered in its prophetic and historical aspects in Heb 10:5–10.[194] The writer argues that the ineffective sacrifices of the old covenant have been replaced with the sufficient sacrifice of Jesus. The cultic arrangements of the Levitical

---

[190] Lane, 171.

[191] Ibid., 204. First, the contrast between the heavenly and earthly tabernacle is demonstrated to supplement the distinction between the new and the old. Secondly, the covenant under which the Levitical arrangement was instituted has been treated by God as obsolete. The new covenant shows the eschatological superiority of Christ's ministry and God's intention to replace the old arrangement with new one eschatologically.

[192] Ibid., 209.

[193] Ibid.

[194] W. Lane, *Hebrews 9–13*, WBC (Dallas: Word Books, 1991), 257.

law, with its annual provision for a Day of Atonement, have been set aside. He appeals to Ps 40:6–8 to show that the incarnation and active obedience of the divine Son had been prophesied in Scripture.[195] In other words, it provided the exegetical support for the thesis that the offering of the body of Jesus was superior to the offerings prescribed by the law. Therefore, Jesus's sacrifice fulfilled the human vocation enunciated in the Ps 40. Jesus embraced the will of God in solidarity with the human family; the new people of God have been consecrated to the service of God. Lane understands Jesus's sacrifice in the light of the Day of Atonement. He stayed with Egyptian Exodus to appreciate the contribution of the prophets.

S. Lehne, *The New Covenant in Hebrews* (Sheffield: JSOT, 1990)

Lehne examined the role of the new covenant idea in Hebrews from the standpoint of the author and his first readers.[196] Lehne discussed consequences of belonging to the new covenant community and the nature of the new covenant cult focusing on some passages in Hebrews. In doing so, Lehne claimed that Hebrews is a study "concerning the relationship of the old and new covenants".[197]

Lehne pointed out that all of Hebrews could be described as an extended examination of the relationship between the old and the new covenantal orders and their representatives.[198] Lehne argued that "Jesus is consistently portrayed as a new form, and an eschatologically superior form, of God's word". He pointed out that the focus on Jesus's person in chapters 1–7 parallels the focus on Jesus's work in chapters 8–10. Lehne also pointed out that the blessing of the new covenant is perfection. According to him, the theme of perfection provides the link between the comparative scheme of revelatory agents and the new covenant idea. Thus the new covenant motif is implicitly linked to the author's treatment of revelation in Hebrews.

---

[195] Ibid., 262.

[196] S. Lehne, *The New Covenant in Hebrews* (Sheffield, Sheffield Academic Press, 1990), 11.

[197] Ibid., 66. Lehne pointed out that the term "covenant" suggests continuity between Christianity and Judaism, yet "new" indicates an element of discontinuity.

[198] Ibid., 24–8. Cf. The promises made to Abraham are connected to both old and new covenants.

Lehne argued that the author depicts the new covenant cult analogously to the old covenant cult.[199] In this sense the new covenant existed from all eternity, but was fully revealed and realized only in Christ. According to Lehne, both the old covenant and Christ's new covenant are based on a sovereign act of God on behalf of his people (Heb 8:8–13) who are thereby summoned to become a cultic assembly bound by God's word (Heb 12:18–24), both are initiated/sealed by a bloody ceremony involving the death of the victim (9:15–22), both covenantal orders require allegiance and obedience to God on the part of their members who are otherwise punished, and both are grounded in the promise of an inheritance (Heb 9:15).

Lehne classified negative and positive consequences of new covenant membership with a schematic overview.[200] The classification shows readers of the letter to Hebrews the intimate link between the reality of the new covenantal order and its effect upon their conduct and lives. In regard to this matter, Lehne saw that the patriarchs had the role of exemplars for the addressees. Abraham and the selected group of ancestors in Heb 11 are portrayed as models of endurance, patience, and faith in the promises of the unseen, heavenly world. The cloud of witnesses proleptically belonged to the new covenantal order by foreseeing it and greeting it from afar (Heb 11:13). New covenant members are therefore enjoined to become *mimetai* of their qualities (Heb 6:12).

Lehne claimed that the new covenant concept plays an important role in Hebrews.[201] He wanted to depict the Christ event in continuity with and as the perfect fulfillment of the cultic heritage of Israel by creatively reinterpreting the category of covenant from a cultic perspective. He also wanted to succeed in presenting Christ as the permanent, definitive, and superior replacement of that same heritage by stressing the elements of newness and drawing a contrast to the former system.

---

[199] Ibid., 97–98. Lehne views the old covenant as a God-given reflection in sketchy, "embryonic form", of the celestial prototype of the new covenant.

[200] Ibid., 104–106.

[201] Ibid., 119.

Lehne pointed out that the exposition about the Christ event can be regarded as a kind of "historical prologue" for the "stipulations" governing life under the new covenant. That is, the Lord's action which took the Israelites by the hand and led them out of Egypt (Jer 31:32; Heb 8:9) stands at the beginning of the Decalogue as the foundation for every commandment (cf. Exod 20:2), and Christ's death and exaltation to God's right hand are presupposed by all the injunctions in Hebrews. Lehne did not pay sufficient attention to the paschal theme itself. She did not think that Christ's death was paschal as the Passover alone preceded the exodus.

B. Lindars, New Testament Theology: The Theology of the Letter to the Hebrews (Cambridge: Cambridge University Press, 1991)

Hebrews chooses to use the designation "son", and says "a son", not "the son", in pointing out that he was appointed the heir of all things in these last days. Lindars comments that "Son" is messianic based on Ps 2:7 in Heb 1:5 and "first-born" in Heb 1:6 looks to be a literary allusion to Ps 89:27.[202] The "first-born" is introduced to the world of humanity in the whole process of the saving events of which Jesus is God's agent. However, the Messiah must die before achieving his messianic work. Lindars sees that the Day of Atonement is used in Hebrews as a model to develop the sacrificial death of Jesus.[203] The important source utilized was the prophecy of the Suffering Servant in Isa 53 in Heb 7:25 and 9:28.

In Heb 3, God's promise of the land of Canaan in the Old Testament is contrasted with the promise of salvation in the New Testament. Moses is described as God's servant, whereas Jesus is God's Son. Hebrews adduces the example of Moses from Num 12:7, where Moses is singled out for his faithfulness. Jesus is a better example to follow and his role ranks higher than that of Moses. Lindars sees that Moses was an example of the fidelity which can be seen in Jesus.

---

[202] Ibid., 35–7.
[203] Ibid., 36.

Lindars saw that the sacrifice of Christ represented the inauguration of the new covenant of Jer 31:31–4.[204] This is quoted in Heb 8:8–12 and Heb 10:16–17 in short form. The author of Hebrews refers to Jesus as "the mediator of a new covenant" in Heb 9:15. The new covenant theme was thus available in connection with the sacrificial death of Jesus as atonement for sins. Lindars built up his argument on this basis, concluding that the sacrifice of Jesus has produced a permanent situation in which no further act of atonement is necessary. Lindars linked the annual ceremony of the Day of Atonement described in Lev 16 with the model of the covenant sacrifice in Exod 24.[205] The whole point of the Day of Atonement is that it takes away the sins of the preceding year for which individual atonement has not been made, so long as repentance is sincere.[206] The latter shows how this act of atonement has lasting effect, which provides a constant resource to deal with the consciousness of sin, which so deeply troubles his readers. Thus, what he intends to say is that everything that is essential for atonement has been done through the sacrifice of Christ.

The author of Hebrews links the mercy and compassion of Jesus with the theme of priesthood.[207] He understands that sins are bound to arise, and that is why he is insistent on the compassionate nature of Jesus as high priest. He argues that everything which could not be achieved by the Jewish sacrificial system for removing the barrier of sin has been actually achieved by Jesus. Therefore, Lindars considers three principal strands of that sacrificial system to be important themes in the author's presentation of the priesthood of Jesus:[208] (1) the author of Hebrews argues that the ceremonial of the Day of Atonement, which is performed by the high priest, has found its fulfilment in Jesus; (2) The priesthood of the Messiah uniquely qualifies him to perform the sacrifice which is required for atonement for sins; (3) Christ's sacrifice opens the era of salvation in which further sacrifices for sins are no longer required. This introduces the eschatological concept of the inauguration of the new covenant.

---

[204] Ibid., 79–84.

[205] Ibid., 84. In fact, the Day of Atonement is not explicitly used in connection with the sacrificial death of Jesus elsewhere in the New Testament, but it is a perceptive move.

[206] Ibid., 85.

[207] Cf. Heb 2:17; 4:14–16; 5:1–14; 7:1–28.

[208] Lindars, *Theology*, 58–72.

It has been also pointed out that Spirit (רוּחַ) in the Old Testament refers to an attribute of God which may be objectified as a separate being.[209] In New Testament times the word was used to denote angelic spirits. According to Lindars, therefore, Spirit (רוּחַ) means the power of God as an active force.[210] He says that it is a mistake to apply to the word the later dogmatic definitions of the personality of the Spirit which belong to Trinitarian theology.[211] Concerning using the definite article with the word, Lindars points out that the omission of the article indicates the notion of divine influence when the context is concerned with the Spirit's gifts. In Heb 2:4 and 6:4, the Greek texts omit the definite article before "Holy Spirit". Lindars comments that both texts are reminiscent of the claim of Peter on the Day of Pentecost that the eschatological outpouring of the Spirit prophesied by Joel has been fulfilled in Acts 2:14–33. On the other hand, when the Greek includes the article, it indicates that the real author is the Holy Spirit (Heb 3:7; 9:8; 10:15).[212]

Lindars regarded the Day of Atonement as the primary example of what an act of atonement should be. He did not combine the ritual with the Passover. He also saw Jesus as personally pre-existent in Hebrews. According to him, Jesus is the human expression of the pre-existent Son of God. Lindars missed the importance of the Davidic figure for the letter to Hebrews.

M. E. Isaacs, *Sacred Space: An Approach to the Theology of the Epistle to Hebrews* (Sheffield: Sheffield Academic Press, 1992)

Isaacs pointed out that the author of Hebrews has a preoccupation with the profane versus the holy.[213] From the stance of Israel's wilderness period, this preoccupation with sacred space is worked out in terms of both her entry into the promised land and entry into the inner sanctum of the desert tabernacle, together with the covenant and priesthood upon which these two means of access were based. The author inherited notions of sacred space whereby this was identified with the land, Jerusalem, Zion, and the sanctuary.

---

[209] F. Baumgörtel, "Spirit in the OT," in *TDNT* VI, 359–68. Cf. Judg 11:29 means that God endued Jephthah with his own power.

[210] Lindars, *Theology*, 57.

[211] Ibid.

[212] Ibid.

[213] M. E. Isaacs, *Sacred Space: An Approach to the Theology of the Epistle to the Hebrews* (Sheffield: Sheffield Academic Press, 1992), 62.

Isaacs understood that, in the understanding of the Israelites, the land was not merely a political but a religious heritage.[214] The land-promises are embedded in Israelite consciousness because sacred territory was regarded to be located geographically on earth and was a type of the beatific state in heaven. Isaacs also pointed out that this is the principal topic of Heb 3:7–4:13. Thus Heb 3:7–11 cited from Ps 94:7–11 refers to God's threat to disinherit Israel for her lack of trust and her desire to return to a place of bondage rather than go forward to the land of promise.[215]

Isaacs pointed out that the Epistle to the Hebrews describes certain similarities between Jesus and Moses. The author of Hebrews is emphatic in contrasting prophet with son based on Heb 1:1–2.[216] Isaacs argued that Jesus had a superior relationship to God as Son; on the other hand, Moses functioned as a faithful witness to what is to be God's final word—Jesus. Isaacs went to say that in Heb 3:2–5, Num 12:7 is cited from the LXX. This means that among the wilderness generation Moses alone was faithful. Thus, Isaacs concluded that the author of Hebrews was aware of the unique role ascribed to Moses, and wished to demonstrate that Christ has superseded Moses.

Isaacs pointed out that the most important mediatorial figure in Judaism in the period of the Second Temple was the high priest.[217] The priest's specific role of offering all or part of the victim sacrificed by the worshipper was intended to sanctify the offerer through the offering, thereby admitting the secular into the orbit of the sacred. Therefore, Isaacs related the role played by the high priest in the Day of Atonement ceremonies to the offering.

Isaacs saw that in his death Jesus has carried out the true work of the true priest performed on the Day of Atonement. That is, she did not combine the Day of Atonement with the Passover. Isaacs focused on the type of the exodus from Egypt. Therefore, she identified Moses as the type of Jesus, but missed the Davidic emphasis.

---

[214] Ibid., 78.
[215] Ibid., 79. Isaacs regarded Ps 94 as a midrash on Num 14:1–35.
[216] Ibid., 134.
[217] Ibid., 144.

D. J. Pursiful, The Cultic Motif in the Spirituality of the Book of Hebrews (Lampeter: Mellen, 1993)

D. J. Pursiful researched the cultic motif in the spirituality of the letter of the Hebrews.[218] Pursiful argued that spirituality is an aspect of lived experience, and claimed that biblical spirituality may imply the study of spirituality expressed in Scripture.[219] He tried to unfold his work exegetically, with attention to the relevant passage of Hebrews studied in a historical-critical fashion, without attempting a systematic study of cultus as a theme in biblical spirituality in general.

Pursiful pointed out that the author of Hebrews portrays Christ's cultic role as universally effective. The passion of Christ is expressed as necessary instruction leading to obedience and finally to perfection (5:8–9). Heb 9:15–17 describes the necessity of death for the confirming of a covenant.[220] Jesus's suffering outside the walls of Jerusalem in Heb 13:11–13 is compared to the disposal of the carcasses of sacrificial animals.[221] Thus, Jesus's suffering and death may be seen as an integral part of Christ's ritual accomplishment. Jesus experienced death for the sake of everyone (2:9).

Pursiful saw that Christ's movement into the heavenly realm in Heb 9:11–25 closely paralleled the movement of the high priest on the Day of Atonement as he passed beyond the curtain into the holy of holies. Like the high priest in the Old Testament, Christ's entrance was accomplished through the blood which attained access. Another possible cultic connection with the death of Jesus was the time of its occurrence—the Passover;[222] and yet Pursiful believes that this opportunity of interpretation is never addressed in Hebrews.

---

[218] D. J. Pursiful, *The Cultic Motif in the Spirituality of the Book of Hebrews* (Lampeter: Mellen, 1993), 41. According to Pursiful, cult and cultus are used with no discernible difference in the literature surrounding ancient Jewish religious practices in general and Hebrews in particular. The terms are combined in the adjectival form "cultic", also he used "ritualistic" as a synonym for "cultic".

[219] Ibid., 24.

[220] Ibid., 66–7. In previous covenants, this would have been the symbolic death of the covenant-maker through the sacrifice of an animal; in the new covenant, however, Christ himself died not in symbol but in truth.

[221] Ibid. The author of Hebrews pushes the imagery to an even cruder and more shocking level by linking the death of Jesus to the burning of the corpses after their blood has already been applied.

[222] Cf. Matt 26:2; 1 Cor 5:7.

Hebrews' use of the Day of Atonement explains the typology of a ritual of passage in two distinct ways.[223] The Old Testament rite from which the author draws his imagery is a ritual of passage of the cyclical, corporate type. The Day of Atonement imagery also shows a distinctive reinterpretation of the traditional Hebrew understanding of expiation. As it stands in the Old Testament, defilement and purgation follow one another in a never-ending oscillatory cycle.

Pursiful argued that the letter was built around the type of the exodus, but he missed the cultic interplay between the two exoduses which the New Testament writers make. He also demonstrates that much of the material in Hebrews is based on the Day of Atonement liturgy provided by contemporary Jewish patterns of celebration. Thus, he completely missed any paschal theme that might be present.

Analysis

There have been many academic studies of the letter of Hebrews and, as might be expected, each of these works is defined by its own characteristics and interpretations. For the purpose of my research, I have restricted myself to an investigation and analysis of those texts which place a primary focus on the exodus motif.

Of those texts that I have examined in detail, it appears that most commentators focus on the Egyptian Exodus and have neglected the importance and relevance of the Babylonian Exodus. Because of these material facts, it is my belief that these works severely restrict themselves in terms of their depth and breadth of study and investigation.

Therefore, I would argue that in these works there is no suggestion that the author of Hebrews shared the creativity of the early church in linking the narrative of the Egyptian Exodus with the new exodus promises of the eighth century prophets. I would also argue that these works fail to identify the Davidic emphasis in Hebrews, and furthermore have not paid sufficient attention to the paschal theme in the letter. It is my assertion that, when taken

---

[223] Pursiful, *The Cultic Motif,* 79.

together, the works that I have surveyed have failed to identify the cultic interplay between the Egyptian and Babylonian Exoduses.

Chapter 3: The Deliverance Theme

Introduction

Those whom God has called will receive the promised eschatological inheritance, which concerns the enjoyment of eternal deliverance.[224] The Old Testament shows that God brought the exiles back to the land of their fathers when they turned from their evil ways. Thus, the New Testament writers appropriate this specialized usage of deliverance to designate the establishment of God's reign at the end of time. During the time that John was in prison, he sent messengers to ask if Jesus was indeed the one who was expected for Israel.[225] Jesus answered with a clear allusion to Isaiah.[226] Paul understood Jesus as Christ, and proclaimed that if anyone is in Christ, he is a new creation.[227] The author of Hebrews asserts that Christ is identified with humanity by describing his liberating work for all human-beings.[228] He argues that Christ had to partake of the same nature as us in order effectively defeat an enemy, the devil, who had the power of death.

There are some scholars who think that the term "deliverance" reflects Israel's hope of rescue by her God from pagan oppression in the first century.[229] For first-century Jews the inauguration of the age to come would mean liberation from Rome, the restoration of the Temple, and the free enjoyment of their own land. Deliverance summarizes the entire future hope. This would be the gift of Israel's God to his whole people, all at once. Individual Jews would find their

---

[224] Heb 1:14; 3:1; 5:9; 9:15; 10:36.

[225] Matt 11:2-19; Luke 7:18-35.

[226] Cf. Isaiah, passim. "The blind receive sight, the lame walk, those who have leprosy are cursed, the deaf hear, the dead are raised, and the good news is preached to the poor."

[227] 2 Cor 5:17.

[228] Heb 2:9.

[229] E. P. Sanders, *Judaism: Practice and Belief, 63 BCE—66 CE* (London: SCM, 1992), 278. N. T. Wright, *The New Testament and The People of God* (London: SPCK, 1992), 330, 334. According to them, deliverance was a matter of a new world, the renewal of creation. Within this, Israel's God would call some from within the nation to be a new Israel, the spearhead of the divine purpose. This renewed people were to be the holy, pure, renewed human beings, living in a covenant fidelity which would answer to the covenant faithfulness of the creator God, and which would end in the renewal, i.e. resurrection, of human bodies themselves. If this was to happen then Israel's God had to deal with her sins. The end of exile, in fact, would be seen as the great sign that this had been accomplished. The promise of forgiveness and that of national restoration were thus linked causally, not by mere coincidence.

own deliverance through their membership within Israel, that is, within the covenant. According to them, covenant membership in the present was the guarantee of deliverance in the future.

Others have linked "deliverance" to other Mediterranean cultures. Bultmann understood that the deliverance that had been produced by Christ's sacrifice was victory over the cosmic powers, especially over death.[230] It was bestowed upon the gnostic ("knower") who has come to knowledge of himself, of his heavenly home, and of the way back to it, when at death the self separates from body and soul and is released to soar into the heavenly world of light.[231] However, Bultmann believed that an earthly bound Jesus was incapable of delivering the knowledge which would lead to salvation.[232] Bultmann's view of soteriology is anthropocentric in character. He is not concerned with cosmological speculations. According to Packer, Bultmann's interest in "personal history" is not far removed from a demythologized gnostic concept of man.[233]

However, the author of Hebrews often cited the Old Testament passages,[234] which implies that the understanding of deliverance in Hebrews follows the Old Testament pattern. Therefore, I will first study some views of deliverance related to ideas current in the first century. Then I will show how deliverance is related to the Passover motif. I will then look at ideas of deliverance in the Old Testament, the Intertestamental Literature, and the New Testament. Finally, I will exegete the Epistle to the Hebrews in the light of Old Testament and Intertestamental Literature understanding.

---

[230] R. Bultmann, *The Theology of the New Testament*, trans. K. Grobel, Vol.2 (London: SCM, 1968), 157. According to Bultmann, deliverance is generally termed forgiveness of sin, release ($αvπολυτρωσις$, "redemption"), justification, sanctification, or purification, when it is being described in its effect on believers.

[231] Ibid., 165.

[232] R. Bultmann, *The Theology of the New Testament*, 3-32.

[233] J. I. Packer, "Reviews and Notices" *EQ* 31 (1959), 225-27 [225].

[234] Passim.

Some Views of Deliverance

In Hellenism

In Hellenistic society deliverance was emancipation from the demonic world-rulers, especially from death. The oldest tradition of Hercules that has been preserved links him to the capture of Death.[235] This account provided the core of the classical legend of Hercules's rescue of Alcestis by wrestling with Death.[236] According to this tradition, the idea of "deliverance" approaches that of σωτήρ ("saviour"). Above all, σωτήρ is one of the most popular designations for deified rulers.[237] The ruler is σωτήρ because he brings peace and order.

Knox[238] has reasoned that the depiction of Jesus as the champion (ἀρχηγός) who crushed the tyrant who possessed the power of death. Knox's proposal is supported by Manson who thinks that the designation of Jesus as the champion (ἀρχηγός) in a context depicting him as protagonist suggests that the author intended to present Jesus to his readers in language that drew freely upon the Hercules tradition in popular Hellenism.[239]

However, Manson's and Knox's understanding has been challenged by Cullmann, who points out that the Old Testament calls God "Saviour."[240] That is, the term σωτήρ is generally the saviour of the people in the Old Testament and Judaism. According to Cullmann, therefore, Jesus as σωτήρ is connected

---

[235] Homer, *Iliad* 5.394–400; cf. Pindar, *Olympian Odes* 9.33

[236] Apollodorus Mythographus, *Bibliotheca* 1.106

[237] Cf. Here gods, but also heroes, and above all rulers are called "saviours," because they deliver men from all kinds of physical distress such as sickness and infirmity, dangers such as shipwrecks, and especially from the terrors of war and an uncertain existence.

[238] W. L. Knox, "The Divine Hero Christology of the New Testament," *HTR* 41 (1948), 239. According to Knox, "Hellenistic Judaism was always receiving from its surroundings a coloring of popular religious language, and contributing to the general amalgam from the Septuagint and the prayer of the Hellenistic synagogue." He goes on to say that "all that we have is the use of a common stock of ideas, ultimately religious, but adopted by rhetoric and popular philosophy and carried over into the liturgical and homiletical language of the Hellenistic world, including that of the Church."

[239] W. Manson, *The Epistle to the Hebrews: Christ's and Ours* (Richmond: John Knox, 1958), 103–4.

[240] O. Cullmann, *The Christology of the New Testament* (London: SCM, 1963), 239. The Hebrew words יֵשַׁע, מוֹשִׁיעַ, and יְשׁוּעָה all of which come from the same root, are translated σωτήρ in the Septuagint. The Psalms (24:5; 27:1; 35:3; 62:2,6; 65:5; 79:9) and all parts of Isaiah (12:2; 17:10; 43:3, 11; 45:15, 21; 60:16; 62:11; 63:8) give God this title most often, but it occurs also elsewhere and may be traced through the whole of the Old Testament (Jer 14:8; Micah 7:7; Hab 3:18; 1 Sam 10:19; Deut 32:15) and Jewish literature (1 Macc 4.30; Wisd 16:7; Ecclus 51.1; Baruch 4.22; Judith 9:11).

with the Jewish and Old Testament concept rather than with the Hellenistic one.[241] He concluded that Greek influence is to be judged more with respect to form than to content. The New Testament writers had to distinguish their doctrine of deliverance from current ideas which were in relation to the mystery cults. The evidence is seen by pointing to the apostle's debt to biblical salvation-history centered in God's mighty deed of redemption in Christ. According to Nanos,[242] the New Testament can be read as Jewish correspondence, written by and for Jews and Gentiles concerned with the Jewish context of their faith in Jesus as the Jewish Messiah. Holland supports Nanos's view, saying that Greek influence began to pervade the thinking of the church in the second century AD—after the New Testament documents had been written.[243] He concludes that this second-century process of Hellenization was the result of two momentous events:[244] "The first was the division that took place between the church and Judaism."[245] "The second was the emergence in the second century of Gentile leaders within the church."[246] Neither factor influenced the writing of the New Testament documents. In the writings of the New Testament the church remained faithful to their Jewish heritage.

---

[241] Cullmann, *Christology*, 241; Cf. R. Bultmann, *Theology*, Vol. 1, 79. Bultmann saw that the early Christian texts called Jesus "Saviour," and the title was related to the Hellenistic concept.

[242] M. Nanos, *The Mystery of Romans* (Philadelphia: Fortress, 1997), 4.

[243] T. Holland, *Contours of Pauline Theology: A Radical New Survey of the Influences on Paul's Biblical Writings* (Fearn: Christian Focus, 2004), 16.

[244] Ibid.

[245] This separation happened in the latter part of the first century.

[246] These men brought their Hellenistic intellectual training with them and they unwittingly read it into the Christian Scriptures. They used the Greek text of the Old Testament along with the emerging New Testament canon that was also written in Greek. Rather than appreciating the Hebraic mindset that lay behind these writings, they treated them as "authentic" Greek literature, the same as the Greek texts by which they had been educated. They soon began to lose sight of the Old Testament background to the New Testament writings and in its place inserted a Hellenistic scheme of thought. It thus follows that the Hellenization of the Christian gospel happened in the second century, much later than New Testament scholars had assumed.

Gnosticism

The precise dating of gnostic teaching is disputed; in essence the gnostic claimed deliverance by an immediate knowledge of God.[247] This knowledge was intellectual as against moral, and esoteric in being confined to an elite circle of initiates. It gives the gnostic ("knower") his consciousness of superiority to the world.

Gnosticism taught a dualism of soul and body[248] and a hierarchy of spiritual and angelic intermediaries between God and man.[249] The gnostic is the "spiritual man," the "pneumatic," who disdainfully looks down upon others who do not bear within them the spark of light but are mere "men of soul," "men of flesh or men of matter." Conscious of being already emancipated by his gnosis, he demonstrates this freedom either by asceticism or by libertinism, or even by a peculiar combination of both. By a meditative contemplation which culminates in ecstasy, he is able even now to enjoy the world of light which he is to enter after death, and he can demonstrate the power of the Spirit that dwells within him by miraculous deeds.

In Gnosticism deliverance means emancipation from the demonic world-ruler, from sin, and especially from death by coming to "know" in response to a "call" from the divine world expressed in the so-called "gnostic-redeemer myth".[250] How, then, can people be saved? It is the result of a light-person sent by the highest god[251] who comes down from the light-world bringing gnosis. He "wakes" the sparks of light which have sunk into sleep or drunkenness and "reminds" them of their heavenly home. He teaches them concerning their superiority to the world and concerning the attitude they are to adopt toward the world. He dispenses the sacraments by which they are to purify themselves and fan back to life their quenched light-power or at least strengthen its

---

[247] S. Petrement, *A Separate God; The Christian Origins of Gnosticism*, trans. C. Harrison (London: Longman and Todd, 1990), 129. According to Petrement, knowledge is religious knowledge, a revealed religious teaching to which one adheres. That is to say that it is closer to what we call faith than what we call knowledge. Moreover, the earliest Gnostics mentioned by the heresiologists seem to have spoken of faith as much as knowledge, and hardly made any distinction between them.

[248] R. E. Watts, "The new exodus" in *What Does It Mean to be Saved?* ed. J. G. Stackhouse, Jr. (Grand Rapids: Baker, 2002), 38.

[249] Petrement, *Separate*, 171–2; R. Bultmann, *Theology*, Vol. 1, 109.

[250] Bultmann, *Theology*, Vol. 1, 177.

[251] Ibid. It is called the son and "image" of the Most High.

weakened state—by which, in other words, they are "reborn." He teaches them about the heavenly journey they will start at death and communicates to them the secret passwords by virtue of which they can safely pass through the stations of this journey—past the demonic watchmen of the starry spheres.

In attempting to understand how the New Testament authors reflect the religious milieu that they shared with the emerging Gnosticism, Bultmann pointed out how the exalted Redeemer will draw after himself his own;[252] he is himself the "way."[253] The idea is expressed in Hebrews by the term "pioneer."[254] Christ is the pioneer-guide to heaven; being "made perfect" by attaining heaven,[255] he is also the "perfecter" of his own.[256] Bultmann held that by studying the gnostic documents the background of the theology of the New Testament could be identified and so its history could be plotted and understood. Thus, he saw that Paul and John borrowed this redeemer myth from Gnosticism, and applied it to Jesus to produce New Testament Christology. Wisse also observed that John can be understood as participating in the same speculative freedom as the gnostic writers.[257] Perkins supports Wisse's ideas, saying that this gnostic methodology is the key to understanding other New Testament themes.[258] Their mistake was to assume that the gnostic texts on which they relied were evidence of the state of Gnosticism in the first century. Recent scholarship has demonstrated that this was not the case. Gnosticism was only in its embryonic stage in the first century. Rather than Christians borrowing from Gnosticism, it was Gnosticism that borrowed from Christians.[259]

---

[252] Cf. John 12:32.

[253] Cf. John 14:6.

[254] Heb 2:10; 12:2 cf. Acts 3:15; 5:31; 2 Clem. 20:5—same word in all five cases.

[255] Heb 2:10; 5:9

[256] Heb 12:2.

[257] F. Wisse, "Prolegomena to the Study of the New Testament and Gnosis," in *The New Testament and Gnosis: Essays in honour of Robert M. Wilson*, ed. A. H. B. Logan and A. J. M. Wedderburn (Edinburgh: T&T Clark, 1983), 143. According to Wisse, the author of the Fourth Gospel obviously did not feel bound by the early traditions about Jesus which were incorporated in the Synoptic Gospels, and his reinterpretation of Jesus is in many ways as daring as that found in gnostic gospels. As we see from their writings, gnostics had little difficulty affirming the incarnation or the virgin birth, though as in the case of the author of the Gospel of John and many others in the early church, the real interest was in the divine presence.

[258] Perkins, *Gnosticism*, 31-2.

[259] Holland, *Contours*, 52.

Deliverance in the Old Testament

Casey pointed out that the exodus is the event which orders and gives shape to God's people.[260] Dunn acknowledges that it is a crucial metaphor of deliverance.[261] However, some understand the deliverance from Egypt in entirely political terms. Wright asks why, if Israel was liberated from Egypt and placed in her own land, is everything not now perfect?[262] According to Wright, the deliverance from Egypt was not a deliverance from sin. The old relationship established in Adam's disobedience was not cancelled by the exodus. Therefore, Wright relates the fall and restoration of Israel to the exile; that is, he points out that Israel's sin caused her exile; the exile itself is to be understood as a sacrifice, and the return from exile is as a "resurrection".[263]

In fact, there was another exodus, which was from Babylon. The Israelites also saw the second exile as God's punishment for their sins and found great difficulty in thinking that there could be a new start—and yet this is the very thing that the prophets had promised.[264] It would be just like when the Jews left Egypt, for there would be a second exodus. The exiles would return telling of the deliverance of God (Isa 52:7-10).

What then is deliverance itself in the light of the Passover? Some see deliverance as equivalent to the forgiveness of sins. According to Cullmann,

---

[260] J. Casey, "The Exodus Theme in the Book of Revelation Against the Background of the New Testament," *Con* 189 (1987), 42.

[261] J. Dunn, *The Theology of Paul the Apostle* (Cambridge: Eerdmans, 1998), 329.

[262] N. T. Wright, *The New Testament and the People of God* (London: SPCK, 1992), 216.

[263] Ibid, 272-79. Wright points out that the exile itself was seen a 'death'. He also sees that Israel's forgiveness will mean her national re-establishment (p. 293). It seems to me that Wright has confused resurrection with forgiveness if return from exile is equivalent to her national re-establishment. If so, her national re-establishment is not her forgiveness but the result of her forgiveness.

[264] In spite of the collapse of the royal family, the prophets predicted that a descendant of David would be raised up (Isa 11:1). He would lead the people from their captivity back to the Promised Land (Isa 11:11). He would be anointed with the Spirit of the Lord for this task (Isa 61:1-2). He would lead the people through the wilderness (Hos 2:14). The pilgrimage through the desert would be under the protection of the Holy Spirit (Isa 44:3), just as the pilgrimage from Egypt had been. There would be miracles (Mic 7:15) like when they came out of Egypt, and the desert would be transformed as nature shared in the re-creation of the nation (Isa 55:13). Unlike when the people came out of Egypt when their flesh was circumcised, this time the hearts of the people would be circumcised (Jer 31:31-34). Finally, when the people arrived back at Jerusalem, they would build a magnificent temple that the descendant of David would dedicate (Ezek 44-45). Into this temple all the nations would come to worship Israel's God (Isa 2:1-5). The Lord would come into his temple (Isa 4:2-6) and the wedding between God and his people would be celebrated with a great cosmic banquet (Isa 54:1-8).

suffering for the forgiveness of sins is understood entirely from the divine ratification of that suffering in Jesus's exaltation as κύριος.[265] Vos also pointed out that the idea of redemption is associated with the forgiveness of sins.[266] That is, the ransom was paid to God, and the deliverance secured was a deliverance from the bondage of guilt. He further observed that in 1 Timothy 2.6 the vicarious character of the redemptive transaction has found unequivocal expression in the use of the prepositive ἀντί-, "who gave himself ἀντίλυτρον for all."[267] Vos applied the idea of deliverance to the commercial forensic representations, not to the Passover. If deliverance means forgiveness of sins, then it is very close to the Day of Atonement, for according to Wright, the forgiveness of sin was celebrated annually on the Day of Atonement.[268]

It has been argued earlier that the original Passover has the meaning of forgiveness of sin and restoration. After the exodus from Egypt, the Israelites wandered in the desert for forty years. Of course they did not have the doorframe on which blood was put in the desert. Instead they were given a tabernacle for removing sins. In the matter of the forgiveness of sins they could no longer daub the blood of a lamb on the top and on both sides of the doorframe, but instead they gathered together in the tabernacle, where sacrifices were made.

However, Dunn sees that the Passover is already associated with atonement.[269] And this link is firmly forged in the words used by Jesus at the Last Supper.[270] The language in the Passover meal is unavoidably sacrificial and signifies atonement. Howard also acknowledges that the sin offerings mentioned during the Passover of Ezek 45:25 lie behind the description of Jesus being the Lamb of God spoken of by John the Baptist in John 1:29.[271] He claims that the link

---

[265] Cullmann, *Christology*, 243.

[266] G. Vos, *Redemptive History and Biblical Interpretation* (Phillipsburg, NJ: Presbyterian and Reformed Publishing, 1980), 371.

[267] Ibid.

[268] Wright, *People of God*, 276.

[269] Dunn, *Theology*, 216–7.

[270] Ibid. The same tendency to run together different metaphors and descriptions of Jesus' death, thereby blurring older distinctions, is clearly evident elsewhere in the early churches (1 Pet 1:18–19; John 1.29). Paul's language in 1 Cor 5:7 suggests that the same evolution of imagery was already well advanced in his theology.

[271] Howard points out that the midrash on Exod 12 describes the Passover as an atoning sacrifice: Howard, "Eucharist", 331–2. Dunn sees that the Passover is already associated with atonement in Ezek 45:18–22: Dunn,

between the two feasts was so widely understood in Second Temple Judaism that John the Baptist's hearers would have had no difficulty in understanding the statement that the Lamb of God takes away the sin of the world. In addition to these scholars' arguments, Holland would add that the sacrifices of the Day of Atonement were absorbed into the Passover for deliverance in Ezek 45.[272] Ezekiel saw the prince's main function as being to provide sacrifices for the sins of the community and to build the eschatological temple.

If scholars are right in making a link between the Day of Atonement and Passover on the basis of Ezek 45, then, we would think that readers of the Gospels were not only expected to understand this fifth century BCE association, but that the readers of Paul's letters were also. This means that there must have been a widespread appreciation of the significance of Ezekiel's description as a key to understanding the achievements of the death of Christ. Restoration and forgiveness were celebrated together annually at Passover and on the Day of Atonement.

To sum up, a great exodus must take place to bring about both forgiveness of sins and the restoration of his people to their inheritance. This deliverance, as shown in the exodus, involves the forgiveness of sins and the restoration of God's people to their inheritance in the community which Christ established in his paschal death. The eschatological deliverance is deliverance from the kingdom of darkness to the eternal presence of God himself, where no sin could be tolerated and where no evil could gain entrance.[273] Thus, deliverance in the new exodus points to the greater reality that Christ would establish. What is jointly obtained by faith in Christ is the remission of sins and an inheritance among them that are sanctified.

In the prophetic period the hope for deliverance finds expression in the anticipated *Day of Yahweh* in which judgment would be combined with deliverance.[274] The experience of the exile gave concrete imagery and a

---

Theology, 216.
[272] Holland, *Contours*, 163.
[273] Ibid, 168. In relation to deliverance, according to Holland, Isaiah says that Yahweh would deliver Israel (Isa 42:6; 51:5), protect her on her pilgrimage as she returned to her inheritance (Isa 58:8), and safely establish her in her inheritance (Isa 32:1; 54:14; 62:1–2).
[274] Isa 24:19; 25:6–8; Joel 2:1, 28–32; Amos 5:18; 9:11.

concrete setting for the expression of this hope as a new exodus.[275] Therefore, I will examine the various prophets' thinking about this deliverance in turn.

Isaiah

Isa 40–55 provides a framework for deliverance mediated through Isaiah's use of exodus typology to depict Israel's deliverance from exile.[276] The exile is to be seen both as a punishment for the nation in its wickedness, and as in some sense a vocation to be a righteous bearer of sin and evil. In these chapters the restoration of Jerusalem is clearly to the fore.[277] Zion's waste places will become like Eden as Yahweh effects a new creation (51:3, cf. 41:17–20). Watts[278] and Stuhlmueller[279] assess that, when considered in combination with the warrior imagery and the interpretation of the first exodus as a creation event, both are in proclamations. Chapter 54 comprises something of a climax with its picture of glorious Zion (52:7–9; 54:11), now re-established in righteousness, knowing divine protection and vindication and whose accusers will all be overthrown (54:14).[280] Finally God invites his people to return to the New Jerusalem, that is, salvation in Isa 55:1–5.

The servant acts out the tribulation and future restoration of Zion in the context in 52:7–10. Then God calls for a "way" for the Lord to be prepared in the wilderness, for his saving activity (40:3–5; 43:19). He will sustain them in the wilderness more fully than in the exodus, ensuring they do not hunger, and providing streams in the desert (41:17–20; 43:19–21; 49:9–10). The wilderness will be transformed to celebrate the release of God's people (43:19: 49:10–11; 55:12–13). God will pour his refreshing and restoring Spirit on his people (44:3) so that they own him as their Lord (44:5); he himself will teach them and lead them in "the way" (54:13; 48:17), thus opening the eyes of the blind and the ears of the deaf.

---

[275] Isa 43:14–16; 48:20; 51:9; cf. Jer 31:31–34; Ezek 37:21–28; Zech 8:7–13.

[276] R. E. Watts, *Isaiah's New Exodus in Mark* (Grand Rapids: Baker, 1997), 369–74.

[277] R. E. Watts, "Consolation or Confrontation? Isaiah 40–55 and the Delay of the New Exodus," *TynBul* 41 (1990), 31–59; R. F. Melugin, *The Formation of Isaiah 40–55* (New York: Walter de Gruyter, 1976), 85. Melugin sees this prefigured in Isa 40:1–11.

[278] Watts, *Mark*, 297.

[279] C. Stuhlmueller, *Creative Redemption in Deutero-Isaiah,* AnBib 43 (Rome: Pontifical Biblical Institute, 1970), 145.

[280] R. E. Clements, Beyond Tradition-History: Deutero-Isaianic Development of First Isaiah's Themes, *JSOT* 31 (Sheffield: JSOT Press, 1985), 108.

Jerusalem's restoration is primarily a matter of the return of Yahweh's glorious presence. It is both the goal of the new exodus and the hallmark of the restoration; hence the same kind of self-designation which in 40:9f characterized the coming of Yahweh appears in 62:11. The image of light as God' glory (60:1, 3, 19; 62:2) stands in stark contrast to the present gloom and darkness (59:9). The description of the city's splendour (60:17f; cf. 54:11f) is only outshone by her spiritual glory with its emphasis on righteousness, salvation. This new creation of a New Jerusalem is greeted by great joy in 65:18.

Jeremiah

Jeremiah tells us that the forgiveness of sins is deliverance. God, in the new era, "will forgive their iniquity, and ... will remember their sin no more".[281] God forgave on the condition of repentance, and this was the very basis of forgiveness given by the prophet. In Jeremiah, we are also looking to the community of the end-time, to a situation when the kingdom of God has finally come and God is all in all.

When, therefore, Jeremiah prophesied Israel's return, it was of the return of Israel that he spoke. We cannot construe his prophecies in narrow nationalistic terms, since he is operating within a framework of ideals. Therefore, we see that the notion of the new covenant in Jeremiah is tied to a notion of the renewal, not only of the land, but of creation itself to a new heaven and a new earth.

In Jer 7:21, the whole system of institutionalized worship bound up in the means of national response, namely the cult, is condemned. For Israel the temple was the focus of the Sinaitic and the Davidic traditions. Since it was the focal point of the land, and represented the cumulative revelation which had been offered to Israel, Jeremiah argued that it was the responsibility of the people to protect the temple (and thus basically the land whose focal point it was). Similarly, the destruction of both the land and temple was imminent if they did not mend their ways. In Jer 22 a review of the kingship exercised by the sons of Josiah is conducted, and it is found to be a universal failure. It is

---

[281] Cf. The forgiveness of sins in the Old Testament was bound up, other than in exceptional instances, with the system of institutionalized approach through sacrifice.

even said of the boy king Jehoiachin, the soon to be exiled son of the infamous Jehoiakim, that if he were a signet ring on Yahweh's hand, Yahweh would pluck him off and commit him to exile. Then Jeremiah states the inauguration of the new covenant in Jer 31:31-34, which is set within chapters 30-31. These two chapters deal with the return of the divided nation from exile and the consequences of that return.[282]

Ezekiel

The same central line of thought is continued in Ezekiel.[283] He pictures the transformation of the stony heart into a heart of flesh by the indwelling of God's spirit in man. Ezek 37:1-14 shows that the people will be raised to life, brought back from exile, and given a new beginning. God will cleanse the people from their sins, giving them a new heart and spirit.[284] Ezekiel goes on from this inward new creation to the outward one, when Yahweh the great shepherd of his people brings in the new age of peace in nature and mankind, guaranteeing his gracious presence in the new temple. Jerusalem will be rebuilt, and the temple and the land will be restored (Ezek 40-48).[285] These visions of a salvific future go beyond the merely political and social to involve a new religious relationship with God. They hold out the hope of enjoying the Lord's intimate presence in the temple as a renewed people freely living again with God in their own country (Jer 31:17).

Furthermore, Ezek 45:18-25 tells us how the prince will offer an abundance of sacrifices for the sins of the people. It is also noted that a Davidic prince is to

---

[282] Jer 30:1-3 asserts the certainty of a return, 30:4-11 promises restoration under messianic leadership, vv. 12-17 indicate the disciplinary nature of the punishment received by the exiles, vv. 18-22 treat of the restoration of Jerusalem/Zion. Jer 31:1-6 draws support for the projected return from the unexpected grace displayed to Israel in the first Exodus, vv. 7-22 specifically relate to the return of the North, vv. 23-26 deal with the restoration of the South, while vv. 27-30 which leads into the new covenant section have in mind the restitution of the total nation. Jer 31:31-34 deals with the new covenant, vv. 35-37 locate the certainty of such a renewed covenant within the purposes of creation itself (and the impossibility of their being frustrated), while vv. 38-40 logically conclude the subject of the renewed people of God, with which these chapters have been dealing, by referring to the building of the New Jerusalem.

[283] Cf. Ezek 11:19; 36:25; 37:17-23.

[284] Ezek 36:22-32.

[285] Wright, *People of God*, 264. The prophets who look ahead to the restoration of Jerusalem and the rebuilding of the temple see in this event the refounding of the Garden of Eden. M. E. Tate, "The Comprehensive Nature of Salvation in Biblical Perspective," *ERT* (1999) 23.3, 208. In Ezek 36:24-25 the Babylonian exiles receive a divine promise of future saving action in terms of a new exodus-like experience.

provide a sacrifice for the sins of the covenant community.[286] What is important is that the sacrifices offered on the Day of Atonement were performed during the Passover. This means that the Passover is not only recalling redemption, but also anticipating atonement.[287]

To sum up, since the exile was the punishment for sins, the only sure sign that the sins had been forgiven would be the clear and certain liberation from exile. This is the major national context within which all individual cases of dealing with sin must be understood.[288]

Deliverance in the Intertestamental Literature

In the intertestamental period the expectation of deliverance as described by the prophets still circulated among the Jews. However, since the dominion of the foreigners over Israel continued, the term acquired a political and nationalistic connotation (Ps Song 9:1; 12:6). In a passage which is of uncertain date and provenance, T. Zeb. 9:8. (b d g) announces, "And after that your God himself shall shine forth as the light of righteousness, and salvation and mercy shall be in his wings. He will liberate all the prisoners of Belial, and every spirit of error shall be scattered."[289] A similar prophecy appears in the Assumption of Moses.[290] This tendency is continued in the Pseudepigrapha.[291] The Qumran texts also place emphasis on this expected deliverance (1QM 1, 12; 14, 5). Interestingly, the War Scroll at Qumran twice uses imagery drawn from this very passage in its paean to the mighty Yahweh-Warrior who comes to deliver his people.[292]

Similarly, the book of Tobit[293] speaks of a real post-exilic restoration of which the previous one was simply a foretaste:

---

[286] Holland, *Contours*, 161.
[287] Ibid.
[288] Sanders points out that national survival looms much larger than does individual life after death: Sanders, *Judaism*, 278.
[289] Cf. T. Levi 18.10–12
[290] 10:1–10; cf. 10QMelch 2.13
[291] W. Wink, *Naming the Powers: The Language of Power in the New Testament*, Vol. I (Philadelphia: Fortress, 1984), 24. E.g. 1 Enoch 19:1; 80:7; 99:7; Jub. 1:11; 2:17; 11:4; 12:20; 22:17
[292] 1QM 1, 12; 12, 10–14; 14, 5 and 19, 2–8.
[293] Wright, *People of God,* 270, sees Tobit as being written probably in the third century BCE.

> But God will again have mercy on them, and God will bring them back into the land of Israel; and they will rebuild the temple of God, but not like the first one until the period when the times of fulfilment shall come. After this they all will return from their exile and will rebuild Jerusalem in splendour; and in it the temple of God will be rebuilt, just as the prophets of Israel have said concerning it. Then the nations in the whole world will all be converted and worship God in truth.[294]

The so-called first book of Baruch, probably composed around the same period, clearly reflects the same perspective:

> For you are the Lord our God, and it is you, O Lord, whom we will praise. For you have put the fear of you in our hearts so that we would call upon your name; and we will praise you in our exile, for we have put away from our hearts all the iniquity of our ancestors who sinned against you. See, we are today in our exile where you have scattered us, to be reproached and cursed and punished for all the iniquities of our ancestors, who forsook the Lord our God.[295]

The relationship is also made explicit in the LXX. Psalm 95:5, in announcing (ευαγγελιον) the coming salvation of God, reads "all the gods of the nations are "δαιμονια" (אלהימ). In Isa 65:3 and 11 the LXX specifically adds the mention of demons: "they ... burn incense on bricks τοῖς δαιμονίοις" and "prepare a table to δαιμονίοις" (cf. Tg. Isa.).

Thus, the literature of the Jews during this period, known as the intertestamental or Second Temple period, clearly shows the faith which they had. They clung to the hope that God would yet fulfill the promises he had made to them through the prophets. Wright has understood that, for many Jews, Israel's exile had not ended and would not end until God redeemed his people.[296] Rowland remarks that reference to the last things in Jewish writings of this period is almost always accompanied by the notion, recurring in various

---

[294] Tob 14:5–7. Fragments of Tobit have been found at Qumran.
[295] Bar 3:6–8. This forms the conclusion of the first, and perhaps the older, section of the book.
[296] N. T. Wright, *Jesus and the Victory of God* (London: SPCK, 1996), 126-7; 203-4. Cf. Wright, *People of God*, 268-72.

forms, that a period of special distress and affliction must precede the dawn of salvation.[297]

Deliverance in the Synoptics and the Epistles

We have seen a strong expectation of deliverance within the Old Testament and throughout the intertestamental literature. Obviously this hope was powerful and sustained Israel throughout her suffering; so what we next need to establish is whether this hope of deliverance had any significant influence on the writers of the Gospels and the Epistles.

Matthew

The Lord's Prayer[298] originates from within the very heart of Jewish longing for the kingdom, and is shot through with Jesus's own reinterpretation of what that kingdom meant.[299] Marshall accepted that the prayer was certainly original to Jesus;[300] Fitzmyer was uncertain.[301] Hagner pointed out that it may actually be the prayer that Jesus taught, not so much the exact form of words, but the shape and pattern, the basic content.[302] Wright concludes that liturgical use in the early church has obviously affected the texts as we now have them.[303]

The first petition in the Lord's Prayer is for Yahweh to sanctify his own name; as Fitzmyer points out,[304] this evokes the prophecy of Ezek 36, in which the gift of the new heart and spirit to Yahweh's people will be the means of his

---

[297] C. C. Rowland, *The Open Heaven: A Study of Apocalyptic in Judaism and Early Christianity* (New York: Crossroad, 1982), 159. Cf. in the Old Testament this is also reflected in e.g. Ezek 38:20; Hos 4:3; Zeph 1:3; Dan 12:1, and arguably some of the 'servant' passages in Isa 40–55. The idea of portents appearing immediately before the final moment is reflected in e.g. Sib. Or. 3.795–807; Josephus, *War* 6.289, 299.

[298] Matt 6:9–15; Luke 11:2–4.

[299] Wright, *Victory*, 293.

[300] I. H. Marshall, *The Gospel of Luke: A Commentary on the Greek Text* (Exeter: Paternoster, 1978), 456.

[301] J. A. Fitzmyer, *The Gospel According to Luke (X–XXIV)*, Anchor Bible, Vol. 28a (Garden City, NY: Doubleday, 1985), 897. It is already notorious that the Jesus Seminar allowed only the opening phrase *Our Father* to be certainly original to Jesus, and ruled out hints of 'apocalyptic' ideas altogether: see J. D. Crossan, *The Historical Jesus: The Life of a Mediterranean Jewish Peasant* (Edinburgh: T&T Clark. 1991), 294. Crossan doubts that it contains "apocalyptic" elements, but rejects the authenticity of the prayer because of an a priori, seeing well enough where the real issue lies: "The establishment of such a prayer seems to represent the point where a group starts to distinguish and even separate itself from the wider religious community, and I do not believe that point was ever reached during the life of Jesus."

[302] D. A. Hagner, *Matthew 1–13* (Dallas: Word Books, 1993), 145.

[303] Wright, *Victory*, 293.

[304] Fitzmyer, *Luke*, 898.

sanctifying his name in his people. Prayer for forgiveness, and the accompanying promise of forgiveness within the community, is part of the whole emphasis on the theme of deliverance. And the prayer for deliverance from the time of trial and from the evil one likewise belong very closely with Jesus's proclamation of the kingdom as the announcement of the great moment that Israel had been longing for.[305] The time of great testing was coming upon Israel, and Jesus intended his people to be protected from it. The real enemy was not Rome,[306] but the evil one, who was to be watched and guarded against constantly. The whole prayer fits into the context of Jesus's ministry, which restores his people and forgives sins. Those who prayed this prayer were becoming true Israelites, those whom the covenant God would vindicate.[307]

Mark

Mark begins with John the Baptist saying that he is "the voice of one crying in the wilderness, 'prepare the way of the Lord.'"[308] John took the words from the prophecy of Isaiah that announced the coming of the descendant of David to fulfill God's promises.[309] In fact, Isa 40:1–11 appears to have been regarded by various traditions within Judaism as a classical passage for Isaianic salvation.[310] Thus, by citing the passage, what John intends is to show that the eschatological deliverance that Isaiah had predicted was at last breaking into human history.[311]

---

[305] Wright, *Victory*, 292–94.

[306] Wright, *People of God*, 300. Sanders, *Judaism*, 278. For first-century Jews this could only mean the inauguration of the age to come, liberation from Rome, the restoration of the Temple, and the free enjoyment of their own Land.

[307] Wright, *People of God*, 300.

[308] Mark 1:2–3. "It is written in Isaiah the prophet: "I will send my messenger ahead of you, who will prepare your way"—"a voice of one calling in the desert, 'Prepare the way for the Lord, make straight paths for him.'" The other Synoptics use Isa 40:3 to relate John to Jesus, but again the central concern seems to be the coming reign of God (cf. Matt 3:3, 7–12; Luke 3:6–17). Cf. F. M. Cross, *The Ancient Library of Qumran* AA 272 (Garden City, NY: Doubleday, 1961), 78. The most celebrated examples are those at Qumran (1QS 8, 12b–16a; 9, 17b–20a) where Isa 40:3 functioned as a programmatic statement of the community's self-understanding in fulfilling the necessary preparations for the 'way' of God's return.

[309] Isa 40:3–5. Cf. In fact, both John the Baptist and Jesus began their ministries by quoting Isaiah; the former citing Isa 40:3–5(cf. Luke 3:4–6) and the latter citing Isa 61:1–2 (Luke 4:18–19).

[310] Watts, *Mark*, 84.

[311] Holland, *Contours*, 27.

This understanding is confirmed by the question John asked when he sent messengers to Jesus to ask if he was the Christ. Jesus replied by pointing to the signs of Isaiah (Luke 7:21–22).[312] Jesus also commended John saying that he fulfilled the prophecy of the one sent before the Lord to prepare his way (Luke 7:27). Clearly John the Baptist set his ministries in the context of the Isaianic predictions of deliverance.

Thus, Mark's use of the Isaiah ascription and the "iconic" function of the Isa 40:3 text within various Jewish traditions indicate that the overall conceptual framework for his Gospel is the Isaianic new exodus, the prophetic transformation of Israel's memory of her founding moment into a model for her future hope. This suggests that for Mark the long-awaited coming of Yahweh as redeemer has begun, and with it, the inauguration of Israel's eschatological comfort: her deliverance from the hands of the nations.

Luke

Jesus began his ministry by quoting Isa 61:1–2 in Luke 4:18–19. The various isolated events now imply the coming of a new age that is in continuity with the ancient Israelite traditions.[313] The various components expressed in the Isaianic quotation provide categories for the organization of events in the Jesus traditions: (1) to bring good news to the poor; (2) to proclaim release to the captives; (3) to restore sight to the blind; (4) to let the oppressed go free; and (5) to proclaim the year of the Lord's favor. Turner[314] has argued that the first four phrases express the same concern: the oppressed situation of Israel, the people of God. All five, therefore, are concerned with the salvation of Israel from her low estate. This theological and political reading is confirmed by the reference to "the poor" in a non-social sense in Luke 2:34. One may also add that all five clauses refer to the same arrival of the salvation of God in the context of Isaiah's prophecies.[315] In the light of Luke 7:22, however, a literal

---

[312] Ibid. These were the very signs that Isaiah wrote of that would accompany the new exodus when it finally happened.

[313] This is embodied in the statement in Luke 4:21: Σήμερον πεπλήρωται ἡ γραφὴ αὕτη ἐν τοῖς ὠσὶν ὑμῶν ("Today this Scripture has been fulfilled in your hearing").

[314] M. M. Turner, *Power from on High: The Spirit in Israel's Restoration and Witness in Luke-Acts* (Sheffield: Sheffield Academic Press, 1996), 250.

[315] The vocabularies of εὐαγγελίζω and πτωχοῖς and the metaphors of sight/blindness and freedom/captivity play an important role in Isaiah.

sense cannot be totally excluded, although the broader meaning of the message should be retained. Luke emphasizes his understanding of the new era as a legitimate continuation of the history of the people of God. These clauses should therefore be understood as the manifestations of the arrival of salvation for Israel.[316]

Romans

Rom 3:21–26 has been widely examined in an attempt to find the paradigm used by Paul, which relates to deliverance. The reference to the ἱλαστήριον in v. 25, which has been widely assumed to reflect the Day of Atonement, was translated "propitiation".[317]

Others questioned the Day of Atonement setting, arguing that if this was the model Paul followed, he would have used more imagery that reflected the festival.[318] Barrett suggested that the reference to the ἱλαστήριον links the death of Jesus with the death of the Maccabean martyrs in 4 Macc 17:22.[319] The Maccabean martyr prayed that his death would provide ἱλαστήριον ("propitiation") for the nation's sins. The Jewish martyrs found, in Isaac's willingness to die, the inspiration they needed to be faithful to death.[320]

---

[316] D. W. Pao, *Acts and the Isaianic New Exodus* (Grand Rapids: Baker, 2000), 74. In Luke 7:18–20, a question is raised concerning the exact nature and meaning of Jesus' ministry. Jesus' response alludes again to Isa 61:1 where the arrival of the new era is characterized as one in which "the blind receive their sight, the lame walk, the lepers are cleansed, the deaf hear, the dead are raised, the poor have good news brought to them." The reappearance of the Isaianic scheme reflects the hermeneutical importance of Isa 61 for the identity of the early Christian movement.

[317] F. Buchsel, "ἱ'λασκομαι", in *TDNT* III.314. The Apostolic Fathers use the term as "propitiate"; R. Nicole, "C. H. Dodd and the Doctrine of Propitiation," *WThJ* 17 (1955), 131–32; M. Black, *Romans, The New Century Bible Commentary* (London: Marshall, Morgan & Scott, 1973), 60–61; G. E. Ladd, *A Theology of the New Testament* (London: Lutterworth, 1974), 423–36; L. Morris, *The Atonement. Its meaning and Significance* (Leicester: IVP, 1983), 166–76; L. Morris, *The Apostolic Preaching of the Cross: A Study of the Significance of some New Testament Terms* (London: Tyndale, 1972), 179–213. P. Stuhlmacher, *Reconciliation Law and Righteousness, Essays in Biblical Theology* (Philadelphia: Fortress, 1986), 86. Cf. C. H. Dodd, "Hilaskesthai [Gr], Its Cognates: Derivatives and Synonyms in the Septuagint," *JTS* 32(1931), 352–360. Dodd claims that ἱλαστήριον meant 'expiation'.

[318] F. Buchsel, "ἱλαστήριον," [hilastērion] in *TDNT* III, 310–23. In support of this challenge it was pointed out that the public (προέθετο) display of the sacrifice of Christ (v. 25) is contrary to the privacy of the sacrifice of the Day of Atonement.

[319] C. K. Barrett, *A Commentary on the Epistle to the Romans*, Vol. 1 (London: SPCK, 1957), 217–8. D. Hill, *Greek Words and Hebrew Meanings: Studies in the Semantics of Soteriological Terms* (London: Cambridge University, 1967), 41–5; Wright, *Victory*, 607.

[320] See 4 Maccabees 6:29. N. T. Wright, *The Messiah and the People of God* (Unpublished Thesis submitted to Oxford University for the degree of Ph. D., 1980), 37

However, Dunn points out that God who presented Christ as ἱλαστήριον points back directly to the cult.[321] Holland argues that the material should not be used to interpret Paul's thinking.[322] Instead Holland claims that there was propitiatory value in the blood of the Passover lamb.[323] He concludes that there is only one cultic event in which redemption is celebrated, and that is Passover. If he is right, the Passover involves the propitiation of God's wrath and redemption from the enemy. As pointed out earlier, Ezekiel, who was one that the New Testament authors followed, mentions the Day of Atonement sacrifices in the context of the eschatological temple offered during the Passover.[324] The eschatological Passover will propitiate for the sins of the people. Furthermore, the prophet tells how the prince will offer an abundance of sacrifices for the sins of the people in Ezek 45:25.[325]

The link between atonement and Passover on the basis of Ezek 45 penetrated Jesus's self-understanding about the Messiah. Jesus clearly regarded his death as atonement in Luke 22:19–20, and the timing of his death was deeply significant both for himself and for the early church. According to Holland, this paschal tradition was evidently in place well before Paul's conversion, as evidenced in the use he makes of traditional material.[326] Therefore, Rom 3:20–26 should be understood in the light of the Passover setting.

The question is: what is "a righteousness from God" in Rom 3:21 in the Passover setting? Being righteous before God is not only a matter of being

---

[321] Dunn, *Theology*, 215; D. G. Dunn, *Romans*, WBC, Vol. 38A (Dallas: Word, 1988), 170. Dunn also saw that the text in Romans has to be interpreted in the light of new exodus motif.

[322] Holland, *Contours*, 160. According to Holland, the dating of 4 Maccabees is put by some as late as AD 70. Therefore, it is wise not to place too much weight on its statements. This leaves some uncertainty as to whether Paul could expect his readers to follow allusions to the Maccabeans.

[323] Holland, *Contours*, 171; R. E. Brown, *The Gospel According to John*, Vol. 1 (Garden City, NY: Doubleday, 1970), 62. Brown understands that the Passover has expiatory value because by that time lambs were sacrificed within the Temple area by the priests. C. H. Dodd, *The Interpretation of the Fourth Gospel* (Cambridge: Cambridge University Press, 1953), 234. Dodd also thought that there was probably expiatory significance in the Passover ritual in pre-Mosaic periods, but it had been stopped long before New Testament times.

[324] Dunn, *Theology*, 216. According to Dunn, the Passover is already associated with atonement in Ezek 45:18–22. Howard, "Eucharist," 331–2. Howard also acknowledges that the sin offerings mentioned during the Passover of Ezek 45:25 lie behind the description of Jesus being the Lamb of God spoken of by John the Baptist in John 1:29. 10 He points out that the midrash on Exod 12 describes the Passover as an atoning sacrifice.

[325] To see the Davidic leader making sacrifices for the temple and the people would naturally lead Paul's thinking in the inevitable direction of the cross. It was all part of the testimony of the law and the prophets.

[326] Holland, *Contours*, 165.

declared innocent, it is one of the key Old Testament concepts related to Israel's return from exile. Isaiah said that Israel was declared righteous as a result of her return. The prophet's view of righteousness was not just forgiveness; it also meant that Israel was restored to her inheritance. Therefore, the term righteousness is equivalent to deliverance or salvation.

In this passage (Rom 3:21–25), furthermore, two terms enforce ἱλαστήριον to be interpreted in the Passover setting. First in regard to προέθετο in Rom 3:25, God presented (προέθετο) Jesus as a propitiation (ἱλαστήριον). The word προέθετο means publicly displayed.[327] Of all of the sacrifices that the Levitical law legislated for, there was only one that was displayed for all to see, and that was the Passover. The lamb's blood was daubed on the doorposts and the lintel. In other words, the lamb was presented. As has already been noted, the early church, through the influence of Ezek 45:25, saw the anticipated eschatological Passover to be a sacrifice of propitiation, and so the natural setting for the passage becomes obvious. Secondly, Paul says that God had in his forbearance (πάρεσιν) left the sins committed beforehand unpunished. According to Dunn, the term πάρεσιν has the more legal sense of "letting go unpunished, remission of penalty."[328] He understands πάρεσιν in the light of court room imagery, but Holland argues that the term has an echo of the Passover with ἱλαστήριον.[329]

On the Passover night the angel of death passed over the homes of the Jewish people leaving them unpunished. Paul is saying that the reason God has dealt so patiently with sin throughout history is not that he was indifferent, but rather that he had a plan to deal with sin which was greater than anyone could

---

[327] F. Buchsel, ἱλαστήριον in *TDNT* III, 320. Buchsel says that we cannot be sure of the meaning of προέθετο but then goes on to say that it refers to the apostolic preaching in which Jesus was set before the eyes of man. O'Neill agrees with this and adds that it refers also to the cross and Eucharist: J. C. O'Neill, *Paul's Letter to the Romans* (London: Penguin, 1975), 76. Stibbs says it refers to the public nature of Jesus' death: A. M. Stibbs, *The Meaning of the Word "Blood" in Scripture. The Tyndale New Testament Lecture,* 1947 (London, Tyndale Press, 1948), 21. In addition, Shedd says that the middle voice is insisted upon; thus, "for God set forth Himself": W. G. T. Shedd, *A Critical and Doctrinal Commentary on the Epistle to the Romans* (Minneapolis: Ausburg, 1978), 79.

[328] J. D. G. Dunn, *Romans,* 173. Cf. BAGD, πάρεσιν

[329] Holland, *Contours,* 171; see also: J. Reumann, "The Gospel of the Righteousness of God in Pauline Interpretation in Rom 3:21–31," *Int* 20(1966), 43–6. Reumann points out that πάρεσιν is unique in the New Testament and therefore its meaning can only be decided on by the context. Πάρεσιν reflects Passover for it is the great act in which God passed over the sins of the people.

have dared imagine. The Son of God as ἱλαστήριον deals with all the sins of his people, past, present, and future.

Galatians

Holland points out that the cultic event in Gal 1:4 is overtly presented in terms of a sin offering because of the phrase ὑπὲρ τῶν ἁμαρτιῶν ἡμῶν ("for our sins").[330] Longenecker adds that the following word ὅπως signals purpose ("in order that"), and so interprets the functional Christology of v. 4a ("Christ gave himself for our sins") soteriologically ("in order to rescue us").[331] He goes on to say that the verb ἐξέληται denotes not removal but rescue from the power.[332] That is, a sin offering is fused with the imagery of redemption and is in a new exodus context. So the deliverance spoken of here is not removal from the world but rescue from the evil that dominates it.

Colossians

The Christ hymn in Colossians has divided scholarship in terms of identifying possible sources for its background. Some have thought it to be a Greek hymn in praise of Wisdom,[333] others a Jewish one in praise of Wisdom.[334] But still

---

[330] Holland, *Contours*, 174.

[331] R. N. Longenecker, *Galatians*, 41, Word Biblical Commentary (Dallas: Word, 1990), 8.

[332] Ibid.

[333] E. Käsemann, *Essays on New Testament Themes* (London: SCM, 1964), 149. Käsemann pointed out that the hymn was adopted by the early Christian community and after adaptation used as a confessional statement for baptismal candidates. He also held that creation and redemption formed part of the myth of the primeval man and Redeemer. Talbert locates the origin of the myth in Mediterranean antiquity: C. H. Talbert, "The Myth of the Descending-Ascending Redeemer in Mediterranean Antiquity" *NTS* 22(1976), 418.

[334] This view has become widespread as the result of the work of Davies. According to Davies, Paul carried his training in Rabbinic Judaism with him when he became a follower of Jesus. For Paul, the Torah was not merely a legal code for the Jews, but a divinely appointed way of life. Davies linked the concept of Christ as the new Torah to Christ being the wisdom of God. Referring to Col 1.15, he said: 'Judaism had ascribed to the figure of wisdom a pre-cosmic origin and a part in the creation of the world. It becomes probable, therefore, that Paul has here pictured Christ on the image of wisdom': W. D. Davies, *Paul and Rabbinic Judaism* (London: SPCK, 1955), 151. Davies utilized the work of Burney to prove his own thesis. Burney had before argued that firstborn in Col 1:15 is a direct reference to Proverbs 8:22: F. C. Burney, "Christ as the ARCHE of Creation," *JTS* 27 (1926), 160–77. Burney argued that the term *reshith* in Proverbs 8.22 was used in rabbinic Judaism as the key to the *bereshith* that begins the Hebrew Bible. This latter *bereshith* of Genesis 1 was correspondingly interpreted as meaning 'by wisdom' (Burney, ARCHE, 160–8). Thus Davies pointed out that "it is natural to infer that when in the Epistle to the Colossians Paul calls Christ the *prototokos pases ktiseos* he is thinking of him as the *reshith* of creation": Davies, *Paul and Rabbinic Judaism*, 151–2. Davies continued to appeal to Burney's work to show the link Col 1:15-18 has with Genesis 1:1. Burney claimed that the Colossian passage is "an elaborate exposition of *bereshith* in Gen 1:1 in the rabbinic manner." So Davies argued that firstborn and wisdom were synonymous terms in Paul's thought. Taken together, Jesus is the New Torah, the Torah being wisdom itself, which in turn was

others have thought that it has to be interpreted from the perspective of Old Testament theology.[335]

Klijn sees the language of Col 1:12–14 to be reflecting the LXX description of the exodus or Isa 63:15–19.[336] Martin also says that the Christian confessional hymns (Col 1:15–29; Phil 2:6–11; 1 Tim 3:16) "stayed in the liturgical tradition of the Old Testament in which the exile in Egypt and journey to the promised land were the major themes."[337] Wright points out that Col 1:12–14 reminds us, in particular, of the imagery of the exodus, in which Israel's God showed himself to be God of the whole world by defeating both the Egyptians and the mighty waters of the sea.[338] According to him, the new exodus was the act of New Creation, bringing the chosen race to a new birth out of chaos and slavery.[339] Holland points out that Col 1:12–14 speaks of being delivered from the kingdom of darkness and being brought into the kingdom of light.[340] The Passover is the hymn's inevitable setting because redemption (v. 14), in the original exodus, was through the Passover sacrifice. Therefore, the hymn must be read in a redemptive context. Shogren adds that 1:13 is not about individuals entering the Kingdom of God, but about the church corporately.[341]

To sum up, the hymn celebrates the Passover echoing the Day of Atonement because we find propitiation to be in the original Passover sacrifice. It is also a confessional statement of the creativity of Israel's God because the new exodus is about Yahweh's new creation. As Shogren points out, the hymn has to be read through a corporate lens.

---

begotten before all things, and involved in creation. Davies continued his argument by considering some other Pauline passages (1 Cor 1:24, 30, 10.4; Rom 10:26).

[335] E. Schweizer, *The Letter to the Colossians*, trans. A. Chester (London: SPCK, 1982), 61. Schweizer says that the expression "visible and invisible" in the hymn is Semitic rather than Greek. See also: J. D. G. Dunn, "Some Reflections of Issues of Method: A Reply to Holladay and Segal," *Semeia* 30 (1984), 100.

[336] A. F. J. Klijn, "The Study of Jewish Christianity," *NTS* 20 (1974), 419.

[337] R. P. Martin, 'Some Reflections on New Testament Hymns,' in *Christ the Lord, Studies Presented to D. Guthrie*, ed. H. H. Rowden (Leicester: IVP, 1982), 139. According to Martin, the promised land of the Old Testament becomes the kingdom of God in the New Testament.

[338] N. T. Wright, "Theology and Poetry in Colossians 1:15–20," *NTS* 36 (1990), 452–54.

[339] Ibid. The same impression is given by the verses (21–23) which follow the poem, in which the God of all the earth (v. 23) has become responsible for the reconciliation of the Colossians and their grafting into his true people (v. 22).

[340] Holland, *Contours*, 280.

[341] G S. Shogren, "Presently Entering the Kingdom of Christ: The Background and Purpose of Col 1:12–14," *JETS* 51 (1988), 180.

Deliverance in the Epistle to the Hebrews

We have seen that the ritual of the Day of Atonement was absorbed into the Passover in Ezek 45. There Ezekiel saw that the prince's main function was to provide sacrifices for the sins of the community and to build the eschatological temple. This implies that deliverance means not only the forgiveness of sins, but the restoration of what was being lost. That is, it involves the forgiveness of sins and the restoration to his people of their inheritance in the community which Christ established.

What is Deliverance in Hebrews?

What then is deliverance in Hebrews?[342] The exodus event provides an illustration of what deliverance means. On that day Israel had two different experiences, that is, forgiveness of sins and restoration. As time passed by, however, the former was emphasized, as seen from the Day of Atonement, but the latter was not. Thus, the forgiveness of sins illustrated on the Day of Atonement was part of deliverance, not deliverance itself. The picture of the forgiveness of sins is delineated by means of the sacrifice on the Day of Atonement, but restoration of inheritance is not found in it. It is found in the Passover along with the forgiveness of sin.

As we have seen earlier, in the exodus, the Passover victim became a propitiation for the people; the Passover meant redemption from the Egyptian tyranny. This formula of deliverance penetrates the thought of the author of Hebrews. Therefore, deliverance has to be understood in the light of the new exodus. The author sees deliverance as both forgiveness and restoration.

In Heb 2:17, the author understands that Jesus' ministry is to be as a high priest who makes propitiation (ἱλάσκεσθαι) for the sins of the people. Buchsel sees that the term, ἱλάσκεσθαι in Heb 2:17, has to be understood with the

---

[342] Cf. W. Foerster, "σώζω" [sozo] in *TDNT* VII, 977–978. The principal Hebrew term translated "deliverance" is *yeshuah* and its cognates. Its basic meaning is "bring into a spacious environment" (cf. Pss 18:36; 66:12), but from the beginning it carries the metaphorical sense of "freedom from limitation" and the means to that; i.e. deliverance from factors which constrain and confine. It can refer to deliverance from disease (Isa 38:20; cf. v. 9), from trouble (Jer 30:7) or enemies (2 Sam 3:18; Ps 44:7). In the vast majority of references God is the author of this deliverance. Thus God delivers his people from Egypt (Exod 14:13) and their sons from Babylon (Jer 30:10); he rescues his people (Hos 1:7) and he alone can save them (Hos 13:10–14); there is no other saviour besides him (Isa 43:11).

background of the Day of Atonement.[343] Hughes points out that the language and imagery used in this verse are those of the Day of Atonement.[344] He goes on to say that this is another way of expressing what has been said in Heb 2:10 about the pioneer of our salvation being made perfect through suffering. According to Hughes, deliverance means the forgiveness of sins.

However, we examined the idea that God, presenting Christ as ἱλαστήριον points back directly to the cult, as argued in Rom 3:21–26. We also saw that in the Old Testament redemption is celebrated in only one cultic event, which is the Passover. Like Rom 3:21–26, therefore, Heb 2:17 should be interpreted in the light of Ezek 45. The prophet tells how the prince will offer an abundance of sacrifices for the sins of the people in Ezek 45:25.[345] The Davidic prince makes these paschal atoning sacrifices. Therefore, Jesus's ministry as high priest, i.e. as the Davidic high priest, is to make propitiation (ἱλάσκεσθαι) for the sins of the people. The Passover involves propitiation to God and deliverance from the enemy. As pointed out earlier, Ezekiel, who the New Testament authors follow, mentions sacrifices in the context of the eschatological temple offered during the Passover.[346] The eschatological Passover will propitiate for the sins of the people. The Son of God as ἱλαστήριον deals with all the sins of his people: past, present, and future.

If the author of Hebrews absorbs the ritual of the Day of Atonement into the Passover for deliverance as in Ezek 45, the salvation in Heb 2:10 should be interpreted in the Passover setting. In verse 10, the reference to πολλοὺς υἱοὺς εἰς δόξαν ἀγαγόντα ("in bringing many sons to glory") relates to God's ultimate

---

[343] F. Buchsel, "ἱλάσκεσθαι" [hilaskesthai] in *TDNT* III, 314–16. Bruce, Hebrews, 41. The verb ἱλάσκεσθαις found here and in Luke 18:13, the substantive ἱλαστήριον ("place or means of propitiation") in Heb 9:5 and in Rom 3:25.

[344] P.E. Hughes, *A Commentary on the Epistle to the Hebrews* (Grand Rapids: Eerdmans, 1977), 122. On that occasion the Levitical high priest entered into the holy of holies with the atoning blood and sprinkled it on the mercy seat, and it is viewed as the place of propitiation. In Greek, ἱλαστήριον as in 9:5 below. The only other occurrence of this term, another cognate of ἱλάσκεσθαι in the New Testament is in Rom 3:25, where it is used of Christ, probably without intending any reference to the mercy seat, but with exactly the same sense, it would seem, as in 1 John 2:2 and 4:10, where Jesus Christ is described as the propitiation (ἱλασμὸν) for our sins.

[345] To see the Davidic leader making sacrifices for the temple and the people would naturally lead Paul's thinking in the inevitable direction of the cross. It was all part of the testimony of the law and the prophets.

[346] Dunn, *Theology*, 216. According to Dunn, the Passover is already associated with atonement in Ezek 45:18–22. Howard also acknowledges that the sin offerings mentioned during the Passover of Ezek 45:25 lie behind the description of Jesus being the Lamb of God spoken of by John the Baptist in John 1:29. He points out that the midrash on Exod 12 describes the Passover as an atoning sacrifice. See: Howard, "Eucharist," 331–2.

purpose to lead many people to glory. The participle ἀγαγόντα ("bringing") would best agree with the contiguous noun τὸν ἀρχηγὸν ("the champion") in case, gender, and number. If this is so, this would mean that it is the Son who brings many sons to glory, as the pioneer of their salvation. The goal of Christ's leadership is entrance into the glory (δόξῃ) and honour (τιμῇ) depicted from Ps 8:6 (LXX) which is cited in v. 7. It is Jesus who is "the champion" who secured the salvation of his people through the sufferings he endured in his identification with them and, more particularly, through his death. It is suggested by some scholars, such as Schreiner,[347] that the motif of God's leading of many sons is familiar from the OT, particularly in connection with the exodus from Egypt where the divine initiative is repeatedly underlined.[348] Lane sees that the exodus motif, especially from the two Old Testament passages,[349] would tend to bring them together in the writer's thought. Bruce relates "glory" (δόξῃ) to the phrase in v. 10 "their salvation" (τῆς σωτηρίας αὐτῶν).[350] Koester sees glory as the consummation of the salvation.[351] Jeremias points out, therefore, that the adjective πολλοὺς ("many") includes all those to whom the saving work of Jesus applies.[352]

If salvation in Heb 2:10 has to be understood in terms of the new exodus, then what does salvation in Hebrews mean? It is that people become brothers with Jesus according to God's plan. Bultmann points out that, in Ps 8 cited in Heb 2:6–7, the title "the Son of man" was attributed to the Jewish Messiah after borrowing characteristics from his gnostic rival.[353] Longenecker challenged Bultmann's proposal concerning this origin of the title Son of Man because of lack of evidence.[354] Cullmann claimed that Son of Man was the most personal

---

[347] J. Schreiner, "Führung-Theme der Heilsgeschichte im Alten Testament," *BZ* 5 (1961), 2–18.
[348] Exod 3:8, 17; 6:6–7; 7:4–5, *passim*.
[349] Lane, *Hebrews*, 56. Cf. Isa 41:8–10 and Jer 31:31–32.
[350] Bruce, *Hebrews*, 42. However, Bruce sees salvation to be forgiveness of sin.
[351] C. R. Koester, *Hebrews: A New Translation with introduction and Commentary* (New York: The Anchor Bible, 2001), 228. According to him, Glory has two important aspects; honour and divine presence.
[352] J. Jeremias, "πολλοί" in *TDNT VI*, 536–42.
[353] Bultmann, *Theology*, Vol. 1, 164–83. Bultmann identified the gnostic redeemer myth as the origin of the Son of Man, claiming that it was the invention of the early church.
[354] R. N. Longenecker, "The Melchizedek argument of Hebrews: A Study in the Development and Circumstantial expression of New Testament thought," in *Unity and Diversity in the New Testament Theology* (Grand Rapids: Eerdmans, 1978), 161–85.

title of Jesus and the one he deliberately chose for himself.[355] According to him, the idea of the Son of Man, at its ultimate source, includes the idea that this figure of man represents all men.[356] Borsch says that Jesus refers to himself as an eschatological figure.[357] Holland points out that the Son is spoken of as the messianic figure who was promised to Israel and who would rule creation.[358] As the representative of God amongst men, Christ was responsible for the well-being of his brothers. That is, Christ has liberated his people from sin and its power and, having fulfilled all his various roles as the Redeemer, he completes his work by making those he has rescued his brothers.

Therefore, deliverance under the new exodus involves two themes: the forgiveness of sins and restoration; the former means that believers are to be holy, the latter that they become brothers of Jesus. Becoming a brother of Jesus can be expressed as becoming Abraham's descendants. The term ἁγιάζων ("holy") in Heb 2:11 is understood under the imagery of the temple.[359] Cleansing from defilement (that is, forgiveness of sins) is the necessary corollary to the concept of holiness as consecration. In Old Testament times, certain people, selected vessels and appointed days were "set apart" for God's use.[360] The reference to ὅ ... ἁγιάζων here is to Jesus, who is named explicitly in 13:12 as the one who consecrates his people to the service of God through his own blood, even as 10:14 describes Christians as those who are being consecrated (οἱ ἁγιαζόμενοι) by his one sacrifice.[361] Only one who is himself fully consecrated to the service of God (cf. 10:5–10) may exercise the power of making others holy. In Heb 2:11, the description of Jesus as "the one who consecrates" and of Christians as those who need consecration sufficiently defines the radical difference between the transcendent Son of God and those

---

[355] Cullmann, *Christology*, 137.

[356] Ibid., 141.

[357] F. H. Borsch, *The Son of Man in Myth and History* (Philadelphia: Westminster Press, 1967), 238. The eschatological role of the Son of Man is attested by sayings such as those about the "day of the Son of Man" (Luke 17:22), "the coming of the Son of Man" (Matt 24:27, 37), and about his "coming in the glory of his Father with the holy angels" (Mark 8:38).

[358] Holland, *Contours*, 108.

[359] R. Brown, *The Message of Hebrews* (Leicester: IVP, 1982), 63.

[360] Cf. Leviticus, *passim*; especially Lev 16:6–34, Heb 9.

[361] Lane, *Hebrews* 47A, 58. According to Lane, the designation ὅ ... ἁγιάζων "he who consecrates," seems to reflect the concept of God in the Pentateuch, where he identifies himself with the formula "I am the Lord who consecrates you" (Exod 31:13; Lev 20:8; 21:15; 22:9,16, 32; cf. Ezek 20:12; 37:28).

who are "sons." Therefore, Jesus sanctified his people by becoming one with his people in his humanity and by making his people one with himself (2:11). He who sanctifies and those who are sanctified are all of one stock (NEB). They "are of the same family" (NIV).

Restoration, which is the second aspect of deliverance, is made clear in Heb 2:12–16. It is emancipation from him who holds the power of death—that is, the devil. In this way, people under the devil's rule can now become Abraham's descendants. Abraham was told in Gen 15:13 that his descendants would go into Egypt and would be oppressed there for 400 years. The period of oppression was to be finished by the judgments that God would bring on their oppressor. Thereafter Abraham's descendants would leave captivity greatly enriched. The reference to Abraham's descendants in Heb 2:16 seems to be an allusion to Isa 41:8–10,[362] where the faithful remnant is the object of God's comfort. The passage from Isaiah was appropriate to the situation of the hearers in Hebrews.

Verse 12 cites from Ps 22:22 which the early church saw as a reference to her Messiah.[363] Hewitt comments that verses 22 and 23 of the Psalm implied some great deliverance of the Psalmist from his sufferings, but here it refers to Jesus's exaltation. Christ declared the Lord's name, that is, God's name to his spiritual brothers. Declaring someone's name for the Jew means making known their status and character, in so declaring God's name Christ revealed the exact representation of his being (Heb 1:3). The context emphasizes not the declaration of Christ, but of his brothers. Following the LXX the author uses the word ἐκκλησίας for congregation, and Bruce says that congregation is synonymous with brothers. Those whom the Son of God—the representative head of a new mankind[364]—is pleased to call his brothers are the members of his church.

---

[362] Isa 41:8–10 "But you ... Abraham's descendants, upon whom I took hold ... do not fear, for I am with you ... and I have helped you."
[363] C. R. Koester, *Hebrews*, 230.
[364] C. H. Dodd, According to the Scriptures: The Sub-Structure of New Testament Theology (New York: Scribner's, 1953), 20.

In v. 13, "I will put my trust in him" is quoted from Isa 8:17 LXX.[365] In the Old Testament text Isaiah relied on God, but, according to Hewitt,[366] the author sees a higher reference to Christ who declares his confidence in God, which is proof of his humanity, and in so doing identifies himself with his brothers. v. 13b is taken from Isa 8:18, where Isaiah referred to himself and his two sons, Shear-jashub ("Remnant will return") and Maher-shalal-hash-baz ("Hasten booty, speed spoil"), as those who do not turn away from the living God. According to Bruce, Isaiah's name and the names of his two sons reminded the people of the dominant theme of his message.[367] His sons' names were the expression of his own obedient trust in God, his confidence that what God had said would surely come to pass. Hewitt says that the author regards the prophet as a type of Christ, and his children as a type of the believing remnant whom he came to save.[368] Taken together, Isaiah's words about his children might be understood in an extended sense as the words of Christ about his people. In him, they are the "many sons" who are being brought to glory (v. 10), whom he is not ashamed to call "brethren" (v. 11), "the children" God has given him (v. 13), delivered by him from bondage and death (v. 15). Thus this context has to be understood in the light of the exodus. His solidarity with them is affirmed by means of the term "children."[369]

Furthermore, the Greek ἐπιλαμβάνεται ("he takes hold") in Heb 2:16 may support this point of view. The term ἐπιλαμβάνεται suggests the rescue and redemption of God's people,[370] and its use for the cognate ἀντιλαμβάνεται found in Isa 41:9 may reflect the formulation of Jer 31:31–32, where the exodus is described in terms of God's taking Israel by the hand in order to lead her out of bondage.[371] Hewitt reasons that the verb ἐπιλαμβάνεται is derived from Jer

---

[365] C. R. Koester, *Hebrews*, 231.
[366] T. Hewitt, *Hebrews* (London: Tyndale, 1973), 71-2.
[367] Bruce, *Hebrews*, 40. Isaiah's own significant name means that "Yahweh is salvation".
[368] Hewitt, *Hebrews*, 72.
[369] Bruce, *Hebrews*, 48. The description of Christians as the "children" or "sons" of Christ is peculiar to this epistle among the New Testament writings; yet Old Testament precedent for it might be found not only in the words of Isa 8:18 but in a statement about the suffering servant in Isa 53:10: "when he makes himself an offering for sin, he shall see his off-spring" (RSV).
[370] E. K. Simpson, *Words Worth Weighing in the Greek New Testament* (London: Tyndale Press, 1946), 27.
[371] D. Peterson, *Hebrews and Perfection: An Examination of the Concept of Perfection in the Epistle to the Hebrews* (Cambridge: Cambridge University Press, 1982), 62.

31:9, where God takes the Israelites by the hand to rescue and lead them out of Egypt.[372] Lane says that this text, which is also cited in Heb 8:9, and the new exodus motif, which the two Old Testament passages share, would tend to bring them together in the writer's thoughts.[373] Following the theme of deliverance from bondage to the Devil and fear of death, Heb 2:16 suggests that Christ "takes hold" of the "seed of Abraham" to rescue them in this way. The phrase "seed of Abraham" is probably chosen with Isa 41:9 in mind but also with regard to the promises of Gen 3. The author of Hebrews sees that after the Gen 3 event all people are under Satan's control. But he insists that through Jesus's death, our enemy, the devil, who wields the power of death, was rendered ineffective.

The opening verses of this epistle have made it clear that Christ came to obtain our purification (1:3), but in one sense cleansing alone is not enough. In that act of purification, we are also "set apart" for the use of God. We are cleansed in order that we might "serve the living God" (9:14). In this service we are one with Christ and he is pleased to call us "brothers".

The Deliverance of God's People Through Christ's Death

This theme of deliverance is developed further in Heb 9:11–28. The basis for the exposition in the passage is the religious conviction that Christ on the cross is seen by our author as part of a whole redemptive movement initiated by the grace of God.[374] In doing so, the author of Hebrews points out that the same sacrifices repeated endlessly year after year never make perfect those who draw near to worship because they are the shadow of reality. The author rather appeals to a typological parallel between the Passover sacrifice and the self-offering of Christ. In other words, Heb 9 should be interpreted in the light of Ezekiel's vision in Ezek 45.

The author points out that Christ was sacrificed, having obtained eternal redemption in Heb 9:12, and through the sacrifice of the body of Jesus Christ once for all we have been made holy in Heb 10:10. Some have linked the death

---

[372] Hewitt, *Hebrews*, 74–75. Koester, *Hebrews*, 232.
[373] W. Lane *Hebrews* 47A, WBC (Dallas: Word, 1991), 64.
[374] S. S. Smalley, "The Atonement in the Epistle to the Hebrews" *EQ* XXXIII (January–March 1961), 37.

of Jesus with the death of the Maccabean martyrs in 4 Macc 17:22.[375] Wright argues that the Israelites in the first century anticipated a Messiah who would first cleanse or rebuild the temple.[376] His work was also to forgive their sins, and that this would involve innocent or righteous suffering. Hence the stories of the sufferings of the martyrs are described in 2 Maccabees as having the effect of dealing with the nation's sin in the present time.[377] With regard to the doctrine of martyrdom, furthermore, the author of 4 Maccabees takes martyrdom as a substitutionary atonement that expiates the nation's sin and purifies the land.[378]

The martyrs, therefore, went gladly to their suffering and death, believing that they would be raised to new life in the future.[379] Their sufferings would make a way through the present time of wrath to the salvation which lay beyond, while their tormentors were storing up wrath for themselves.[380] According to Wright, Jesus identified himself with the sufferings of Israel and believed that relieving them was his vocation. Jesus, thus, kept the death of the Maccabean martyrs in his mind for the deliverance of his country; he died to get rid of the sufferings of Israel following the death of the Maccabean martyrs. Wright, finally, sees redemption in the first century as liberation from Rome.[381] If we accept this

---

[375] W. R. Farmer, *Maccabees, Zealots, and Josephus: An Inquiry into Jewish Nationalism in the Greco-Roman Period* (New York: Columbia University Press, 1956), 201–204; Barrett, *Romans*, 217–8; Hengel, *Atonement*, 60–1. Wright, *Victory*, 582.

[376] Wright, *Victory*, 604.

[377] Ibid., 582. Cf. 2 Macc 6:12–17; 7:18–19.

[378] M. McNamara, *Intertestamental Literature* (Wilmington, DE: Michael Glazier, 1983), 234. "They became the cause of the downfall of tyranny over their nation. By their endurance they conquered the tyrant, and thus their native land was purified through them (4 Maccabees 1:11)." The dying Eleazar prays to God: "Be merciful to your people and let our punishment suffice for them. Make my blood their purification, and take my life in exchange for theirs" (6:28–29). In an exhortation the eldest brother says to the others: "Fight the sacred and noble battle for religion. Thereby the just Providence of our ancestors may become merciful to our nation and take vengeance on the accursed tyrant" (9:23–24).

[379] 2 Macc 6:30; 7:9, 11, 14, 16–17, 22–3, 29, 30–8. Wright, *Victory*, 588. Wright also sees that the biblical context for the stories of suffering and martyrdom in the Second-Temple period is the prophecy of Isaiah; particularly chapters 40–55.

[380] 2 Macc 7:36–8; 4 Macc 6:27–9, 9:23–4, 17:20–2, 18:3–4. Wright, *Victory*, 583. There are three strands of belief which run through these accounts. First, the fate of the martyrs is bound up with the fate of the nation as a whole. Second, as a result, their suffering forms as it were the focal point of the suffering of the nation, continuing the theme of exile-as-the-punishment-for-sin which we find in the great prophetic writings such as Jeremiah, Ezek, Isa 40–55 and Daniel, but now giving it more precise focus. Third, this representative exilic suffering functions redemptively. C. K. Barrett, "Background", 11–15. Hengel, *Atonement*, 60–1.

[381] Wright, *Victory*, 594, 598. According to Wright, Jesus believed that Israel's exile had arrived at its climax. He

tradition and also accept that it is behind the theology of the writer to the Hebrews then it is a possible key to the assessment being made.

However, there are scholars who argue that the materials Wright used are not applicable to Jesus because there is no certainty that the rabbinic material existed before Jesus.[382] Wright also agrees that 4 Maccabees was written in the middle of the first century.[383] Therefore, it is wise not to place too much weight on its statements with this uncertainty. Even if it is accepted as early enough to be contemporary with Jesus,[384] we do not know whether it was known to Jesus or his hearers.

Israel has the two exoduses relating to deliverance, that is, one from Egypt and the other from Babylon. The former is applied to the death of Jesus by the New Testament writers. The latter provided the promises of a new covenant that fulfilled the type of the first exodus.[385] Through the two exoduses, of course, Jesus's vicarious death is seen, but martyrdom theology, as used by the Maccabees, is not found. Therefore, that martyrdom theology might have been linked to messianic expectation in a sect of second temple Judaism is true, but since it was not a mainstream theology of the Old Testament, Wright may be making a little too much of its significance for the New Testament's writing about Jesus.

Although evidence that the death of Jesus should be explained by martyrdom theology is thin, there is far more substantial support for the New Testament writers" linking it with the Day of Atonement. Despite this, Heb 10:10 cannot be explained by the sacrifice of the Day of Atonement alone. We have earlier found that forgiveness of sins and redemption are the two parts of the Passover. The Passover Lamb in the Passover provided the Israelites with deliverance.[386] The theological origin of the word "redemption" in the Old

---

understood the book of Daniel to be referring to the great climax in which YHWH would defeat the fourth world empire and vindicate his suffering people.

[382] Holland, *Contours*, 49.

[383] Wright, *Victory*, 583. T. Holland, *Contours*, 160. Holland sees that the dating of 4 Maccabees is put by some as late as 70 CE.

[384] McNamara, *Literature*, 237. McNamara sees that the date of composition as during or after the period 20–54 CE when Cilicia was joined to Syria and Phoenicia (4 Maccabees 4:2).

[385] Holland, *Contours*, 153–54.

[386] On the paschal victim, I will argue at the end of this chapter in excursus.

Testament is God delivering Israel initially from Egypt and secondly from Babylon. The word is not found in the Day of Atonement context,[387] but in that of the Passover.[388]

Hence in Heb 9–10, the author utilizes the imagery of the Day of Atonement for the forgiveness of sins, and then uses the Passover imagery to explain the redemptive significance of Jesus's death. The author's methodology is exactly the same as Ezekiel's vision in Ezek 45.[389] The influence of Ezekiel on the New Testament writers is seen in that the prophet is regarded as the source of the idea that the church was the temple of the living God. Also, the tabernacle imagery, seen in the letter to the Hebrews, is recognized as being based on the eschatological temple described by Ezekiel.[390] Therefore, Heb 9–10 can be linked to the Passover motif via the remodeling of the significance of the feast described by Ezek 45:25. The passage merges the Passover with the sacrifice of the Day of Atonement. Thus the merger of redemption with atonement, found in Heb 9:12, follows the structure of Ezek 45:25 in which the sacrifices of the Day of Atonement are brought into the orbit of Passover ritual.[391] Therefore, Ezek 45:25 teaches how the prince will offer an abundance of sacrifices for the sins of the people during Passover. What is important is that Ezekiel saw the importance of the raising up of a Davidic prince,[392] and the prince's main function was to provide sacrifices for the sins of the covenant community.

In the Targum on Zech 9:11, the Passover lamb is referred to as the blood of the covenant. It considers the blood of the Passover lamb as the covenant blood that brought about Israel's release from the "waterless pit" (Egypt). Goppelt concludes that Jesus' blood, his death, like the blood of the Passover lambs, means sparing, deliverance and redemption from death, slavery, and the wrath of God.[393]

---

[387] C. Brown, *The New International Dictionary of New Testament Theology*, Vol. l (Exeter: Paternoster, 1986), 192.

[388] A. Motyer, *Look to the Rock* (London: IVP, 1996), 49.

[389] C. Mckay, "The Argument of Hebrews," *CQR* 168(1967), 325.

[390] Holland, *Paschal*, 64.

[391] Ibid.

[392] Ezek 34:23–24; 37:24–25.

[393] L. Goppelt, *Typos: The Typological Interpretation of the Old Testament in the New* (Grand Rapids: Eerdmans, 1982), 114.

It is clear that Jesus regarded his death as atonement,[394] and equally clear that the timing of his death was deeply significant both for himself and for the early church.[395] Therefore, there is unity between Jesus's understanding of the purpose of his death and the explanation found in Hebrews. So there is a link between atonement and the Passover. This is further upheld by the reference to "eternal redemption" (Heb 9:12). Yahweh's Old Testament acts of redemption not only delivered the Hebrews to be his people, but it also justified his character as the covenant-keeping God to the nations of the earth. For the New Testament writers, it is redemption that brings humanity out of the spiritual bondage in which they have been incarcerated since they broke covenant with Yahweh.

As Yahweh had promised to act to deliver Israel, and declared that his salvation would come through his servant David, so his covenant faithfulness is blazed abroad through his redemptive act in the giving up of his own Son to death. In terms of Christ's sacrifice on the cross, Lane comments that it requires no repetition or renewal; his exaltation and entrance into the real sanctuary consecrates the eternal validity of his redemptive ministry.[396] He goes on to say that eschatological redemption may be associated with that sustained offer of decisive purgation that is extended through Christ to the human family. Therefore, eschatological redemption refers to God's final act of redemption which focused on the death of Jesus, so making him to be "Christ our Passover".

Jeremias sees that Heb 9:20 and 10:29 take the blood of the covenant in the Sinai event as a prototype of Jesus's blood of the covenant.[397] That is, the phrase "blood of the covenant" in Heb 9:20 and 10:29 is in verbal agreement with Exod 24:8.[398] If this is so, as the older divine order at Sinai was sealed with blood— for this is clearly what sprinkling with blood meant originally (Heb 9:18)— so the new order is established with the blood of Jesus, i.e. by the sacrifice of his life.[399] However, the sprinkling of blood was not interpreted in

---

[394] Luke 11:20.
[395] M. Dibelius, *Jesus: A Study of Gospels*, trans. C. B. Hedrick & F. C. Grant (London: SCM, 1963), 85.
[396] Lane, *Hebrews* 47b, 239. However, Lane understands the passage in the light of the Day of Atonement.
[397] J. Jeremias, *The Eucharistic Words of Jesus* (New York: Macmillan, 1955), 173.
[398] C. R. Koester, *Hebrews*, 419.
[399] J. Behm, "$αἷμα$" [aima] in *TDNT* I, 174.

the New Testament period as a sealing of the covenant, but as a sacrifice for the sin of the people.[400] Therefore, it would seem that Jesus's blood is the blood of the covenant because his atoning death prepares mankind to be received into God's covenant.

Lane thinks that the author may have coined the word αἱματεκχυσίας in Heb 9:22 as a comprehensive term for the application of blood.[401] Jewish sources indicate that in a cultic context the reference is not to the slaying of the sacrificial victims,[402] but to the final disposal of the blood upon the altar in order to effect atonement.[403] The term seems to stress the surpassing potency of blood as a religious force for dealing with defilement. Thornton says that the contrast between the two halves of v. 22 is not between purgation ἐν αἵματι ("with blood") and αἱματεκχυσίας ("the application of blood") but rather between the restrictive σχεδὸν ("almost") and the inclusive οὐ ("no/none").[404]

Therefore, the declaration in v. 22b is the third of three postulates that have been formulated in a similar way to stress the crucial importance of sacrificial blood: blood provides access (v. 7); blood purges the people (v. 19); blood cleanses cultic implements (v. 21); blood purges almost everything under the old law (v. 22a). On each occasion the writer used χωρὶς ("without") and casts his statement negatively. In the light of the emphasis in this context, only the blood of Christ can cleanse the human conscience.

Heb 9:26 is also to be understood in the light of the desert tabernacle.[405] Jesus was expressed as a manifestation of the way into the holy of holies. In Heb 10:19–20 Christ's earthly flesh is described as the curtain (καταπέτασμα)[406] through which he inaugurated the new way. Manson says, therefore, that the innermost reality of God's cultic relations with man was revealed when Christ's

---

[400] Jeremias, *Eucharist*, 173.

[401] Lane, *Hebrews*, 246.

[402] I.e. "the shedding of blood"; so RSV, NEB, NIV; cf. J. Swetnam, *Jesus and Isaac: A Study of the Epistle to the Hebrews in the Light of the Aqedah* (Rome: Biblical Institute, 1981), 186–87.

[403] Cf. Exod 29:12; Lev 4:7,18, 25,30,34; 8:15; 9:9 LXX, where αἷμα ("blood") and ενχυννει ("to pour out") are used in conjunction with the pouring out of blood upon the altar.

[404] T. C. G. Thornton, 'The meaning of αἱματεκχυσία in Heb IX. 22,' *JTS* 15 (1964), 63–65.

[405] J. Swetnam, "Sacrifice and Revelation in the Epistle to the Hebrews: Observations and Surmises on Hebrews 9:26," *CBQ* (1968), 228.

[406] It is instructive to notice how close is the connection in the New Testament between the word καταπέτασμα and the body of Christ: Matt 27:51; Mark 15:38; Luke 23:45; Heb 6:19; 9:3; 10:20.

earthly body was pierced in sacrificial death.[407] If this is so, according to Swetman,[408] the Christ who has been manifested is the Christ who has been sacrificed.

In Heb 10:1–10, the author insists that the Old Testament sacrifices could not remove the consciousness of sins (10:2), instead those sacrifices were an annual reminder of sin (10:3). However, offerings and sacrifices, before the revelation to Moses at Sinai, were a key to a relationship with God, from Cain and Abel to the ratification of the Mosaic covenant by sacrifice before the tabernacle was built (Gen 4:2–12). They remained central to the ritual systems of the tabernacle and the first and second temples and, therefore, to the Old Testament theology of God's presence and his relationship to ancient Israel as his kingdom of priests.[409]

Averbeck defines the sin offering as the primary blood atonement offering.[410] Lev 16:29–34 is a summary of the consequence of the sin offerings on the Day of Atonement. That is, the scapegoat sin offering cleansed the people from their sins (vv. 29–31), and the slaughtered sin offerings for the priests and the people cleansed the tabernacle from the impurity of their sins (vv. 32–33). However, the sin offering could also be brought for physical impurities that had nothing to do with moral failure.[411] In the text, as we have seen, the author appears to have merged the system of the sin offerings on the Day of Atonement into Passover, as previously done in Ezek 45.

Deliverance from the Power of Death

Heb 2:14–15 shows that the purpose of the incarnation is victory over the devil as the one who wields the power of death and the liberation of his prisoners. It should be recognized that the power of death is held by the devil, God's most

---

[407] Manson, *Hebrews*, 67.

[408] Swetman, "Sacrifice," 231.

[409] R. E. Averbeck, "Offerings and Sacrifice" in *Evangelical Dictionary of Biblical Theology*, ed. W. A. Elwell (Grand Rapids: Baker, 1996), 574–81.

[410] Ibid., 577. According to Averbeck, the focal point of the sin offering ritual was blood manipulation and the way it was done was different when it was brought for the priest and whole congregation as opposed to the leader and the common people (cf. Lev 4:6–7, 17–18). Sin offerings were executed on several unique occasions; for example, the consecration of the priests (Exod 29:14, 36; Lev 8:2, 14), and the inauguration of altar worship (Lev 9:2–7, 8–11, 15–17).

[411] Averbeck, "Offerings and Sacrifice", 577.

potent enemy, only in a secondary and not in an ultimate sense.⁴¹² Therefore, God is described as the divine warrior, who arms himself in order to defend his people from humiliation and enslavement.⁴¹³

The phrase τὸ κράτος ἔχοντα τοῦ θανάτου ("the power of death") in Heb 2:14 is a key to understanding Heb 2:14–15.⁴¹⁴ The destructive power of death is thought to rule life and rob it of its true quality. The death which awaits man holds fear (Heb 2:15; Rom 8:15). It has been said that death is equated with sin, and both are personified as the devil, which is Satan.⁴¹⁵ Some have pointed out that Heb 2:14–15 has been influenced by the passage of Isa 49:14–26.⁴¹⁶ In this passage of Isaiah, Yahweh is called "the Mighty One of Jacob" (v. 26) who vows to overcome Israel's foes. Longman pointed out that "The Mighty One of Jacob" in the Old Testament is an epithet of the divine warrior.⁴¹⁷ The whole section is important in that, immediately following the installation of what appears to be a new "servant" Israel,⁴¹⁸ it introduces the more positive themes of chapters 49–55.⁴¹⁹ This part of Isaiah consists almost entirely of future orientated promises of the new exodus salvation as inaugurated by the new, unknown "servant".⁴²⁰ Longman goes on to point out that, seen from the perspective of the Old Testament, Jesus is described as the "Mighty One" who would bring deliverance.⁴²¹ Watts has suggested that the Isaianic depiction of Israel's deliverance by the downfall of the oppressing nations' idols, illustrates

---

[412] Hughes, *Hebrews*, 112.

[413] Longman III and Reid, *Warrior*, 31.

[414] W. Michaelis, "κράτος" [kratos] in *TDNT* III,907. The devil controls death. Death is subject to him. He uses it as an instrument. Death is in the devil's service and is his myrmidon.

[415] Bruce, *Hebrews*, 49. The prince or angel of death is identified with the devil—that is, Satan. Bruce comments on 1 John 3:8 that the particular work of the devil most prominent in that context is sin. The association between sin and death is close enough for the destruction of death to be included in the purpose of the Son of God's appearance. Furthermore, death is the last of the enemies destined to be brought low by Christ in 1 Cor 15:26, in ultimate fulfillment of Ps 110:1. Cf. Rom 7:2–3; Rom 8:1.

[416] Watts, *Mark*, 149. Lane, *Hebrews* 47A, 60. He sees that the remarkable formulation in Heb 2:14–15 appears to draw upon the older prophetic tradition of God as the champion of his people as set forth in Isa 49:24–26. Cf. Schoors, Savior, 106; Melugin, *Formation*, 148.

[417] Longman III & Reid, *Warrior*, 111.

[418] Ibid., 62. Melugin, *Formation*, 70; H. G. M. Williamson, 'The Concept of Israel in Transition" in *The World of Ancient Israel*, ed. R. E. Clements (Cambridge: Cambridge University Press, 1989), 141-61; Watts, "Consolation," 54.

[419] Melugin, Formation, 151.

[420] Watts, "Consolation," 56.

[421] Longman III & Reid, *Warrior*, 62.

Jesus's warfare against the evil spirits.[422] What is important is that the deliverance motif from the Egyptian Exodus appears in the Isaiah text.[423]

Some words in Heb 2:14–15 support this new exodus motif. Hewitt sees καταργήση ("he might destroy") in verse 14 as a reference to salvation, first in relation to the great enemy from whom the believer is delivered, and second in relation to the bondage from which the Christian is emancipated.[424] Regarding καταργήση Delling says that Satan is "condemned to inactivity or ineffectiveness in relation to the Christian".[425] However, neither Hewitt nor Delling saw the term in the light of the new exodus. It was in this context that God rendered impotent the devil who had the power of death, and freed God's people from the horror of death. The term ἔνοχοι Heb 2:15 has a negative meaning "held in slavery."[426] The slavery springs from the fear of death. The term ἀπαλλάξῃ in Heb 2:15 is derived from ἀπαλλάσσω which means "to alter by removal," "to do away."[427] According to Buchsel, ἀπαλλάξῃ means "to liberate."[428] It reminds us of the context of the exodus.[429]

Therefore, the Christological perspective developed in Heb 2:10–16[430] has its clearest anticipation in this passage from Isaiah. Continuity in tradition may be traced from the prophetic depiction of God as the champion who rescues the captives of an evil tyrant. The author affirms that what God had pledged to do as Israel's redeemer, Jesus has accomplished. Jesus is the protagonist who broke the devil's power and so secured deliverance for the people of God. This

---

[422] Watts, *Mark*, 135.

[423] Cf. Peterson, *Hebrews*, 62. Peterson sees the background of 2:14–15 to be the picture of Gen 1–3 and the teaching of Prophetic and Apocalyptic writers about the restoration of paradise in the End-time, the victory over death and sin and Satan. Implicit in this context is the assumption that death is the divine punishment for sin, which Satan wields as a power over man's life within the divine economy.

[424] Hewitt, *Hebrews*, 74.

[425] G. Delling, "ἀργός, ἀργέω, καταργέω," in *TDNT* I, 453.

[426] R. Kratz, "ἔνοχοι," in *Exegetical Dictionary of the New Testament*, Vol. 1, ed. H. Balz and G. Schneider (Edinburgh: T&T Clark, 1995), 457. Kratz points out that the term ἔνοχος has the basic meaning held in something, in the figurative sense subjected, exposed, subject to. It is most often used forensically: guilty, liable. However, the term here is not used with connotations of judicial language or a figurative meaning.

[427] F. Buchsel, "ἀπαλλάσσω," in *TDNT* I, 252.

[428] Ibid.

[429] C. L. Rogers Jr and C. L. Rogers III, eds., *The New Linguistic and Exegetical Key to the Greek New Testament* (Grand Rapids: Zondervan, 1998), 520.

[430] It is clear that the author to Hebrews sees deliverance as liberation from other powers to enable the Christian to live henceforth under the power of God.

fruitful approach to the incarnation and death of Jesus was designed to strengthen the hearers by reminding them of their liberated status. They are no longer to be paralyzed by the fear of death, even when they experience imperial opposition.

Can such an author's thought, that the devil holds the power of death and man is held in slavery by his fear of death, be justified from the Bible? Kennedy points out that there is a kind of personification of Death, resembling that of the Greek Hades, in Ps 40:14.[431] Sometimes, the dead are described as if they exist in the underworld almost beneath the sway of another tyrannical power. Thus, in ancient literature it is hard to distinguish between a person and a personification. Animistic ideas lie deep in the naive, popular consciousness.

Bousset would also relate the figures of θάνατος (Death) (cf. Rev 20:13) and the angel of Hades closely to that of the devil, finding in them personal opponents of God.[432] The prince of death is identified with the devil, that is, Satan. It can be deduced that the particular work of the devil is sin, and as a result the devil leads humans to death.[433] As mentioned earlier, the association between sin and death is close. Therefore, the purpose of the Son of God's appearance was to destroy the devil's work.

Sanders points out that sin is a power to which one dies and, more importantly, it is a power to which one may yield one's members and as such it is placed in direct opposition to God, almost as an equivalent power.[434] Holland points out that the Targum certainly makes the equation, identifying the angel of death in Exod 12 with Satan.[435] The Book of Wisdom also testifies to Satan being the opponent of God.[436] Such thinking has penetrated into the

---

[431] H. A. A. Kennedy, *Paul's Conception of the Last Things* (London: Hodder &Stoughton, 1904), 108.

[432] Bousset groups together such passages as Isa 25:7; 4 Ezra 8:53; Apoc. Bar. 21:23; Test. Levi 18; 1 Cor 15:26, 55, all of which treat of the destruction of death at the end: W. Bousset, *Die Religion des Judentums in Neutestamentlichen Zeitalter* (Berlin: Reuther und Reichard, 1906), 241.

[433] Cf. Wisdom 1:13: "God did not make death, and he does not delight in the death of the living. For he created all things that they might exist ... and the dominion of Hades is not on earth."

[434] E. P. Sanders, *Paul, the Law, and the Jewish People* (Minneapolis: Ausburg Fortress, 1971), 71-2. Cf. Rom 6:13, "do not yield your members to sin ... but yield yourselves to God."

[435] Holland, *Contours*, 102-3.

[436] "God did not make death, and he does not delight in the death of the living. For he created all things that they might exist ... and the dominion of Hades is not on earth" (Wisdom 1:13).

"God created man for incorruption, and made him in the image of his own eternity, but through the devil's envy

thinking of the New Testament writers. Holland points out that Paul links sin and death with the law of the husband in Rom 7–8.[437]

Since death is equated with sin, and both are personified as the devil, this context fits our passage, Heb 2:14–15. Relating to death and sin, Isa 28:15 shows that the covenant Israel bound herself in whom she forsook Yahweh was a covenant with death.[438] Watts sees the passage as addressed to the nobles of Judah who have scorned Isaiah's advice and made a treaty with Egypt because השקר ("the falsehood") and כזב ("lie") round out the names attributed to the treaty-partner, Egypt.[439] This means that they have signed a treaty with that god. Tromp points out that מות ("death") and שאול in verse 15 are the names of the Canaanite god of the underworld and fertility.[440] In addition to Tromp's research, Bright would add that, since the pact was with Egypt, the reference is probably to Egyptian deities of similar character, such as Osiris or Seth in whose names the pact was sealed.[441] If this is the background of the author's thinking in interpreting the passage, it is natural to use this passage when unbelievers have rejected the mercy of Yahweh. Grech supports Bright's observation, in saying that the New Testament authors' world-picture was not so different from that of Isaiah as to render a hermeneutical translation necessary.[442] Thus, Isa 28 has to be interpreted in the light of the new exodus and the corporate perspectives.[443]

In fact, the covenant referred to by Isaiah is manifestly the very opposite of the covenant of Yahweh.[444] At the time of Isaiah no developed doctrine of Satan

---

death entered the world, and those who belong to his party experience it" (Wisdom 2:23).

[437] Ibid., 103. So there are passages such as 1 Cor 15:45–55 and Rev 20:14, in which death is personified as the last enemy and is destroyed by Christ.

[438] Cf. Isa 28 known as "stone passages" would have been well known in the early church. The New Testament writers speak about the covenant Yahweh would establish through his servant in Matt 21:42–44; Mark 12:10; Luke 20:17; Acts 4:11; Rom 9:32; 1 Pet 2:4–6.

[439] J. D. W. Watts, *Isaiah 1–33*, WBC (Waco, TX: Word, 1985), 362–63.

[440] N. J. Tromp, *Primitive Conceptions of Death and the Nether World in the Old Testament* (Rome: Pontifical Bible Institute, 1969), 99.

[441] J. Bright, "Isaiah," in *PCB*, 489–51

[442] P. Grech, "The 'Testimonia' and Modern Hermeneutics," *NTS* 19 (1972–73), 322.

[443] The phrase "it passes over" is used in Kethibh עבר and in Qere יעבר.

[444] Cf. The concept of a covenant with other gods is not unique to Isaiah. Exod 23:32 warned the Jews not to make covenants with other gods. In this one verse there is enough evidence to establish that the Old Testament saw the possibility of a covenant with other gods than Yahweh.

existed. Death was the great enemy. It cut man off from the covenant community and from his God. It was therefore natural for the author of Hebrews to see that he could legitimately expand its reference point to Satan, for he is, in reality, the enemy man has bound himself to in a covenant relationship. Thus, what is important in Isa 28 is that the step, from seeing death as the great enemy to a personal, evil opponent of Yahweh, had already been taken by Isaiah himself. The unbelieving Jews had placed themselves in covenant with this sworn enemy of Yahweh, and the author of Hebrews is merely adapting the theology of this passage, taking it beyond the unbelieving Jews of Isaiah's day and applying it to the whole of mankind.

The Corporate Nature of Deliverance

God's deliverance from the bondage to celestial powers focused primarily on the deliverance of the community, and not on any particular individual. Sanders, commenting on Paul's understanding, points out that the power of sin was so great that one must die to be set free of it.[445] He goes on to say that Christ's death makes the way for it. People who become united with Christ share his death and thus escape bondage, and they then share his life, being free from the power of sin. However, Sanders fails to appreciate the corporate and covenantal dimension of Paul's thought. Keck also notes that sin entails participation in a domain marked by sin's enslaving power, whose consequence is death.[446] Keck also does not emphasize the corporate. Humans are not just sinners; they are enslaved by the power of sin. These comments may help us understand Hebrews if they share a common presupposition about sacrifice and Jesus's death. According to Bultmann, the redeemed appear as brothers of the Redeemer in Heb 2:11, 17, though they can also be called his children, since he has the priority.[447] But Bultmann understood the text of Hebrews in the light of the gnostic teaching of the "kinship" between the Redeemer and the redeemed by virtue of their mutual heavenly origin, although he saw the text mentioned to be corporate.

---

[445] E. P. Sanders, *Paul, Past Masters Series* (Oxford: Oxford University Press, 1996), 79.

[446] L. E. Keck, "What Makes Romans Tick" in *Pauline Theology*, Vol. 3, ed. D. M. Hay and E. E. Johnson (Minneapolis: Fortress, 1995), 25.

[447] Bultmann, *Theology*, Vol. 1, 177.

We have argued that death, like sin, is a personification of Satan. It is the great enemy of God. That is, a new division has come into existence. There is one who holds the power of death and another who can destroy him.[448] This concept is not individualistic, as is so often held, but it is corporate, speaking of the state of unredeemed humanity in its relationship to Satan (sin). This is the model that the author of Hebrews follows relating to Israel's deliverance from Egypt. In that historical deliverance Israel was redeemed through the death of a representative, her firstborn. By the substitution of a lamb, her covenant with Egypt and her gods was terminated and a new life under the headship of Moses began. Thus, the corporative theme of the new exodus model exists in Heb 2:14–15.

Two words κεκοινώνηκεν and μετέσχεν in the statements of v. 14a indicate that any semantic difference between the verbs that refer to "the children" and to "the Son" respectively ought not to be pressed here. The meaning of the two roots is virtually synonymous; both describe a full participation in a shared reality.[449] The author of Hebrews insists that Christ partook of flesh and blood "in like manner" with "the children," so that his humanity was as genuine as theirs. The distinction lies in the variation of the verbal tenses. The perfect tense of κεκοινώνηκεν ("share") marks the "original and natural" state of humanity, while the aorist tense of μετέσχεν ("shared") emphasizes that the Son assumed human nature "at a fixed point in time, by his own choice."[450] By means of this distinction the transcendent character of the incarnate Son is maintained precisely in a context in which the accent falls upon his full participation in the human condition. The addition of the adverb παραπλησίως ("in just the same way") which signifies total likeness, underscores the extent of the identity of the Son's involvement in the conditions of human experience common to other persons.[451] It anticipates the inferential statement of v. 17, that an "obligation was upon him to be made like his brothers in every respect."

---

[448] Cf. In the version of the author of Romans, this is interpreted that 'there are those who are in Adam and those who are in Christ.'

[449] J. Y. Campbell, "κοινωνια and its Cognates in the New Testament," *JBL* 51 (1932) 353, 355, 363.

[450] Bruce, *Hebrews*, 41, n. 55.

[451] R. Williamson, *The Epistle to the Hebrews* (London: Epworth, 1965), 82.

Furthermore, the implications of the solidarity affirmed in Heb 2:1–13 are developed in the balanced clauses of a periodic sentence. Hughes points out that the purpose of these quotations here is to confirm the truth that those whom Christ redeems are rightly called his brothers.[452] Thus the exposition is related organically to its biblical support by the repetition of the expression τὰ παιδία ("the children") contributed by the previous quotation. Since "the children" share a common human nature αἵματος καὶ σαρκός ("blood and flesh"), it was necessary for the one who identified himself with them (v. 13) to assume the same full humanity (μετέσχεν τῶν αὐτῶν). This assertion grounds the bond of unity between Christ and his people in the reality of the incarnation. In the incarnation the transcendent Son accepted the mode of existence common to all humanity.

Conclusion

To sum up, the exodus is an event which models biblical thinking on deliverance. In the exodus there were two aspects to what Israel experienced: atonement and redemption. Soon after this the event of the Day of Atonement was initiated and so redemption was celebrated in the annual memorial in the Passover. From this development the theme of redemption related to the exodus and that of atonement related to the Day of Atonement.

Ezekiel saw that the original exodus had the means to teach atonement and redemption. He absorbed the sacrifice on the Day of Atonement into the ritual of the Passover. Specifically, the sacrifice of the Day of Atonement was performed at the feast of the Passover. In Ezekiel's account of this eschatological Passover it is a prince from David's line who produces the sacrifices to cleanse Israel from her sin.

The author of Hebrews followed this model for deliverance in Heb 2:10–18, which focuses on the descent from Abraham and his messianic kingship as the basis of his saving work. Christ provides not only purification for sins, but also a new status for those who have been saved out of slavery to the fear of death. That is, deliverance in Hebrews is both restoration and the forgiveness of sins. The former involves becoming a brother of Jesus, the latter is having sins

---

[452] Hughes, *Hebrews*, 109.

washed away by means of the blood of Jesus. Becoming a brother of Jesus speaks of the messianic community and is therefore corporate.

Excursus: The Meaning of the Paschal Lamb Implied to the Firstborn in the Passover.

We have explored the Passover as a setting for the theme of deliverance used by the New Testament writers. If the Passover was dominant in the cultic and theological thinking of the writers of the NT, it needs to make us focus on the Passover for it was the paschal lamb which substituted for the firstborn of the Israelites. That is, the lamb was killed as a substitute for Israel's firstborn.

In Heb 1:6 Christ is spoken of as God's firstborn (πρωτότοκος) whom he has brought into the world. He had earlier been described as the express "image of the invisible God" and "the one who, after cleansing his people from their sins, has sat down on the right hand of the majesty on high." The passage says that the firstborn, as the heir, is related to redemption, and the firstborn is united with all the people of God (Heb 12:23). So we need to clarify why the Passover lamb was killed in the Passover and the relation between the lamb and firstborn (πρωτότοκος). We also need to understand the role of πρωτότοκος and his significance in the Passover setting. We will also consider how πρωτότοκος is applied to Christ in the New Testament setting.

There are a number of questions that need to be clarified relating to the Passover. First, why was the Passover lamb killed at the Passover? The paschal lamb was the Passover offering on behalf of the firstborn. In other words, the Passover lamb was vicariously slain for the firstborn. Therefore, Holland points out that the paschal lamb and the firstborn converge to become one and the same entity.[453] The firstborn, at that time, was designated to represent the family. It was the family as a whole that the firstborn represented. This, then, was bound up with the family's deliverance from the angel of death. The firstborn's life was threatened because he represented the family. The role of the firstborn is representative.

Then why was it the firstborn, and not the father, who represented the family? Trumper proposed that, as the Passover event took place after 400 years of

---

[453] Holland, *Contours*, 239.

exile in Egypt, it is reasonable to construe that we might find some significance in the role of the firstborn in that nation's understanding.[454] According to him, the firstborn's special significance in Egypt is shown in the text of King Unas. When the dead king successfully made his way into heaven, the gods saw him arriving and stated, "He is God the firstborn of the firstborn."[455] Yahuda also commented on the position of the firstborn and their prerogative rights and privileges according to Egyptian hierarchical conceptions.[456] In Egypt the firstborn, the crown prince, had divine rank like the king himself. As soon as he succeeded to the throne, he was appointed by the gods in person as the heir of Horus, the god king, and was given the title of "Sa-Ra-en-Khetef."[457] In addition to both scholars' arguments, Holland noted that the dynasty depended upon the survival of the firstborn son of Pharaoh.[458] The firstborn's significance became even greater than his father's, for the future of the nation, the throne, and even Ra himself, was then focused upon the welfare of the new son of Ra. The father's death would be by no means as calamitous as the death of his firstborn. The firstborn's representative role was more crucial than that of his father, until such time as he himself had fathered a son. Taken together, it could be argued from this that the significance of the firstborn might be rooted in Egyptian religious belief. However, despite its attractive possibilities, it will be seen that Israel had her own firstborn tradition dating back to the Patriarchal period.

Secondly, what is the meaning of the death of the paschal lamb (the firstborn) in the Passover? It has been pointed out that the paschal victim has not been regarded as a sin-offering or regarded as a means of expiating or removing sins by most scholars. Gray sought to isolate various ancient features of the Passover by focusing on its later customs.[459] According to him, the blood ritual

---

[454] V. L. Trumper, *The Mirror of Egypt in the Old Testament* (London: Marshall Morgan & Scott, 1911), 119–21.

[455] Ibid, 120.

[456] A. S. Yahuda, *The Accuracy of the Bible* (London: William Heinemann, 1934), 85. Primogeniture was in no other country of such great significance as in court life in Egypt, and in no other hierarchy did the firstborn of the king have such privileges as in Egypt.

[457] Ibid. It means "the son of Ra from his body."

[458] Holland, *Contours*, 254.

[459] Gray, *Sacrifice*, 337–82. Gray pointed out that the Passover was originally observed by nomadic Israelites on the night of the full moon nearest the spring equinox. The victim was cooked and its blood smeared on the door posts.

had an apotropaic purpose; it was intended to protect those within from some power outside by providing a "reinforced closed door". De Vaux argued that the Passover sacrifice was to guarantee the prosperity of the flock, by nomadic or semi-nomadic shepherds in order.[460] It occurred prior to the tribal migration, and required neither a priest nor an altar. An important feature of the feast was the smearing of blood on the tent-poles in order to drive away evil powers.[461]

However, despite all scholarly endeavours to explain the origins of the Passover, no real equivalent exists outside of the OT. According to Selman, the attempts of scholars to derive the main Passover ritual from apotropaic blood ritual in Israel's nomadic period, and unleavened bread from Canaanite agricultural practices, remain uncertainly founded on internal literary analysis of Old Testament texts.[462] Engnell rejected the view that various features of the Passover were originally a nomadic festival.[463] The fact that a lamb was used in the Passover is no proof that it has to have nomadic roots. Haran points out that there is no reason to delete the term פסח ("Passover") in Exod 34:25.[464] Similarly, McConville points out that it is not necessary to remove all references to unleavened bread in Deut 16.[465]

Taken together, almost all the Pentateuchal sources link the Passover with the Israelite exodus.[466] Furthermore, almost every passage which refers to the Passover associates it with either the Feast of Unleavened Bread or with the eating of unleavened bread.[467] In the light of these observations it is apparent

---

[460] R. de Vaux, *Ancient Israel: Its Life and Institutions* (London: Darton Longman & Todd, 1965), 484-93.

[461] Ibid.

[462] M. J. Selman, "Sacrifice in the Ancient Near East," in *Sacrifice in the Bible*, ed. R. T. Beckwith and M. J. Selman (Grand Rapids: Baker, 1995), 101.

[463] I. Engnell, *A Rigid Scrutiny: Critical Essays on the Old Testament* (London: SPCK, 1970), 190. He pointed out that the command to put the blood on the door posts and lintel does not fit a nomadic situation, because it assumes a settled community with more permanent types of houses.

[464] M. Haran, "The Passover Sacrifice" Studies in the Religion of Ancient Israel, VTSup 22 (Leiden: Brill, 1972), 96-101.

[465] J. G. McConville, *Law and Theology in Deuteronomy, JSOTS* 33 (Sheffield: JSOT Press, 1984), 99-123.

[466] Among all the references to the Passover in the Pentateuch, only in Lev 23:5-6 is there no mention of the exodus. Apart from Exod 12:1-13:16, the two events are linked together in Exod 23:15; 34:18; Num 9:1; 33:3; Deut 16:1, 3, 6.

[467] Only two passages mention the Passover without making any reference to unleavened bread: Num 33:3, a brief chronological remark, and 2 Kgs 23:21-23, a short description of the Passover celebrated by Josiah. Passover and the Feast of Unleavened Bread are linked together in Exod 12:1-13:16; 23:15-18; 34:18-25; Lev 23:5-6; Deut

that the task of reconstructing the history of the Passover will continue to present a major challenge, especially if scholars insist that the meaning is to be found outside of Israel's own tradition. Therefore, we shall treat seriously the biblical tradition which links the origin of the Passover with the Israelite exodus from Egypt.

At the heart of the first Passover ritual is the slaying of a lamb, the smearing of its blood on the door posts, and the eating of its meat. The detailed instructions for this ritual parallel closely those relating to sacrifices. Thus, Alexander states that the slaughter of the animal atoned for the sin of the people and the blood smeared on the door posts purified those within the house.[468] Jeremias pointed out that the language in the Passover is unavoidably sacrificial and signifies atonement.[469] Stalker sees a sacrificial intention behind the purpose of the death of the firstborn noting that the word "set apart" in Exod 12:12—which literally means "cause to pass over"—is linked with sacrificing children to Molech in 2 Kgs 16:3 and Ezek 20:31.[470] Holland points out that the blood of the Passover lamb, which substitutes for that of the firstborn, had propitiatory value.[471]

Therefore, the concept of atonement, while not mentioned specifically, underlies the offering of the Passover sacrifice. On the occasion of the Passover the Israelites had, of necessity, to mark their houses with sacrificial blood. Obviously the blood of the sacrifice played a significant part in preventing the death of the male firstborn. That is, the firstborn of the Israelites were inherently no different from the male firstborn of the Egyptians. Without the atoning blood of the sacrifice they too would have been struck dead by the "destroyer".

16:1–16; 2 Chr 30:1–21; 35:1–19; Ezra 6:19–22. Passover and the eating of unleavened bread are associated in Exod 12:1–13:16; 23:18; 34:25; Num 9:2–14; 28:16–17; Deut 16:1–8; Josh 5:10–11; Ezek 45:21.

[468] T. D. Alexander, "The Passover Sacrifice," in *Sacrifice in the Bible*, ed. R. T. Beckwith and M. J. Selman (Grand Rapids: Baker, 1995), 8.

[469] Jeremias, *Eucharistic*, 222–26.

[470] D. M. Stalker, *Ezekiel: Introduction and Commentary* (London: SCM, 1968), 221.

[471] Holland, *Contours*, 171. Brown understands that the Passover has expiatory value because by that time lambs were sacrificed within the temple area by the priests: R. E. Brown, *John*, Vol. 1, 62. Dodd also thought that there was probably expiatory significance in the Passover ritual in pre-Mosaic periods, but it had been stopped long before New Testament times: C. H. Dodd, *Interpretation*, 234.

The Passover seems to be associated with atonement in Ezek 45:18–22.[472] In Ezek 45:25 the prophet tells how the prince will provide sacrifices for the sins of the people during the Passover. He is focusing on the importance of the Passover for treating the sins of the people. What Ezekiel wanted to emphasize was what the Son of David would do; that is, provide atonement during the Passover.[473]

The sacrificial meaning of the Passover was appreciated in the intertestamental literature[474] and even the New Testament period. The instances from the Dead Sea Scrolls are particularly interesting, because the Qumran community had separated itself from the temple until better times arrived, and was thus actually substituting spiritual sacrifice for literal to a degree which even the Jews of the dispersion, who could visit the temple only occasionally, did not equal.

Howard acknowledges that the sacrifices mentioned during the Passover of Ezek 45:25 are linked to the description of Jesus being the Lamb of God spoken of by John the Baptist in John 1:29.[475] He points out that the midrash on Exod 12 describes the Passover as an atoning sacrifice. He concludes that this idea was so widely understood in Second Temple Judaism that John the Baptist's hearers would have had no difficulty in understanding the statement that the Lamb of God takes away the sin of the world.

Thirdly, we need to ask where the New Testament writers went for their understanding of redemption linked with the Passover. Redemption is another important theological idea associated with the Passover. It could be used for manumission of a slave;[476] the same meaning is found of this word in the

---

[472] Dunn, *Theology*, 216; Holland, *Contours*, 162; Howard, "Eucharist," 331–2.
[473] Holland, *Contours*, 161.
[474] Sir 35:1–3; Test. Lev 3:6; IQS 8, 9.
[475] Howard, "Eucharist," 331–2.
[476] F. Buchsel, "λύτρον" [lutron] in *TDNT* IV, 340. Deissmann argues that in 1 Cor 6:20 Paul focused on the process adopted for the release of a person from slavery. He points out that in both classical and Hellenistic Greek, redemption is used of the price paid to redeem something that is in pawn, of the money paid to ransom prisoners of war, and of money paid to purchase the freedom of a slave. More especially the word was also used for sacral manumission of a slave. In the Ancient Near East, a slave could pay a sum of money into the treasury of the local temple and through this means the god of that temple technically purchased him. The slave was freed from his old master because he had become the property of the god: G. A. Deissmann, *Light from the Ancient East*, trans. L. R. M. Strachan (New York: Hodder & Stoughton, 1927), 320–31.

LXX.[477] According to Ladd, when writing of redemption Paul mainly used the Greek word, ἀπολύτρωσιν.[478] Several times the price of redemption is expressed in this context.[479] Redemption is also expressed by the verb ἀγοράζω ("to buy" or "purchase").[480] In both 1 Cor 6:19–20 and 7:22–23, the cost of purchase is not stated; it is clearly in the author's mind in view of the fact that both times he refers to the price.[481] That is, this can be nothing other than the death of Christ. With regard to the doctrine of redemption Morris argues that the payment of a price is a necessary element in the redemption idea; and Christ has paid the price of our redemption.[482]

However, Buchsel argues that the original sense of the root λύτρον is watered down and only the general sense of "liberation" remains instead of ransom.[483] Dunn rejects Morris' argument, which is that the concept of "redemption" included the idea of paying a price.[484] It was occasioned more by the subsequent Anselmian interpretation than by the image itself or the scriptural background evoked by Paul. He concludes that the stronger influence was certainly that of Israel being ransomed (from slavery) in Egypt, prominent in Paul's principal quarry for scriptural texts in Isaiah.[485] It is mentioned first in Exod 6:6 where it is used in the context of the release of slaves (cf. 21:8). The concept reappears in 13:14–16 where it is linked to the future redemption of the male firstborn in commemoration of the Passover. In this context two aspects are prominent:[486] (a) as a consequence of the Passover all the firstborn of the Israelites, both human and animal, owe their lives to the Lord; they belong uniquely to him and this has to be acknowledged in a special way; (b)

---

[477] Morris, *Apostolic*, 10.
[478] Ladd, *Theology*, 433. This is a rare word, occurring only eight times outside the New Testament.
[479] Cf. Rom 3:24; Eph 1:7; Heb 9:15.
[480] Ladd, *Theology*, 434; Morris, *Apostolic*, 53–55.
[481] Ladd, *Theology*, 434. Morris, *Apostolic*, 53–55. However, according to Dunn it is less clear whether the verb "buy" (ἀγοράζω) or "buy from/back" (ἐξαγοράζω), has similar redemptive overtones: J. D. G. Dunn, *Theology*, 228. McLean also points out that it is true that the verbs themselves do not necessarily carry such an implication: B. H. McLean, *The Cursed Christ: Mediterranean Expulsion Rituals and Pauline Soteriology*, JSNTS 126 (Sheffield: Sheffield Academic, 1996), 127–31.
[482] Morris, *Apostolic*, 58.
[483] Buchsel, "ἀπολύτρωσις," in *TDNT* IV, 355.
[484] Dunn, *Theology*, 228.
[485] E.g. Isa 43:1, 14; 44:22–24; 51:11; 52:3. Cf. Dunn, *Romans*, 169.
[486] Alexander, "Sacrifice," 17.

since all the male firstborn belonged to the Lord, this required that each life be offered up to the Lord in sacrifice. However, in the case of human beings and non-sacrificial animals it was possible to offer a sacrifice. This is apparent from the brief remark about the redemption of every firstborn donkey in 13:13: if the donkey is redeemed it lives; otherwise it must be put to death. Here redemption involves the offering of a sacrifice.

Passover controlled not only Israel's self-consciousness, but her existence. Israel could not identify herself apart from the fact that Yahweh had redeemed her. Indeed, it was the one festival about which Jews had exhaustive knowledge, and her principled system was founded on the fact of Yahweh's mercy toward her in redeeming her from slavery (Deut 24:17). Now if Passover is at the heart of Israel's self-identification and understanding, and since most of the writers of the New Testament documents were Jews, then it should not be surprising to find that this same imagery is at the heart of the eschatological salvation to which Israel had been looking forward.

Furthermore, in the Old Testament the Jewish kings celebrated the great Passover events.[487] Indeed, according to Ezekiel the king was to be the main figure in the eschatological celebration of the Passover.[488] This has been taken up by the gospel writers in the way they emphasize that Jesus died in the context of the Passover as King of the Jews. In other words, the use of the title "firstborn from the dead" is drawing these redemptive threads together.[489]

Taken together, the Passover involves propitiation to God and redemption from the enemy. According to Holland, there is only one cultic event in which redemption is celebrated, and that is Passover.[490] Ezekiel, who was a prophet the New Testament authors used, mentions the atoning sacrifices of the Day of Atonement in the context of the eschatological temple offered during the

---

[487] 2 Kgs 23:23; 2 Chron 30:15–17.
[488] Ezek 45:21–25.
[489] M. Wilson, "The Promise of the 'Seed' in *The New Testament and the Targums, JSNT* 5 (1979), 6. He says that Ps 89 is behind New Testament redemptive themes; F. F. Bruce, *Commentary on the Epistles to the Ephesians and Colossians* (Grand Rapids: Eerdmans, 1957), 197. This puts Ps 89:27, "I will also appoint him my firstborn, the most exalted of the kings of the earth," into a redemptive context.
[490] Holland, *Contours*, 160.

Passover.[491] The eschatological Passover will thus propitiate for the sins of the people.

There are people who apply sacrificial ideas in Greek and Roman literature to the atonement, drawing attention to the theme of a dying hero who gives his life for people.[492] Occasionally, those Greek heroes who die for their people are said to die for the nation's laws. Hengel considers that this idea came into Judaism from Greek sources in the intertestamental period. Hengel compares this with the Maccabean heroes, who gained an everlasting name by dying, not just for their people, but for their God and his laws (1 Macc 2:50–51, 64; 6:44; 2 Macc 13:14).[493] Hengel sees this idea reflected in John 15:13 and Rom 5:7. However, the sacrifice of Jesus did not just expiate a particular crime or avert a particular earthly calamity, like the death of Greco-Roman heroes.

Wright supports Hengel's thought, saying that the fate of the martyrs was bound up with the fate of the nation as a whole, and that this representative, exilic suffering functions redemptively.[494] According to Wright, the biblical context for the stories of suffering and martyrdom in the second-Temple period is the prophecy of Isaiah, particularly in chapters 40–55, and in the figure of the servant.[495] Thus he points out that Dan 11–12 in particular should be regarded as one of the earliest extant interpreters of the servant figure in Isaiah. That is, Daniel saw the martyrs of his own day as at least a partial

---

[491] According to Dunn, the Passover is already associated with atonement in Ezek 45:18–22: Dunn, *Theology*, 216. Howard also acknowledges that the sin offerings mentioned during the Passover of Ezek 45:25 lie behind the description of Jesus being the Lamb of God spoken of by John the Baptist in John 1:29. He points out that the midrash on Exod 12 describes the Passover as an atoning sacrifice: Howard, "Eucharist," 331–2.

[492] Hengel, *Atonement*, 28–32. M. de Jonge, "Jesus' Death for Others and the Death of the Maccabaean Martyrs" in *Text and Testimony* (A. F. J. Klijn), ed. T. Baarda, A. Hilhorst, G. P. Luttik Luizen, and A. S. van der Woude (Kampen: J. H. Kok, 1988), 142–51; M. de Jonge, *Jesus, the Servant-Messiah* (New Haven: Yale University Press, 1991), 155; A. J. Droge and J. D. Tabor, *A Noble Death: Suicide and Martyrdom among Christians and Jews in Antiquity* (San Francisco, CA: Harper and Francisco, 1992), 96.

[493] Hengel, *Atonement*, 8. According to Hengel, in Greek and Roman literature the hero dying for his people is often spoken of in sacrificial terms and is said to atone for them. At these points religious language is certainly used, and it is sacrificial in character.

[494] Wright, *Victory*, 583.

[495] Ibid, 588–89. According to Wright, Isa 40–55 is not about a detached atonement theology, but the prophecy that Yahweh would comfort and restore his people after their exile, would pour out his wrath upon the pagans who had held them captive, and would return in person to Zion to reign as king. Especially, the chapters (54–55) which come after the fourth song celebrate in no uncertain terms Israel's restoration, the renewal of the covenant, and the forgiveness of the sins which led to exile; and chapter 55 throws open the invitation to all and sundry to come and join in the blessing.

fulfilment of Isa 53.[496] Here Wright's weak point is found—redemption, rather than atonement, is focused on the Passover. 1 Cor 5:7 is a proof that the Passover victim was understood by Paul to be a sacrifice.[497]

According to Holland, however, the fact that the Day of Atonement was amalgamated with the language of Passover was basic to the early church's cultic thinking.[498] It is well known that John's gospel appears to differ from the Synoptics in giving the day that Jesus died as the day of the Passover (15th Nisan).[499] John apparently emphasizes that the crucifixion took place on the day of the preparation of the Passover.[500] Smalley points out, "if Jesus is represented as dying on the day of the preparation of the Passover, then his death coincides with the slaughter of the sacrificial Passover lambs; and this is theologically suitable in a gospel which uniquely designates Jesus 'the Lamb of God'".[501] This very point is emphasized at John 19:36: "these things took place that the scripture might be fulfilled, 'Not a bone of him shall be broken'". Here "these things" refer to all that the previous verse had in mind, namely, the death of Jesus.[502]

Both Rom 3:24–26 and Heb 9:1–10 have been shown to be the same in a comparison of the themes.[503] Holland points out the term ἱλαστήριον in Rom

---

[496] The allusion from Dan 12:3 ("those who justify the many") to Isa 53:11 ("he shall justify the many") is a sign that the whole passage about the suffering righteous ones, from 11:31 to 12:10, may be influenced by Isa 52:13–53:12. It is observed by the following scholars: J. A. Montgomery, *A Critical and Exegetical Commentary on the Book of Daniel*, ICC (Edinburgh: T&T Clark, 1927), 459, 472; N. W. Porteous, *Daniel: A Commentary* (London: SCM, 1965), 171; A. Lacocque, *The Book of Daniel* (London: SPCK, 1979), 243, 245, 249, and M. Fishbane, *Biblical Interpretation in Ancient Israel* (Oxford; Oxford University Press, 1985), 482–99.

[497] It reads: "Christ our Passover has been sacrificed for us."

[498] "The material is handled, both in Paul and in Hebrews, in such a way that the convergence is taken as understood." Holland, *Contours*, 163.

[499] For recent discussions concerning the relationship between John and the Synoptics on this point, see R. T. France, "Chronological Aspects of 'Gospel Harmony'," *VoxEx* 16 (1986), 43-54; R. T. Beckwith, "*Cautionary Notes on the Use of Calendars and Astronomy to Determine the Chronology of the Passion*", *Chronos, Kairos, Christos*, eds. J. Vardaman and E. M. Yamauchi (Winona Lake, IN; Eisenbrauns, 1989), 183–205.

[500] Cf. Reference to the Passover in John appears early in the passion account (13:1), and later passages (e.g. 18:28, 39; 19:14, 31, 42)

[501] S. S. Smalley, *John: Evangelist and Interpreter* (Exeter: Paternoster, 1978), 24.

[502] P. M. Head, "The Self-Offering and Death of Christ as a Sacrifice in the Gospels and the Acts of the Apostles" in *Sacrifice in the Bible*, ed. R. T. Beckwith and M. J. Selman (Grand Rapids: Baker, 1995), 122-3. The quotation comes from Exod 12:46, and there refers to the eating of the Passover lamb.

[503] D. J. Moo, *Romans 1–8,* The Wycliffe Exegetical Commentary (Chicago, IL: Moody, 1991), 246. However, Moo failed to see the absorption of Day of Atonement into the Passover.

3:25 was translated as propitiation and the early church saw the anticipated eschatological Passover to be a sacrifice of propitiation through the influence of Ezek 45:25.[504] It is natural, therefore, that just as the Jews in Egypt on the Passover night had to put their faith in the efficacy of the blood of the Passover lamb, the blood of Christ, the Christian Passover victim (1 Cor 5:7), is where the faith of those who are threatened with judgment must be placed. The blood of Christ speaks of his death.

Ezekiel's influence has been noted throughout the New Testament. The statement, *peace with God*, in Rom 5:1 is linked with Ezek 37:26, which says that "I will make a covenant of peace with them".[505] Holland points out that the argument of Rom 8, relating to the resurrection, is a summary of that found in 1 Cor 15. According to Schneider, 1 Cor 15:3–20 was an echo from Ezek 37 and was influenced by Passover.[506] Furthermore, Ezek 37 was read at the Passover celebration. Ezek 37 provided Paul with a key type of the resurrection when Yahweh's Spirit breathed into an army of bones and gave them life. Therefore, Ezekiel seems to have had significant influence on the argument of Paul, which his readers are expected to recognize. If it is right, then it is also reasonable to suggest that the significance of the paschal offering made by the Davidic king in Ezek 45:25 would have been widely recognized.

According to the Targum on Zech 9:11, the blood of the Passover lamb that was slaughtered at the exodus from Egypt was also referred to as the blood of the covenant. It considers the blood of the Passover lamb as the covenant blood that brought about Israel's release from the "waterless pit" of Egypt. Goppelt concludes that Jesus's blood, like the blood of the Passover lambs, means sparing, deliverance, and redemption from death, slavery and the wrath of God.[507]

Returning to Heb 1:6, Michaelis[508] sees the firstborn as corresponding to the son of 1:2 and the series of quotations stressing sonship in 1:5. He takes the

---

[504] Holland, *Contours*, 170–1.
[505] Ibid., 164. Dunn, *Romans*, 247. Dunn links Rom 5:1 with Ezek 37:26; 45:25
[506] B. Schneider, "The Corporate Meaning and Background of 1 Cor 15:45b—ὁ ἔσχατος Ἀδὰμ εἰς πνεῦμα ζῳοποιοῦν" *CBQ* 29 (1967), 156–59.
[507] Goppelt, *Typos*, 114.
[508] W. Michaelis, "πρωτότοκος" [prototokos] in *TDNT* VI, 880. Cf. D. R. De Lacy, "The Form of God in the Likeness of Men: A Study in Pauline Christology," Ph.D. diss., University of Cambridge, 1974, 19.

title as a reference to the pre-existent Lord who is praised in the Christ-hymn of 1:3 and who is designated as first-born of all creation in Col 1:15. Sabourin[509] saw the origin of the title prototokos to be in Exod 13:11–16, but he did not recognize the passage in redemptive imagery. Helyer[510] pointed out that in Heb 1:6 there is an echo of the Davidic oracle in Ps 89:27 which stands in close connection with Ps 2:7 and 2 Sam 7:14, cited in the previous verse. On this accounting, then, the firstborn is the one who is qualified for world sovereignty and the expression is equivalent to the "ruler of kings on earth" (Rev 1:5). Nevertheless, Helyer failed to see the significance of the Passover as the setting to interpret the title. Bowman[511] links the firstborn to Christ the paschal victim, but he says that the deliverance results from the death of the Saviour himself. He virtually calls Jesus "God's firstborn" in a paschal context, but does not pin significant theological implications on it.

Levenson identified the death of the firstborn as a paschal offering.[512] He saw the Aqedah as a foundation story for the festival of Passover, but he failed to see how it is part of the paschal theology of the early church. Helyer[513] further claimed that there was a new exodus background to the use of the term πρωτότοκον in Heb 1:6 and 12:23. Holland[514] concluded that the church of the firstborn exists as a result of Christ's redemptive activity when he gave himself for his people as the paschal victim. In Heb 12:23 the writer tells his readers that they have come to the church of the firstborn. It is the church that belongs to the firstborn, for it exists as a result of his redemptive activity when he gave himself for her as the paschal victim.[515]

To sum up, in the original Passover the paschal lamb substituted for the firstborn who in turn represented his family. The lamb, on behalf of the

---

[509] L. Sabourin, *Christology: Basic Tools in Focus* (New York, NY: Alba House, 1984), 84.

[510] L. R. Helyer, "The prototokos title in Hebrews," *SBT* (1977), 16.

[511] J. Bowman, *The Gospel of Mark: The New Christian Jewish Passover Haggadah* (Leiden: Brill, 1965), 314. He points out that deliverance is not produced by the death of the firstborn of the Egyptians, not even the death of Pharaoh's firstborn, nor at the price of the foreign oppressor. According to him, "The death of the firstborn in Mark's Christian Jewish New Haggadah of the Passover achieves the deliverance of the people enslaved to the Law and the Temple."

[512] J. D. Levenson, *The Death and Resurrection of the Beloved Son: The Transformation of Child Sacrifice in Judaism and Christianity* (New Haven: Yale University, 1993), 198.

[513] Helyer, "πρωτοτόκος," 16.

[514] Holland, *Contours*, 129.

[515] Heb 9:11–15, 24–28.

Israelite firstborn, was thus killed for all the family. Here the Passover carries the meaning of the cultic language and the theological theme, i.e. atonement and redemption. This propitiatory element was dropped as Israel celebrated Passover as a memorial of redemption. Alongside the Passover, the Day of Atonement, which was set up following the Passover, was kept for the atonement of Israel's sin.

In the sixth century BCE the prophet Ezekiel prophesied about the final Passover offered by the Son of David, saying that it would be similar in achievement to the original Passover. The sacrifice of the Day of Atonement offered by the prince was put into the orbit of Passover celebration. Jesus built on this understanding and Paul continued what Jesus taught. The New Testament writers together inherited and developed this understanding.

Chapter 4: The Pilgrimage Theme

Introduction

Hebrews uses the term παρεπίδημοί ("sojourners") in Heb 11:13, of those who live by faith. The author of Hebrews connects this with the idea of a journey to a city to come. Walker points out that Hebrews has been mainly influential in the development of the metaphor of Christian existence as a pilgrimage.[516] Käsemann argued that the existential necessity of pilgrimage for bearers of revelation means that Israel's journey through the wilderness is an antitype of Christianity.[517] He understood Hebrews to be based on the gnostic redeemer-myth of the Urmensch.[518]

Johnsson sees that key elements of the phenomenology of a religious pilgrimage have been taken up and transformed in Hebrews' view of Christian existence.[519] Pederson added some points to Johnsson's theory, and claimed that some of the themes of the journey are traced in the Bible.[520] However, Wright wants to give pilgrimage a theological meaning while making it clear that this is only of secondary significance.[521] He relates a particular religious experience that occurred on his first visit to the Church of the Holy Sepulchre, after which he realized that he had become a pilgrim.[522] He concludes that such

---

[516] P. W. L. Walker, *Jesus and the Holy City: New Testament Perspectives on Jerusalem* (Grand Rapids: Eerdmans, 1996), 201-34. R. Jewett, *Letter to Pilgrims: A Commentary on the Epistle to the Hebrews* (New York: Pilgrim, 1981), 17.

[517] E. Käsemann, *The Wandering People of God*, English trans. (Minneapolis: Augsburg, 1984), 7. Käsemann saw that the basic presupposition of the text is that one possesses the ευαγγελιον on earth only as ενπαγγελια. But then it follows that the form of existence in time appropriate to the recipient of the revelation can only be that of wandering (pilgrimage).

[518] Ibid., 87-96.

[519] Johnsson, "The Pilgrimage Motif," 244-7.

[520] D. J. Pederson, "The Pilgrim Gospel: The Old Testament as a Theology of Journey," *TTJ* Vol. II, No 1 (1990, Nov), 150. He goes on to say that the central issue revolves around the normality of homelessness in biblical faith.

[521] N. T. Wright, *The Way of the Lord: Christian Pilgrimage Today* (London: SPCK, 1999), 9-10. Wright contrasts 'a geographical pilgrimage' with 'the pilgrimage that really counts' and in conclusion reminds us that whether or not we have 'the chance to go on an actual pilgrimage ... all of us are summoned to go on this inside-out pilgrimage, following in the way of the Lord' (cf. Ibid., ix, x).

[522] Ibid., 4-7.

Christian pilgrimages take place in the space and time between the life of Jesus and God's restoration of the whole creation.[523]

However, God still deals with his people in the last days as he dealt with Israel in the wilderness. In other words, things that happened to Israel are types of the experiences of the church.[524] The earthly Canaan and the earthly Jerusalem were temporary object-lessons pointing to the saints' everlasting inheritance. In the new exodus, which the prophets predicted would release Israel from Babylon, the people will once again begin their sojourn by passing through the sea.[525] Their pilgrim progress through this world had as its goal a home elsewhere.

This pilgrim theme has been part of the Israelites' consciousness throughout all generations—Old Testament people, intertestamental people, even New Testament people. Thus, we will first explore how the pilgrimage theme is related to the Passover. If the theme can be shown to be part of the Passover event, we shall examine how the authors applied the theme to the Passover in the Old Testament, intertestamental literature, and the New Testament documents. In particular we will examine four passages in Hebrews concerning this matter.

Pilgrimage and Passover

Pilgrimage as an Essential Element of Israel's Obligation

Before exploring the Old Testament, intertestamental literature, and New Testament to identify the way that the pilgrimage theme is used in them, we shall examine the relationship of our subject, the Passover, with the pilgrimage.

---

[523] Ibid., 8. Wright sees his conclusion as "a characteristically Pauline position of now-and-not-yet". But this is not a compelling claim. His position in fact simply reverses the emphasis of the "already" and "not yet" dialectic not only of Paul but also of Hebrews and John. The period of "not yet" until the consummation of Christ's lordship over the cosmos does not for them reintroduce what had been transformed but provides the opportunity to live out ahead of time in all places the new reality guaranteed by Christ's present rule in the heavenly realm.

[524] L. Goppelt, *Typos: The Typological Interpretation of the Old Testament in the New*, trans. D. H. Madvig (Grand Rapids: Eerdmans, 1982), 4–5.

[525] Isa 432, 16; 4427.

The Old Testament writers' perspective is that the journey to the promised land was a pilgrimage.[526] The journey to the land of Canaan is portrayed as a procession of Yahweh from Sinai. It is from the place of the feast referred to in Exod 5:1, which was the place of Yahweh's appearing in the wilderness, to Mt Zion, which is the place of his settled dwelling in the heart of the land he has given to his people (Ps 68:18). Johnsson[527] and Pederson[528] have set out the religious "structure" of pilgrimage. Both scholars relate pilgrimage to (1) a separation, (2) a journey to a sacred place with difficulties, (3) incorporation rites on arrival at the goal, and (4) an eschatological concept. However, they fail to appreciate that pilgrimage is linked with the Passover.

The Israelites went on pilgrimage three times a year to their central sanctuary, where they celebrated their occupation of the promised land. Durham says that the Hebrew verb חגג in Exod 5:1 emphasizes a religious journey to an appointed place more than it signifies a "feast."[529] He sees that, although there is no mention here of a three-day journey, the request is for permission to undertake a religious pilgrimage at the command of Yahweh. Merrill draws attention to the fact that the two strands were already interwoven into the exodus accounts: Moses had requested of Pharaoh that the people be allowed to leave Egypt for the express purpose of undertaking a pilgrimage to the desert, there to hold a feast to Yahweh.[530] Dumm[531] further points out that this

---

[526] The place of the "festival" referred to in Exod 5:1: "Let my people go," says Yahweh through Moses to Pharaoh, "so that they may celebrate a festival to me in the wilderness". "Festival" here is חגג, just like the three annual feasts required in Exod 23:14–18; Deut 16:1–17; Lev 23 (Passover-Unleavened Bread, Feast of Weeks, Feast of Tabernacles).

[527] Johnsson, "The Pilgrimage Motif," 244–7.

[528] Pederson, "Pilgrim," 150 argues that (1) God initiates journeys according to His sovereign plan; (2) excessive attachment to an earthly home leads to spiritual blindness; (3) true rest is future; and (4) people most open to the gospel are on the move physically or emotionally. He goes on to say that the central issue revolves around the normality of homelessness in biblical faith.

[529] J. I. Durham, *Exodus*, WBC (Waco, TX: Word, 1987), 62.

[530] A. L. Merrill, "Pilgrimage in the Old Testament: A Study in Cult and Tradition," *EIATS* (1974), 46–46. Compare Exod 3:12; 5:1.

[531] D. R. Dumm, "Passover and Eucharist", *Worship* 61 (2003), 205. He examines the meaning of "wilderness" and concludes that "wilderness" is land that is still relatively free of human control. Such land may be desert-like, as is the case with the Sinai Peninsula, but it could also be a jungle. In the context of Exodus, this largely unknown and uncontrolled land is sharply contrasted with Pharaoh's Egypt, which was noted for its order and neatness. "Thus the wilderness came to symbolize for Israel the mystery of God. They were being called from a place of human order and slavery to God's country, full of God's mysterious presence and open to exquisite freedom."

"pilgrimage-feast" has a religious meaning for travellers. In the light of later developments, according to him, the travellers are seen to be all the later generations of Israelites (and of Christians too) who pledge themselves to a journey through history in response to God's call.

Furthermore, McConville[532] interprets "festival" (חג) in Exod 5:1 as "pilgrimage-feast." This included the three annual pilgrimage-feasts required in Exod 23:14-18; Deut 16:1-17; Lev 23 (Passover-Unleavened Bread, Feast of Week, Feast of Tabernacles). He points out that pilgrimage expresses a strong attachment to place.[533] It is based on Israel's memory of its deliverance from slavery in Egypt, its formation as the covenant people of Yahweh at Mt Sinai, Yahweh's gift of land to them by the dispossession of others, and his dwelling among them in the central sanctuary. McConville[534] highlights that one of Joshua's first acts on entering the land was to keep the Passover, as a sign that the time of wilderness and manna was at an end and the time of land and cultivation had come (Josh 5:10-12). If McConville is correct, pilgrimage is a process based on Israel's memory of its deliverance from slavery in Egypt at the Passover.

Jeroboam l, the first king of the separate northern kingdom of Israel, wished to end the pilgrimages of his subjects to Jerusalem and so set up alterative shrines at Dan and Bethel.[535] Pilgrimage to these shrines was criticized by the prophet Amos,[536] not because they were an alternative to Jerusalem, but because pilgrimage had become a religious symbol for obeying God. King Hezekiah's efforts to gather all the inhabitants of Judah and the defunct northern kingdom to one Passover celebration in Jerusalem were partly successful.[537] Furthermore, one of the aims of King Josiah's reforms was to highlight the Passover pilgrimage to Jerusalem.[538] After the exile, pilgrimages were usually limited to attending the Passover.[539] Thus, pilgrimage can be defined as an

---

[532] G. McConville, "Pilgrimage and 'Place': An Old Testament View," in *Explorations in a Christian Theology of Pilgrimage*, ed. C Bartholomew and F. Hughes (Farnham: Ashgate, 2004), 17.
[533] Ibid.
[534] Ibid.
[535] 1 Kgs 12:28-30
[536] Amos 4:4-5; 5:5-6; 8:14
[537] 2 Chr 30:1-13
[538] 2 Kgs 23:21-23; 2 Chr 35:1.
[539] cf. Luke 2:41

essential element of Israel's obligation to celebrate Passover through which she recalled Yahweh's saving activity from Egypt.

Pilgrimage in the Psalms and Prophets

Psalms

In the book of Psalms, the worshippers' regular journey to the holy place is to meet Yahweh. These Psalms recall and celebrate the original journey to the land (Ps 68:7–10; 81:1–10). In doing so, they openly rejoice in Yahweh's victory over other peoples (Ps 68:21–3) and proclaim the superiority of Mt Zion over other holy mountains (Ps 68:15–16).

Sabourin sees that Pss 113–18 are related to the three pilgrimage feasts.[540] Allan points out that Pss 113 and 114 are traditionally sung prior to the Passover meal; Pss 115 through 118 are sung afterwards.[541] The superiority of Yahweh is celebrated in Ps 113. It is he who is above all things (Ps 113:4–5) and who is able to elevate the poor and weak to positions of eminence (Ps 113:7–9). Merrill links the events to Yahweh's redemption of Israel from Egypt.[542] He also connects the pilgrimage festival song to the return of the Babylonian exiles to Zion.[543] The allusion to cult and temple (Ps 115:9–12) and

---

[540] L. Sabourin, *The Psalms: Their Origin and Meaning* (New York: Alba House, 1974), 188–89.

[541] L. C. Allan, *Psalms* 101–150, WBC, Vol. 21 (Waco, TX: Word, 1983), 99–100.

[542] E. H. Merrill, "Pilgrimage and Procession Motif of Israel's Return," in *Israel's Apostasy and Restoration*, ed. A. Gileadi (Grand Rapids: Baker, 1988), 265.

[543] Ibid., 265. According to Merrill, major elements of pilgrimage, derived from the three most relevant categories of psalms—"Songs of Pilgrims (120–134)," "Pilgrim Psalms," and "Hallel-Psalms (Pss 113–118)"—are listed as follows with the passages from the prophets that appear to show dependence on them, or at least concepts shared with them.

A. Goal of Pilgrimage
  1. Zion/Jerusalem (Ps 84:5, 7; 122:3, 6; 125:1; 126:1; 128:5; 129:5; 132:13; 133:3; 134:3; compare Zeph 3:16–17; Jer 3:14; 31:6; Zech 1:16–17)
  2. The Temple (Ps 84:2, 10; 122:1; 116:28–29; 132:5–7)
B. Purpose of Pilgrimage: Payment of Offerings/Vows/Tribute (Ps 116:14, 18–19; 118:27; 126:6; compare Zeph 3:9–10; Jer 31:8–9; Ezek 20:40–41; Hag 2:6–9; Isa 60:4–7; 66:20).
C. Universal and Scattered Origins of Pilgrimage (Ps 120:5; compare Amos 9:9; Hos 11:11; Mic 7:12–13; Jer 3:18; Zech 8:1–8; Isa 11:11–12; 19:23–25; 43:5–6)
D. Path of Pilgrimage
  1. Building of the Highway (Ps 84:5; compare Isa 35:8–9; 40:3–4; 42:14–17; 62:10)
  2. Irrigation of the Desert (Ps 84:6; 114:8; compare Isa 11:15; 41:17–20)
    3. Drying of the Rivers (Ps 124:4–5; compare Isa 11:16)
    4. As an Ascent (Ps 122:4; compare Mic 4:1–8; Isa 2:1–4)
E. Mode of Pilgrimage

to creation theology (Ps 115:15–16) confirms this connection, because Isaiah makes clear that it is the Creator—Yahweh—who is able to restore his people to the land and to re-establish worship in the new temple in Zion.[544]

Furthermore, the Songs of Ascent (Ps 120–134) show us the fullest available picture of Old Testament pilgrimages. These fifteen psalms were sung on pilgrim processions to Jerusalem and occurred there at the festival.[545] When the Songs of Ascent are read in sequence, they suggest the experience of pilgrims travelling from a distant land.

In these psalms the pilgrim proclaims that he has come from far away Meshech and Kedar (Ps 120:5), places whose inhabitants hate peace (Ps 120:6–7).[546] Though the journey has been long and hard, Yahweh has been his keeper and shade (Ps 121:5–6). Then we have the joyful arrival at Jerusalem: "I was glad when they said to me, Let us go to the house of the Lord, our feet are standing within your gates, O Jerusalem" (Ps 122:1–2 NRSV). Pss 123–133 are full of prayers, oaths and invocations spoken by pilgrims at the festival, followed by a farewell blessing of the temple servants by the departing pilgrims to complete the cycle: "May the Lord, maker of heaven and earth, bless you from Zion" (Ps 134:3).[547]

Isaiah

Pilgrimage imagery is used in a variety of ways by Isaiah. Isaiah's pilgrimage imagery is unmistakable in its depiction of future salvation. The amalgamation of deliverance and pilgrimage themes in the prophet's writing should not be surprising. This juxtaposition of themes appears first in Isa 11:11–16.[548] Here the prophet bases the exilic return of the remnant on second exodus

---

1. As a Stream (Ps 126:4; compare Mic 4:1–8; Isa 2:1–4)
2. With Divine Protection (Ps 84:11; 113:7–9; 115:9–11; 116:6, 8; 118:5–14; 121:3–8; 124:1–3, 6–8; 125:1–2; compare Isa 25:9–10; 52:7–12)
3. With Song and Rejoicing (Ps 118:15, 24; 126:5–6; 132:9; compare Jer 31:10–14; Zech 8:22–23; Isa 30:29; 35:10; 49:13; 51:11)

[544] see Isa 40:26–31; 42:5–9; 44:24–28; 51:9–16

[545] *Dictionary of Biblical Imagery*, eds. L. Ryken, J. C. Wilhoit, and T. Longman III (Leicester: IVP, 1998), 644. These psalms are an excellent index to the values and preoccupations of pilgrims on their journey.

[546] These place names constitute a merism, namely, "everywhere". See M. Dahood, *Psalms* III 101–150 (Garden City, NY: Doubleday, 1970), 197.

[547] Merrill, "Procession," 264.

[548] J. D. W. Watts, *Isaiah* 1–33, WBC 24 (Waco, TX: Word, 1985), 178.

deliverance (11:16b). Verses 12–14 show us that God gathers the dispersed of Israel and Judah.[549] Moreover, in vv. 15–16 the way will be arranged through water and desert, so that the exiles will be able to make their way with ease from Assyria—symbolic of the entire hostile world (11:16).[550] But the Isaianic return transcends an exodus redemption because Assyria and Egypt themselves are included in the return.[551] Isaiah thus joins the other prophets in announcing the complete dimensions of Yahweh's salvation.

The cultic character of the return to Zion is spelled out in Isa 25. Watts points out that the term "wonder" in Isa 25:1 is the word used in Exod 15:11 for the exodus.[552] By means of many wonders God brought his people into his citadel in v. 6. Yahweh's feast will be held in Zion for all nations. The phrase "on this mountain" in Isa 25:6 decides on the location from 24:23, stressing both the identical locality of the throne and the banquet, and the timing of the banquet with the throne appearance.[553] Merrill points out that a feast of Yahweh roots the passage in pilgrimage thought.[554] Mount Zion is the destiny of pilgrimage.

Isaiah describes the special preparation of the way of return in 40–55.[555] In Isa 41:17–20, the prophet speaks of the pilgrim way as a desert route which will be rejuvenated by springs of water and an abundance of flora. Westermann sees a parallel between Isa 41:17–20 and Isa 42:14–17.[556] He comments that the prophet depicts the process of road-building that Yahweh carries out in order to facilitate the return of his people as salvation.[557]

---

[549] Ibid. According to Watts, the result is the unification of the kingdom and re-establishment of its sovereignty over its neighbours, i.e. the return to the conditions of the United Kingdom which David established.
[550] Ibid., 178–9.
[551] Isa 19:23–25; 35:8; 49:11; 62:10.
[552] Watts, *Isaiah 1–33*, 330. Watts also points out that the term was used in Ps 77:14; 78:11; 88:10. God does for his worshippers in judgment and redemption.
[553] Ibid., 331.
[554] Cf. Isa 45:14; 60:3–4; 66:12. Merrill, "Procession," 268. See also Otto Kaiser, *Isaiah 13–39* (Philadelphia: Westminster, 1974), 199–200.
[555] Cf. In Isa 40:4 the valleys are exalted and the mountains levelled.
[556] Westermann, *Isaiah 40–66* (London: SCM, 1969), 106–7. Westermann shows how YHWH'S opposite works of irrigation and drying up in the respective texts are two sides of his preparation of the pilgrim way to Zion.
[557] Ibid.

Some scholars see Isa 51:9–11 as illustrating the expected redemption from Babylon in terms of mythic creation.[558] Merrill points out that the prophet adds in it exodus imagery (51:10) and a scene of joyous procession to Zion (51:11).[559] Watts understands that the imagery comes from the exodus.[560] He comments on v. 10 that "the arm of Yahweh" is identified with "the drying up a sea," which may indicate the crossing of the Reed Sea of Exod 14:21.[561] Therefore Isa 51:9–11 sketches God's work for the future deliverance in the light of the exodus event. The prophet wanted to say that deliverance comes from the Creator, God, who continues the creative process, and his plan is to rebuild Zion's Temple and to restore Israel's freedom to worship there.

This pilgrimage feature is reinforced in the passage of 52:7–12. After introducing the messenger of good news who comes to the exilic community at his request, Yahweh commands his ransomed ones to leave their bondage. These are not prisoners escaping for their lives but pilgrims about to embark on a joyous procession to Zion.[562] The remarkable thing is that they are urged to protect their ritual cleanness because their journey is a pilgrimage.

Jeremiah

The idea of a pilgrimage to Zion of both the remnant of Israel and the nations is stressed also by Jeremiah. References to gathering to Zion in Jer 3:14 may seem to indicate a restoration of proper government in Zion.[563] According to

---

[558] J. Muilenburg, *The Book of Isaiah*: Chapters 40–66, IB (New York: Abingdon, 1956), 5:401; F. M. Cross, *Canaanite Myth and Hebrew Epic* (Cambridge, MA: Harvard University Press, 1973), 107–8. According to these scholars, this means that Isaiah used mythopoeic language well known to his hearers/leaders in order to communicate Yahweh's sovereignty over natural and political chaos.

[559] Merril, "Pilgrimage," 269. According to Merril, it is reminiscent of the colourful vocabulary of the pilgrim psalms.

[560] J. D. W. Watts, *Isaiah* 34–66, WBC 25 (Waco, TX: Word, 1987), 211. According to Watts, from Isa 40 onward Yahweh's new act of deliverance is expressed by means of the imagery.

[561] Ibid. Watts calls the Red Sea the Reed Sea. He also sees "the arm of Yahweh" to be a mythical reference. ים("sea") was one of the gods in Ugaritic myths who played out the mythical drama of the seasons. Exod 15:1–15 is an ancient hymnic version of the event in which Yahweh's "right hand" (v. 12) and "arm" (v. 16) play major roles.

[562] The idea of YHWH going before them to lead and behind them to guard (Isa 52:12; compare 58:8) not only suggests procession as opposed to the haste of exodus, but highlights the caricature of Babylonian procession seen in Isa 46:1–2. There, in what Brueggemann sees as an obvious reference to the Akitu festival, the prophet describes the humiliation of Marduk and Nabu, who do not lead but are themselves led by their captors. See Walter Brueggemann, *The Prophetic Imagination* (Philadelphia: Fortress, 1978), 73–4.

[563] G. L. Keown, P. J. Scalise, and T. G. Smothers, *Jeremiah* 1–25, WBC 26 (Waco, TX: Word, 1991), 60.

Keown, Scalise, and Smothers, the notion of the restored government is enforced by the following two verses (vv. 16–17).[564] Verse 16 indicates that the ark would stop having any important role in the faith of this future Israel because in the future Jerusalem itself would symbolize God's presence in the larger context of the world of nations.[565] Thus Jeremiah presents the new exodus as a procession to the temple in order to render homage to Yahweh.

The merger of exodus and pilgrimage is highlighted in Jer 16:14–15; 23:7–8, where the prophet proclaims that it will no more be said, "'As surely as Yahweh lives, who brought the Israelites up out of Egypt,' but they will say 'As surely as Yahweh lives, who brought the descendants of Israel up out of the land of the north and out of all countries where he had banished them.'" (NIV) Weinfeld points out that Jer 16:14–15 is an example of re-interpretation of the exodus tradition.[566] Keown, Scalise, and Smothers understand the two verses to be about deliverance, with God promising that the people will return to their land.[567] They will come in joyous procession (Jer 31:8–9), making their way to Yahweh in Zion (31:6). That this is a second exodus is evident from the fact that the return is characterized by the elements of pilgrim procession: song, offerings of grain and livestock, and unbridled joy (31:10–14).

Ezekiel

Ezekiel, the great prophet of the exile, also refers to Israel's return in terms of pilgrimage. In chapter 20, following a description of the return couched in language of a new exodus (vv. 33–39),[568] Ezekiel speaks of Yahweh's holy mountain, the seat of Yahweh's dominion, where he will receive the offerings of his returning people (vv. 40–41).[569] They will know that he is Yahweh and will confess him before all nations (vv. 42–44; compare 28:25–26; 36:32–38).

---

[564] Ibid.

[565] Ibid., 61.

[566] M. Weinfield, "Jeremiah and the Spiritual Metamorphosis of Israel," *ZAW* 88 (1976), 17–8.

[567] G. L. Keown, P. J. Scalise, and T. G. Smothers, *Jeremiah*, 332.

[568] W. Zimmerli, *A Commentary on the Book of the Prophet Ezekiel*, Chapters 1–24 (Philadelphia: Fortress, 1979), 415. As Zimmerli shows, however, the exodus of the exiles will transcend that of Moses because of its widespread points of origin.

[569] Here occurs a mingling of exodus and Zion themes, a prime characteristic of the exilic restoration as viewed in terms of pilgrimage and procession (ibid., 417).

In Ezek 37, Yahweh is depicted as the creator of new life. The prophet indicates that exile is a graveyard; to live again is to return to the land.[570] In fact, Yahweh's own desire was to put his people back on their feet. The repeated promise to bring his people home appears in verses 12 and 21. Allen points out that the promise in v. 12 functions as a goal, and in v. 21 as a starting point for a new work of God.[571] Furthermore, Ezekiel sees those who return to the land as a larger grouping;[572] see verse 11, "all the house of Israel" and the use of the terms "Israelites" and "tribes of Israel" (vv. 16, 19, 21, cf. v. 28).

Zechariah and Haggai

Zechariah also writes of a day of glory subsequent to the building of the second temple. It will be a day in which Yahweh again chooses Zion as his dwelling place (Zech 1:16–17). The nations will assemble there and become, with Israel, his own people (2:8–13). Israel herself will be gathered from the whole earth (8:1–8) and will undertake the celebration of the stated festivals (8:19).[573] Devotion to Yahweh will spread, and the nations will join in joyful procession to make their way to Zion (8:22–23).[574] In an unmistakable reference to a pilgrim journey, Zechariah speaks of the nations undertaking annual observance of the Feast of Tabernacles, a procession that is mandatory if they are to enjoy divine favour and blessing (14:16–19).[575]

That all the prophecies are not fulfilled by the return of 538 BCE is clearly evident from the testimony of the late postexilic prophets Haggai and Zechariah. The return as an exodus must have appeared to be a reality by their time (520 BCE), but promise of restoration for cult and ceremony, centered in

---

[570] L. C. Allen, *Ezekiel 20–48*, WBC 29 (Waco, TX: Word, 1990), 187.

[571] Ibid., 195. Allen understands that the same figurative verb for uniting occurs in both, with reference to the joining of the bones in the vision and the joining of the sticks in the symbolic act (vv. 7, 17).

[572] See v. 11, "all the house of Israel" and the terms "Israelites" and "tribes of Israel" (vv. 16, 19, 21, cf. v. 28).

[573] The fasts of Zech 8:10 refer to the commemoration of the tragic events surrounding the fall of Jerusalem and destruction of the temple (see respectively Jer 39:2; 52:12–14; 2 Chr 25:25; Jer 52:4). They will be turned into ritual feasts associated with pilgrimage to Zion: see D. L. Petersen, *Haggai and Zechariah 1–8* (Philadelphia: Westminster, 1984), 314–15.

[574] As Petersen observes (ibid., 316), "The majority of commentators understand this oracle to be part of a larger tradition, the pilgrimage of nations to Jerusalem" (see especially Isa 2:1–4; see also Smith, *Micah-Malachi*, 239, who speaks of this promise of pilgrimage as "a part of the continuing strand of the Zion traditions").

[575] Smith, *Micah-Malachi*, 291-93 describes this entire passage as the "The Pilgrimage of the Nations to Jerusalem."

the temple, was unfulfilled. Haggai thus chided the people for not rebuilding the temple (Hag 1:7–8), and when the meager edifice was finished, he spoke of a day when the house would be filled with Yahweh's glory and become the repository of the sacrificial gifts of his pilgrim people, Israel and the nations alike (Hag 2:6–9).[576]

Pilgrimage in the Intertestamental Literature

The Apocrypha functions as a historical hyphen to study developments between the Old Testament and the New Testament periods. Although its writings are not part of the canonical books, they give information from various forms of Judaism in the Second Temple period. The pilgrimage theme appears in this literature also.

The Rabbinic literature preserves the tradition of the remnant as a temporary sojourner on earth who is on his way to his true home. The aim of the Haggadah was defined as bringing heaven nearer to men and lifting men up to heaven.[577] According to Goppelt, the Haggadah fulfills its calling, on the one hand, by glorifying God and, on the other hand, by comforting Israel.

The Tannaim strived to relate Israel's history to the times. According to the Tannaim, Israel's stay in the wilderness, before their sin with the golden calf, was regarded as the time of the nation's first salvation and the prototype of the future salvation.[578] Eliezer ben Hyrcanus says that Israel will be nourished miraculously just as in the exodus from Egypt.[579]

1QS seems to have been written for the community as a true pilgrim. The men of the community expected the Prophet and the Messiah of Aaron and Israel. The Rule tells us that they are to walk in the primitive precepts until those who were expected came (9:11). After that it points out how the Master should act in different circumstances and how the worship is performed (9:12–10:8).

---

[576] Haggai teaches that "they will come with the wealth of all nations" (2:7 NASB); that is, the nations will bring their treasures as tribute to YHWH. Despite D. L. Petersen's reservations, this should be compared to Isa 60:5–11, a passage to be taken without question as a pilgrimage text. See Petersen, *Haggai and Zechariah* 1–8, 68.

[577] Goppelt, *Typos,* 26. Halakah is in common traditional law, all other material falls in the domain of Haggadah. Haggadot are for the most part the historical and ethical-religious teachings that have been developed by means of a rather free adaptation of sacred Scripture.

[578] Goppelt, *Typos,* 29.

[579] Ibid, 35.

Philo understood the story of Abraham's call as follows: "impelled by an oracle calling him to leave his native land and family and paternal home, and move to another country, he made eager haste to do so, considering that speed in giving effect to the command was as good as its full accomplishment; in fact, it looked as though he was returning to his homeland from foreign parts and not leaving his homeland for foreign parts".[580] Furthermore, Philo draws a parallel between the Israelites in the wilderness who wanted to give up the struggle and return to Egypt, and weary athletes who drop their hands through weakness,[581] a parallel used in the letter to the Hebrews.[582]

Pilgrimage in Gospels and the Epistles

The image of pilgrimage is also latent in the Gospels, especially the Synoptics, all of which underscore Jesus's final pilgrimage to Jerusalem. In Mark this pilgrimage is repeatedly emphasized by reminders of Jesus's final journey (Mark 8:27; 9:33–34; 10:1, 17, 32, 46, 52), which becomes the dominant image of discipleship. This motif is elaborated in Luke and continues in John.

The Gospels

Mark

Swartley emphasizes the structural function of the term ὁδός in Mark's gospel.[583] He argues that this ὁδός is placed so as to elucidate both Mark's literary structure and important themes. Taylor sees Mark's use of ὁδός as having a significant role, that of creating a sense of transition from Galilee to Jerusalem.[584] Perrin points out that the ἐν τῇ ὁδῷ in Mark 8:27 is linked with

---

[580] Philo, On Abraham, 62
[581] Philo, De Congressu, 164.
[582] Philo interprets the story of Abraham's call and migration in a thoroughgoing allegorical manner. According to Philo, the visible world is the image (ἀπεικονισμ, Op. Mund. 16), radiance (ἀπαυνασμα, Plant. 50), and copy (μιμημα, Plant, 50) of that world because the world of ideas is designated as its archetype (ἀρχετυπος, cf. Op. Mund. 16, 71).
[583] W. M. Swartley, "The Structural Function of the Term 'Way' (Hodos) in Mark's Gospel" in The *New Way of Jesus: Essays Presented to Howard Charles*, ed. W. Klassen (Newton, KS: Faith and Life, 1980), 73–86. Cf. E. Best, "Discipleship in Mark: Mark viii: 22–x:52," *SJT* 23 (1970), 323–37.
[584] V. Taylor, *The Gospel According to Mark,* TC (Grand Rapids: Baker, 1981), 374. C. E. B. Cranfield, *The Gospel According to St. Mark*, CGTC (Cambridge: Cambridge University Press, 1959), 268, 335. Michaelis, "ὁδος" [odos] in *TDNT* V, 66.

the teaching on discipleship by the phrase ὀπίσω μου ἐλθεῖν in 8:34.[585] Watts also sees that ἐν τῇ ὁδῷ in 9:33 connects a passion prediction with teaching on discipleship.[586]

Thus, Mark's use of ὁδός is not simply "a way", but a journey. This sense of journey has been linked with the passion teaching of Jesus to teach the disciples that the "Way" is the way of suffering discipleship reflecting Jesus's own "way of the cross".[587] Kelber points out that Mark combines his οδος motif with "entrance into the kingdom of God".[588] He derives terminology from the Deuteronomic phrase of "entering into the land" (LXX Deut 1:8; 4:1; 6:18; 16:20). Kelber concludes that the οδος theme in Mark 8:27–10:52 is modeled on the exodus οδος journey into the promised land and that Mark's use of ἐν τῇ ὁδῷ is intended to draw attention to the section as the explanation of the new exodus "Way" spoken of in Mark 1:2 with its citation of Exod 23:20 and repetition of ὁδός terminology.[589] Swartley also confirms the programmatic function of Mark 1:2 and the exodus-journey of the "Way" section.[590] He notes further that the abundant use of ἐξερχομαι and εἰσερχομαι is suggestive of Israel's Exodus motif and entrance-motif. Swartley proposes that exodus typology and discipleship materials alternate throughout Mark 8:27–10:52.[591] He concludes that "Mark presents in this section of his Gospel 'The Way of Discipleship (Suffering and Cross) that leads to the Promised Land, the Kingdom of God'".[592] Marcus also affirms the understanding of Mark's use of ὁδός in this section, arguing that it ought to be understood in terms of

---

[585] N. Perrin, "The Literary Gattung 'Gospel'—some observations," *ExpT* 82 (1970), 6.
[586] Watts, *Mark*, 125.
[587] Perrin, "Gospel", 6.
[588] W. H. Kelber, *The Kingdom in Mark* (Philadelphia: Fortress, 1974), 67. Cf. Mark 9:1, 43, 45, 47; 10:15, 23–25.
[589] Ibid., 67.
[590] Swartley, "Way," 75.
[591] Ibid., 80-2. Swartley observes that the Exodus account and Mark's Transfiguration are both bracketed with "entrance-formulas" (Exod 23:23–33; 33:1–3; Mark 9:1, 43–47), and finds an Exodus echo in Mark 9:1. Cf. R. H. Gundry, *Mark: A Commentary on His Apology for the Cross* (Grand Rapids: Eerdmans, 1993), 440–42. Gundry argues that a survey of Mark's use of ὁδός throughout the Gospel does not support the idea of a special theological sense in 8:27–10:52, and is there is not any link between the "way" in 1:2 and 8:27–10:52. According to Gundry (Mark, 442), ὁδός means simply the road on which an event takes place irrespective of the direction or destination of travel.
[592] Ibid., 82.

Deutero-Isaiah's presentation.[593] Thus Mark's "Way" section is not "about the human way to the kingdom (βασιλεία) but rather about God's way, which is his βασιλεία his own extension of kingly power".[594] Watts points out that Mark's use of ὁδός is in keeping with the idea of an Isaianic Yahweh-Warrior at work among a Jewish diaspora.[595] If Watts's claim is acceptable, Mark's use of ὁδός is the way of Yahweh's deliverance of his people from the powers of the nations and their idols.

Luke

Egelkraut, the form critic, pointed out that Luke created the journey motif as a literary device to enable the inclusion of a surplus tradition.[596] However, Egelkraut's claim was challenged by Dawsey who suggest that Luke himself emphasized Jesus's pilgrimage, interweaving it as he did with the memory of Israel's Exodus.[597] Evans compared Luke 9:51–18:14 with Deuteronomy, and suggested that Luke 9 parallels Deut 26.[598] In this model, Jesus on his way to Jerusalem anticipates the Passover festival by remembering the exodus event.

Jesus comes to declare release to the captives and set at liberty those who are oppressed.[599] For this purpose, Jesus passed through Samaria on his way to the Jerusalem feast. The Samaritans were not going to accept such a band of pilgrims destined for Jerusalem. They have no knowledge of the nature of Jesus's resolute orientation to Jerusalem.

---

[593] J. Marcus, *The Way of the Lord: Christological Exegesis of the Old Testament in the Gospel of Mark* (Louisville: Westminster John Knox, 1992), 33.
[594] Ibid.
[595] Watts, *Mark*, 135-6, According to Watts, if Mark's "Way" section is compatible with the journey of Isaiah's new exodus "Way", for in both cases Jerusalem is the goal.
[596] H. L. Egelkraut, *Jesus' Mission to Jerusalem: A Redaction Critical Study of the Travel Narrative in the Gospel of Luke, Lk 9.51–19.48* (Frankfurt: P. Lang, 1976), 41-44. R. Bultmann, *The History of the Synoptic Tradition* (Oxford: Blackwell, 1972), 334-38. Form criticism has held the ready answer that the formlessness of the travel narrative resulted from the material that was available to the author of the Gospel.
[597] J. M. Dawsey, *Jesus' Pilgrimage to Jerusalem* (Auburn, AL: Auburn University Press, 1987), 232. According to Dawsey, the author combined the memory of the Exodus with the Passover pilgrimage in order to show how Jesus is the new Moses. However, Holland (*Contours*, 99) points out that Moses is rarely mentioned in the Gospels. Rather it is the son of David.
[598] C. F. Evans, "The Central Section of St. Luke's Gospel," *Studies in the Gospels: Essays in Memory of R. H. Lightfoot*, ed. D. E. Nineham (Oxford: Blackwell, 1955), 50. However, Egelkraut, *Mission*, 57, asked whether it was fair to say that the Promised Land is here identified with Judea and Jerusalem.
[599] D. P. Moessner, "Luke 9.1–50: Luke's Preview of the Journey of the Prophet Like Moses of Deuteronomy," *JBL* 102 (1983), 575.

John

In John's Gospel, the author's perspective on pilgrimage to a sacred place is provided in the climax of Jesus's dialogue with the Samaritan woman in 4:21–26.[600] She recognized Jesus as a prophet, and said that "our ancestors worshipped on this mountain,[601] but you say that the place where people must worship is Jerusalem." In Jesus's reply he sides clearly with the Jewish tradition: "You worship what you do not know; we worship what we know; for salvation is from the Jews."

Thus, Jesus's reply is put between two very surprising assertions which announce an eschatological change. It affects both the previously erroneous Samaritan view and the previously correct Jewish view. The first prediction is that "the hour is coming when you will worship the Father neither on this mountain nor in Jerusalem" (4:21), and the second announcement is that "the hour is coming, and is now here, when the true worshippers will worship the Father in spirit and in truth" (4:23). The arrival of that hour is further signalled when in response to the woman's statement of her knowledge that the Messiah is coming, Jesus's claim incorporates and transcends that title as he employs the formula of divine self-revelation, "I Am [is] the one who is speaking to you" (4:26).

It is in and through Jesus that God is now revealing himself and seeking worshippers. The place of the Name—here "I Am" (cf. 4:26)—is now an embodied location, the person of Jesus. Jesus now makes possible the worship of the Father in Spirit and in truth. Walker understands that Jesus is the holy place of worship and so to go on pilgrimage is to come to Jesus.[602] Thus the goal of pilgrimage; temple worship, has been transformed Christologically.

---

[600] Cf. R. Bultmann, *The Gospel of John: A Commentary*, trans. G. R. Beasley-Murray (Oxford: Blackwell, 1971), 191–2. According to Bultmann, the point of this story originally lay in the question of the relation of the Jews to the Samaritans.
[601] Gerizim, whose temple had been destroyed earlier in 128 BCE.
[602] Walker, *Holy*, 191

The Epistles

Romans

Dunn points out that the phrase "who follow in the footsteps" (στοιχοῦσιν τοῖς ἴχνεσιν) in Rom 4:12 may already have been used of Abraham in Jewish circles.[603] Barth saw those "who follow in the footsteps" as pilgrims.[604] He understood that such persons were prepared for surrender and dissolution, ready to decrease in honour, ever tireless in descending the ladder of renunciation and death.[605] Therefore, Barth concluded that people as pilgrims perpetually return to the starting-point of that naked humanity which is poverty and utter insecurity.[606] Pilgrim image is present in Rom 5:1–5 and 8:35–39 and is identified in the language of walking in the Spirit and being led by the Spirit (Rom 8:4, 14).

Galatians

In Gal 4:21–5:1 Paul points out that Hagar and Sarah represent two covenants. Hagar is said to represent Mount Sinai and seen as corresponding to the present Jerusalem. On the other hand, Sarah corresponds to the Abrahamic covenant that finds its fulfilment in Christ. Sarah also corresponds to the Jerusalem above. On this basis, Paul does not seem to view the present earthly Jerusalem as the holy city that is the focus of God's presence on earth; rather he imagines that his readers will be familiar with the notion of a Jerusalem above.

Longenecker sees that Gal 4:27 is linked with Isa 54:1, which was a prominent oracle in Jewish eschatological expectation.[607] It depicts a glorified Jerusalem and its temple as the centre of the world to which all nations will make

---

[603] Dunn, *Romans* 38A, 390. Cf. Gen *Rab.* 40.12. Compare 2 Cor 6:16, Col 3:7 and 1 Pet 2:21. στοιχοῦσιν originally meant "draw up in line," so "be in line with, hold to, follow" (BGD); ἴχνεσιν, "footprint," "the trace left by someone's conduct or journey through life" (*TDNT* III, 402). On the basis of the phrase, according to Dunn, faith in pilgrimage is something active, which embraces an element of obedience.

[604] K. Barth, *The Epistle to the Romans*, trans. E. C. Hoskyns (London: Oxford University Press, 1965), 132.

[605] Ibid.

[606] Ibid.

[607] R. N. Longenecker, *Galatians* 41, WBC (Dallas: Word, 1990), 215.

pilgrimage in the last days. Even though idealizing the future city, it remains compatible with Israel's national hopes for the earthly Jerusalem.[608]

The Jerusalem to come already exists in heaven. The Jerusalem above stands for the salvation and freedom of the age to come that can be experienced now by faith.[609] However, for Paul it is no longer the case that the inheritance promised to the descendants of Abraham is the land of Canaan with its centre in an earthly Jerusalem. The inheritance which now comes to those who are descendants of Abraham by faith is the heavenly Jerusalem.

Therefore, what is implicated? First, pilgrims are to look to the Jerusalem above, since Christ their Lord is now in heaven. Secondly, in becoming part of God's people through Christ and the Spirit, Gentile pilgrims have already participated in the fulfilment of the pilgrimage of the nations to Jerusalem. The scriptural texts saw the salvation of the end-times with its pilgrimage of the Gentiles in terms of a "centripetal" movement in which all the nations would make their journey to a renewed and glorified Jerusalem.

First Corinthians

Paul calls Israel in her wilderness wanderings "our forefathers" in 1 Cor 10:1. All that happened to them occurred as examples and it was "written down as warnings for us, on whom the fulfillment of the ages has come" (1 Cor 10:11). In terms of the clause "the Israelites were under the cloud," Paul reasons that it is a reference to the saving and sheltering protection of the cloud in Exod 14:20.[610] For believers, this earth is not their homeland, but rather foreign territory. Paul again wrote to the Philippians; "your citizenship is in heaven".

---

[608] Cf. Isa 65:17–25 tells us that Jerusalem is created as part of the new heavens and the new earth and the depiction of its glory is mixed with motifs of paradise. Furthermore, what is seen about the eschatological Jerusalem in Galatians is found in the apocalypses of 2 Baruch. In 2 Baruch Jerusalem is to be restored and transformed in the age to come (6:9; 32:2–4), while at the same time it is seen as already prepared and preserved in the presence of God (4:2–6). In 2 Baruch, the existence of the heavenly city serves to guarantee the destiny of the earthly city.

[609] A, T. Lincoln, "Pilgrimage and the New Testament," in *Explorations in a Christian Theology of Pilgrimage*, ed. C. Bartholomew and F Hughes (Aldershot: Ashgate, 2004), 32. According to Lincoln, the Scriptures and other Jewish texts saw the salvation of the end-times with its pilgrimage of the Gentiles in terms of a 'centripetal' movement in which all the nations would be gathered or make their journey to a renewed and glorified Jerusalem.

[610] Goppelt, *Typos*, 144–45.

Paul frequently depicts the Christian as an athlete, self-disciplined and concentrated, as he strives to gain a glorious and unfading crown,[611] and he himself movingly testifies as he faces the ordeal of his own martyrdom in the world's arena.[612]

First Peter

Peter's first epistle also takes its place in the pilgrimage literature of the Bible. The Christian communities addressed are pictured as pilgrims and aliens, sojourning in exile[613] because of social alienation and general persecution by society. The author himself reflects this stance toward the world when he says that he writes from "Babylon" (1 Pet 5:13), again alluding to the previous history and pattern of God's pilgrim people. Peter continued to say that it was not with perishable things such as silver or gold that you were redeemed from the empty way of life handed down to you from your forefathers, but with the precious blood of Christ.

Pilgrimage in Hebrews

The book of Hebrews repeatedly explores the Christian life through images of pilgrimage, often returning to biblical heroes who undertook a faith pilgrimage.[614] Abraham obeyed God and "a place that he was to receive as an inheritance," looking for "the city that has foundations, whose designer and builder is God" (Heb 11:8–10). His offspring all died in faith as "strangers and exiles on the earth" because they were "seeking a homeland," a "better country, that is, a heavenly one" (Heb 11:13–16). Many other heroes of the faith are pictured as wandering in deserts and mountains and caves, yet never receiving the promise because "God had provided something better" (Heb 11:38–40).

In the light of this pilgrimage, Christians are exhorted to throw off everything that hinders as they journey toward their goal, which is not the earthly Zion

---

[611] 1 Cor 9:24–27; Gal 2:2; Phil 1:29; 2:16; Col 1:29; 2:1; 1 Tim 1:12; 2:5; Acts 20:24.

[612] Cf. 2 Tim 4:6–8, "I have fought the good fight, I have finished the race, I have kept the faith. Henceforth there is laid up for me the crown of righteousness, which the Lord, the righteous judge, will award to me on that Day, and not only to me but also to all who have loved his appearing."

[613] Lincoln, "Pilgrimage," 34. In 1 Pet 1:1; 2:11 the term παρεπιδήμοις is used.

[614] Johnsson interprets the pilgrim passages in Hebrews in the light of Partin's theory about pilgrimage: Johnsson, "The Pilgrimage Motif," 246.

but "the city of the living God, the heavenly Jerusalem" (Heb 12:1, 22). In similar fashion Christ is portrayed as a forerunner; he is the "founder of their salvation" (Heb 2:10 ISV) as well as the "author and perfecter of our faith" (Heb 12:2).

Thus, we will further investigate Hebrews with regard to the pilgrimage theme. In Heb 3–4 we will consider that, although the readers faced impending danger as a temporal discipline, they had a goal for their journey; in Heb 6:1–12 we shall argue that they as a community, rather than focusing narrowly on individuals, are called to spiritual growth; and in Heb 12 we will discuss what the goal of pilgrimage is. We will then sum up our observations.

Impending Danger, but with Purpose: Heb 3–4

In his use of Ps 95 the author of Hebrews has applied early Jewish exegetical principles in his treatment of this Old Testament text.[615] In doing so, he sought to reorient Old Testament texts to the situation of his readers without altering their actual sense to their original audience. Thus, the Old Testament background of Heb 3:7–4:11 can help to explain the spiritual condition of those warned based on the word "falling away" (ἀποστῆναι) (3:12), and the meaning of "rest."

In Ps 95 David cited the unbelief and the judgment of the wilderness generation as a warning for the people of his day. So by using David's psalm the writer of Hebrews passed the same warning on to Jewish believers, their descendants in the first century. For the typological comparison to apply to his readers, the spiritual condition of the wilderness generation must closely correspond to the spiritual condition of the audience of this epistle.

---

[615] Lane, *Hebrews 1–8*, cxix–cxxiv. H. W. Bateman IV, *Early Jewish Hermeneutics and Hebrews 1.5–13* (New York: Lang, 1997), 9–21, 59–77, 93–116. The author of Hebrews utilized Hillel's exegetical rule known as *gezera shawa* ("verbal analogy") by appealing to rest in Gen 2:2 in order to explain the meaning of rest in Ps 95. Furthermore, the author followed the midrashic practice of selective editing in his citation of Ps 95:10. By changing the demonstrative pronoun from "that (ἐκείνη) generation," as found in the Septuagint, to "this (ταύτῃ) generation" (Heb 3:10), he was able to apply more forcefully the warning of Ps 95 to his readers' situation. This minor modification produces a rhetorical effect without altering the meaning of the original verse. Another example is the author's repeated use of "today" (σήμερον) from Ps 95:7 in order to modernize the Old Testament text as well as stress the urgency of its warning to his audience (Heb 3:7, 13, 15; 4:7).

As Johnsson has pointed out,[616] though there is not one specific term in Heb 3-4 that directly bears on the idea of pilgrimage, the setting supports the idea of movement towards a goal. Thus, I will examine the condition of the readers of Hebrews in relation to the exodus generation in the Passover setting.

Pilgrimage in the Passover Setting

The setting of Ps 95 explains the spiritual condition of the Israelites in the wilderness, so it provides an interpretive key to understanding the spiritual condition of those warned in Heb 3-4. Enns divides the Psalm into three parts;[617] verses 1-5 deal with God's cosmic creation as motivation for worshipping Yahweh,[618] verses 6-7a follow by speaking of another act of "creation," the exodus, which also inspires the faithful to worship,[619] finally verses 7b-11 conclude the psalm by warning the readers against unfaithfulness. This exodus imagery in vv. 6-7a makes vv. 1-5 more immediate for the readers of this psalm. According to Enns, what is explicit in 7b-11 is barely concealed in vv. 1-7a. He concludes that it is the creation/re-creation theme in the first half that serves to connect it to the second.[620]

Enns pointed out that the psalmist chose the incident at Meribah and Massah as a paradigm for his warning.[621] The author of Hebrews borrowed the

---

[616] Johnsson, "The Pilgrimage Motif," 240.

[617] P. E. Enns, "Creation and Re-creation: Psalm 95 and Its Interpretation in Hebrews 3:1-4:13", *WTJ* 55 (1993), 256. Enns seems to deal with Ps 95 as a whole. However, some form-critics have argued that Ps 95 is composed of two songs that were sung in the cult. See T. K. Cheyne, *The Book of Psalms* (London: Kegan, Paul, Trench&Co., 1888), 265. W. O. E. Oesterley, *The Psalms*, Vol. 2 (New York: Macmillan, 1939), 419. M. Buttenweiser, *The Psalms: Chronologically Treated with a New Translation* (New York: KTAV, 1969), 798. G. H. Davies, "Psalm 95," *ZAW* 85 (1973), 183-87. According to these scholars, in Ps 95 the first half, vv. 1-7a, is an exhortation to praise Yahweh; the second half, vv. 7b-11, is a word of warning against hardening one's heart and ends on an altogether sour note: "As I swore in my wrath: 'surely they shall not enter my rest.'" This second half follows abruptly upon the first, apparently without the slightest indication that these two halves belong together.

[618] Enns, "Creation," 256. The motive of worship is based on the fact that Yahweh is the greatest God. What makes him the greatest is not only his ownership of creation (v. 4), but also the fact that he is the creator himself.

[619] Enns, "Creation," 258. According to Enns, verses 6 and 7a parallel vv. 1-5 in structure. Verse 6 corresponds to vv. 1-2: "come, let us worship, bow down, kneel". Verse 7a corresponds to vv. 3-5 by providing the motive for worship: "for (כי) he is our God, i.e. we are the people of his pasture, the sheep of his hand."

[620] Ibid., 260-263. Enns sees the return from Babylon as a second Exodus (for example, Isa 52:4; Hos 9:3). The first Exodus is unambiguously tied to the second Exodus. Both are acts of re-creation; both are acts of redemption. Enns further observed that both creation and redemption language are used to describe God's acts of deliverance, be it the Exodus or the return from Babylon.

[621] Ibid., 264-269.

expression "harden your hearts" (3:8, 13, 15; 4:7) from Ps 95:8 to describe the sin of the Israelites. The Hebrew word תַּקְשׁוּ in the Psalm and its Greek equivalent σκληρύνητε in the Septuagint denote a "hardening" of the will (i.e. stubbornness) against listening to and obeying the Lord.[622] The author of Hebrews identified this hardening of their hearts with "the provocation" or "rebellion," as "the testing" or "trial" (τοῦ πειρασμοῦ) which is equivalent to "Massah" (מסה).[623] Meribah and Massah identify the time immediately after Israel's deliverance from Egypt when they first "tested" the Lord over the lack of water and doubted his presence among them at Rephidim (Exod 17:1–7). The name "Meribah" was used again forty years later when they "rebelled" over a lack of water at Kadesh (Num 20:2–13). The psalmist undoubtedly intended both events and the intervening "forty years" (Ps 95:10; Heb 3:9) to confirm the consistent pattern of "go[ing] astray in their heart" (Ps 95:10; Heb 3:10).[624] However, he also had in view their rebellion after the spies returned to Kadesh-Barnea (Num 14), for the expression "[God] swore in [His] anger" (Ps 95:11) could refer only to God's oath ("as I live") by which he prohibited their entrance into the land (Num 14:20–35; Deut 1:34–40).

The author of Hebrews focused on the events of Kadesh-Barnea as evidenced by his repeated reference to God's oath (Heb 3:11, 18; 4:3) and his warning that their "bodies fell in the wilderness" (3:17; 4:11; cf. Num 14:29, 32–33). Therefore, the sin (Heb 3:17) of unbelief (3:12, 19; 4:2) and disobedience (3:18; 4:6, 11), warned against in Heb 3–4, must correspond in meaning to the "rebellion" (Num 14:9; Deut 9:23–24) and unbelief (Num 14:11) of Israel at Kadesh-Barnea.

---

[622] Deut 9:6, 13; Neh 9:16–17, 29; Jer 7:26; 17:23; 19:15. L. Koehler and W. Baumgartner, *The Hebrew and Aramaic Lexicon of the Old Testament*, trans. M. E. J. Richardson (Leiden, Brill, 1996), 3:1152; and W. Bauer, W. F. Arndt, and F. W. Gingrich, *A Greek-English Lexicon of the New Testament and Other Early Christian Literature*, 2nd ed., Rev. F. W. Gingrich and F. W. Danker (Chicago, IL: University of Chicago Press, 1979), 756. The use of the Greek term σκληρύνητε in the New Testament indicates that even the disciples were capable of a "hardened heart" (Mark 8:17).

[623] Bruce, "Hebrews," 64.

[624] This corresponds to the Lord's account of the "ten times" they had tested him (Num 14:22). Whether ten discrete events were in view or this was an idiomatic way of saying "many times", the point is clear that they exhibited a consistent pattern of rebellion. See R. B. Allen, "Numbers," in *The Expositor's Bible Commentary* (Grand Rapids: Zondervan, 1990), 2:820.

Goppelt argues that Israel's downfall in the rebellion, by which they forfeited salvation, is used to warn the church about the possible loss of salvation.[625] Marshall supports Goppelt's claim by saying that the exodus generation had received the good news and as such were God's people. Yet because they became disobedient and distrustful and consequently did not enter into rest, there remained for them only the possibility of judgment. Hence, they depict the dangers facing those who fall from faith and obedience, which are the conditions of salvation.[626] That is, Goppelt and Marshall regard the exodus generation as a redeemed people who forfeited salvation through their stubborn rebellion and unbelief displayed in the wilderness. Grudem argues that Heb 3–4 does not warn its readers against the loss of salvation, because the exodus generation was never truly saved.[627] Grudem points out that, though the people of Israel "had been 'redeemed' from Egypt, they had never believed," and therefore, "were never saved in the first place."[628]

However, there are other scholars who see the exodus generation as genuinely saved believers who are in danger of forfeiting future blessing and of undergoing the physical discipline of God's wrath and who yet will escape eternal judgment.[629] Gleason[630] examines the six occurrences of אמן[631] in Exod

---

[625] Goppelt, *Typos*, 172–73.

[626] I. H. Marshall, *Kept by the Power of God*, rev. ed. (Carlisle: Paternoster, 1995), 136–40. For a similar position see G. R. Osborne, "Soteriology in the Epistle to the Hebrews," in *Grace Unlimited*, ed. Clark H. Pinnock (Ada, MI: Bethany House, 1975), 144–66.

[627] W. Grudem, "Perseverance of the Saints: A Case Study from Hebrews 6:4–6 and the Other Warning Passages in Hebrews," in *The Grace of God, the Bondage of the Will*, ed. T. R. Schreiner and B. A. Ware (Grand Rapids: Baker, 1995), 1:160–61.

[628] Ibid.

[629] J. C. Dillow, *The Reign of the Servant Kings: A Study of Eternal Security and the Final Significance of Man* (Hayesville, KS: Schoettle, 1992), 93–110. M. A. Eaton, *A Theology of Encouragement* (Carlisle: Paternoster, 1995), 215; R. T. Kendall, *Once Saved. Always Saved* (Chicago, IL: Moody, 1983), 153–55; T. K. Oberholtzer, "The Warning Passage, Part 2: The Kingdom Rest in Hebrews 3:1–4:13," *BibSac* (April, 1988), 188. J. D. Pentecost, "Kadesh-Barnea in the Book of Hebrews," in *Basic Theology Applied: A Practical Application of Basic Theology in Honor of Charles C. Ryrie and His Work*, ed. Wesley and Elaine Willis and John and Janet Master (Wheaton, IL: Victor, 1995), 127–35.

[630] R. C. Gleason, "The Old Testament Background of Rest in Hebrews 3:7–4:11", *BibSac* 157 (July–September 2000), 286–8. Exodus 4 begins with Moses doubting whether the people would "believe" him (vv. 1–9) and ends with their belief in Yahweh (v. 31).

[631] H. Wildberger, "אמן," in *Theological Lexicon of the Old Testament*, ed. E. Jenni and C. Westermann, trans. M. E. Biddle (Peabody, MA: Hendrickson, 1997), 1.142–45. The word אמן, translated "believed," means in the Hiphil form" to have faith, to trust (in)" and was used in the Old Testament to express full confidence and genuine faith in Yahweh.

4, marking the people's faith as central to the argument of the chapter. He points out that the exodus generation was a redeemed people who participated in the Passover. According to him, the genuineness of the people's faith is evidenced not only by their immediate worship (4:31; 12:27), but also by their obedience related to the specific commands regarding the preparation of the Passover sacrifice (12:28, 50). After that the exodus generation feared an attack by the Egyptians, but the Lord promised them "salvation" (14:13). Here the word ישועה is used for only the second time in the Old Testament to predict their deliverance. Following their rescue, the author declared that the Lord indeed "saved [ויושע] Israel that day" (v. 30). In response to their deliverance, the text states, "they believed in [אמן⁶³² plus ב] the Lord" (vv. 30–31). Kaiser states that it indicates their entrance into a relationship of trust in Yahweh.⁶³³ Childs⁶³⁴ sees the condition of the exodus generation who were rescued from Egypt as the "salvation" (ישועה, Exod 15:2) by which the Israelites were "redeemed" (v. 13) and "purchased" (v. 16).

In summary, although the views considered have different opinions about the efficiency of salvation, what is important for our study is that pilgrimage is based on salvation occurred at the exodus.⁶³⁵ Thus the author's use of pilgrimage of Ps 98 shows that he recognizes that the present condition corresponds to the exodus generation.

Pilgrimage in the Face of Impending Danger

The author's warning against "falling away [ἀποστῆναι] from the living God" (Heb 3:12) is often understood as an obstinate rejection of salvation equivalent to eternal damnation from faith in God.⁶³⁶ Gleason, however, understands that ἀποστῆναι ("to fall away") is not a technical term for absolute apostasy, but that

---

⁶³² Wildberger, "אמן," 1.142–45.
⁶³³ W. C. Kaiser Jr., *Toward Rediscovering the Old Testament* (Grand Rapids: Zondervan, 1987), 122–24. This form is also used of Abraham who believed in the Lord, and He reckoned it to him as righteousness" (Gen 15:6). The genuineness of their faith and praise is expressed in the Old Testament (2 Chr 20:20; Ps 106:12; Jonah 3:5).
⁶³⁴ B. S. Childs, *The Book of Exodus* (Louisville: Westminster, 1974), 248–50.
⁶³⁵ We pointed out earlier that salvation is linked to the Passover.
⁶³⁶ B. M. Fanning, "A Theology of Hebrews," in *A Biblical Theology of the New Testament*, ed. R. B. Zuck (Chicago, IL: Moody, 1994), 408; and McKnight. "Warning Passages," 39–41; P. Ellingworth, *The Epistle to the Hebrews: A Commentary on the Greek Text* (Grand Rapids: Eerdmans, 1993), 222.

it simply denotes movement away from a point of reference,⁶³⁷ it is best to determine the meaning of this warning in light of the events of Num 14 alluded to throughout the passage. Undoubtedly the author used ἀποστῆναι to echo Moses's warning to the people at Kadesh-Barnea: "Do not rebel [ἀποστῆναι] against the Lord" (Num 14:9 LXX).⁶³⁸ The term ἀπιστῆμί is also associated with failing to obey God's voice in Jer 3:13–14 and Dan 9:9 and trusting in mankind rather than God in Jer 17:5.

In Heb 3:12, ἐν τῷ with the infinitive ἀποστῆναι is used exegetically to further explain "an evil, unbelieving heart."⁶³⁹ The adjective ἀπιστίας ("unbelieving") corresponds to the Lord's question to Moses at Kadesh, "How long will they not believe in Me?" (Num 14:11; cf. Deut 1:32; 9:23; Ps 106:24). The adjective πονηρά ("evil") occurs twice in the description of the "evil [πονηρά] congregation" at Kadesh-Barnea (Num 14:27, 35) but nowhere else in the Pentateuch.⁶⁴⁰ The phrase "the living God" corresponds well to the exodus theme of God's life-sustaining presence guiding his people (Exod 13:21–22; 15:13–17; 17:6–7; 23:20, 23; 33:14–15; 40:34–38; Num 10:33–34; 11:16–25; 14:7–9). The readers were cautioned not against a complete absence of faith in God but more specifically against the failure to believe that God would sustain their lives in the face of impending danger (cf. Exod 14:7–9).⁶⁴¹ They were warned that their lack of faith would draw them away from the life-sustaining presence of God, their only source of "mercy" and "grace" to aid them in time of need (Heb 2:18; 4:16).

---

⁶³⁷ Gleason, "Hebrews 3:7–4:11," 291. The term ἀποστῆναι, is used in the New Testament to declare that Anna never "left" the temple (Luke 2:37), the angel "departed" from Peter (Acts 12:10) and Mark "deserted" Paul and Barnabas (Acts 15:38).

⁶³⁸ Cf. Later in the passage the same word is used for those who "rejected" the land (Num 14:31).

⁶³⁹ James Hope Moulton and Nigel Turner, Syntax, Vol. 3 *A Grammar of New Testament Greek* (Edinburgh: Clark, 1963), 146.

⁶⁴⁰ C. R. Koester, *Hebrews: A New Translation with Introduction and Commentary* (New Haven: Yale University Press, 2007), 258.

⁶⁴¹ Salvation of the Exodus generation from Egypt was not forfeited, for they were never allowed to return to their former bondage under Pharaoh. Instead, God "carried" them along in the wilderness "as a man carries his son" (Deut 1:31), caring for them for forty years.

Furthermore, Heb 10:26–39 contains important present and eschatological instructions for the addressees. It focuses on the topics of sin during worshipful pilgrimage.⁶⁴² The warning opens with the connective γὰρ ("for"), indicating that the same readers, the new covenant people, were in view as in 10:19–25.⁶⁴³

Rice pointed to "apostasy as a motif and its effect on the structure of Hebrews."⁶⁴⁴ Concerning the matter of apostasy, McCown pointed out that the parenetic sequence found in 5:11–6:12 can be identified in Heb 10:19–31.⁶⁴⁵ Toussaint understood the metaphor of fire, employed in 10:27 (cf. 6:8), as a reference to the fire of hell.⁶⁴⁶ Thus Toussaint thinks that the author cited from Isa 26:11 to explain what the judgment involves.⁶⁴⁷ The awesomeness of this judgment is emphasized by the vocabulary.

> The terror of the expectation is brought out by a more literal rendering of the words, 'a certain fearful expectation of judgment' (ASV); the indefinite 'a certain' leaves it somewhat open to the reader's imagination to fill in the gruesome details of that judgment."

Therefore, it has been suggested that such a judgment in this passage would be a condemnation.

---

⁶⁴² R. Jewett, *Pilgrims*, 173–183.

⁶⁴³ T. K. Oberholtzer, "The Warning Passages in Hebrews: The Danger of Willful Sin in Hebrews 10:26–39," *BibSac* 145 (Oct, 1988), 411. In Heb 10:19–25 the readers are again referred to as ἀδελφοί ("brethren"), pointing to the fact that they are related to the new covenant blood, that is, they are believers. They were to have confidence to enter the very presence of God, the ἁγίων ("holy place"), through the blood of Christ. Through the blood of Christ, the Christian obtains confidence.

⁶⁴⁴ G. E. Rice, *Apostasy as a Motif and Its Effect on the Structure of Hebrews*, Andrews University Seminary Studies, 1985 (Spring), Vol. 23, no. 1, 29–35.

⁶⁴⁵ W. G. McCown, *Ο ΛΟΓΟΣ ΤΗΣ ΠΑΡΑΚΛΗΣΕΩΣ: The Nature and Function of the Hortatory Sections in the Epistle to the Hebrews* (PhD diss., Union Theological Seminary, 1970), 50–69. According to McCown, in 6:4–8 and 10:26–31, there is a severe warning concerning the danger of apostasy.

⁶⁴⁶ S. D. Toussaint, "The Eschatology of the Warning Passages in the Book of Hebrews," *GTJ*, Vol. 3 (Spring, 1982), 67–80.

⁶⁴⁷ Toussaint, "Eschatology," 70 says that Isa 26:11 contrasts the righteous with the wicked. Specifically, the lost are referred to as "enemies." The Greek term υπεναντιος in Heb 10:27 describes what is "opposed to, opposite or contrary to."

However, Oberholtzer challenged Toussaint's idea, by saying that the metaphor of fire against the background of the Old Testament is Yahweh's anger toward his failing covenant people in Isa 9:18–19; 10:17.[648] He pointed out that there is nothing in the context to indicate that the writer has shifted to the soteriological topic of eternal damnation.[649]

As it was pointed out earlier, the addressees are ἀδελφοί ("brethren") in Heb 10:26, pointing to the fact that they are related to the new covenant blood, that is, they are believers. They cannot be lost in hell, for the believer's eternal destiny is certain from the moment of salvation.[650] Thus the willful sin mentioned in 10:26 may result in temporal discipline from the one and only living God. Those who forsake the assembling must now await the discipline of the Lord (Heb 12:5–11). They have willfully chosen to so live that they will be disciplined by the Lord.

The temporal discipline resulting from defection is further described in v. 29 where the author gives three reasons why this willful defection deserves greater judgment. The defecting individuals had trampled underfoot the Son of God,[651] regarded unclean the blood of the covenant by which they were sanctified,[652] and insulted the Spirit of grace.[653] The sin mentioned in 10:26 is applied to Heb 10:28–29 resulting in temporal discipline from the one and only living God.

---

[648] Oberholtzer, "Hebrews 10:26–39," 414.

[649] Ibid., 414.

[650] John 5:24; 10:27–30; Eph 1:1 John 5:13

[651] The word καταπατήσας ("trampled underfoot") means to treat with contempt of the most flagrant kind. By aligning themselves with sectarian Judaism they treated the Son of God with contempt.

[652] They considered Christ's blood profane because they viewed it as no different from the blood of any other person. They considered the blood of Christ, which forms the basis of the new covenant, to be commonplace. And yet the blood of Christ is the means by which the defecting individual was sanctified (ἐν ᾧ ἡγιάσθη). Heb 10:10 and 14 also refer to the sacrifice of Christ by which the readers had been sanctified.

[653] The defectors were also disciplined because they had ἐνυβρίσας("insulted") the Spirit of grace. This verb suggests treating with "utter contempt." This insulting the Spirit was an insult against the work of the Holy Spirit, whose gifts had been manifested among the readers, according to 2:4. Dunham writes of this threefold rejection: "Is the sin of a blood-bought believer less insulting or outrageous to God than the grossest unbeliever? It is not. It is far more serious. A child insulting his father is more wounding than a neighbor child insulting the same man."

Furthermore, the writer expresses his present situation in Heb 10:39.[654] Koester considers that the term ἀπώλειαν ("destruction") used in verse 39 should be understood as utter and eternal perishing.[655] However, Hatch and Redpath pointed out that there are 111 instances of the term in the Septuagint, as a translation of 21 Hebrew words; one meaning is desolation (Ezek 32:15) and another is physical death (Esth 7:4).[656] Therefore, in regard to the previous warnings and the immediate context of Heb 10:26–38, according to Oberholtzer,[657] it seems best to understand ἀπώλειαν in verse 39 as referring to temporal physical discipline.[658]

The warnings seem to refer to the possibility of temporal discipline for those who deliberately sin. Heb 11 serves as an encouragement to those who patiently endured in spite of a variety of difficult life situations. In Heb 12 the topic of discipline resurfaces. The readers in 12:4–11 were reminded that they had not suffered to the extent Christ suffered.[659] For the readers to mature in Christlikeness, they must endure sufferings. Discipline is designed by God to produce the fruit of holiness and righteousness in his children (12:10–11).

God imposes discipline on his children to produce his desired effect. A final form of discipline for a continually disobedient child of God may be the loss of physical life.[660] Continual sin and rejection of the Lord's discipline may lead to physical death. Among the readers of Hebrews there seem to have been varying degrees of discipline in process. However, the final goal of discipline is restoration, as described in Heb 12:12–13.

In summary, their redemption from Egypt was not forfeited, for they were never allowed to return to their former bondage under Pharaoh. God carried them along in the wilderness "as a man carries his son" (Deut 1:31), caring for

---

[654] Cf. His use of ἡμεῖς("we") in verse 39 is emphatic as seen in the change from the second person plural "you" in verse 36.
[655] C. R. Koester, *Hebrews*, 462.
[656] E. Hatch and H. A. Redpath, eds. *A Concordance to the Septuagint*, (Grand Rapids: Eerdmans, 1991), 151–52.
[657] Oberholtzer, "Hebrews 10:26–39", 414.
[658] cf. 3:1–4:13; 5:11–6:12; 10:27–31; 12:4–11. Cf. The writer reassured his readers that they were of those who have faith to the "preserving of the soul."
[659] The discipline of the recipients appears as a divine corrective for their dullness of hearing and spiritual immaturity (5:11–6:20). This educational process moves from lesser to greater intensity, as seen in the terms "to reprove", "to discipline", and "to scourge".
[660] 1 Cor 11:27–30; 1 John 5:16–17

them by feeding, clothing, guiding, and protecting them for forty years. The Old Testament passage relates to the metaphor of fire ($\pi\upsilon\rho\grave{o}\varsigma$) which is found in Heb 10:27, which is applied to Christian temporal discipline.

Pilgrimage with Purpose

The term κατάπαυσιν ("rest") occurs eight times (and the verb καταπαύω occurs three times) in Heb 3–4, its meaning is crucial to the entire passage. The word is used in Ps 95:11 to indicate the rest forfeited by the people of Israel when they rebelled in the wilderness (Heb 3:11, 18–19; cf. Num 14). Some see "rest" as a spiritual rest. Von Rad understood it as "a gift which Israel will find only by a wholly personal entering into its God."[661] Enns challenges von Rad's thought, by saying that "my rest" in Ps 95 is God's creation rest referred to in Gen 2:2.[662] Attridge comments that in certain contexts καταπαύω refers to God's creative activity.[663] Davies says that the root in Genesis is שָׁבַת: in Gen 2:2, whereas the psalmist used the term מְנוּחָה in Ps 95:11. It is tempting to equate rest with the temple, suggesting that the psalm is pre-exilic and tied to the Jerusalem temple.[664] Thus Ps 95:11 is best understood as a warning against forfeiting the right to worship before the presence of the Lord[665] in his holy sanctuary and enjoy the covenantal blessings.[666] The noun מְנוּחָה in Ps 95 denotes a "resting place" in the sense of the "dwelling place of God."[667] It is derived from the primary root verb מנחה which signifies being "settled down" in a secure place, safely out of reach from one's enemies.[668] The word and its

---

[661] G. von Rad, "There Still Remains a Rest for the People of God: An Investigation of a Biblical Conception," in *The Problem of the Hexateuch and Other Essays* (New York: McGraw-Hill, 1966), 99.

[662] Enns, "Creation," 264.

[663] Attridge, *Hebrews*, 128. Attridge cites Wis 9:2 and 13:4 as examples, as well as Isa 40:28; 43:7; 45:7 and 9, which in the MT read ברא.

[664] G. H. Davies, "Psalm 95," 183–87.

[665] Cf., We see that the message of the first of Ps 95 is:
    A. Let us praise Yahweh [the maker] (vv. 1–2)
    B. because of his creation. (vv. 3–5)
    A'. Let us praise Yahweh, our maker (v. 6)
    B'. because we are his. (v. 7a)

[666] Bruce, *Hebrews*, 63. The use of מְנוּחָה in Ps 95 fits its pattern found elsewhere in the Old Testament. The psalm's twofold division between a call to worship (vv. 1–6) and a warning to worshipers (vv. 7–11) indicates its liturgical purpose to invite people into the sanctuary of Yahweh.

[667] Koehler and Baumgartner, *Hebrew and Aramaic Lexicon of the Old Testament*, 2.600.

[668] Ibid., 2.680.

cognates often speak of the Lord granting his people rest in the promised land (Deut 3:20; Josh 1:13; 22:4; 1 Kgs 8:56).[669]

After Israel's settlement in the land the term מנוח came to denote God's "resting place" on Zion (Ps 132:8, 13–14; Isa 11:10), in the temple (1 Chron 28:2; cf. 2 Chron 6:41), as a synonym for his throne (Isa 66:1). Hence Israel's rest and Yahweh's resting place were linked by worship. The people were "rested" מנחה in the land for the purpose of worshiping Yahweh. The land became Yahweh's "resting place" מנוחה where he promised to dwell in order to bless his people (Deut 12:5–11). Then he was enthroned on his "resting place" מנוחה on Zion (1 Chron 23:25; Ps 132:13) in the temple (1 Chron 28:2), where he should be worshipped. Furthermore, the verb מנחה was commonly used to signify the "dedication" of certain items before the presence of the Lord for liturgical purposes (e.g. manna in Exod 16:33–34; Aaron's linen tunic in Lev 16:23; Aaron's rod in Num 17:4; and the firstfruits of the harvest in Deut 26:4, 10). So both the noun מְנוּחָה and its verb מנחה became part of the worship vocabulary of Israel, describing all aspects of Israel's celebration of the Lord's life-sustaining presence in their midst.

Therefore, the privilege to "enter into My rest" (Ps 95:11) is best understood as the right to worship before the personal presence of Yahweh (vv. 2, 6), which could be forfeited by hardened, rebellious hearts like those of the exodus generation (vv. 8–10). This fits the argument of Heb 3–4 in which the author encouraged his readers that if they would hold fast to their hope (Heb 3:6) and their assurance (v. 14) in Christ they could "draw near with confidence to the throne of grace" (i.e. God's resting place) to receive help (4:16), blessing (6:7), and reward (10:35).

The author in Heb 10:35 moved from the readers' past endurance of persecutions to their present persecutions with the term οὖν ("therefore"). They were encouraged not to throw away their confidence, which will result in

---

[669] In Deut 12, the land was promised to the people of Israel as their "resting place" (מְנוּחָה, v. 9), not to do as they pleased (v. 8) but rather to worship before the presence of the Lord (vv. 5–7, 11–14). This "rest" (מנחה) was realized under Joshua after the conquest (Josh 23:1; cf. 21:43–44; 22:4), by David after his defeat of the Philistines (2 Sam 7:1), and then by Solomon at the dedication of the temple (1 Kgs 5:3–5; 8:56; 1 Chron 22:7–10). In each case the Lord gave His people rest from their enemies in order for them to worship him and to enjoy the blessings he had promised them in the land.

μεγάλην μισθαποδοσίαν ("a great reward"). The term μισθαποδοσίαν[670] derived from μισθος and ανποδιδωμι, looks at a payment of wages. Hughes[671] explains, "the relationship of the present pilgrimage to the future reward is the relationship of faith to hope, as the quotation which follows teaches (vv. 37 and 38) and the next chapter so amply illustrates." The "great reward" is the eschatological possession mentioned in verse 34.

Verse 36, which could be a summary statement for the epistle, exhorts the readers to endure their trials patiently and not abandon their assembling together (cf. v. 25). If the readers endured, they would accomplish God's will and receive his promise of blessing. The reward is stated in 10:36, it is to receive ἵνα τὸ θέλημα τοῦ θεοῦ ποιήσαντες ("what was promised on endurance"). In Hebrews the "promise" refers to a variety of subjects: entrance into rest (Heb 4:1); inheritance of the promises related to Abraham (6:12–13); eternal inheritance (9:15); a land (11:9, 11); and a future reward (10:34–36; 11:13, 39). Each of these has an eschatological sense and is conditional to persevering in obedience to the will of God.

Summing Up

Ps 95 is an argument couched in exodus language to warn the people against unbelief. The Old Testament background to Heb 3–4 indicates that those warned by the author were genuinely redeemed like the people of Israel in the exodus. Therefore, the writer of Hebrews applies the warning of Ps 95 to his community by means of an interpretation of the passage that brings out the eschatological dimension of his exegesis, thus making it speak directly to the new exodus community in its period of wilderness wandering.

Using Ps 95 the author of Hebrews warns the believers that their lack of faith and confidence in Christ could potentially result in their loss of physical life, as it had in the case of the exodus generation (Heb 3:17–19). The readers were cautioned not against a complete absence of faith in God. This new exodus community would lose in the opportunity to worship God joyfully in the safety of his presence and to enjoy the covenantal blessings.

---

[670] The term which in the NT occurs only in Hebrews (2:2; 10:35; 11:26). In 2:2 it is used of punishment and in the other two references it has the positive idea of blessing.

[671] Hughes, *Hebrews*, 432–4.

His "resting place" is now in his heavenly sanctuary where Jesus Christ has "sat down" (1:3; 8:1; 10:12; 12:2) to serve "in the presence of God". If they remain faithful (3:6, 13), though the earthly temple will "disappear" (8:13), the readers can still "enter his resting place" (4:1, 3, 10–11) and "draw near with confidence to the throne of grace" (4:16) to "continually offer up sacrifices of praise" and good works (13:15–16). God's presence would become to them a place where sins are exposed, punishment is given, and discipline is received.

Pilgrims are Ones who are Called to Spiritual Growth: Heb 6:1–12

Why did the author of Hebrews exhort the readers to "press on to maturity" in Heb 6:1. They, as pilgrims, were ones who were called to spiritual growth.[672] Therefore the author's exhortation "let us press on" (6:1) is best understood as a continuation of his pilgrimage motif into chapter 6 with the fate of the exodus generation in view (6:4–6).

Heb 6:4–6 has attracted most scholarly attention because it remains one of the most puzzling passages. The bulk of attention devoted to these verses has focused on the issues of the precise identification of the status of those in vv. 4–5 and the nature of the sin they have committed in v. 6. Therefore, scholars continue to debate whether the subjects of the warning are genuine members of the faith community, who through falling away (v. 6) subsequently lose this status, or whether this falling away only results in the loss of rewards, or whether failure to persevere is evidence that the initial faith was not genuine in the first place, or whether the passage should be understood at a corporate level, addressing the covenant community rather than individuals. Therefore, I will examine in which context this passage should be understood and who were addressed whether a community or an individual.

---

[672] D. G. Peterson, "The situation of the Hebrews 5:11–6:12," *RTR* 35 (1976), 14–21, investigated Hebrews as a document of early Christian pastoral care, especially concerning Heb 5:11–6:20 as "the key text for the interpretation of Hebrews." However, Käsemann, *Wandering*, 184–94. Käsemann found in 5:11–6:12 a main support for the gnostic interpretation of Hebrews. He pointed out that in Gnosticism, as in the mystery religions, those who are about to receive the primary revelation (the λογος τελειος, i.e. the word for those who are "perfect") are questioned concerning their worthiness and the testing to which they have been exposed. Lane, *Hebrews* 1–8, 135, challenged Käsemann's thought, by saying that the decisive technical vocabulary of Gnosticism is absent from Hebrews.

Pressing on to Maturity

An understanding of Heb 6:1–12 is impossible without a clear view of the nature of the sin that could place the readers beyond the possibility of repentance. This sin is designated in Heb 6:6 by a participle of the Greek verb παραπίπτω, which has a broad range of meanings including "to fall beside, to fall in one's way, to fall aside, to mistake or err."[673] Because παραπίπτω lacks a modifier in verse 6, its precise connotation is difficult to determine from the immediate context.[674]

Παραπίπτω in the Septuagint is used as a general term "to sin".[675] Five of the eight occurrences of παραπίπτω in the Septuagint are in Ezekiel (14:13; 15:8; 18:24; 20:27; 22:4). Michaelis observes that in each of these references "the context shows that what is at issue is a culpable mistake, or sin."[676] In four of these five occurrences in Ezekiel (all except 22:4) παραπίπτω is equivalent to the Hebrew word מעל ("to act unfaithfully").[677] This is confirmed by its occurrence with the most common Hebrew word for sin (חטא) twice in Ezekiel (14:13; 18:24). Therefore, παραπίπτω denotes a serious sinful act or attitude against God. The exact nature of the sin must be determined from the context.

Some scholars understood that παραπεσόντας refers to total apostasy from the faith.[678] Osborne pointed out that final perseverance depends on human requirements accomplished through the help of God and fellow believers.[679] The view that the judgment of apostasy (vv. 7–8) speaks of eternal

---

[673] Liddle and Scott, *A Greek-English Lexicon* (New York: Harper, 1883), 526.

[674] There is no mention about what they fell from or fell into in Heb 6:6.

[675] W. Michaelis, "παραπίπτω" [parapito] in *TDNT* VI, 171.

[676] Ibid., 170. Παραπίπτω is used a bit differently in Esth 6:10, where it denotes the king's command to Haman: "Do not fall short [παραπίπτω] of your word" (author's translation). However, its final two occurrences in the Septuagint (Wis. 6:9; 12:2) correspond to Ezekiel's meaning "to commit an error" or "to sin."

[677] F. Brown, S. R. Driver, and Charles A. Briggs, *A Hebrew and English Lexicon of the Old Testament* (Oxford: Clarendon, 1903). 591.

[678] Lane, *Hebrews 1–8*, 142. According to Lane, the term in Hebrews is equivalent to the expression ἀποστῆναι ἀπὸ θεοῦ ζῶντος "to fall away from the living God," in 3:12. R. Shank, *Life in the Son* (Springfield, MO: Westcott, 1961), 229–34. H. O. Wiley, *The Epistle to the Hebrews* (Kansas City, MO: Beacon Hill, 1959), 216. C. E. Carlston, "Eschatology and Repentance in the Epistle to the Hebrews", *JBL*, Vol. lxxviii (1959), 297. Cf. The Shepherd of Hermas held that sins committed before baptism would be forgiven, but that there would be no second forgiveness (Mand. IV.iii; see also Vis. II.ii and Sim. VI.ii).

[679] G. Osborne, "Soteriology in the Epistle to the Hebrews," in *Unlimited Grace*, ed. C. H. Pinnock (Minneapolis: Bethany, 1975), 144–66. Marshall, *Kept*, 137–53.

condemnation conflicts with the security of the believer taught in Hebrews.[680] Furthermore, they fail to account adequately for the impossibility of recovery mentioned in 6:6, for they are unwilling to admit that the apostates who have lost their salvation are forever beyond the possibility of repentance.[681]

According to Fishbane, the exodus event became a lens of historical perception and anticipation.[682] Gleason points out that παραπίπτω is best understood as expressing a decisive refusal to trust God which results in a general state of spiritual retrogression paralleling the experience of the Israelites at Kadesh-Barnea.[683] The incident at Kadesh-Barnea provides the model for the author's depiction of the subjects of Heb 6:4–6 and such an analysis yields important semantic results. Thus, the author of Hebrews defines the readers' situation in terms of the experience of the Israelites as they wandered in the wilderness on their way to the promised land. Like their Old Testament counterparts, the audience of Hebrews is also on a pilgrimage to the promised land and stands on the threshold of the fulfillment of God's promises.

Gleason[684] points out that in light of the Old Testament blessing-curse motif, the judgment in view in Heb 6:7–8 is best understood as the forfeiture of blessing and the experience of temporal discipline rather than eternal destruction. Furthermore, it may also have in view the impending destruction of Jerusalem. As indicated in Heb 6:7–8, those who do not "fall away" are like the ground that "brings forth" useful vegetation and they receive blessing. On

---

[680] e.g. 7:25; 9:14–15; 10.14

[681] Regarding this weakness Roger Nicole's critique is classic. "If Heb 6 proves anything about losing salvation, it proves too much! A wise Arminian might do well not to quote this text, since before the end of the discussion he may have to concede that he does not understand it, and that he is unable to point to concrete cases where it applies. This, we should think, would be better than to abandon to damnation all those who are viewed as apostates": "Some Comments on Hebrews 6:4–6 and the Doctrine of the Perseverance of God with the Saints," in *Current Issues in Biblical and Patristic Interpretation*. ed. Gerald F. Hawthorne (Grand Rapids: Eerdmans, 1975), 357. However, some like Marshall avoid this problem by acknowledging that the apostate may "go so far in sin" that "God may not permit him an opportunity of repentance" (*Kept*. 150).

[682] M. A. Fishbane, *Text and Texture: Close Readings of Selected Biblical Texts* (New York: Shocken, 1979), 121. Cf. also Wright, *People of God*, 36.

[683] Gleason, "Hebrews 6:4–8", 82 notes the parallels as follows: "For example, when they arrived at Kadesh-Barnea, they had already seen the pillar of fire and cloud over the tabernacle ('been enlightened'), eaten of the manna ('tasted of the heavenly gift'), experienced the Spirit on the seventy elders ('made partakers of the Holy Spirit'), and witnessed the giving of the Law at Sinai and the miracles of Moses ('tasted the good word of the Lord and the powers of the age to come').

[684] Ibid., 86–90.

the other hand, those who do "fall away" are denied God's blessing. Therefore, believers who "fall away" by refusing to press on to maturity will be denied the blessings that come with faithful obedience. Berkouwer concluded that the author is not trying to disturb and threaten our assurance of salvation, he is giving the church an admonition, the purpose of which is to lead to a more secure walk in the way of salvation.[685]

Corporate Concept

Bruce sees that the figure of Heb 6:7-8 comes from the parable of the vineyard in Isa 5,[686] an origin that Verbrugge supports.[687] Verbrugge has argued that 6:4-8 does not describe individual members of the church but local covenant communities.[688] Verbrugge's argument is clear, and he shows an obvious enthusiasm for its potential. His essential argument derives from the illustration found at 6:7-8 which, he argues, stems from Isa 5:1-7. The major conclusion he draws is that, since Isa 5:1-7 is concerned not with individual Israelites but with Israel as a nation, then it follows that the extension of this parable into the new covenant also applies not to individuals but also to local covenant communities. This places the interpretation of Heb 6 directly within the context of God's relationship to his people as a covenant community. Thus the writer of Hebrews is telling us we must understand this in terms of God's dealing with his covenant people as a community.

We also can see the corporative concept in the passage itself. It is the blessing-curse motif in Heb 6:7-8, εὐλογίας and κατάρας. These are precisely the two words used in Deut 11:26-28 where God places before his covenant people two options: blessing for obedience and curse for disobedience.[689] The point to note here is that Moses is speaking to the total covenant community, to the people of God as a whole.

---

[685] G. C. Berkouwer, *Faith and Perseverance*, trans. R. Knudsen (Grand Rapids, MI: Eerdmans, 1958), 119.
[686] Bruce, *Hebrews*, 124.
[687] V. D. Verbrugge, "Towards a New Interpretation of Hebrews 6:4-6", *CTJ* 15 (April 1980), 64-65. According to Verbrugge, both Isaiah and Hebrews make it plain that the field is well-cultivated. Isaiah gives a full description of all that the owner did for the field in order that it might produce the best grapes possible; Hebrews gives a general phrase indicating that, since it is well-cultivated, the owners can expect a good, useful crop.
[688] Ibid.
[689] P. C. Craigie, *The Book of Deuteronomy*, NICOT (Grand Rapids: Eerdmans, 1989), 212-3.

The author gave many indications throughout the epistle that his intended readers were Jewish Christians. The way the writer addressed them as "holy brethren, partakers of a heavenly calling" (3:1), "partakers of Christ" (3:14), and "dear friends" (6:9), and his constant use of "we" (e.g. 2:1–3; 4:14–16) and "us" (e.g. 4:1, 11, 16) indicates that they are the members of the new-covenant community.[690] They were baptized; it is implied by the repeated reference to their "confession" (3:1; 4:14; 10:23). They were also undergoing persecution and economic deprivation because of their faith (10:32–34; 12:4; 13:3).

In Heb 10:26 the author gives another warning to the whole community: "If we go on sinning willfully." This makes clear that those choosing to sin do so voluntarily. The writer included himself in the warning by using the pronoun ἡμῶν ("we"). He understood himself as one of the "brethren" mentioned in verse 19.[691] This warning is addressed to "brethren"; to those who have entered into the Holiest.

Eschatological Statement

The illustration in Heb 6:7–8 forms the eschatological statement in the warning.[692] The author applied his warning in Heb 6 to the pronouncement of judgment on the land that bears no fruit (vv. 7–8). Gleason points out that in light of the Old Testament blessing-curse motif, the judgment in view in Heb 6:7–8 is best understood as the forfeiture of blessing and the experience of temporal discipline.[693] According to him, the author's pattern of drawing from the Old Testament suggests that the source of his imagery is to be found in Gen 3:17–18 and Deut 11:26–28. The "curse" on the land in Heb 6:8 clearly alludes to Gen 3:17–18, which records God's declaring that the growth of "thorns and thistles" is part of the curse for Adam's disobedience. Deut 11:26–28 indicates that God offered the survivors of the wilderness generation two

---

[690] If this letter were addressed to unbelievers within a mixed audience rather than primarily to believers, one could expect the author to express more uncertainty about their spiritual condition and to appeal more to their need for genuine conversion. However, the author's goal was to exhort all (13:22) to take confidence in what God had already done for them in Christ (3:6; 4:16; 10:19, 35) and to urge them to hold fast to the hope they already confessed in Christ (3:6, 14; 4:14; 6:18; 10:3).

[691] Verbrugge, "Interpretation," 71.

[692] T. K. Oberholtzer, "The warning passage in Hebrews; Part 3: The Thorn-Infested Ground in Hebrews 6:4–12" *BibSac* 145 (July-Sep, 1988), 324. The conjunction γαρ ("for") links the illustration of 6:7–8 with the previous section, showing that the readers of 5:11–6:6 are still in view.

[693] Gleason, "Hebrews 6:4–8," 86–90.

options: blessing for obedience or a curse for disobedience.⁶⁹⁴ Disobedience would result in the devastation of the land. Since the blessings of obedience were experienced in relationship to the land (28:1–6), the destruction of the land meant the withholding of those blessings.

Likewise, in Heb 6:7–8 the author referred to the land of promise by the word γῆ. There the word γῆ declares that the sacred land of the Jews will be a place of cursing and judgment. If the soil yields useful produce, it receives God's blessing (Heb 6:7). If the soil produces thorns and thistles, it becomes disqualified, worthless, and is near to being cursed. The analogy is lucid—obedience in the life of a believer results in blessing; disobedience in the life of a believer results in a useless life for God and the possibility of receiving temporal discipline from the Lord (12:5–11). The specifics of this temporal discipline are not stipulated, but God's discipline of his children is for the purpose of bringing them back to usefulness and productivity (Heb 12:5–11). In Heb 6:5–8 temporal judgments for disobedience are in view, but an eschatological perspective appears implicit also. Terms such as ἀδόκιμος ("worthless") and καῦσιν ("burning") imply eschatological loss.⁶⁹⁵

Believers' soteriological status is settled on the basis of grace through faith alone. They will never be judged to determine their eternal destiny. However, the Scripture teaches that believers will be evaluated for reward or loss of reward for their motives, thoughts, and actions as disciples of Christ.

For the recipients of Hebrews, failure to press on to maturity might result in temporal discipline. It seems reasonable from Heb 3:1–4:13 that this might sometimes include the loss of physical life. Therefore it is clear that present unfaithfulness will result in loss of reward at the judgment seat of Christ. The result for the believer is not loss of eternal salvation but a forfeiting of reward. According to Verbrugge, the combination of blessing and curse fits more closely with Deut 11:26–28.⁶⁹⁶

---

⁶⁹⁴ Craigie, *Deuteronomy*, 212–3. These are further elaborated in Deut 28–29 with lists of blessings and curses. The final curse is on the land, which will be "a burning waste, unsown and unproductive, and no grass grows in it." (29:23).

⁶⁹⁵ T. K. Oberholtzer, "Hebrews 6:4–12," 326.

⁶⁹⁶ V. D. Verbrugge, "Towards a New Interpretation of Hebrews 6:4–6", *CTJ* 15.1, April (1980), 67. Gleason, "Hebrews 6:4–8," 86. There God offered the survivors of the wilderness generation two options: blessing for

Summing up

The falling away (παραπεσόντας) in Heb 6:6 was committed by Christians, not non-Christians. Their immediate problem was rather a passive drifting away from the word of Christ (2:1), a persistent lethargy to press on to maturity (5:11–6:2). They faced the danger of falling into a permanent state of immaturity through a willful once for all refusal to trust God to deliver them from their present troubles, rather than a total rejection of Christ. Thus the problem in this passage is the failure to grow and mature as a Christian, not the public rejection of Christ's work by attributing it to Satan.[697]

The author includes himself in the warning by using the pronoun ἡμᾶς ("we"), in 2:1 and ἀδελφοί ("brothers") in 3:12. The reader's focus of attention is upon the church as a corporate body, as a covenant community. Thus, the writer addresses the readers as members of the new covenant community.

In Hebrews reward awaits the faithful at the end. Those who have trusted God's promise are those who are about to receive a deliverance. Deliverance offered by the Son is eternal, and this eternal salvation is what the obedient believers look forward to inheriting. The things promised by God have an eschatological sense.

The Goal of Pilgrimage: Heb 12

The Righteous—the People of Yahweh Waiting for Deliverance

The righteous are called to live by faith while expecting deliverance from the Lord. The writer in Heb 10:37–38 drove his point home by a free citation of

---

obedience or a curse for disobedience. These are further elaborated in Deut 28–29 with lists of blessings and curses. The final curse is on the land, which will be "a burning waste, unsown and unproductive, and no grass grows in it" (29:23). Disobedience would result in the devastation of the land. Since the blessings of obedience were experienced in relationship to the land (28:1–6), the destruction of the land meant the withholding of those blessings. Likewise, in Heb 6:7-8 the author referred to the land of promise by the word γῆ. The word γῆ declares that the sacred land of the Jews will be a place of cursing and judgment rather than safety for those Jewish believers who desired to return to Judaism.

[697] According to the Gospels (Matt 12:31; Mark 3:28–29; Luke 12:10), two important facts must be noted about the nature of the unpardonable sin. First, it was committed by unbelievers (i.e. Pharisees), not believers. And second, it involved accusing Jesus of being in league with Satan. This sin was committed by the Pharisees when they wilfully rejected the Holy Spirit's work through the Messiah. They saw a great miracle and heard Jesus's own teaching, but they called good evil (Isa 5:20) by attributing the miracle to the devil. The person who commits this sin is not ignorant, but chooses in the face of irrefutable facts to reject God, to call God the devil.

Hab 2:3–4[698] and Isa 26:20 from the Septuagint.[699] Hab 2:3–4 depicts the people of Yahweh as waiting for the deliverance of the Lord and destruction of their enemies, the Babylonians.[700] In the midst of this difficult situation, the righteous are called to live by faith while expecting deliverance from the Lord.

The quotation from Hab 2:3 follows the Greek of the Septuagint version.[701] By quoting from Habakkuk, there is a transposition of the two clauses as they appear in the original.[702] Hughes says that this transposition does no violence to the thought of the prophet.[703] Bruce observes that it has the advantage of allowing "my righteous one" to become the subject of both parts of the verse in a manner particularly suited to the situation which the author is addressing.[704] Toussaint sees that by quoting Hab 2:3–4 the author refers to the one who draws back.[705] He understands that this points to an apostate. However, Oberholtzer points out that the subject of shrinking back in Heb 10:38 is clearly "My righteous one," that is, a believer. "Shrinking back" in this

---

[698] Hab 2:3–4 in the Septuagint, "Because the vision is yet for an appointed time, and it will appear at length and not in vain: if he is late, wait for him; because he will surely come, he will not delay. If he draws back, my soul has no pleasure in him, but my righteous one will live by faith (faithfulness)." Cf. The Targum of Jonathan renders the passage: "Behold, the prophecy will be for an appointed time, and its term is fixed; it will not be in vain. If there is a long period of waiting for the event, keep looking out for it; behold, it will come in its appointed time, and will not be late. Behold, the wicked say to themselves, 'None of these things are happening'; but the righteous will be established by their truth." Cf. Hab 2:3–4 "διότι ἔτι ὅρασις εἰς καιρὸν καὶ ἀνατελεῖ εἰς πέρας καὶ οὐκ εἰς κενόν· ἐὰν ὑστερήσῃ, ὑπόμεινον αὐτόν, ὅτι ἐρχόμενος ἥξει καὶ οὐ μὴ χρονίσῃ. ⁴ ἐὰν ὑποστείληται, οὐκ εὐδοκεῖ ἡ ψυχή μου ἐν αὐτῷ· ὁ δὲ δίκαιος ἐκ πίστεώς μου ζήσεται." in the Septuagint, Heb 10:37–38, "ἔτι γὰρ μικρὸν ὅσον ὅσον, ὁ ἐρχόμενος ἥξει καὶ οὐ χρονίσει· ³⁸ ὁ δὲ δίκαιός μου ἐκ πίστεως ζήσεται, καὶ ἐὰν ὑποστείληται, οὐκ εὐδοκεῖ ἡ ψυχή μου ἐν αὐτῷ".

[699] Jewett, *Pilgrims*, 189–90. According to him, verse 37a is designed to depict an extremely short time until the eschatological fulfilment, while 37b is altered so that the coming one refers explicitly to the returning Christ.

[700] R. L. Smith, *Micah-Malachi*, WBC (Waco, TX: Word, 1984), 106. D. W. Baker, *Nahum, Habakkuk and Zephaniah: Tyndale Old Testament Commentaries* (Leicester, IVP: 1988), 59.

[701] Cf. On this passage the Septuagint is different from the Hebrew of the original text. In the latter, "If it seems slow, wait for it; it will surely come, it will not delay"; it seems not to a person but to a vision of divine judgment and vindication. Whereas in the Septuagint the reference is clearly to a person who is coming: "If he seems late, wait patiently for him; for he will surely come and he will not delay": E. B. Pusey, *The Minor Prophets*, VI (London: SPCK, 1907), 74. According to Pusey, "but the vision had no other existence or fulfilment than in him Who was the Object of it, and Who, in it, was foreshadowed to the mind. The coming of the vision was none other than His Coming."

[702] Cf. Hab 2:4: "Behold, he whose soul is not upright in him is puffed up; but the righteous shall live by his faith"; whereas Heb 10:38: "but my righteous one shall live by faith, and if he shrinks back, my soul has no pleasure in him."

[703] Hughes, *Hebrews*, 436.

[704] Bruce, *Hebrews*, 274

[705] Toussaint, "Eschatology," 75.

situation meant failure to hold fast, abandonment of the assembly, loss of confidence and failure to endure. Oberholtzer concludes that the author wanted to be sure that the readers understood the eschatological ramifications of their present endurance in obedience to the will of God.[706]

The author of Hebrews applied the passage in Hab 2 to his readers by referring to the imminent return of Messiah,[707] his defeat of his enemies and their deliverance from their enemies and their participation in ruling as "partners" with the king. The readers were assured of the return of the Messiah, who would deliver them from their enemies. In their present persecutions (Heb 10:32–36) the recipients of Hebrews, like Habakkuk's audience, were enjoined to "live by faith" in light of the Messiah's coming deliverance.

Furthermore, the first words of the quotation μικρὸν ὅσον ὅσον ("a very little while") in Heb 10:37 are borrowed from Isa 26:20 (Septuagint),[708] an eschatological text, which is a part of "Isaiah's little apocalypse." Watts identified Isa 26:1–21 to be about Judeans on pilgrimage to Jerusalem.[709] Isa 26:20 relates to the day of the Lord, the tribulation period, during which Israel will find safety "for a little while" until the Lord's wrath is accomplished.[710]

Thus, the writer to the Hebrews quoted from Habakkuk 2:3-4 to link the Isa 26:20 phrase "in a very little while" with the second advent of Christ. The point in quoting Isa 26:20 was to encourage the audience not to allow the difficulty of their persecutions, during the "very little while," to cause them to forfeit their heavenly rewards or eschatological possessions. The eschatological deliverance for the readers of Hebrews will begin with the rapture of the church and be consummated at the second advent of the Messiah.

The author develops how the righteous live by faith in Heb 12. There the verb διώκετε in Heb 12:14 implies an earnest pursuit, underscoring the urgency with which this pastoral directive is addressed to the community. The stress falls on active Christian effort in response to the divine gifts, which are atonement and

---

[706] Oberholtzer, "Hebrews 10:26–39", 415.
[707] E. B. Pusey, *The Minor Prophets* (London: SPCK, 1907), 74. Jewett, *Pilgrims*, 190.
[708] C. R. Koester, *Hebrews*, 461.
[709] Watts, *Isaiah* 1–33, 335-42.
[710] Dan 9:24–27; Jer 30:7

redemption obtained by Jesus's blood. What is necessary is that believers are to pursue peace and holiness.

Pursue Peace (εἰρήνην) and Holiness (ἁγιασμόν)

In terms of peace, Guthrie[711] reasons that Christians must strive for it with all men, but Bruce[712] and Buchanan[713] regard it simply as being in harmony with the community. Along with them, Hughes sees the blessing of God's peace as flowing through believers into the lives of others.[714]

However, Foerster considers the term "peace" to be a gift of eschatological salvation.[715] According to him, believers are admonished to seek this salvation in Heb 12:14. Lane sees that "peace" is brought about by the redemptive accomplishment of Christ in his sacrificial death on the cross.[716] He goes on to say that it points to the presence of the new age and it is to be pursued because this gift of Christ is given visibility in the solidarity of the community.[717] Lane and Foerster's opinions are acceptable because they see that peace was a result of Christ's sacrifice. That is, it is to be seen as restoration through the Passover.

Concerning holiness, Westcott comments that the word expresses not the positional state or fact of sanctification, but the process of sanctification because, in Koine Greek, nouns ending in -μος describe action.[718] Kistemaker supports Westcott's claim, saying that the believer reflects God's virtues.[719] In doing so, according to him, he becomes more and more like Christ who through the Holy Spirit continues to work in his heart.[720]

---

[711] D. Guthrie, *The Letter to the Hebrews* (Grand Rapids: Eerdmans, 1983), 256–57.
[712] Bruce, *Hebrews*, 362.
[713] Buchanan, *Hebrews*, 216.
[714] Hughes, *Hebrews*, 536.
[715] Foerster, "eivrh,nhn" in *TDNT* II, 412–3. Salvation has come as a historical event through Jesus Christ. This is intimated in Heb 13:20.
[716] Lane, *Hebrews 47B*, 449.
[717] Ibid.
[718] B. F. Westcott, *The Epistle to the Hebrews: The Greek Text with Notes and Essays*, 3rd ed. (London: Macmillan, 1903), 347–48.
[719] Kistemaker, *Hebrews*, 384–5.
[720] Ibid. Kistemaker understands that we as believers must do everything in our power to obtain holiness.

However, Casey saw the term holiness to refer to the gift of Christ through which believers have been made holy.[721] Lane supports Casey's thoughts, by saying that it is eschatological in character, as the objective gift of Christ, achieved through his sacrificial death on the cross.[722] It does not stress human effort, but derives its peculiar nuance from the cultic argument concerning the efficacy of Jesus' high priestly ministry in 10:29. The importance of holiness is highlighted by the qualifying phrase "without holiness no one will see the Lord." The phrase means that "holiness" is the only way which one can come into the presence of God. Only those who have been made holy through the gift of Christ have access to God.

This admonition to "pursue holiness" in v. 14 anticipates the further development of the sentence in vv. 15–16. It prepares for the subsequent reference to those who are prepared to forfeit the grace of God through spiritual carelessness. It is foundational for the reference in v. 16 to Esau, who was rejected ἀπεδοκιμάσθη (v. 17), preferring something secular to his spiritual birthright and so became the archetype of the secular person.

To sum up, peace and holiness are the possession of believers as a result of Christ's redemptive ministry. In other words, the righteous are called to peace and holiness which is parts of their deliverance achieved by God.

The Sacred Place: Mt. Zion

There is a contrast between Sinai and Zion in Heb 12:18–24. The contrast is not between speakers (Moses and God) but between the revelation at the earthly mountain and the revelation from heaven, the speaker being God in both instances.[723]

Käsemann suggested that the author of Hebrews is working with a tradition which he has adapted.[724] He argued that the gnostic redeemer-myth of the Urmensch supplied the format for Hebrews. Thompson pointed out along with Käsemann that the term, ψηλαφωμένῳ was not found in the biblical accounts; the basic structure comes from tradition, although it is a reflection of Exod

---

[721] J. M. Casey, "Eschatology in Heb 12:14–29," (PhD diss., Catholic University of Leuven, 1977), 90–91.
[722] Lane, *Hebrews 47B*, 450. W. G. McCown, "Holiness in Hebrews," *WesThJ* 16 (1981), 61.
[723] Lane, *Hebrews* 47B, 459.
[724] Käsemann, *Wandering*, 48–51.

19:12–13.⁷²⁵ He suggested that the basic structure, with the comparison of the earthly Sinai and the heavenly Zion, is contained in Gal 4:25–26, Jub. 4:26, and Midrash Tanchuma B.⁷²⁶ He interpreted the Sinai event with an assumption which designates the metaphysical dualism.⁷²⁷ Such a view corresponds to the perspective that is found in Plato, where the sense-perceptible world was distinguished from the intelligible world; for Plato that which is touchable belongs to the sphere of sense-perception.⁷²⁸ We argued earlier that Plato's thought did not enter that of the author of Hebrews anywhere.

Bruce pointed out that the description of the terrors of Sinai in Heb 12:18–21 is based on the account in Exod 19:16–19; 20:18–21, with Moses's reminiscence of the scene forty years later in Deut 4:11.⁷²⁹ The word ψηλαφωμένῳ ("to what may be touched") was used as a contrast between Sinai and Zion. Casey also proposes that the Sinai event was physical and tangible,⁷³⁰ but the mountain was so filled with the holiness of the Lord who manifested himself there that for man or beast to touch it meant certain death. It means that the people were unable to draw near to God under the old covenant because of their sinfulness.⁷³¹ Therefore, the Israelites pleaded to hear God's voice no more, and in response to their request God desisted from speaking to them except through Moses (Exod 19:16–19; 20:18–21; Deut 5:23–28). Jones comments on vv. 18–21 that under the Sinai covenant there was the sense of a huge distance separating the worshipper from God, and a numinous awareness of the God who was unapproachable, an experience of blazing fire, black clouds, gloom,

---

⁷²⁵ J. W. Thompson, "That Which Cannot be Shaken: Some Metaphysical Assumptions in Hebrews 12:27", *JBL* 94 (1975), 582. According to Thompson, ψηλαφωμένῳ serves in a much wider way to describe the entire Sinai theophany. The list of phenomena is cited from Deut 4:11 and Exod 19:12–13. It is probable that the author is working with a tradition which enumerates the Sinai phenomena and which had the intent of indicating the awesome character of the Sinai theophany. The author interprets the fire from a metaphysical standpoint, according to which material objects can only be inferior agents for the expression of the nature of God.
⁷²⁶ Ibid, 581.
⁷²⁷ Cf. Thompson saw that it is apparent, from the contrast between ψηλαφωμένῳ and the heavenly Zion, that ψηλαφωμένῳ has the primary meaning of "earthly" or "sense-perceptible".
⁷²⁸ Philo, De Cher 57, 73.
⁷²⁹ Bruce, *Hebrews*, 371. Cf. Exod 19:18. "Mount Sinai was wrapped in smoke, because the LORD descended upon it in fire; and the smoke of it went up like the smoke of a kiln, and the whole mountain quaked greatly. And as the sound of the trumpet grew louder and louder Moses spoke, and God answered him in thunder" (RSV)
⁷³⁰ Casey, "Eschatological in Heb 12:14–29," 322.
⁷³¹ K. J. Thomas, "The Old Testament Citations in Hebrews", *NTS* 11 (1964–65), 317.

whirlwind, loud noise, and a frightening sound of words.[732] In Heb 12:19 the readers are reminded of the request, prompted by a voice whose words (ῥημάτων) were terrifying, of those in Exod 19 that no further message (λόγον) be spoken to them. They are also reminded of the blood which speaks (λαλοῦντι) better than that of Abel (12:24). It is this motif of God's speech, prevalent in the earlier chapters of Hebrews, which is picked up by the warning in Heb 12:25. The readers are exhorted not to refuse the one who is speaking (λαλοῦντα). Then, they are warned not to refuse the one who is warning them (χρηματίζοντα) from heaven. This warning is heard through Scripture and throughout the writer's own exposition. To sum up, Mount Sinai typifies not only the Mosaic law-giving and the institution of the Aaronic priesthood, but also the wanderings of that generation which was under a cloud of condemnation, because of its infidelity and ingratitude.

Vv. 22-24 contrasts with the Sinai event in the previous passage. The verb προσεληλύθατε ("you have come") is in the perfect; it refers to a communion into which they enter when Christianity is grasped, not to some communion into which believers enter after death.[733] Lane reasons that it illustrates clearly the experience of encountering God through Christ, in the metaphor of pilgrimage to the city of God.[734] Therefore, προσεληλύθατε denotes the advancing direction of faith in the light of an objective goal, the transcendent blessing secured for Christians by the death of Jesus as mediator of the new covenant.

The first three designations[735] in v. 22 are synonymous and are various expressions as a unit.[736] Mount Zion in Jerusalem was called the house which the people of God inhabited, and the place where the tribes of Israel gathered together. It was also called the foundation of the glorified heavenly city.[737] Therefore, the city of God called Mount Zion, the heavenly Jerusalem,

---

[732] P. R. Jones, "The Figure of Moses as a Heuristic Device for Understanding the Pastoral Intent of Hebrews", *RevExp* 76 (1979), 101.

[733] Hewitt, *Hebrews*, 200-01.

[734] Lane, *Hebrews* 47B, 465.

[735] Mount Zion is called the city of the living God (Ps 9:11; Joel 3:17), and the heavenly Jerusalem (Gal 4:26; Rev 3:12; 21:2).

[736] Montefiore, *Hebrews*, 229-30; Westcott, *Hebrews*, 413; See the extensive article on "Zion-Jerusalem" by G. Fohrer and E. Lohse in Kittel, TDNT.

[737] E.g. Isa 28:16; 54:11 LXX.

represents the kingdom of God in a metaphor, it is also referred to as "the place" (11:8), "the heavenly home land (11:16), "the unshakable kingdom" (12:28), and "the abiding city which is to come" (13:14) which Christians belong to under the new covenant. Namely, Mount Zion exemplifies the establishment of the unique and everlasting priesthood of Christ, the fulfillment in him of all the promises of the new covenant.

With reference to μυριάσιν ἀγγέλων, πανηγύρει[738] ("to innumerable companies of angels") the word πανηγύρει denotes a joyful gathering in order to rejoice in a festival.[739] It reminds us of the "thousand thousands" whom Daniel saw serving God, and "ten thousand times ten thousand" who stood before Him (Dan 7:10).[740] Innumerable companies of angels are here described as united in festal gathering to celebrate the glorious triumph of Mount Zion. We know how exalted the status of the heirs of salvation is from the fact that the Son of God who passed by angels to partake of flesh and blood, is with mankind.

In terms of the phrase "the assembly of the company of the redeemed," Clement argued that the "assembly of the firstborn" is actually a title of majesty referring to the highest angels as the "first-created" of God's creative activity.[741] However, the title "firstborn" was given to the Israelites when God brought them out of Egypt; their names were written in the heavenly register. Moreover, "firstborn" is an apocalyptic title applied to the redeemed community. Therefore, this phrase has been thought by some commentators to signify the saints who are members of the church triumphant, and tells us that the church is rooted in a relationship of men and women of faith under the old covenant.[742]

In v. 24, the author wants to teach that the pilgrim community is based on the blood of Christ and the efficacy of the new covenant. The blood of Jesus, as the blood of a better covenant, is the means of eternal redemption (9:12), the final putting away of sins (9:26), the purging of an evil conscience (10:22), perfecting and sanctifying all to whom it is applied in contrast to Abel's blood

---

[738] Holmes, M. W. *The Greek New Testament: SBL Edition* (Heb 12:22). Bellingham: Lexham, 2011–2013.

[739] R. Williamson, *Philo and the Epistle to the Hebrews* (Leiden: Brill, 1970), 64–70.

[740] Bruce, *Hebrews*, 375. Cf., 1 Enoch 40:1; Rev 5:11

[741] Clement of Alexandria, Extracts of Theodotus 27.3–5; Hermas, Shepherd, Vision iii. 4.1.

[742] Bruce, *Hebrews*, 375; Montefiore, *Hebrews*, 231; Lane, *Hebrews* 47B, 468.

which speaks of vengeance, and judgment demanded by his murder.[743] Therefore, v. 24 tells us of the realization of the eschatological covenant through the death of Jesus. Citizenship of the heavenly Jerusalem has come through the blood of Jesus, the high priest's perfect sacrifice. Holland understands the expression to refer to the community that belongs to the firstborn, i.e. Christ (Heb 1:6).[744]

The sacred place which is the goal of the Hebrews is the dwelling place of God par excellence. The real city which is "to come" (13:14) already is, because it belongs to the realm of the invisible, not made with hands, whose builder and maker is God (11:10, 8:1–5, 9:11).[745]

Summing Up

The recipients of Hebrews were enjoined to "live by faith" in light of the Messiah's coming deliverance. The righteous are those waiting for deliverance from the Lord. In other words, the eschatological deliverance for the readers of Hebrews will begin with the rapture of the church and be consummated at the second advent of the Messiah.

The people of God are to pursue peace and holiness because they belong to the attributes of God. Both peace and holiness are brought about by the redemptive accomplishment of Christ in his sacrificial death on the cross. Especially without holiness no one will see the Lord. Therefore, Heb 12:14–17 shows why the community must hold fast to the objective gifts of peace and holiness and why the community must guard against apostasy.

Both events are presented by means of the metaphor of a pilgrimage to the heavenly city of God. The Sinai event emphasizes its intrinsic inadequacy, whereas the Zion event indicates the experience of encountering God through Jesus. The author stressed that the latter is only the blood of Christ that can lead people to God's kingdom.

---

[743] Hughes, *Hebrews*, 552.
[744] Holland, *Contours*, 272–3.
[745] The manner in which Hebrews combines both linear and vertical modes is shown at 10:1: "the law has but a shadow of the good things to come instead of the true form of these realities." Likewise, throughout chapter 11 faith is directed toward both the invisible and the future.

Conclusion

Throughout the Bible the faithful who follow God are pictured as either literal or figurative pilgrims. They are people journeying rather than settled, still looking for the spiritual place that will satisfy them. The patriarchs considered their status to be that of pilgrims: Abraham said to the sons of Heth, "I am a stranger and a sojourner with you," and Jacob also, in old age, speaks of the long course of his life as "the days of the years of my pilgrimage." The manner of their existence was altogether that of one who did not belong in the land, a migrant rather than a permanent inhabitant. As the wilderness was no more the home of their descendants in Moses's day who journeyed from Egypt to Canaan, neither Canaan was their home as they sought the country of their heart's desire.

Furthermore, the prophets predicted that Israel would be released from Babylon, and that the people would once again begin their sojourn by passing through the sea. It is true that the prophets describe the return of the remnant of Israel to their homeland as a process predicated on a great redemptive act of YHWH akin to that of the new exodus. The return itself is not merely a wandering through wilderness toward a land flowing with milk and honey. It is, rather, a pilgrimage, a solemn and yet joyous procession of YHWH's redeemed to the high and holy precincts of Zion. The language of the prophets in describing this procession becomes transmuted from that of exodus and redemption to that of pilgrimage and worship.

This pilgrim theme has been part of the Israelites consciousness throughout all generations—throughout the Old Testament, the Intertestamental period and finally the New Testament. It is apparent, therefore, that Hebrews displays a pilgrimage motif. This motif does not simply exist alongside the other major descriptions of Christianity, the cult—it harmonizes and blends with it. This is because the believers of Hebrews are viewed as a cultic community on the move. Pilgrimage in Hebrews is in the face of impending danger, but it has purpose. Pilgrims as a community are ones who are called to spiritual growth. Its goal is to reach the sacred place, the city of God called Mount Zion. Peace and holiness the gifts of God, are there.

Chapter 5: The New Covenant Theme

Introduction

The idea of covenant was prominent in Judaism.[746] Its basis was the promises made by Yahweh to the patriarchs; they were about land and its prosperity.[747] The fulfillment of the covenant was understood to be the exodus (Exod 2:24), and the Torah was regarded as the covenant document.[748] In Jeremiah's day the covenant theme was topical because of the solemn renewal of the covenant that had been made by the king and the leaders of the nation in the eighteenth year of Josiah.[749] Then, Jeremiah foretold the new covenant which is set in contrast with the covenant which Yahweh made with the people of Israel when he delivered them from the land of Egypt.[750] There was also a belief, in Second Temple Judaism, that Israel's God had renewed his covenant at last.[751] It was expected that their God would act in the future to liberate Israel from her continuing exile.[752] The book of Jubilees celebrated the special status of Israel as a result of the covenant.[753] That is, the covenantal idea also spread to the different movements within Second Temple Judaism.

The term "covenant" was directly translated into the Hebrew term ברית and Greek by the word διαθήκη.[754] The question has long been debated whether

---

[746] G. Vos, *The Teaching of the Epistle to the Hebrews* (Philipsburg, NJ: The Presbyterian & Reformed Publishing Company, 1975), 27. Vos pointed out that the idea was eclipsed in the New Testament. According to him, other ideas took its place, namely the ideas of the church and of the kingdom of God. That is, through the coming of the Messiah the people of God have received a new form of organization instead of the Berith organization. This new organization yielded the ideas of the church, Christ, and the kingdom of God. The covenant idea does not pass out altogether, of course, for it still merits an occasional reference in the New Testament. Wright, *People*, 262. W. Eichrodt, *Theology of the Old Testament*, Vol. 1, trans. J. A. Baker (London: SCM, 1969), 36–7. Eichrodt takes covenant as the central idea of the Old Testament.

[747] Gen 12, 15, 17, 22, etc.

[748] Wright, *People*, 260–1. According to Wright, the covenant document, grounded upon the faithfulness of Israel's God, provided for his people the way of life by which they should express their corresponding fidelity to him. Wright goes on to say that the book of Deuteronomy is the major work of covenant theology which stands at the head of a long line of subsequent writings on this theme (the Deuteronomic history, Jeremiah, etc.).

[749] 2 Kgs 23:3

[750] The ratification of that earlier covenant is recorded in Exod 24:1–8, a passage to which specific reference is made in Heb 9:18–20.

[751] E.g. CD 6.19

[752] Wright, *People*, 209.

[753] E.g. Jub. 14:19; 15:1–34, esp. 30–2, 34; 22:15–19, 23.

[754] The word διαθήκη occurs 33 times in the NT. Cf. P. Golding, *Covenant Theology: The Key of Theology in*

ברית (διαθήκη) should be turned into "testament" or "covenant." In fact, the major point of confusion in these two concepts of "covenant" and "testament" arises from the fact that both a "covenant" and a "testament" relate to "death." Death is essential to both, to activate a will (testament) and to inaugurate a covenant (i.e. the death of the covenant sacrifice).

What is important, then, is that neither translation ("testament" and "covenant") of the term ברית (διαθήκη) required a different setting from the Day of Atonement; both were merely an adjustment in understanding what was happening in connection with the death of Christ. Both terms ברית and διαθήκη are related to death, which activates a will (testament) and inaugurates a covenant. Therefore, a "mediator" is required in both contexts. Yet our concern is to understand the role of the ברית in both the Day of Atonement setting and the Passover setting.

The New Covenant and its Context

The Day of Atonement Setting

Westcott says that the death of a sacrificial victim is an essential part of the ceremony for the establishment of a covenant.[755] He points out that the man who brings the sacrifice identifies with the animal victim of the sacrifice.[756] That is, the contextual connection of Heb 9:16 with the preceding verse lends support to the assumption that "covenantal" arrangements provide the framework for understanding the author's argument. Robertson, who interprets Heb 9:16–17 in the light of the death of Christ the maker of the new covenant,[757] says that the key to understanding the significance of these verses

---

Reformed Thought and Tradition (Fearn: Christian Focus, 2004), 80. The Hebrew word ברית is equivalent to two Greek words, συνθήκη and διαθήκη. The former was the common word for compact or treaty, and was in fact the word chosen by other Greek translators such as Aquila and Symmachus to render ברית. The Septuagint, however, deliberately avoided συνθήκη, because it suggested an agreement arrived at by negotiation between equal partners. Instead, they consistently used διαθήκη which means literally "a disposition for oneself," and which in everyday usage bore the general sense of "statute" or "ordinance," and then the specialized sense of "last will" or "testament". In fact, the nuances of διαθήκη are quite different from those of συνθήκη. It emphasizes the divine initiative in the covenant, and in the sovereign, gracious and authoritative nature of its provisions.

[755] Westcott, *Hebrews*, 263–70. Cf. W. G. Johnson, "Defilement and Purgation in the Book of Hebrews" (Unpublished dissertation, Vanderbilt University, 1973). 206–75, 290–338. J. J. Hughes, "Hebrews 9.15ff," 32–35.
[756] Ibid.
[757] Robertson, *Covenant*, 140.

lies in an analysis of the relation of death and a διαθήκη which unites the entire progress of thought in these passages.[758] In Heb 9:15, the author of the Hebrews indicates that a death has taken place for the forgiveness of sins committed under the first covenant, which is the Mosaic covenant. As the relation of death to "covenant" seems to be the subject of Heb 9:18–20,[759] it seems appropriate that the term διαθήκη in Heb 9:16–17, which is a parenthetical paragraph, is understood in the light of the same meaning. However, both Westcott and Robertson failed to link the term διαθήκη relating to the death of Christ with the Passover for redemption. Robertson's thinking is supported by McComisky who sees that the author speaks of the promise as a will or testament in Heb 9:16 that it is valid only when the testator has died.[760] He links his understanding of the term διαθήκη with surrounding passages as follows:[761]

> Such a death has occurred under the new covenant (v. 15); it is the death of Christ (v. 14). But a death occurred under the old covenant as well (v. 18); it is to be found in the symbolic shedding of the blood of animals (vv. 19–22). Under the new covenant, the blood of Christ establishes the "better promises" enacted by his death (9:28).

Campbell also argues that the central feature of the covenant idea is inadequate to express the new relationship of believers to God by virtue of the atoning death of Christ.[762] The glory of the new covenant is that it has been sealed by the blood of Christ Himself. Campbell understands Heb 9:16–17 to refer to the Day of Atonement. He goes on to say that the text enforces the author's exposition of the covenantal significance of the death of Christ.

Simpson says that Jesus as "the mediator of a better covenant" is presented in an example of the profound enhancement conferred on expressions already in vogue by the Christian revelation.[763] He goes on to say that the Greek word

---

[758] Ibid, 138

[759] In these verses "blood" and διαθήκη echo the inauguration ceremony of Sinai. The ceremony at Sinai instituted a covenantal relationship. The sprinkled "blood of the covenant" solemnly consecrated God and Israel to one another for life and death.

[760] T. E. McComisky, *The Covenant of Promise* (Nottingham: IVP, 1985), 168–69.

[761] Ibid.

[762] Campbell, "Covenant or Testament?" *EQ* 44 (1972), 111.

[763] E. K. Simpson, "The Vocabulary of The Epistle To The Hebrews," *EQ* XVIII (July, 1946), 188.

translated "mediator" is shown by the papyri to have been a common business term "in the sense of arbitrator or go-between."[764] However Lang sees the concept of mediator in the covenant idea.[765] Lehne points out that the term μεσίτης ("mediator") is always connected to the new covenant (8:6; 9:15; 12:24; cf. 7:22) and functions analogously to assure the addressees that Christ's person and work guarantee the superior effectiveness of the new covenant and make its blessings available to his followers.[766] Bruce also links the concept of mediator to the covenant, saying that "Christians have one who does not remain in the realm of ideas but is the incarnate Logos, one who preserved his purity while treading the common ways of this world and sharing our human lot."[767] He sees Christ as the mediator in the covenant which Yahweh made with the people of Israel.[768] Oepke sees that the primary meaning is everywhere that Jesus transcends and replaces the mediator of the old covenant, Moses 8:5; 9:19; 12:21.[769] Oepke concludes that the better covenant is better than the covenant God made with their forefather in the exodus because the old covenant was a covenant which Moses mediated, whereas the new one is the covenant which Jesus, who is superior to Moses, mediated. Oepke also understood the new covenant in the light of the Sinai setting.

The Passover Setting

Casey says that the Passover was the most emphasized sacrificial concept used by the early church due to its association with the death of Jesus.[770] Gray says that the Passover is not only the most frequently mentioned festival in the Old Testament but also in the New Testament.[771] In Heb 9:12–13, the author speaks of Christ having obtained eternal redemption which is part of the

---

[764] Ibid.

[765] F. Lang, "Abendmahl und Bundesgedenke im NT," *En Th* 35 (1975), 537.

[766] S. Lehne, *The New Covenant in Hebrews* (Sheffield: Sheffield Academic Press, 1990), 102

[767] F. F. Bruce, *Hebrews*, 157. Cf. Although he came to earth "in the likeness of sinful flesh", and lived among sinners, he is set apart from sinners, "in a different class from sinful men"; and is now exalted above all the heavens to share the throne of God.

[768] Ibid.

[769] Oepke, "μεσίτης" 620. According to Oepke, the author did not coin the theological concept μεσίτης independently on the basis of Hellenistic presuppositions. He took it from the Jewish or Christian tradition. Hence "mediator" is a pertinent translation.

[770] R. P. Casey, "The Earliest Christologies" *JTS* 9(1958), 272

[771] G. B. Gray, Sacrifice in the Old Testament: Its Theory and Practice (New York: KTAV, 1971), 383.

Passover; at the same time he uses imagery which is distinctive of the atoning sacrificial system of the Day of Atonement.

Furthermore, "I will be to them for God and they shall be to me for a people" in Heb 8:10 is close to Lev 26:12.[772] Most Old Testament scholars refer to the statement in Lev 26:12 as "the covenant formula".[773] Webb points out that it expressed an exclusive covenant bond between Israel and her God in relation to leaving Egypt and establishing a covenant at Sinai.[774] Thus, many Old Testament references place the covenant formula as part of the exodus narrative.

Holland proposes that Ezekiel saw the significance of the raising up of a Davidic prince.[775] Mckenzie saw that Ezek 34:23–24 and 37:24–25 are clear references to a Davidic prince who will once again be king over Israel.[776] Ezekiel saw the prince's main function was to build the eschatological temple and to provide sacrifices for the sins of the covenant community.

How then do we relate the Davidic prince to the mediator? De Lacy understands the concept of mediation as only a variant of the concept of high priest.[777] Merrill examines the function of Old Testament royal priesthood.[778]

---

[772] W. J. Webb, *Returning Home: New Covenant and Second Exodus as the Context for 2 Corinthians 6:14–7:1* (Sheffield: JSOT, 1993), 36.

[773] W. Eichrodt, *Ezekiel. A Commentary*, trans. C. Quin (Philadelphia: Westminster, 1970), 515; W. Zimmerli, *Ezekiel 2. A Commentary on the Book of The Prophet Ezekiel*, Chapters 25–48, trans. J. D. Martin (Philadelphia: Fortress, 1983), 277; M. Greenberg, *Ezekiel*, 1–20 (Garden City, NY: Doubleday, 1983), 254; W. L. Holladay, *Jeremiah 1: A Commentary on the Book of the Prophet Jeremiah* (Philadelphia: Fortress, 1986), 262; K. Baltzer, *The Covenant Formulary: In Old Testament, Jewish, and Early Christian Writings*, trans. D. E. Green (Philadelphia: Fortress, 1971), 102. Baltzer comments, "the relationship between Yahweh and Israel...can be reduced to the formula, "I will be your God, and you will be my people"".

[774] Webb, *Returning*, 38. Cf. Exod 6:7; Lev 26:12–13; Deut 4:20.

[775] T. Holland, *Contours*, 161–63. Ezek 34:23–4; 37:24–5 etc. cf. also the mention of the Davidic prince in 44:3; 45:7, 22; 46:2,4,8 etc. who is to officiate over the messianic eschatological sacrifice. Cf. W. H. Brownlee, "Messianic Motifs of Qumran and the New Testament" *NTS* 3(1956–57), 21. He examined the eschatological nature of Passover in Qumran.

[776] J. L. McKenzie, "Royal Messianism," *CBQ* 19 (1957), 45; D. I. Block, "My Servant David: Ancient Israel's Vision of the Messiah", in *Israel's Messiah: In the Bible and The Dead Sea Scrolls*, ed. R. S. Hess and M Daniel Carroll R. (Grand Rapids: Baker, 2003), 48. Remarkably in Ezekiel the servant is not the agent of Israel's regathering and return to the land. These both are direct actions of Yahweh, after which the servant is installed to function as a symbol of the new realities, that is, the fulfillment of Yahweh's eternal promises to Abraham, to Israel, and to the Davidic dynasty.

[777] D. R. de Lacy, "Jesus as Mediator," *JSNT* 29 (1987), 101; O. Cullmann, *The Christology of the NT* (London: SCM, 1959), 89.

He argues that David functioned as a messianic type not only with respect to kingship but also in terms of priesthood.[779] He goes on to say that the priesthood of Christ is typified by that of David who in turn was not a priest of an Aaronic order, but of the order of Melchizedek. He concludes that the priestly role of the kings in Israel and Judah is not well documented following Solomon's early years, but that it continued and was implicitly identified as appropriate, as may be seen in one example at least, that of Uzziah (2 Chr 26:16–23).[780] In Ezek 45:25 the prophet tells how the prince will offer an abundance of sacrifices for the sins of the people. What is significant is that these offerings will not be made on the Day of Atonement, but that these sacrifices will be offered during the Passover. In other words, Ezekiel has the Davidic prince making these paschal atoning sacrifices.

Ezekiel's picture of the Messiah accords fully with other prophets who also identify the messianic figure as Davidic: Jer 23:5 speaks of raising up for David "a righteous Branch"; Amos 9:11 of restoring the fallen tent of David; Isa 9: 6–7 of a child upon the throne of David;[781] and Isa 11:1 refers to "a shoot from the slump of Jesse."

Taken together, the covenantal concept was closely linked with the exodus. In the new exodus a Davidic prince will provide paschal sacrifices. It has been said that with regard to covenant Hebrews seems to be following the pattern of

---

[778] E. H. Merrill, "Royal Priesthood: An Old Testament Messianic Motif", *BibSac* 150 (Jan–Mar, 1993), 61. Merrill points out that the burning of incense was limited to the priests, the descendants of Aaron; the high priests presupposed other kinds of priests, the royal priesthood itself.

[779] Merrill, "Royal," 57. Davidic royal priesthood occurs in 2 Sam 6 (cf. 1 Chr 15), which recounts the procession of the ark into Jerusalem from Kiriath-Jearim. The entire enterprise was at the initiative of David and though the regular Aaronic order of priests and Levites was involved, David himself was in charge, leading the entourage and, clothed in priestly attire, offering sacrifice and issuing priestly benediction. A similar exercise of priestly prerogative is evident at the inauguration of the reign of Solomon who went to Gibeon (1 Kgs 3:1–9; cf. 2 Chr 1:1–6). Though he obviously did not slay and present the enormous numbers of animals unaided, the narrative is clear in its insistence that he, the king, functioned as a priest. On this occasions Solomon presided over the cultic festivities and personally participated in them. Cf. E. H. Merrill, *Kingdom of Priests: A History of Old Testament Israel* (Grand Rapids: Baker, 1987), 238–42. R. de Vaux, *Ancient Israel*, 2 Vols. (New York: McGraw-Hill, 1961), 1:113–14.

[780] This king of Judah was unfaithful ("acted treacherously") to the Lord, and entered the temple of the Lord to burn incense on the altar of incense (v. 16, NIV). Cf. R. de Vaux, *Israel*, 1:114. According to de Vaux, while it might appear at first glance that Uzziah's sin was that of arrogating priestly privilege that is not the case at all, for the rebuke of the Aaronic priest Azariah centered on Uzziah's having overstepped the bounds of priestly ministry to which he was limited and infringed on that of the Levitical priests.

[781] G. W. Grogan, "The New Testament and the Messianism of the Book of Isaiah" *SBET* Vol. 3, no. 2 (1985), 6.

Ezekiel in pulling the sacrifices of the Day of Atonement into the orbit of Passover celebration.[782] Therefore, the Greek term διαθήκη has to be understood as reflecting redemption in the light of the Passover setting.

The Nature of the New Covenant in the Passover Setting

We have argued above that the covenant is the consequence of the Passover. Our concern here is to find the difference between the old and new covenants in their settings. In other words, in what way is the new covenant new?

Some scholars have resolved that its newness is the forgiveness of sins. "For I will be merciful to their iniquities, and I will remember their sins no more" (Heb 8:12). There is, here especially, an evident affinity with the death of Christ. Forgiveness and atonement go hand-in-hand. His "blood" (sacrificial death) establishes the new covenant (Luke 22:20). Surely here, if anywhere, we may find the heart of the distinction between the covenants. But again, the Old Testament evidence is against us. While the forgiveness of those under the Abrahamic and Mosaic covenants was in anticipation of the death of Christ, and hence in a real sense dependent on the new covenant created by Christ's death, the fact of their forgiveness is beyond doubt. Abraham was justified (Gen 15:6; Rom 4:3, 22), but that is a meaningless description without the forgiveness of sins. Though the blood of bulls and goat could not produce forgiveness (Heb 10:4), nevertheless forgiveness was the privilege of Old Testament believers.

Some dispensationalists have held that there are not one but two new covenants in Scripture, one for the Jews and the other for Gentiles.[783] This understanding, however, has mostly been abandoned in recent years because a form of Platonism actually permeates the hermeneutical roots of dispensationalism so we will not need to pursue it.[784]

---

[782] T. Holland, *Paschal*, 65.
[783] C.C. Ryrie, *The Basis of the Premillennial Faith* (New York: Loizeaux, 1953), 119–124. According to Ryrie, the new covenant for the church is alluded to in 2 Cor 3:6, Heb 8:6; 9:15; 10:29; 13:20: The new covenant for Israel is mentioned in Rom 11:27 and Heb 8:7–13; 10:16–17. See also J. D. Pentecost, *Things to Come: A Study in Biblical Eschatology* (Findlay, OH: Dunham, 1958), 124–25.
[784] Cf. "If something as monumental as a new covenant for the church— distinct from Israel's new covenant— had been instituted in the economy of God, one wonders why there is no record of its initiation, and why it is cited with no clear distinction from the new covenant of Jer 31. In Heb 8:6–13 one goes from a reference to the

Glasson notes that all the Jewish literature of the Second Temple Period includes "the national hope", but he is generally sceptical about eschatology dominating the period.[785] Sanders notes that the restoration of Israel figures prominently in Jewish literature.[786] According to him, two points characterize the theme: first the relationship between the expectation of the restoration of all Israel and the survival of a remnant and, secondly, the degree to which there was a definite expectation of the reassembly of "the twelve tribes", as distinct from more general hopes for the freedom of Jews from foreign dominion.

It is well understood that the remnant theme is linked with the theme of judgment and salvation.[787] G. F. Hasel writes on marriage of these themes in materials prior to Jeremiah, "It is a part of the emphasis on judgment and salvation. The final aim of God, however, is salvation and not doom. This is apparent from the emphasis on the survival of a remnant."[788]

The remnant theme is prominent in Amos 3:12. The remnant that is to be saved is often described as the people who are "humble and lowly". According to Mic 2:12, the remnant comprises all Israel. God will "assemble the outcasts of Israel, and gather the dispersed of Judah from the four corners of the earth," specifying the area embraced by Assyria, Ethiopia, and the Aegean coast (Isa 11:11–12). The references, according to Sanders, in Micah to "Jacob" and in Isaiah to both "Israel" and "Judah" point to the fact that all twelve tribes are in mind.[789]

---

better covenant, ascribed to the church in this view, to the covenant of Jer 31, ascribed to Israel. Therefore, the most natural reaction of the readers is to identify the two covenants as one." Cf. Robertson, *Covenants*, 213–14.

[785] T. F. Glasson, "What is Apocalyptic," *NTS* 27 (1980), 100.

[786] E. P. Sanders, *Jesus and Judaism* (Philadelphia: Fortress, 1985), 87.

[787] This is widely recognized as the overarching theme in the book of Jeremiah as may be gathered from the call of the prophet in chapter 1, "to root out, to pull down, to destroy, and throw down (judgment)" and also "to build and to plant (salvation)". See W. H. Schmidt, *Old Testament Introduction*, trans. Matthew J. O'Connell (New York: Crossroad, 1984), 237. E. Achtemeier, *Deuteronomy, Jeremiah, Proclamation Commentaries* (Philadelphia: Fortress, 1978), 73–88.

[788] G. F. Hasel, *The Remnant: The History and Theology of the Remnant Idea from Genesis to Isaiah* (Berrien Springs, MI: Andrew University Press, 1972), 458. According to Hasel, Isaiah speaks both of a remnant that is present from a past event (historical remnant) and of one that will emerge from a future action of God (eschatological remnant).

[789] Sanders, *Jesus and Judaism*, 96.

In the post-biblical literature, for remnant terminology, various terms designate the survivors as "poor" and "lowly". However, the emphasis is on reassembly, freedom from oppression and foreign dominion, punishment of the Gentiles and the like, not on the further winnowing of Israel.[790] The same tendency is seen in the liturgy of the synagogue.[791] What is striking is that in the surviving literature, no group applies either title (the remnant or the true Israel) to itself during its own historical existence.[792] The expectation that all twelve tribes will be assembled is continued in the post-70 period.

In 1QM the final war (in which all twelve tribes will be represented) is against both the Gentiles and the "wicked of the covenant" (1QM 1.2). The general thrust of the commentary on Habakkuk seems to be that the "breakers of the covenant" (1QpHab 2.6) will be destroyed. Much of the text is damaged, but the hatred of the "Wicked Priest" and the "Spouter of Lies" is so severe that it seems to require the assumption that the author or authors of the scroll looked forward to the final destruction of their Jewish enemies.[793] In light of this it is probably best to take 8:1–3 to refer to the salvation of some Jerusalemites ("those who do the Torah in the House of Judah"), who will be saved even when Jerusalem ("the House of judgment") is destroyed, because of their loyalty to the Teacher of Righteousness.

We should finally note that in the scrolls nothing is said about the Jewish Diaspora, but the scrolls maintain the motif of "the twelve". Thus we see all the more that in the first century Jewish hopes for the future would have included the restoration of the twelve tribes of Israel. Sanders points out that it is against this background that we are to understand the motif of the twelve

---

[790] The expectation of the restoration of the twelve tribes is frequent and widespread. Cf. Baruch 4:37; 5:5; Ben Sira 36:11; 48:10; 2 Macc 1:27; 2 Macc 2:18; Ps Sol. 11; 17:28–31; 17:50; T. Mos. 3:4; 4–9; 10:7; 1QM 2.2; 2.7; 3.13; 5.1; 11.13; 13.13; 11 QTemple 18.14–16.

[791] J. Heinemann, *Prayer in the Talmud* (New York: De Gruyter, 1977), 35.

[792] 1QH 6.7: "Thou wilt raise up ... a remnant". 1QM 13,8 and 14,8 are best taken as referring to the eschatological period. Even those who thought that they were the only true followers of Moses, or the only ones who knew the correct interpretation of the covenant and its laws, nevertheless did not think of God's reducing Israel to coincide with their group, but rather of the reassembly of Israel under the covenant rightly understood. See Huebsch, The Understanding and Significance of the 'Remnant' in Qumran Literature; Including a Discussion of the Use of this Concept in the Hebrew Bible, the Apocrypha and Pseudepigrapha (PhD diss., McMaster University, 1981), 250.

[793] This seems to be predicted, for example, in 10:3–5 and 10:9–13.

disciples in the Gospels.[794] Though not every text which looks forward to the vindication of Israel explicitly mentions the number twelve, it is nevertheless true that the expectation of the reassembly of Israel was so widespread, and the memory of the twelve tribes remained so acute, that "twelve" would necessarily mean "restoration".

The New Covenant Theme in the Old Testament

Isaiah

Isaiah speaks the ideal conditions of the time of the end, in which the divine plan of salvation for Israel is realized, as a ברית.[795] In order to link this with the dealings of God in the past, he uses as his guiding motif the idea of the deliverance from Egypt and of divine faithfulness, which brings to completion the work begun in olden time.[796]

In Isa 40–66, there is hope which rises quickly. From the beginning to the end the sound of joy, like the melody of victory, runs through all the chapters. Hades and terror moved backward, the people of God seem to reach the threshold of the kingdom of God, and there is good news to be preached.[797] That is new.[798] It is new exodus imagery.[799] The prophet points out that the old covenant is to be completely overshadowed by the eternal covenant of peace, which Yahweh is about to conclude with his people. After a miraculous wandering in the wilderness he will settle them in their homeland, transforming it into a paradise, and therein establish his dominion anew. It is new to Israel, a more glorious national start for the future compared to past.

This manifestation of the ברית in the last times is no isolated act of a ritual character; it does not represent a new constitution or organization. Rather, it is something embodied in the life of a human person, the servant of God, who is

---

[794] Sanders, *Jesus and Judaism*, 97–98.

[795] Isa 54:10; 55:3; 61.8.

[796] Isaiah has nothing to say about the particular covenant at Sinai, but speaks instead of the deliverance from Egypt (Isa 43:16; 51.9; 52:4), in which Yahweh formed his people for himself (Isa 42:6; 44:21, 24; 46:3).

[797] Isa 42:9; 43:19; 46:9; 48:3, 6–8.

[798] It is a view which is out of Babylon (48:14, 20–21; 52:11–12), it also means something above being out of Babylon. There is a notion that will be made straight in the wilderness and the desert will be turned into pools of water (40:3–5; 41:18; 43:16–19; 48:21; 49:10–11).

[799] J. Bright, *The Kingdom of God* (Nashville, TN: Abingdon, 1953), 171

defined as the mediator of the covenant to the new nation.[800] In him the divine will for the community is revealed as one of vicarious suffering, by which the covenant people with their messianic ruler are united in an unbreakable community and are reconciled with God.[801] Furthermore, by this gathering of the people round a king and raised to sovereignty from suffering, God's own purpose of absolute lordship receives unqualified acceptance.[802] Therefore, God needed his servant.

In 42:6 and 49:8 the servant himself is called "a covenant." If the servant is to function as a covenant, then he will guarantee those promises that effect the realization of the inheritance of God's people.[803] Indeed, it is precisely in his role as covenant-mediator that the *ebed* is to be the "light of the Gentiles" and Yahweh's law is to shine out from the newly created people of God over the whole world, bringing the nations into voluntary subjection to the divine order revealed in it.[804] The promise is to be fulfilled in him.

That is another newness which is out of Babylon.[805] It is new to Israel, and it promises a glorious national renewal and re-creation. The servant is sometimes to be identified with Israel.[806] North regards the servant as the righteous remnant of Israel.[807] Burney[808] understands that the servant was the faithful worshipper of Yahweh upon whom the hope of the nation must be centered, but they failed to see that the servant's work is connected to the restoration of those of Israel Yahweh had kept.

Morgenstern[809] argues for the royal nature of the servant from the application of the term Israel to him in Isa 49:3. It is said by him[810] that the servant is not

---

[800] Isa 42:6; 49:8.

[801] Eichrodt, *Theology*, 62.

[802] Cf. The intimations of this association of the covenant concept with the messianic hope have appeared in Ezek 34:24; 37:25.

[803] McComisky, *Covenants*, 90.

[804] Isa 42:1, 4; 49:6; 55:3–5. The last-named passage shows that, even outside the sections relating to the servant of God, the new covenant still retains its messianic character.

[805] Cf. Isa 48:14, 20–21; 52:11–12).

[806] N. W. Porteous, 'The Theology of the Old Testament,' in *Peake's Commentary on the Bible*, 157. Cf. Isa 42:18–22; 44:1–2, 21; 49:4.

[807] C. R. North, *The Suffering Servant in Deutero-Isaiah: An Historical and Critical Study* (London: Oxford University Press, 1956), 36.

[808] C. F. Burney, "The Book of Isaiah: A New Theory," *CQR* 75(1912), 99–139.

[809] J. Morgenstern, "The Suffering Servant: A New Solution," *VT* 11 (1961), 307.

the people, Israel, but is rather an individual figure, one of royal character, a king of Israel. He sees that the servant songs comprise a drama based on Greek forms.[811] It has been appreciated that the servant imagery used in Isaiah is not based on Greek forms,[812] but rather based on the Davidic leader.

In Isa 52:13–53:12 what is important is said of the servant; the suffering and the victory. The victory of the servant lies beyond suffering. Indeed, the discharge of his mission is impossible without suffering, for suffering is the means by which that mission is to be accomplished.

Then who is the servant? He is the coming Redeemer of the true Israel who through his suffering becomes the true fulfillment of Israel's mission. He is the central performer in the "new thing" that is about to take place. According to Bright,[813] he is identified with the "new Moses" in the new exodus now shortly to begin. However, Watts sees that the servant, the one truly like a Son of Man, is none other than Jesus.[814] He goes on to say that Jesus's unconventional messianic self-understanding is consistent with the misunderstood career of the servant of Isa 53 whose rejection, suffering, and death for the sin of many becomes Yahweh's equally unexpected means of effecting Israel's new exodus.[815] According to Watts, Isaiah's servant teacher would through his ministry effect Israel's new exodus.

---

[810] Ibid., 307–8. According to Morgenstern, the servant is a member of the Davidic family, a potential king of Israel, who offers himself as a sacrifice, the sacrifice regularly offered in ancient times during the course of the festival for the physical salvation of the nation, in order to guarantee the renewal of their food supply during the new year just beginning, but here the self-sacrifice is for the salvation of all mankind.

[811] Cf. The Davidic prince would build a new temple and purge the sins of the people (Isa 53; Ezek 16:62–63; 40–48; Zech 3:9; 13:1

[812] Simpson, "Vocabulary," 188.

[813] J. Bright, *Kingdom*, 151.

[814] R. E. Watts, *Isaiah's New Exodus in Mark* (Grand Rapids: Baker, 1997), 287. Watts understands that the underlying and crucial presuppositional shift that facilitates the contrast finds its impetus in the linking of the concerns of Dan 7 and Isa 53 and 43 with Israel's deliverance. Dan 7, with its Son of Man symbolism, only deals with the fact of suffering Israel's vindication and exaltation—that is, her return from exile. This does not explain how this will come about. Isa 40–55, which also deals with the return from exile, provides the explanation in chapters 43 and 53.

[815] Ibid., 287. The death of Christ in the New Testament is related to reconciliation and the opening of the way of entering into God's presence, themselves key components of the new exodus.

Jeremiah

Jeremiah[816] contrasts the new covenant with the covenant which Yahweh made with the people of Israel when he delivered them from the land of Egypt. The ratification of the old covenant is recorded in Exod 24:1–8. He refers to the old covenant in Jer 31:32, the Sinai arrangement which is the point of departure for the new covenant.[817] Here, the points conveyed are those of its foundation by divine initiative, the redemption which gave rise to it, and the relationship.[818] That is, the images of real significance are the ancient ones of marriage, of the father-son relationship and of the divine role of shepherd which flowed from it.

The new covenant in Jer 31:31–34 contributes to the terms of the promise for those who are governed by the old covenant and to the nature of obedience essential to the maintenance of their relationship to the promise.[819] The expression mentioned by the prophet is again shown in Jer 32:36–41, in verse 40 it is also called an "everlasting covenant." This covenant is without doubt the new covenant of Jer 31. The references to the fact that Yahweh would be their God (32:38) and to the renewed heart (32:39) are found in Jer 31:33 as well.

Jeremiah presents the forgiveness of sins as providing the basic substructure for the new covenant relationship in v. 34. It may be asked if elaborate provision was not made for the forgiveness of sins under the Mosaic covenant. In answer to this question, Robertson points out that the constant renewal of sacrifice for sins under the old covenant gave clear indication of the fact that sin actually was not removed, but was only passed over.[820] He did not explain the difference between the two. McComisky sees that Jeremiah did not deny that sin was forgiven under the old covenant, but that it is this blotting out of sin that is a characteristic of the new covenant.[821] It is understood, in fact, that

---

[816] W. Eichrodt, *Theology*, 59. During the first period of his activity Jeremiah makes no explicit reference to the ברית (cf. chs. 2–6). After the Josianic reform in ch. 11, however, he does accord it more significance and, while still not giving it a central position, yet uses it as one favourite method of conveying his prophetic message.

[817] G. L. Keown, P. J. Scalise, and T. G. Smothers, *Jeremiah 26–52*, Word Biblical Commentary 27 (Dallas: Word, 1995), 182.

[818] H. L. Ellison, "The Prophecy of Jeremiah," *EQ* XXXVII, No. 1 (Jan–March, 1965), 25.

[819] T. E. McComiskey, *The Covenants of Promises* (Nottingham: IVP, 1985), 81.

[820] Robertson, *Covenants*, 283.

[821] McComisky, *Covenants*, 87. The word used here for "forgive" is used throughout the Old Testament. The

the forgiveness of sins in the Old Testament was bound up with the system of institutionalized approach through sacrifice. In Jeremiah all the emphasis is on God's fresh creative activity and the position of greatest prominence is reserved for the relationship of the individual heart to God; in place of an unchanging statutory order he stresses God's redemptive work.

Furthermore, the new covenant is rooted in hope.[822] The greatest statement of hope in Jeremiah provides answers to the theological emergency of the time. Yehezkel Kaufmann refers to Jeremiah's prediction of the new covenant as "the jewel of his prophecy of consolation."[823] Therefore, Jeremiah's contrast is not simply with the Mosaic covenant, but the new covenant with the totality of God's covenantal dealings with Israel previously.[824] A "new" covenant shall replace all of God's previous covenantal dealings. The prophet contrasts the new covenant explicitly with the covenant at the exodus, but implicitly also with the Abrahamic and the Davidic covenants.

Jeremiah's new covenant prophecy includes as an integral aspect of its fulfillment the return of Israel to the land of promise after the Babylonian captivity. According to Robertson,[825] therefore, the consequent "mini-realization" of the new covenant promise inherently indicates that some typological factor must be involved in the fulfillment of new covenant prophecy. He links a new Israel of God constituted on the basis of the heart-revitalization of Jews and Gentiles through the new covenant provisions with the death and resurrection of Christ.[826]

The new covenant predicted by Jeremiah is placed in contrast with the covenant which Yahweh made with the people of Israel when he delivered

---

great difference is in the fact that God will not remember their sin. It is this blotting out of sin that is a characteristic of the new covenant.

[822] Jer 31:27–28 serves to introduce the passage that announces the new covenant; many of the people were about to be taken from their land and transported to Babylon, but Jeremiah envisioned a time of great repopulation. Even though the Lord had brought Israel to disaster, he would eventually reverse his dealings with her and restore her fortunes.

[823] Yehezkel Kaufmann, *The Religion of Israel, From Its Beginnings to the Babylonian exile,* trans. and abridged by Moshe Greenberg (Chicago, IL: University of Chicago Press, 1960), 425.

[824] Robertson, *Covenant,* 281.

[825] Ibid., 298

[826] Ibid., 299

them from the land of Egypt. Dumbrell[827] understands that the expectation of what is about to happen, particularly in the matter of the return from the Babylonian exile, is couched by Jer in 31:31–34. Here, the points conveyed are those of its foundation by divine initiative, the redemption that gave rise to it, and the relationship[828] which flowed from it. This parallelism seems to be employed to provide an analogy for the new covenant. Dumbrell,[829] therefore, says that the new arrangement will be preceded by a redemptive movement of the same character as that to which Jeremiah has so far referred, and to which the exilic prophets refer under the imagery of the new exodus. However, Dumbrell rejects any Christological understanding of the passage. According to Robertson, Jeremiah's contrast is not simply with the covenant which Yahweh made with the people of Israel at the exodus, but the new covenant with the totality of God's covenantal dealings with Israel previously.[830]

To sum up, even though Jeremiah never mentions the Day of Atonement, he emphasizes the forgiveness of sins. Furthermore, he proclaimed hope (restoration). So there is a link between the Day of Atonement and the Passover, and the forgiveness of sin and restoration. Jeremiah anticipates the day in which the actual shall replace the typical. That is, Jeremiah sees the day in which sins actually will be forgiven, never to be remembered again.[831] This parallelism seems to be employed to provide an analogy for the new covenant. Dumbrell,[832] therefore, says that the new arrangement will be preceded by a redemptive movement of the same character as that to which Jeremiah has so far referred, and to which the exilic prophets refer under the imagery of the new exodus. A "new" covenant shall replace all of God's previous covenantal dealings.

---

[827] W. J. Dumbrell, *Covenant & Creation* (Milton Keynes: Paternoster, 2013), 174.
[828] Ellison, "The Prophecy," 25.
[829] Dumbrell, *Covenant & Creation*, 177.
[830] Robertson, *Covenant*, 281.
[831] Ibid., 283.
[832] Dumbrell, Covenant & Creation, 177.

Ezekiel

Ezekiel's vision of the covenant of Israel with God involved restoration from exile.[833] He discusses God's commitment to David in terms of the essential theme of the covenant and dramatizes the relation of the covenantal formula to the Davidic covenant. As covenantal representative, according to Robertson,[834] David substitutes for the whole of the people.[835] That is, Ezekiel saw that the essence of the covenant finds its fulfillment through God's intimate relation with a Davidic prince.[836] He said that the prince would provide the sacrifices for the eschatological temple. In Ezek 45:25, therefore, the prophet tells how the prince will offer an abundance of sacrifices for the sins of the covenant community. In fact, it is pointed out by Betz[837] that in ancient Israel the king was responsible for the sanctuary. It was the king who led all major celebrations of the Passover during the monarchy (2 Chr 30:24; 35:18–19).

Dumbrell[838] has pointed out that Ezekiel's emphasis was upon Yahweh's kingship. Between the poles of judgment with which the book commenced and redemption in new creation terms with which it ends, the kingship is manifested. But kingship and covenant are correlates and we have noted that the restoration passages in Ezek 34–37 are concerned with the imposition of the new covenant,[839] and find a fitting conclusion in the new temple prophecy of Ezek 40–48. Schneiner[840] understood that Ezekiel's idea about the tabernacle

---

[833] Ezek 16:60–63; 34:25–31; 37:26–28. Ezekiel calls this covenant an everlasting covenant (16:60; 37:26).

[834] Robertson, *Covenant*, 48.

[835] Because David belongs to the Lord, all the people belong to the Lord. The essence of the covenant finds its fulfillment through God's intimate relation with the heir to the Davidic throne. According to T. E. McComiskey, *Covenant*, 89, the elements of the promise are clearly set forth in Ezekiel's new covenant. The promise of security in the land is affirmed by the prophet in 34:27; it is set in the context of covenant inverse 25. The corporate concept of the offspring is found in the reference to the people in 34:22–24. The individualistic aspect of the promise of the offspring is found in the ascription of the name *David* to the Messiah (v. 23). This ascription also calls to mind the promises given to David in 2 Sam 7. The promise that the Lord would be their God and they would be his people occurs in verses 30–31.

[836] Ezek 34:23–4; 37:24–5; cf. also the mention of the Davidic prince in 44:3; 45:7,22; 46:2,4,8 etc. who is to officiate over the messianic eschatological sacrifices.

[837] O. Betz, *What do We Know About Jesus?* (Philadelphia: Westminster, 1968), 91.

[838] Dumbrell, Covenant & Creation, 190.

[839] J. L. Mckenzie, "Royal," 45–46. McKenzie saw that Ezek 34:23–24 and 37:24–25 are clear references to a David redivivus who will once again be king over Israel.

[840] B. Schneiner, "The Corporate Meaning and Background of 1 Cor 15,45b—ἔσχατος Ἀδὰμ εἰς πνεῦμα ζῳοποιοῦν[840]," *CBQ* 29 (1967), 159. According to Schneider, Ezek 37 is read during the Passover by rabbis to refer to the final resurrection in the messianic age.

and the prince was linked with the eschatological Passover, and points out that Ezek 37 can be shown to be paschal. Holland concludes that Ezekiel has the Davidic prince making these paschal atoning sacrifices.[841]

The New Covenant in the Intertestamental Literature

The idea of covenant remained central in the period of Second Temple Judaism.[842] So the writers of the intertestamental literature were saturated in it. They used διαθήκη for ברית to indicate a covenant.[843] First and second Maccabees develop this theme of covenant.[844] 1 Macc 1:10–15 indicates that the abandonment of the holy covenant brought about a crisis for the Jews, leading to the resolution of Mattathias, which appears in 1 Macc 2:20 as follows:

"Yet I and my sons and my brothers will live by the covenant of our fathers."

When Mattathias was about to die, he told his sons, "my children, show zeal for the law, and give your lives for the covenant of our fathers."[845] In 1 Macc 4, after taking five thousand infantrymen and a thousand picked cavalry, Gorgias suddenly attacked the camp of the Jews. Then Judas, Mattathias's son, who was called Maccabeus, appeared in the plain with three thousand men, but they did not have armour and swords. Judas told his soldiers, "Do not fear their numbers or be afraid when they charge." He compared the situation to the event at the exodus in 4:9, saying that he (God) will favour us and remember his covenant with our fathers and crush this army before us today.[846]

The Damascus Rule (CD) narrates and comments on God's saving plan in history. It also gives detailed rules for the members of the new covenant in their camps in the land of Damascus. The members of the group referred to themselves in this way:

> But with the remnant which held fast to the commandments of God, He made His Covenant with Israel forever, revealing to them the hidden things in which all Israel had gone astray. He unfolded before

---

[841] Holland, *Contours*, 162.
[842] Wright, *People*, 262.
[843] J. Behm, "διαθήκη" [diatheke] in *TDNT* II, 127.
[844] Cf. 1 Macc 1:15; 2:20, 49–68; 4:8–11; 2 Maccabees 1:2–6; 7:36; 8:14–18.
[845] 1 Macc 2:49–68.
[846] 1 Macc 4:10.

them His holy Sabbaths and His glorious feasts, the testimonies of His righteousness and the ways of His truth, and the desires of His will which a man must do in order to live. And they dug a well rich in water; and he who despises it shall not live. Yet they wallowed in the sin of man and in ways of uncleanness, and they said, 'This is our (way).' But God, in His wonderful mysteries, forgave them their sin and pardoned their wickedness; and He built them a sure house in Israel whose like has never existed from former times till now. Those who hold fast to it are destined to live forever and all the glory of Adam shall be theirs. As God ordained for them by the hand of the Prophet Ezekiel, saying, The Priests, the Levites, and the sons of Zadok who kept the charge of my sanctuary when the children of Israel strayed from me, they shall offer me fat and blood (Ezek 44:15).[847]

To sum up, as Sanders points out, many scholars understand that covenantal ideas were common and ordinary at this time.[848] What is important is that covenant ideas were central to the understanding and thinking of the Jewish community in the Second Temple Period.

The New Covenant Theme in the Gospels and the Epistles

The Gospels

Matt 26:28 (Mark 14:24; Luke 22:20)
In Jesus's own discourses the word διαθήκη occurs only once,[849] in the formula, "This cup is the new διαθήκη. According to Mark, Jesus described the wine as his blood of the διαθήκη. Taylor understands out that Jesus's saying about the διαθήκη in the Synoptics came from Exod 24:8.[850] Meyer claims that it is related

---

[847] CD 3.12–4.2.

[848] E. P. Sanders, *Paul and Palestinian Judaism: A Comparison of Patterns of Religion* (London: SCM, 1977), 420; G. Vermes, *The Dead Sea Scrolls: Qumran in Perspective* (London: Collins, 1977), 169–80; J. D. G. Dunn, *The Partings of the Ways Between Christianity and Judaism and Their Significance for the Character of Christianity* (London: SCM, 1991), 21–3.

[849] Matt 26:28; Mark 14:24; Luke 22:20.

[850] V. Taylor, *Jesus and His Sacrifice: A Study of the Passion Sayings in the Gospels* (London: Macmillan, 1937), 131. M. Casey, *Aramaic Sources of Mark's Gospel*, SNTSMS 102 (Cambridge: Cambridge University Press, 1998), 242.

to Jer 31:31,[851] whereas Behm thinks that both Exod 24:8 and Jer 31:31 were assimilated into the saying. Jesus conceived of his messianic work, fulfilled in his death, from the standpoint of the fulfilment of the prophecy of an eschatological διαθήκη.[852] All the elaborations of the saying in Mark and Matthew may be understood along these lines. Thus Behm sees that διαθήκη is the mighty declaration of the sovereign will of God in history, by which he orders the relationship between himself and men according to his own saving purpose.

Evans considers that Jesus's saying about the significance of the cup and his blood presupposes a collocation of related covenant texts (Exod 24:8; Jer 31:31; Zech 9:11) as well as the Servant Song (Isa 53:12).[853] Jesus has alluded to these passages when he says "my blood of the covenant." But the adjective καινη, "new," which modifies διαθήκη "covenant" (Luke 22:20; 1 Cor 11:25), is derived from Jer 31:31, part of an oracle that anticipates the restoration of the fallen Israel.[854] According to Evans, the clause τὸ περὶ πολλῶν ἐκχυννόμενον ("which is poured out on behalf of many") in Matt 26:28 alludes to Isa 53:12, "he poured out [הערה] his soul to death, and was numbered with the transgressors; yet he bore the sin of many [רבים; LXX: πολλῶν]," a passage drawn from the exodus context in all probability by the similar language in Exod 29:12, "and the rest of the blood you shall pour out [תשפך; LXX: ενχεεις] at the base of the altar." The Aramaic paraphrase of Zech 9:11, "You also, for whom a covenant was made by blood, I have delivered from bondage to the Egyptians; I have supplied your needs in the wilderness desolate as an empty pit in which there is no water" (emphasis indicating departures from the Hebrew), which alludes to the exodus event, may explain why this collocation of scriptures was invoked at the Passover season.[855]

---

[851] B. F. Meyer, "The Expiation Motif in the Eucharistic Words: A Key to the History of Jesus?" *Gregorianum* 69 (1988), 461–87.

[852] J. Behm, "διαθήκη" [diatheke] in *TDNT* II, 133.

[853] C. A. Evans, *Mark 8.27–16:20*, 34B, Word Biblical Commentary (Nashville, TN: Thomas Nelson, 2001), 393. Evans sees that the foundational passage is Exod 24:1–8.

[854] Ibid. C. F. D. Moule, *The Gospel According to Mark*, Cambridge Bible Commentary on the New English Bible (Cambridge: Cambridge University Press, 1965), 115.

[855] See also Exod 24:11, "And they beheld God, and ate and drank," which also lends itself to a Passover setting: V. Taylor, *Jesus and His Sacrifice: A Study of the Passion Sayings in the Gospels* (London: Macmillan, 1937), 545.

In the new covenant following the new exodus motif, the name υἱοῦ Δαυὶδ υἱοῦ Ἀβραάμ ("son of David, son of Abraham") in Matt 1:1, signifies much more than simply pointing to two of the most important persons in the history of Israel who were among the ancestors of Jesus.[856] "Son of David" had become, by the first century and previous eras, a title for the messianic deliverer who would assume the throne of David in accordance with the promise of 2 Sam 7:4-17 (the Davidic covenant), thereby inaugurating a kingdom of perfection and righteousness that would last forever.[857] Jesus is that promised Son of David, and Jesus means "Yahweh is salvation" or "the Lord saves."[858] His ministry will not first be the physical liberation of Israel from its enemies but the spiritual salvation of God's people by removing the alienation from God which their sins have created.[859] Matthew's great stress on fulfillment is anticipated.[860] That is, the figure "son of David" already appeared as the key protagonist of the new covenant in Judaism.

Mark

With regard to the death of the mediator, Mark 10:45 is widely regarded as the key to the soteriology of the Gospel of Mark. Hooker rejected an Isa 53 influence on Mark 10:45 because the term λύτρον ("ransom") is not found in the Isaianic passage.[861] As pointed out earlier, the term λύτρον was related to Yahweh's redemptive activity on Israel's behalf. Hooker saw that the only place where a human life was a literal substitute for another human life was in the case of the substitution of the Levites for the firstborn following the Passover. Her examination illuminated Jesus's understanding of his mission and the

---

[856] R. A. Horsley, *The Liberation of Christmas* (New York: Crossroad, 1989), 55. One common thread involved liberation of Israel from its enemies.

[857] D. A. Hagner, *Matthew* 1-13, 33A, WBC (Dallas: Word, 1993), 9. Cf. This title is a favorite of Matthew's, occurring ten times, compared to four times each in Mark and Luke: R. H. Gundry, *Matthew: A Commentary on His Handbook for a Mixed Church under Persecution* (Grand Rapids: Eerdmans, 1994), 13.

[858] Matt 1:21.

[859] C. L. Blomberg, *Matthew*, The New American Commentary (Nashville, TN: Broadman, 1992), 59.

[860] B. M. Nolan, *The Royal Son of God: The Christology of Matthew 1-2 in the Setting of the Gospel. Orbis biblicus et Orientalis 23* (Gottingen: Vandenhoeck & Ruprecht, 1979), 224-34. The classic intertestamental illustration of the messianic Son of David appears in Pss. Sol. 17.21-18.7—a righteous warrior-king who establishes God's rule in Israel.

[861] M. D. Hooker, *Jesus and the Servant* (London: SPCK, 1959), 74; C. K. Barrett, "The Background of Mark 10:45" in *New Testament Essays: Studies in Memory of T. W. Manson* ed. A. J. B. Higgins (Manchester: Manchester University Press, 1959) 1-18; R. E. Watts, *Mark*, 278; B. Lindars, "Re-Enter the Apocalyptic Son of Man" *NTS* 22 (1975-76), 66.

meaning he projected when he used the Son of Man saying. However, Hooker failed to explore more fully the paschal link. Jesus obviously wanted the significance of his sufferings to be interpreted by the redemptive significance of the feast. As the mediator of God, he gives his life λύτρον ἀντὶ πολλῶν (Mark 10:45), and knows that God will acknowledge his mediatorship. Holland notes that the Mark 10:45 text would have been originally spoken during the Last Supper because of the parallel passage in Luke 22:27.[862] What is important is that Mark 10:45 is related to Yahweh's redemption, and has to be understood in the light of the Passover.

Luke

Behm points out that the song of Zacharias in Luke 1:72 is fully in line with the Old Testament and Judaism.[863] There the term διαθήκη is used of the promise to Abraham. Green points out that the term διαθήκη is used of the history of God's redemptive project.[864] Marshall also says that the word is used in the traditional sense of the declaration of the will of God concerning future deliverance, promise and self-commitment.[865]

The Epistles

Romans

Rom 2:25–3:2 indicates the importance of circumcision. As in Gen 17:9–14, God gave it to Abraham as a sign of the covenant between God and Abraham.[866] Thus circumcision was the single clearest distinguishing feature of the covenant people. However, Paul points out that the circumcision God looks for is not an outward visible cutting of the flesh, but the circumcision of the heart in Rom 2:28–29. In fact, Jeremiah called for it,[867] and Ezekiel promised it.[868] With this new idea Paul begins to answer the question "How is the law to be properly fulfilled?"

---

[862] Holland, *Paschal*, 149. Luke 22:27—ἐγὼ δὲ ἐν μέσῳ ὑμῶν εἰμι ὡς ὁ διακονῶν.

[863] Behm, "διαθήκη" 132.

[864] J. B. Green, *The Gospel of Luke*, NICNT (Grand Rapids, MI; Cambridge: Eerdmans, 1997), 117.

[865] I. H. Marshall, *Commentary on Luke* (Exeter: Paternoster, 1978), 92.

[866] Cf. 1 Macc 1:48, 60–61; 2:46; and 2 Macc 6:10. Jub. 15:25–34

[867] Jer 4:4.

[868] Ezek 36:6–27. Cf. Jub. 1:23.

It is widely accepted that Paul shared the Old Testament perspective that the ultimate relationship between God and his people was like a marriage relationship. Dunn points out that Rom 7:1–6 is bound up with Rom 2:28–28, by saying that "the oldness of the letter" is clearly a reference to the law.[869] The main problem in Rom 7:1–6 is to discover what the law of the husband refers to. Barrett took husband (τοῦ ἀνδρός) in apposition with law (τοῦ νόμου).[870] This seems to be unreasonably forced. Cranfield[871] and Dunn[872] point out that the phrase τοῦ νόμου τοῦ ἀνδρός ("the law of the husband") means the law which gives the husband authority over his wife. Dunn points out, furthermore, that the clause "but if the husband dies, she is free from the law"—not "free from the husband" (ἐὰν δὲ ἀποθάνῃ ὁ ἀνήρ, κατήργηται ἀπὸ τοῦ νόμου)—implies that the law belongs to sin, and that sin is the power which dominates the age of Adam.[873] Therefore, deliverance is necessary. Dunn did not link this deliverance to the exodus.

Holland premises that Paul uses the exodus as the model for deliverance in this context.[874] Then he sees that the deliverance from Egypt was from the power of Pharaoh (the husband); in the new exodus it is from the power of a former husband, which has to be sin.[875] The law of sin and death is the law of the former husband. The law of the old covenant has been broken through the death of the new husband—Christ—who died as the representative of his people. From the illustration, according to Holland, Paul worked out how Yahweh could take the church as his bride, as he had taken Israel.[876] It can happen only if man's covenant with sin can be broken, and this can only be done by death.

---

[869] Dunn, *Romans* 1–8: Dunn sees the term νόμον in Rom 7:1 (cf. 2:14) as the Jewish law, Torah. Moo supports Dunn's idea: D. Moo, *Romans* 1–8, The Wycliffe Exegetical Commentary (Chicago, IL: Moody, 1991), 436. However, Käsemann, Lagrange, and Knox point out that the reference can be to "a general principle of all law." According to Lightfoot, it indicates Roman law.

[870] C. K. Barrett, *The Epistle to the Romans* (London: Adam & Charles Black, 1957), 136. He explained: "in the analogy as a whole the husband represents the law."

[871] C. E. B. Cranfield, *A Critical and Exegetical Commentary on the Epistle to the Romans*, Vol. 1 (Edinburgh: T&T Clark, 1990), 333.

[872] Dunn, *Romans* 1–8, 359–360.

[873] Ibid. Dunn sees that the imagery of Rom 7:3 is bound up with that of Rom 6:18–22.

[874] Holland, *Contours*, 97. Holland sees being released from the law of marriage as exodus from Egypt.

[875] Ibid. Cf. Rom 6:14.

[876] Ibid., 98.

Furthermore, Rom 8 shows us that Christ's death liberates and brings the children of God out of their bondage. He challenged sin at the point where Satan's power was strongest (8:3). This fulfilled the righteous requirements of the law, for it was this event that the law and the prophets had foretold (1:2; 3:21).

Galatians

Paul introduces an illustration from ordinary human experience and compares the promise of God to Abraham with the διαθήκη of a man in Gal 3:15.[877] The many legal terms used in the passage make it clear that he is here using the word διαθήκη in the sense of the council of Jerusalem in Acts 15:7-11. This illustration from the legal sphere throws light on God's dealings in salvation history.

Longenecker believes that in Gal 3:19 Paul's answer to the question "Why the law?" is expressed in terms of five considerations.[878] In v. 20 Paul tells us what it is about mediation that reflects negatively on the law: Cullmann saw that the presence of a mediator implies a plurality that stands in contrast to the oneness of God.[879] Oepke saw that the plurality signalled in ἑνὸς οὐκ has to do with a plurality of persons. According to him, a mediator is required to act as a go-between—in this case between the angel, through whom the law was ordained, and the Jewish people.[880] Oepke's thought was challenged by some saying that angels were never thought of in Judaism as being the principal cause or originators of the Torah, even though the tradition arose as to their being an efficient cause or agents of what took place at Sinai.[881] Lightfoot understood that the plurality signalled in ἑνὸς οὐκ has to do with a duality of parties involved in a mediated arrangement, God on the one hand and the Jewish

---

[877] J. D. G. Dunn, *The Epistle to the Galatians* (London: A&C Black, 1993), 182.
[878] R. Longenecker, *Galatians* 41, WBC (Dallas: Word, 1990), 138. According to him: (1) "it was added"; (2) "because of transgressions"; (3) "until the Seed to whom the promise was given should come"; (4) "it was ordained through angels"; and (5) 'by the hand of a mediator." He then says that each feature or clause needs to be treated separately, though with an eye always to their cumulative impact.
[879] Cullmann, "Pauline Midrash" *JBL* 99(1980), 555-67; H. D. Betz, *Galatians: A Commentary on Paul's Letter to the Churches in Galatia* (Philadelphia: Fortress, 1979), 171-73.
[880] A. Oepke, "μεσίτης" [mesites] in *TDNT* IV, 619.
[881] Longenecker, *Galatians* 41, WBC, 141. Furthermore, this point of view makes Moses only a functionary of the angels, which seems hard to countenance not only for Jews but also for Christians.

people on the other.[882] Lightfoot's idea is supported by Longenecker saying that Moses acted as a mediator in the giving of the law at Sinai.[883] Lightfoot's understanding seems to keep the focus of attention on the inferiority of the law itself without deflecting attention first to either angels or Moses.

Longenecker understands ἐν χειρὶ in Gal 3:19 in terms of a mediator as a Hebraism that means simply "by means of."[884] He understands that the implied subject of the phrase is Moses.[885] Wright[886] and Witherington[887] also insist that ἐν χειρὶ is regularly used of Moses in his role as God's spokesman. However, ἐν χειρὶ μεσίτου does not lay as much stress on the role of Moses as a mediator in the biblical accounts as it does on the act of transmission itself. Hays understood mediator in Gal 3:19 to be Christ,[888] being influenced by such texts as 1 Tim 2:5 and Heb 8:6; 9:15; 12:24. If Hays's view is correct, the second part of v. 20 is a citation of the quintessential confession of all Jews,[889] the great Deuteronomic utterance of the Shema: that "God is one!" (Deut 6:4). The point Paul seems to be making in citing this confession is that "the process of divine redemption requires conformity to the oneness of God."[890] So just as ἑνὸς οὐκ in the first part of the verse drew attention to the law's indirect and contractual nature, here εἷς ἐστιν ("is one") draws attention to the fact that God's true redemptive activity is always direct and unilateral in nature. To desire the former, therefore, is to desire the inferior, whereas God wants to deal with his people directly.

---

[882] J. B. Lightfoot, *Saint Paul's Epistle to the Galatians,* 10th ed. 1890; (repr. London: Macmillan, 1986), 146–47; E. de W. Burton, A *Critical and Exegetical Commentary on the Epistle to the Galatians,* ICC (Edinburgh: T&T Clark, 1921), 191–92.

[883] Longenecker, *Galatians* 41, 143.

[884] Cf. C. F. D. Moule, *An Idiom-Book of New Testament Greek* (Cambridge: Cambridge University Press, 1959), 184.

[885] Longenecker, *Galatians* 41, 141; T. Callan, "Pauline Midrash: The Exegetical Background of Gal 3:19b." *JBL* 99(1980), 549.

[886] N. T. Wright, *The Climax of the Covenant* (Edinburgh: T&T Clark, 1991), 160; J. D. G. Dunn, *The Epistle to the Galatians* (London: A&C Black, 1993), 188–92; J. L. Martyn, *Galatians: A New Translation with Introduction and Commentary* (London: The Anchor Bible, 1997), 357.

[887] B. Witherington III, Grace in Galatia, A Commentary on St Paul's Letter to the Galatians (Edinburgh: T&T Clark, 1998), 256.

[888] R. B. Hays, *The Faith of Jesus Christ: The Narrative Substructure of Galatians 3:1–4:11* (Grand Rapids, MI: Eerdmans, 2002), 197.

[889] Ibid, 142.

[890] H. D. Betz, *Galatians,* 172–73; see also Rom 3:30 where a similar implication is drawn from God's oneness.

Corinthians

The new covenant in 1 Cor 11:25 is based on the new covenant of Jer 31:31.[891] The use of καινὴ διαθήκη in 1 Cor 11:25 occurs in Paul's account of the sayings of Jesus at the Last Supper. Paul's saying differs from that in the gospels. What is important is that Paul described the cup (i.e. its contents) as the new διαθήκη in virtue of Christ's blood.[892] The saying in the Pauline form is to the effect that the blood (or death) of Jesus establishes the new διαθηκη, and that the wine in the Lord's Supper is thus a representation of the new διαθηκη. That is, the wine of the cup signifies Jesus's blood poured out in death, which ratifies the new covenant.

Paul also follows the traditional biblical understanding in 2 Cor 3:6. The mark of the καινῆς διαθήκης is the Spirit (πνεῦμα), in contrast to the old which was characterized by the written letter (γράμματος). The passage reminds us of Jer 31:31, of which Paul now sees the fulfilment.[893] His ministry relates to the divine order of salvation, to the Gospel, and to the ordering of the relation between God and man as thus determined (i.e. to the Christian religion, not to the Law and the Jewish religion—cf. 1 Macc. 2:27 etc.).[894]

The expression the old covenant (τῆς παλαιᾶς διαθήκης) in 2 Cor 3:14 seems to be deduced from Jeremiah's διαθήκη καινὴ and from the Eucharistic tradition of the cup as ἡ καινὴ διαθήκη ratified by Christ's blood (1 Cor 11:25).[895] Paul denotes τῆς παλαιᾶς διαθήκης contracted at Sinai as "old" because he is convinced that Jesus has inaugurated the new covenant of Jer 31:31–34.[896] The designation "old" is not a pejorative evaluation of the content of the Sinai covenant, but an eschatological description of its fulfillment.

When Paul in Gal 4:24 introduces a typological exposition of the story of Hagar and Sarah, saying of these two women who both bore sons to Abraham:

---

[891] G. D. Fee, *The First Epistle to the Corinthians*, NICNT (Grand Rapids: Eerdmans, 1987), 555. Fee points out that 1 Cor 11:25 also mentions the covenant of Exod 24 as that which is being replaced. That is, the old covenant is referred to explicitly and the new implicitly.

[892] Behm, "διαθήκη" 133.

[893] S. J. Hafemann, *2 Corinthians*, The NIV Application Commentary (Grand Rapids: Zondervan, 2000), 129.

[894] Holland, *Contours*, 221. According to Holland, in 2 Cor 3:9 Paul understands that Christ has inaugurated the new covenant.

[895] M. J. Harris, *The Second Epistle to the Corinthians*, NIGTC (Milton Keynes: Paternoster, 2005), 302.

[896] Cf. Ezek 35:26–27.

αὗται γάρ εἰσιν δύο διαθῆκαι, the slave Hagar being the Sinai covenant which sets its members in a state of bondage (δουλεία) and the free woman Sarah being the heavenly covenant which sets its members in a state of freedom (ἐλευθέρα), he has in view the same διαθήκη as in 2 Cor 3, i.e. two orders in the divine history whose essential difference may be seen from the different conditions prevailing in them, Judaism which enslaves on the one hand and Christianity which brings the liberty of the sons of God on the other.[897]

The New Covenant Theme in Hebrews

As we have seen, the covenant theme was a central theme in the Scripture. The author of Hebrews uses the Old Testament covenant concept as a weapon in the battle for the superiority of Christianity over Judaism, and also as a foundation for a new theology of history. The author also contrasts the new covenant with the covenant which Yahweh made with the people of Israel when he delivered them from the land of Egypt. The former governs salvation history and manifests itself definitively in Christ who is the fulfilment of every promise. That is, with regard to deliverance the new covenant is bound up with the exodus.

I will now examine how the author of Hebrews follows the pattern of the prophets, in relation with the new covenant, in the eighth century BCE. I will also explain on what basis Jesus was the mediator of the new covenant. Finally, I will discuss how the author applies the exodus event to his readers in a collective sense.

Διαθήκη in the New Exodus Setting

In Heb 9:15–17 the writer spoke of the new covenant. It was put in force by the death of Christ because the term ברית translated into the Greek word διαθήκη is related to death, which activates a will (testament) and inaugurates a covenant. Therefore, it is essential to the realities of the Old Testament covenantal institutions.

---

[897] Gal 5:1; 4:6; Rom 8.15; 2 Cor 3:17.

In relation to the interpretation of διαθήκη, Deissmann understood it as testament,[898] as does Attridge.[899] Payne accepts that it means a "last will and testament" on the basis of his understanding of the covenant.[900] Koester says that the use of διαθήκη in Heb 9:16 is broad and inclusive, and its meaning is a will or testament, not a formal covenant like the old and new covenant.[901] Kline searches out the pattern of ancient covenant-making for the key to understanding Heb 9:6–17.[902] He turns to the provisions for dynastic succession in the ancient treaties. In this manner, he seeks a basis for justifying a "testament/covenant" play on διαθήκη in Heb 9.[903] He neglects the pledge-to-death which is at the heart of covenant inauguration, which the author to the Hebrews clearly understands to be at the heart of the covenant-making ceremony.

However, as Norton pointed out,[904] both the writer to the Hebrews and his readers were familiar with the Old Testament, and therefore with the idea of "covenant"; and a concept of διαθήκη equivalent to the ברית of the Old Testament was in existence and would have been known to the readers of this epistle.[905] Robertson comments on Heb 9 from the standpoint of a covenantal rather than a testamental position.[906] Golding adds, supporting the view that διαθήκη is equivalent to "covenant", that διαθήκη appears as a promise and dispensation of divine grace, established, confirmed and fulfilled by God, and therefore irreversible and unbreakable.[907]

Clearly the debate is not yet over; it has been pointed out that in all other passages of Scripture, διαθήκη refers to a bilateral or multi-party covenant

---

[898] A. Deissmann, *Light from the Ancient East* (New York: Hodder &Stoughton, 1927), 337–8.

[899] H. W. Attridge, *The Epistle to the Hebrews* (Philadelphia: Fortress, 1989), 255.

[900] J. B. Payne, *Theology of the Older Testament* (Grand Rapids: Eerdmans, 1962), 89.

[901] C. R. Koester, *Hebrews: A New Translation with Introduction and Commentary* (New York: The Anchor Bible, 2001), 417.

[902] M. Kline, *Treaty of the Great King* (Grand Rapids: Eerdmans, 1963), 41.

[903] Ibid.

[904] F. O. Norton, *A Lexicographical and Historical Study of DIATHEKE* (Chicago, IL: Chicago University Press, 1908), 31.

[905] B. F. Westcott, *The Epistle to the Hebrews: The Greek Text with Notes and Essays*, 3rd ed. (London; New York: Macmillan, 1903), 263

[906] O. P. Robertson, *The Christ of the Covenant* (Phillipsburg, NJ: Presbyterian and Reformed Publishing Co, 1980), 140

[907] Golding, *Covenant*, 82.

rather than a unilateral testament or will.[908] Campbell concludes that this persistent problem arises out of two fundamental and erroneous assumptions.[909] First, it is generally thought that the Hebrew concept of ברית means a "compact" or "contract" between two sides. Secondly, it is widely believed that the Greek use of διαθήκη indicates a "will" or "testament" similar to our present-day wills. Campbell goes on to say that the author of Hebrews (and his readers) was well-acquainted not only with the true Old Testament meaning of ברית, but also the contemporary Greek usage of διαθήκη, and that both the Hebrews word ברית and the Greek word διαθήκη express fundamentally the same idea.[910] Therefore, the author did not have to choose between the two different concepts, nor did he have to use one word διαθήκη to synthesize distinct or opposing ideas. Hatch points out that in classical Greek usage the word διαθήκη has at least two meanings: (1) a "disposition" of property by will, which is its most ordinary use; (2) a "covenant" which is a more rare meaning.[911] Arndt and Gingrich also take the view that the Greek διαθήκη can be used both in the testamentary and in the covenantal sense.[912] The term διαθήκη in Heb 9:16–17 was rendered "testament" or "will."[913] Therefore, some scholars favour "covenant,"[914] but the great majority argue in favour of "testament."[915]

Back to the text of Hebrews, the writer of Hebrews explains the necessity of the death of Christ for salvation in Heb 9:15. Christ is the mediator of a new covenant (διαθήκης καινῆς μεσίτης). His death signifies redemption

---

[908] An anonymous lawyer, "A Lawyer looks at Hebrews 9:15-17," *EQ*, Vol. XL (1968), 154.

[909] K. M. Campbell, "Covenant or Testament?", *EQ*, Vol. 44(1972), 107–108

[910] Ibid., 111.

[911] E. Hatch, *Essays in Biblical Greek* (London: Oxford University Press 1989), 47.

[912] W. F. Arndt and F. W. Gingrich, *A Greek-English Lexicon of the New Testament* (St. Louis: Concordia, 1957). Cf. H. S. Gehman, "The Covenant: Old Testament Foundation of the Church," *Th.T.*, 7 (1950–51), 39. Gehman sees that that in the New Testament, "testament" is synonymous with "covenant" except in Heb 9:16-17.

[913] The Authorized Version in as many as fourteen instances renders it as "testament", and other cases as "covenant". The Revised Version has greatly modified this tradition. Tyndale, ASV, NEB, Douay, and Confraternity (and also in the Dutch, German, French, and Spanish versions).

[914] The New American Standard Version goes the whole way, and translates διαθήκη in every instance as 'covenant'. Westcott, *Hebrews*, 263–70; J. J. Hughes, "Hebrews 9.15ff and Galatians 3:15ff: A Study in Covenant Practice and Procedure." *NovT* 21 (1979), 32–35; Robertson, *Covenant*, 140.

[915] Bruce, Calvin, Deissmann, Lenski, Meyer, Moffat, Robinson. Cf. H. S. Gehman, "The Covenant: Old Testament Foundation of the Church", *Th.Z.*, 7(1950/51), 39. Gehman pointed out that the general opinion is that "in the New Testament, 'testament' is synonymous with 'covenant' except in Heb 9:16–17".

(ἀπολύτρωσιν) from the transgressions (παραβάσεων) which were committed under the first διαθήκη so that Christ is the mediator of a new covenant, that those called according to the promise (ἐπαγγελίαν) may receive the eternal possession assigned to them, i.e. the promised enjoyment of eternal salvation.[916] In this verse διαθήκη is plainly a religious concept; the two different διαθήκη are the same as those referred to in Jer 31:31–34.[917] But what is the necessary connection between the death of Christ and the new διαθήκη?

Heb 9:16–22 explains the necessity for the death of Christ.[918] Lane sees that vv. 16–17 enunciates a general principle based on the procedure for the ratification of a covenant, and vv. 18–22 shows that this procedure was illustrated in the case of Sinaitic covenant mediated by Moses.[919] He points out, then, that the meaning of διαθήκη in vv. 16–17 is qualified by its meaning in v. 15, where the proper frame of reference for the interpretation of v. 15b is the death of the covenant-victim whose blood sealed and ratified the covenant.[920] He concludes that the writer has employed διαθήκη in a consistent way in 9:15–18 to mean "covenant."[921] However, Lane understands the death of Christ in the light of the Day of Atonement. Pursiful also sees διαθήκη as "covenant" in Heb 9:15–17, and asks the result of the death of the one who made διαθήκη in Heb 9:16.[922] He claims that in the ancient world covenants were made with a sacrifice that might be understood to represent the death of some party to the transaction.[923] He also thinks that the imagery of the Day of Atonement ritual is a primary paradigm in this context.

Vos generally understands διαθήκη as covenant.[924] He saw that the author meant a sovereign disposal of God by using the word διαθήκη in Heb 8.[925]

---

[916] J. J, Hughes, "Hebrews 9.15ff and Galatians 3:15ff: A Study in Covenant Practice and Procedure." *NovT* 21 (1979), 38, 47–49.

[917] Lane, *Hebrews 9–13*, 241.

[918] This block of exposition is tied to the preceding verse by the explanatory γαρ, "for" in v. 16 and by the inferential particle ὅθεν "this is why," in v. 18.

[919] Lane, *Hebrews 9–13*, 242.

[920] Ibid.

[921] Ibid. Lane also indicted that both διαθήκη and θανάτου in v. 15 are reiterated in vv. 16–17, which strongly suggests that διαθήκη continues to be used uniformly to mean "covenant".

[922] D. J. Pursiful, *The Cultic Motif in the Spirituality of the Book of Hebrews* (Lampeter: Mellen Biblical Press, 1993), 78.

[923] Cf. A. Nairne, *Epistle of Priesthood* (Edinburgh: Clark, 1913), 365; Johnsson, "Defilement and Purgation," 314.

[924] Vos, *Hebrews*, 29. Cf. Vos saw διαθήκη in Heb 9:16–17 as testament. He understood that verse 16 and 17 form

According to Vos, the διαθήκη is a means to bring on perfection, not moral perfection, but the perfection of consummation, of bringing a person to his goal, to the ideal state. However, Vos did not link the concept of covenant to the Passover, thus he failed to appreciate that the perfection of consummation was redemption in Christ. Interpreting Heb 8:8–12, Bruce saw the new covenant foretold by Jeremiah in contrast with the covenant which Yahweh made with the people of Israel when he delivered them from the land of Egypt.[926]

Furthermore, Bruce linked Jesus's saying[927] in the Last Supper (Mark 14:12–26) to Heb 8:8–12. The paschal context of the incident would have made his disciples link his words with "the blood of the covenant" which God established with his people Israel in the days of Moses on the basis of the Ten Commandments (Exod 24:8).[928] He saw Moses as a type of the eschatological savior, Jesus. What is important in the new διαθήκη is that the term has to be interpreted as "covenant" in the setting of the Passover.

Dunhill sees the shape of the rite in Heb 9:15–22 to be drawn from the Sinaitic rite in Exod 24:3–8.[929] The shape of the rite seems to have followed that of the Day of Atonement. Dunhill points out that the writer turns to a different source, the Passover in Heb 11:28, for a more positive model of a covenant-rite. He sees that this first Passover must be distinguished from every act of repetition.[930] The Septuagint translated the term πεποίηκεν in Heb 11:28 as

---

a sort of parenthetical expression.

[925] The author represents God as the enacting Person: Heb 8:6, "a better covenant, which hath been legislatively enacted (νενομοθέτηται "laid down as law") upon better promises." In 8:8 the writer uses συντελέσω; in 8:9 and 9:20 ἐπ.

[926] Bruce, *Hebrews*, 170. According to Bruce, the ratification of that earlier covenant is recorded in Exod 24:1–8, a passage to which specific reference is made in Heb 9:18–20.

[927] Cf. Mark 14:24. "This is my blood of the covenant, shed for many" Matt 26:28 adds "unto remission of sins". Neither Matthew nor Mark (according to the most probable reading) records the adjective "new" before "covenant" in this word of institution, as is done by Paul (1 Cor 11.25) and the longer text of Luke (Luke 22:20); but the new covenant is intended, whether "new" is expressed or only implied. The phrase "for many" may echo Isa 53:1 (cf. the phrase "a covenant of the people" in association with the first and second Servant Songs, Isa 42:6; 49:8): J. Jeremias, *The Eucharistic Words of Jesus*, trans N. Perrin (New York: Charles Scribner's Sons, 1955), 151.

[928] Bruce, *Hebrews*, 178.

[929] The laws are read, the blood is brought into contact with symbols of God and the people. The slaughtered beasts would be permissible for burnt-offerings and peace-offerings such as Moses offered.

[930] J. Dunnill, *Covenant and Sacrifice in the Letter to the Hebrews* (Cambridge: Cambridge University Press,

"keep" rather than "institute." Buchanan translated it as "instituted."[931] Westcott chose "kept" but added: "The Passover then instituted and kept remained as a perpetual witness of the great deliverance."[932] Dunhill continues to say that the term "the sprinkling" πρόσχυσιν in 11:28 is related to the Passover.[933] He concludes that the writer is interchanging expiatory and covenantal motifs, and treating the Passover as an annual reenactment of a foundational covenant-sacrifice. Passover was used in the intertestamental and Christian periods,[934] and it is probable that there was at least an element of covenant-renewal in the composite New Year feast in Solomon's Temple. Dunhill argued that the Day of Atonement attracted to itself description as "the Day" in which the covenant of salvation based on the Passover is complete. It points not only backward to creation, for there were then no sins to need atoning, but forward to the final redemption in the new age.

Casey considers that the Passover was the most emphasized sacrificial concept relating to the death of Christ.[935] In Heb 9:11–13 the writer shows how Christ fulfills all the sacrificial requirement of the Mosaic covenant. Verse 14 tells us how the blood of Christ will purify our hearts from deeds that lead to death in harmony with the principles of the old covenant. The concept of redemption in v. 15 is thus absorbed into the writer's sacrificial categories. The statement in v. 16 is clarified and amplified in v. 17. These general considerations explain why Christ had to die in order to become the priestly mediator of a new covenant. The ratification of a covenant required the presentation of sacrificial blood (cf. v. 18). Such blood is obtained only as his sacrificial death ratified or "made legally valid" the new covenant promised in Jer 31:31–34. Because he

---

1992), 128.

[931] Buchanan, *Hebrews*, 198.

[932] B. F. Westcott, *Hebrews*, 177.

[933] Most translations (including RSV, NEB, JB) render πρόσχυσιν inadequately as "sprinkling". The noun does not appear in the Septuagint, but the verb is normally used to denote the act of throwing blood against the altar, proper to holocaust and peace-offering (Exod 24:6, 29:16, Lev 1:5, 3:2). Cf. H. Danby, *The Mishnah* (Oxford: Oxford University Press, 1933), 142, 468. According to Danby, it is notable that in the Mishnah, whereas the act of sprinkling, with its expiatory overtones, had been introduced into the rites for whole-offerings and peace-offerings (Mish. Zeb. 5.4), the blood in the Passover rite was to be tossed against the altar (Mish. Pes. 5.6) in a manner more reminiscent of the peace-offering or the unique covenant-sacrifice (Exod 24) than of the sin-offerings.

[934] R. J. Daly, *The Origins of the Christian Doctrine of Sacrifice* (London: SCM, 1978), 38.

[935] Casey, "Christologies," 272.

died a representative death (see on v. 15b), those whom he represents may receive the blessings mediated through the new covenant. These ideas are deeply embedded in Old Testament covenant practice, where the prerequisite for blessing and the reception of a promised inheritance was obedience displayed in an unbroken relationship with the Lord.

Where, then, is the heart of the new covenant? In what way is the new covenant new? The promise of this eternal inheritance in Heb 9:15 is that of the new covenant cited in Heb 8:8–12.[936] God would form a people, a new nation, under the new covenant, who would not break it, because all of them without exception would know the Lord. The people of the Mosaic covenant were not the kind of people who would keep the covenant, so the Lord could have done one of two things: either change the people or change the covenant. In the event, he chose to do both. He formed a new people and gave them a covenant in keeping with the people he had formed and the period of redemptive history in which he had formed them. The new people are the church of Jesus Christ.

The Term "μεσίτης" in the New Covenant

The writer to Hebrews relates the concept of covenant to the function of the mediator of Christ. The new covenant (διαθήκη) required a new mediator (μεσίτης). Characteristic of all these passages (Heb 8:6; 9:15; 12:24; cf. 7:22) is the linking of μεσίτης with διαθήκη. Two concepts naturally suggesting themselves as determining the meaning of the word διαθήκη are μεσίτης and ἔγγυος.[937]

In fact, the term "mediator" related to the new covenant was used in its theological sense in Judaism. The Old Testament introduces human mediators. Most weakly developed was the religious significance of the king.[938] The king was sometimes called the son of Yahweh (2 Sam 7:14; Ps 2:7), but not in a metaphysical sense. Royal mediation finds central significance only in the future figure of the ideal anointed, the Messiah. The true uniqueness of Old Testament religion as compared with paganism is to be seen in the mediatorial

---

[936] Koester, *Hebrews*, 417.
[937] μεσίτης means mediator and ἔγγυος means one who guarantees.
[938] C. Graham, "The Mediator of the Covenant," *RTJ*, Vol. 11 (1995), 28.

position of the priest and the prophet. Oepke sees that the *munus* triplex becomes progressively the vessel which gradually fits the New Testament concept of the mediator in the course of the development of salvation.[939] He proposes that there are two figures that are related to the *munus* triplex; at the beginning of the history of Israel's religion was Moses,[940] and the other great Old Testament figure was the *Ebed Yahweh* of Isaiah.[941]

Its use in Philo and Paul shows that this development of the mediator concept had already taken place by the 1st century CE. Oepke argues that since the Rabbis have the loan Hebrew word מיסון for the Greek word μεσον, but use a Hebrew term for μεσίτης, Palestinian usage is the starting-point.[942] He reasons that though rabbinic sources are later, it is as well to begin with Rabbinic Judaism. Here, in correspondence with the meaning of סרסור, the sense of "broker," "negotiator," "interpreter," is basic,[943] and the term is used exclusively for Moses as the commissioned agent of God.[944]

Rabbinic Judaism at first shows little understanding of the magnificent and profound development of the mediator concept in the figure of the suffering servant. This is surprising, since from Sir 48:10 it may be deduced, though not conclusively, that the Servant Songs were construed messianically even in the pre-Christian period. The lack of emphasis is very typical in the Targum on Isa 52:13–53:12. Here the *Ebed Yahweh* of the songs is taken to be the Messiah. But no place is found for vicarious suffering within the messianic concept. Instead, the text is consistently reinterpreted in terms of the exaltation of Israel and the overcoming of the nations by force. The vicarious action is reduced to messianic intercession. In the Targum paraphrase the decisive verses run as follows:

---

[939] A. Oepke, "μεσίτης" [mesites] in *TDNT* IV, 611. Graham, "Mediator," 34, According to Graham, the prophet must proclaim what the priest has ascertained and the king must defend the liberty which the prophet announces.
[940] Exod 19:3, 9, 21; 20:18; 34:1, 29; 35:1, 4; Lev 1:1; 4:1; 5:14; 6:1; 11:1; Num 17:10, 27; 21:7; Deut 5:24; 18.16
[941] Isa 42:1–4; 49:1–6; 50:4–9; 52:13–53:12.
[942] Oepke, "μεσίτης", 615.
[943] Cf. Dt.r. 3, 12 on 10.1 (Str.-B., III, 512); Exod r., 3 on 3:13 (Str.-B., III, 556).
[944] The Israelites could not look on the face of Moses because of their sin with the calf. (Str.-B., III, 515, cf. 31). As the Torah was given by the hand of a mediator, so it may be passed on only by an interpreter distinct from the reader (Str.-B., III, 556). Thus the mediator concept is focused in the main on Moses.

3. Hence the glory of all kingdoms will be turned to contempt and disappear; they will be weak and poor. Lo, like a man of sorrows appointed for sickness, and as when the face of the shekinah is turned from us, they will be despised and not accounted. 4. Therefore will he pray for our guilt, and for his sake he will forgive our transgression, while we are reckoned as those who are crushed, rooted out before Yahweh and humbled. 5. And he will build the temple which is desecrated because of our iniquity and abandoned because of our transgression, and through his teaching there will be great peace for us, and when we gather around his words, our sins will be forgiven us ... 7. When he prays he is answered, before he opens his mouth he receives. The strong of the nations he will hand over like a lamb to the slaughter, and like a sheep dumb before the shearer, and before him there is none that opens his mouth or speaks a word ... 10. And before Yahweh it was his good-pleasure to purge and cleanse the remnant of his people, to purify their soul from sin; they will see the kingdom of their Messiah. Their sons and daughters will be many, they will have a long life and if they serve the Torah of Yahweh in his good-pleasure, they will find happiness.

This complete misunderstanding is the more surprising because the idea of vicarious suffering was by no means alien to Judaism,[945] and traditions about a suffering and dying Messiah may certainly be traced back to the 2nd century CE. However, it was very difficult for Judaism to link this with Isa 53.[946]

Apart from the further development in wisdom teaching,[947] the doctrine of divine intermediaries is carried further in Judaism only in so far as the transcendent apocalyptic Messiah developed out of Dan 7:13 and ultimately out of the myth of the primal man.

In the text of Hebrews, Christ is described as the mediator of the new covenant.[948] Therefore, it has been asked on what basis Jesus was the mediator of new covenant? A reference to "the better covenant" in 8:6 precedes the full

---

[945] cf. 4 Macc. 6:28; 17:22.
[946] The Targum may even be polemicizing against the idea of a suffering Messiah.
[947] Sir 24:3; Bar 3:9; Eth. En. 42:1; 91:10 etc.
[948] Heb 8:6; 9:15; 12:24; cf. 7:22

citation of Jer 31:31–34 in 8:8–12. Concerning the covenant mediated by Moses on Mount Sinai (cf. 8:4–6; 9:15–22), the covenant of which Jesus is "mediator"[949] and "surety"[950] is said to be "better" because "'it is enacted on better promises'" (8:6). That is, by his life of perfect obedience and his death, Jesus inaugurated the new covenant of Jer 31:31–34. The writer of Hebrews stresses the imperfect and provisional character of the old covenant in introductory and concluding comments.[951]

Then, what God promised to do with the coming of Christ as mediator was the new covenant. Heb 8:6 teaches us that better promises build a better covenant relationship between us and God and this relationship is what Christ obtains and takes care of as Mediator.

Heb 9:1–10 tells us that the ritual law in the first covenant pointed to the final perfection, and in it there was the Christ event. Some scholars see that the following paragraph describes worship of God in the light of the Day of Atonement.[952] Christ as a mediator entered the Most Holy place by means of his blood which secured salvation (9:11–15). In Heb 9:15 the author proclaimed Christ to be the mediator of the new covenant. He was both a paschal lamb and high priest. Here is a problem! The paschal lamb was offered during the Passover. Holland pointed out that God's eschatological salvation was to be performed not through the Day of Atonement, but through Passover.[953] Therefore, this chapter has to be interpreted in the light of the eschatological temple setting provided in Ezekiel.

In Heb 9:15–20, furthermore, the author explains how Christ is the mediator of the new covenant. He begins with the phrase διὰ τοῦτο ("because of this") which signals to the readers that he is about to draw a conclusion based on his discussion of Christ as sacrifice (9:11–14). It is for this reason, the author says,

---

[949] Heb 8:6; 9:15; 12:24: μεσίτης.

[950] Heb 7:22: ἔγγυος.

[951] Also the contrasts of 8:1-6 have already indicated the basis on which the imperfection of the old covenant is to be understood

[952] P. J. Achtemeier, J. B. Green, and M. M. Thompson, *Introducing the New Testament: Its Literature and Theology* (Cambridge: Eerdmans, 2001), 485. According to them, most of the features of Jesus's priesthood are drawn from the functions of the high priest as one who intercedes on behalf of the people for forgiveness of sins before God, and particularly so on the annual Day of Atonement.

[953] Holland, *Contours,* 98.

that Christ is the mediator (μεσίτης) of a new covenant. He adds that the reason that Christ became the mediator of a new covenant (see 8:6) was that ὅπως ("since") a death has taken place (θανάτου γενομένου), he would become the means of redemption for those who transgressed under the first covenant (τῇ πρώτῃ διαθήκῃ). The phrase "for redemption" (εἰς ἀπολύτρωσιν) signifies the purpose of Christ's death. Taken together, Christ became the mediator of a new covenant "since a death has taken place," and "for the purpose of redemption."

Furthermore, the phrase "redemption from the transgressions" (εἰς ἀπολύτρωσιν τῶν ἐπὶ ... παραβάσεων) is a genitive of separation. Christ's death brings about the forgiveness included as part of the promise of the new covenant, for in the original context in Jeremiah, the means by which forgiveness becomes an eschatological possibility is never stated.[954] God's eschatological salvation was to be performed not through the Day of Atonement, but through Passover.

All of the realities that the writer of Hebrews identifies are surrounded in the Jerusalem where Christians have drawn near in intimate union "to Jesus, the mediator of a new covenant" (Heb 12:24). In eschatological fulfillment of the prophecies of old (Jer 31:31–34; Ezek 37:26, 27), Jesus came as "the mediator of a new covenant" (8:6; 9:15).

The "blood of the covenant" was sprinkled on the people at the inauguration of the old covenant (Exod 24:8), but the blood of animals had only a temporal effect for the people of God (Heb 9:11–22).[955] In Heb 12:24 the author reminds the readers that they have drawn near "to the sprinkled blood, speaking better things than that of Abel." The "sprinkled blood" is a euphemism for the redemptive efficacy of the sacrificial death of Jesus Christ on the cross at Mount Zion. No Hebrew believer would have missed the connection of the sprinkling of blood as the seal of the old covenant, and how the death of Jesus by crucifixion was the establishment and seal of the new covenant. The Hebraic terminology of the believer being "sprinkled with his blood"[956] was

---

[954] Lane, *Hebrews* 9–13, 241.

[955] The author emphasizes again to the Christians in Jerusalem that Jesus "through His own blood" (9:12), "offered Himself without blemish" (9:14), as "the mediator of a new covenant" (9:15), and "the blood of the covenant" (10.29) has "sprinkled our hearts clean" (10.22).

[956] Cf. 1 Pet 1.2

recognized as the redemptive action of forgiveness whereby people could draw near to the presence of God "by the blood of Jesus" (10:19).[957]

The purpose for which Jesus is mediator of a new covenant is in order that "those who are called to an eternal inheritance" (οἱ κεκλημένοι τῆς αἰωνίου κληρονομίας) may receive the promise in Heb 9:15. The term "eternal inheritance" is a reference to eternal salvation. The fact that the term "inheritance" may be an allusion to the promised land ("rest") which the generation of the exodus was to inherit and, according to the author, was an antitype of eternal salvation, the "rest" that remains open to enter (Heb 3–4). These beneficiaries are also said to receive the promise, so that the promise is that of eternal salvation. We also may see 4:1 and 6:17 for previous references to the receiving of the promise of eternal salvation. Thus, "eternal inheritance" stands in apposition to "promise" in the new covenant.

Corporate Concept in the New Covenant

This manifestation of the ברית in the last times is no isolated act of a ritual character, nor new constitution or organization, but something embodied in the life of a human person, the servant of God, who is defined as the mediator of the covenant of the new nation.[958]

The vocative ἀδελφοί in Heb 3:1, 12; 10:19; 13:22 implies that the readers belong to the same household and it signifies their corporate solidarity.[959] The author applies the exodus story to his readers in a collective sense and his exposition of the exodus events is focused in the first instance entirely upon the collective people of God. He addresses the community as if they were Israelites, the covenanted and holy people of God. Thus Heb 3 entails the author's fundamental idea of the church being the new covenant community of God's people and is the true eschatological Israel in continuation of Israel in the OT, and reflects his corporate concern in warning the readers. This corporate concern is evident in the author's references to "holy."

---

[957] Christians remember this time they partake of the Lord's Supper and hear Jesus's words, "this cup is the new covenant in my blood" (Matt 26:28; Luke 22:20; 1 Cor 11:25).
[958] Eichrodt, *Theology*, 61–2. cf. Isa 42:6; 49:8.
[959] Hughes, *Hebrews*, 125.

The author identifies the addressees as those people who are called ἀδελφοὶ ἅγιοι, κλήσεως ἐπουρανίου μέτοχοι in Heb 3:1 (having been called οἱ κεκλημένοι in Heb 9:15). The word "calling" (κλήσεως) is probably related to God's calling of Israel as a holy people in the Old Testament (cf. Isa 41:9; 42:6; 43:1; 45:3; 48:12).[960] Ridderbos says that this designation has "to be understood with reference to the historical calling of Israel."[961] But it would seem that the author obviously replaces the condition of earthly life with a new community identity in the kingdom of God.[962] By employing κλήσεως the author again stresses the corporate identity of his readers as the true people of God in succession to Israel. That the author employs the term ἅγιοι in referring to the addressees is more striking. The term, as noted above, is another Old Testament term which is identified with Israel, the holy people of God having been separated from the ungodly world.

The term "those who are being made holy" τοὺς ἁγιαζομένους in Heb 10:14 (οἱ ἁγιαζόμενοι in Heb 2:11, ἡγιασμένοι in Heb 10:10) is derived from the verb ἁγιάζειν, and the adjective ἁγίοις which comes from the root ἅγιος. The terms echo the Old Testament concept where Israel, God's elect people, is called a "holy people" whom God has chosen out of all the peoples of the world (cf. Exod 19:6; Lev 11:44, 45; Deut 7:6–8 etc.).[963] The holiness of God's people, as stated in Deut 7:6–8, is closely connected to God's election according to his sovereign will. Since God has chosen them as a holy people, holiness is not one of the personal ethical virtues, but a corporate status in which they are placed by God's election.[964] In employing words related to ἅγιος here, the author seems to lay emphasis on this corporate status of his readers.

The author identifies his hearers as those people who have been sanctified through the sacrifice of the body of Jesus Christ. They have been set apart from

---

[960] H. Ridderbos, *Paul: An Outline of His Theology*, trans. J. R. de Witt (Grand Rapids: Eerdmans, 1975), 332–3; W. A. Meeks, *The First Urban Christians: The Social World of the Apostle Paul* (New Haven: Yale University Press, 1983), 85.

[961] Ridderbos, *Paul*, 332.

[962] Bruce, *Hebrews*, 55.

[963] C. K. Barrett, *The First Epistle to the Corinthians*, BNTC, 2nd ed. (London: A&C Black, 1971), 32; G. D. Fee, *The First Epistle to the Corinthians*, NICNT (Grand Rapids: Eerdmans, 1987), 33. As seen in Dan 7:18–25, the concept of the holy people developed in later Judaism. Cf. Ps Sol. 17:28; 1 Enoch 43:4.

[964] H. Conzelmann, *1 Corinthians*, trans. J. W. Lieth, Hermeneia (Philadelphia: Fortress 1975), 22–3. Barrett, *1 Corinthians*, 32–3.

the world for God through Christ Jesus. The author significantly uses the word ἡγιασμένοι in Heb 10:10, the perfect passive participle of the verb ἁγιάζειν. When compared with 10:14 ἁγιαζομένους where the present passive participle of the same verb is used, the perfect participle here may bring into focus specifically the present state of the readers, whereas the present indicates "a timeless designation of the community of faith, it describes the result of Christ's sacrifice, which confers on his people definitive consecration, qualifying them for fellowship with God."[965] Without doubt, the term ἡγιασμένοι proves that the author calls attention to the reader's corporate state of being holy people who have been consecrated to God.[966]

His emphasis on corporate identity is more clearly observed in the perfect tense of the verb τετελείωκεν in Heb 10:14. This word, in combination with the expression εἰς τὸ διηνεκὲς emphasizes the permanent result of Christ's offering. The writer locates the decisive purging of believers in the past with respect to its accomplishment and in the present with respect to its enjoyment. The means by which the community has experienced definitive purging is the sacrificial death of Christ. A decisive purging was the prerequisite of the consecration of the people of the new covenant. It is proper, according to Lane, to interpret the expression τετελείωκεν in the light of the description of the community as "the consecrated ones."[967]

In short, the author's additional expressions ἡγιασμένοι and ἁγιαζομένους over and over again demonstrate the corporate identity of the readers as the true people of God in continuation with Israel in the Old Testament. As Meeks says, "repetitive use of such special terms for the group and its members plays a role in the process of resocialization by which an individual's identity is revised and knit together with the identity of the group."[968] With such special terms ἅγιοι (ἁγιάζειν) and κλήσεως the author clearly emphasizes the corporate identity of the readers as the new people of God in Jesus Christ. Both expressions therefore can be readily read in the context of the author's corporate concern which calls attention to the corporate identity of the readers

---

[965] Lane, *Hebrews* 47B, 268.
[966] Bruce, *Hebrews*, 241.
[967] Lane, *Hebrews* 47B, 267.
[968] Meeks, *Christian*, 86. Cf. Ridderbos, *Paul*, 330–41.

as the holy people of God, that is, those called to be holy by God through the offering of the body of Jesus Christ.

Elsewhere in the New Testament the church is seen to have a, "holy calling" (2 Tim 1:9) and an "upward calling" (Phil 3:14).[969] The church is the community of those whom God has called (Rom 9:15; Eph 4:4; Col 3:15, etc.). It is normally used as an equivalent term to ἐκκλησια in the epistolary openings of Pauline letters.[970] It is also used of believers in terms of universal fellowship, especially in the epistolary closing of the letters[971] and in statements about the collection for the church at Jerusalem.[972] Paul sometimes uses it in the context of the corporate identity of believers in contrast to outsiders.[973] More than that, its usage in Pauline letters suggests that the word ἅγιοι was a special term, which denotes Christians to be a holy people particularly chosen by God from the world, in early Christianity.[974] Paul repeatedly emphasizes the corporate identity of his readers as the people of God.

Conclusion

The covenant theme was a central theme in the Old Testament. The Greek term διαθήκη translates the Hebrew term ברית meaning "covenant." The covenant which Yahweh made with the people of Israel when he delivered them from the land of Egypt is set in contrast to the new covenant of which Jesus speaks. If there is serious correspondence between type and antitype, then the new covenant has to be understood in the light of the Passover/exodus setting.

The new covenant of which Jesus acted as a mediator concerns the promise of the coming kingdom of God. Jesus will give his own blood to effect the covenant, the restoration of Israel, and the kingdom of God. It is the same new covenant as promised by the prophets in the eighth century BCE.

---

[969] Cf. also Rom 1:7; 8:28, 30; 1 Pet 1:15, etc.
[970] Rom 1:7; 1 Cor 1:2; 2 Cor 1:1; Eph 1:1; Phil 1:1; Col 1:2.
[971] Rom 16:15; 2 Cor 13:12; Phil 4:21 (Cf. Rom 16:2; Eph 1:15; 6:18; Phlm 1:5, 7).
[972] Rom 15:25; 1 Cor 16:1, 15; 2 Cor 8:4; 9:1, 12.
[973] 1 Cor 6:1 (cf. Eph 5:3; Col 3:12).
[974] Cf. Acts 9:13; Heb 3:1; 6:10; 1 Pet 1.15; Jude 3; Rev 11:18; 18.20.

The author of Hebrews tells his hearers that they have been sanctified through the sacrifice of the body of Jesus Christ. They have been set apart from the world for God through Christ Jesus. Thus, the term ἅγιοι because in the Old Testament it relates to the community rather than the individual, indicates that the author calls attention to the reader's corporate state of being holy people who have been consecrated to God. Therefore, this letter has to be understood in the light of this corporate perspective.

Excursus: The Term "Perfection" (τελείωσις) in the Paschal Setting

The term perfection (τελείωσις) and its cognates occur fourteen times in the Epistle to the Hebrews.[975] We need to ask what the term and its cognates mean in each context for the background of the epistle and understanding of the goal of the epistle.[976] Delling has argued that the primary influence upon the writer's use of the vocabulary of "perfection" is the LXX, which employs the word τελείωσις with a broad range of meanings found in extrabiblical Greek.[977] He points out that the cultic associations of the noun in Heb 7:11 are related to the use of the cognate verb τελειόω in Heb 7:19.

Käsemann considered perfection in Hebrews to be synonymous with "glorification" or "entrance into the heavenly sphere."[978] He understood the term in the light of the gnostic myth of the "redeemed Redeemer". Käsemann's dependence on the gnostic myth of the heavenly man leads him to conclude that obedience and perfecting are two contrasting stages in the journey of Christ, from heaven to earth and back to heaven again.[979] Similarly, Dey

---

[975] The term appears as the verb 9 times (Heb 2:10; 5:9; 7:19, 28; 9:9; 10:1, 14; 11:40; 12: 23), as the noun 3 times (τελείωσις 7:11; τελειωτις 12:2; τελειότητα 6:1), and as the adjective twice (τελείων 5:14; 9:11).

[976] This term is confirmed by even an examination of the contexts where the words are located: Saints in Christ are perfected (10:14; 11:40; 12:23), for only the divine arrangement mediated by Christ, who is the perfecter of our faith (12:2), may be called perfect (7:11, 19; cf. 9:11), and consequently only his blood can perfect the conscience (9:9; 10:1,14); further, the author calls Christians to perfection (5:14, 6:1), and even Jesus, we are told, experienced perfection through his sufferings (2:10, 5:9, 7:28).

[977] G. Delling, "τέλειος, τελείωσις, τελειώτης, τελειότης" in *TDNT* VIII, 67-87.

[978] E. Käsemann, *The Wandering People of God: An Investigation of the Letter to the Hebrews*, trans. R. A. Harrisville and I. L. Sandberg (Minneapolis: Augsburg, 1984), 91-2.

[979] Ibid. Käsemann sees the perfecting of believers to be associated with transfer to the heavenly assembly in 11:40 and 12:23 and to be understood in similar terms at 7:11 and 7:19. However, 9:9; 10:1 and 10:14 connect the perfecting of believers with the concepts of purification and sanctification accomplished by Christ in his sacrifice (p. 88). Only Christ is "perfecter" (12:1), but believers are perfected by their attachment to him (10:14) and as such may be called τελείων (5:14).

understands perfection in Hebrews in the light of Philo.[980] He points out that "perfection" in Hebrews is to belong to "the other world" as opposed to "the world". It exceeds the phenomenal world to come to God directly and is to participate in the ideal world.[981]

In contrast, Bruce defines perfection as "unimpeded access to God and unbroken communion with Him."[982] According to him, Christ made the way of perfection through his suffering, and the perfect Son of God has become his people's perfection, opening up their way to God, thinking of the Day of Atonement.[983] Delling also understands that "perfection" consists in being able to "draw near to God."[984] According to Lane, however, the meaning of the verb τελειῶσαι in Heb 10:1 is equivalent to the meaning of the phrase τελειῶσαι τὸν λατρεύοντα ("decisively to purge the worshiper") in Heb 9:9.[985] In Heb 10, furthermore, the author of Hebrews points out that the sacrifices prescribed by the law in the old covenant could not make perfect those who draw near to worship.[986] What they try to say is that the old Levitical system could not enable the worshiper to approach God because its sacrifices were impotent to cleanse him from sin.

What is important is that the fulfillment of the promises of the new covenant, through the mediatorship of Christ, makes access to God possible in terms of a relationship with God which was not possible under the former covenant. Therefore, the concept of τελείωσις is an eschatological reality. The fulfillment of the promises of the new covenant involves perfection for Christ as a mediator, the perfection of his redemptive ministry, and for the perfect, complete and entire redemption of the saints.

However, some scholars believe that Judaism in the New Testament period taught that unimpeded access to God was provided under the old covenant. In

---

[980] L. K. K. Dey, *The Intermediary World and Patterns of Perfection in Philo and Hebrews*, S. B. L. Dissertation Series 25 (Missoula, MT: Scholars Press, 1975),

[981] Dey, *World*, 215.

[982] Bruce, *Hebrews*, 43-4.

[983] Ibid.

[984] Delling, "ἀργός, ἀργέω, καταργέω", 67–73.

[985] Lane, *Hebrews 9–13*, 255. Heb 9:9 can be also translated in the light of the Day of Atonement setting.

[986] M. Silva, "Perfection and Eschatology in Hebrews," *WTJ* 39 (1976), 68; G. L. Cockerill, *The Melchizedek Christology in Heb 7:1-28* (Ann Arbor: University Microfilms International, 1979), 85-87. This imperfection was underscored by the declaration in Ps 110:4 of a need for a different kind of priest.

other words, salvation was achieved through keeping the law. So Paul attacked Judaism for its legalism. Paul attacked this legalist position arguing that salvation was not achieved by keeping the law.[987]

Scholars such as Sanders, Dunn, and Wright challenged the legalistic view of Second Temple Judaism understood by the reformer and their heirs, claiming that the Second Temple texts showed that Judaism never saw itself to be a religion of works. Sanders understood that Judaism's whole religious self-understanding was founded on the basis of grace.[988] Paul's criticism of Judaism focused instead on Israel's national pride. Sanders argued that Second Temple Judaism saw itself to be in a covenant relationship with God. That is, God had freely chosen Israel and made his covenant to be their God and for them to be his people. This covenant relationship was regulated by the law, so that rather than law-keeping being thought of as a way of entering the covenant, it was seen instead as the way of living within the covenant.[989] It also included the provision of sacrifice and atonement for those who confessed their sins and thus repented.

Wright, broadly supporting the claims of Sanders's covenantal nomism, noted that the promise of return from exile is fundamental to the covenant made with Abraham in Gen 15.[990] The writer of the Pentateuch saw the initial fulfillment of the covenant in the events of the exodus (Exod 2:25), and thus understood

---

[987] The expression 'works of the law' is found in Gal 2:16; 3:2; 3:5 and 3:10.

[988] E. P. Sanders, *Paul, the Law, and the Jewish People* (Minneapolis: Fortress, 1983), 3–10. His view between covenant and law has been known as "Covenantal nomism". According to Sanders, much of what Paul wrote falls within a framework, "getting in and staying in." That is, the law is not an entrance requirement; but it should be fulfilled.

[989] E. P. Sanders, *Paul and Palestinian Judaism: A Comparison of Patterns of Religion* (London: SCM, 1977), 75, 420, 544. This position is called "covenantal nomism". Covenantal nomism is the view that one's place in God's plan is established on the basis of the covenant and that the covenant requires as the proper response of man his obedience to its commandments, while providing means of atonement for transgression. Obedience maintains one's position in the covenant, but it does not earn God's grace as such. Righteousness in Judaism is a term which implies the maintenance of status among the group of the elect. In fact, the description of covenantal nomism that Sanders has painted was not new. Moore had argued a similar case back in 1927: G. F. Moore, *Judaism in the First Centuries of the Christian Era*, Vols. I–III (Cambridge: Harvard University Press, 1927). The identification of this perspective dramatically altered the way statements of Paul concerning Judaism and the law were to be read. Paul's criticism of Judaism was no longer to be understood as targeted against her legalism, but her national pride. According to covenantal nomism, the Jews considered themselves superior to the rest of the nations because of their unique relationship with God.

[990] Wright, *People*, 260.

the law as the covenant document which provided for his people the way of life by which they should express their answering fidelity to him. According to him, justification is not legal fiction, but about being declared to be within the covenant, a status which was the work of God's grace.[991] Hays also sees Gen 15:6 to have been interpreted in the covenantal setting because Abraham is granted a standing before God normally ascribed only to participants in the Mosaic covenant.[992] He goes on to say that "righteousness" in this context is a relational term which means faithful adherence to the structure of obligations established by the covenant.[993]

Dunn points out that the basic understanding of covenantal nomism is more or less self-evident in the way in which Israel was founded as a nation—that is, by the exodus from Egypt and the giving of the law at Sinai.[994] Then the law given by God is Israel's response to divine grace, not an attempt to gain God's favour as if it were envisaged as being grudgingly given and calculatingly dispensed. According to Dunn, the law gave "identity markers" and "boundaries," to reinforce Israel's sense of distinctiveness and distinguishing Israel from the surrounding nations.[995] This sense of distinctiveness was the sense of privilege. Dunn claims that justification is not a once-for-all act of God; rather it is the initial acceptance by God into a restored relationship. This means that God sustains the relationship, continuing to exercise his justifying righteousness with a view to the final act of judgment and acquittal.[996] Dunn sees that Paul sets in clear parallel "justification" and "salvation" in Rom 5:9–10.[997] However, Dunn comments on the phrase διὰ τοῦ θανάτου τοῦ υἱοῦ αὐτοῦ ("through the

---

[991] N. T. Wright, "Justification: The Biblical Basis and its Relevance for Contemporary Evangelicalism", in *The Great Acquittal*, ed. G. Reid (London: Fount, 1980), 30.

[992] R. B. Hays, "Justification," in *ABD* III (Garden City, NY: Doubleday, 1992), 1129. Paul in Rom 4:3–8 was later to capitalize upon the scrupulous turn of phrase.

[993] Hays, "Justification," 1129.

[994] Dunn, *Romans 1–8*, lxviii. As expressed in Exod 20 and Deut 5, the law (here the Ten Commandments—cf. Deut 4:8 with 5:1) follows upon the prior act of divine initiative. Namely, "I am the Lord your God, who brought you out of the land of Egypt...."

[995] J. D. G. Dunn, "Works of the Law and the Curse of the Law (Galatians 3:10–14)", *NTS* 31(1985), 524. This sense of separateness was deeply rooted in Israel's national consciousness (e.g. Lev 20:24–26; Ezra 10:11; Neh 13:3; Pss. Sol. 17:28; 3 Macc 3:4) and comes to powerful expression in Jub. 22:16.

[996] J. D. G. Dunn, *The Theology of Paul the Apostle* (Cambridge: Eerdmans, 1998), 386.

[997] Dunn, *Romans 1–8*, 259. According to Dunn, to insist that each term (justification/reconciliation/salvation) must be a technical term for one or other aspect and that all three must be sharply distinguished from each other, would be pedantic, theologically unjustified, and pastorally dangerous.

death of his Son") that the idea of reconciliation through a mediator appeared in the case of Moses turning away God's wrath from Israel.[998] In other words, he sees the death of Christ for deliverance as found in the essence of the Jewish martyr theology.

In the OT, furthermore, justification is expressed by the verbal form of the adjective righteous.[999] As a theological concept it has its metaphorical roots in legal language, thus δικαιοσύνη can become a summary description of God's mighty salvific deeds on Israel's behalf.[1000]

In Isaiah, God's righteousness becomes the ground and content of an eschatological hope for the setting right of human historical experience. God will reveal his righteousness in a way which will vindicate Israel's trust in him, thus leading all nations to acknowledge his cosmic lordship.[1001] In contexts such as these, the idea of God's righteousness becomes strongly associated with the ideas of deliverance and vindication; the latter notion is further reinforced by the LXX rendering of צְדָקָה/ קדצ as δικαιοσύνη. In Isa 50:7–9, for example, a passage full of legal imagery, the prophet describes God as "he who vindicates me" (ὁ δικαιωσας με) before all accusers and adversaries.

According to Holland, Isaiah described three aspects of this righteousness or justification.[1002] Isaiah said that Yahweh would deliver Israel,[1003] protect her on her pilgrimage as she returned to her inheritance,[1004] and safely establish her in her inheritance.[1005] These three themes are the outworking of Yahweh's righteousness, his saving activity, and his justification of Israel. Isaiah also pointed out that Yahweh's salvation is about the return from exile in which both Yahweh and Israel are justified.

Holland goes further than Dunn's definition about justification, by saying that it is about God's salvation, about the creation of the covenant.[1006] According to

---

[998] Ibid., 260. Ps 106:23; Josephus, *Ant.* 3.315; Wis 18:20–25; Sir 45.23.
[999] Job 11:2; 25:4; Ps 51:4; 143:2; Isa 43:26; 45:25.
[1000] Ps 71:15–19; 98:2
[1001] Cf. Isa 51:4b–5 LXX.
[1002] Holland, *Contours*, 208.
[1003] Isa 42:6; 61:5.
[1004] Isa 58:8.
[1005] Isa 32:1; 54:14; 62:1–2.
[1006] Holland, *Contours*, 190–97.

him, this salvation is about God taking responsibility for his people and eventually carrying them into the experience of eschatological salvation. Some passages tell us that Israel was justified when she was released from her bondage.[1007] Justification is related to entering the kingdom of God. This New Testament perception was influenced by the Old Testament. In the Old Testament justification spoke of Israel being released from exile and being brought to her inheritance.[1008]

Wright and Dunn see the work of law as a reference to the boundary markers of Judaism. Holland tackles their interpretation by saying that law is evidence of separation.[1009] Israel was a prisoner of sin. Christ is the end of the law so that there may be righteousness for everyone who believes. Holland points out that Paul clearly describes an attempt to gain righteousness as a result of keeping the law.[1010] Some of those texts clearly state that the law condemns. Justification must have some bearing on how people are delivered from this condemnation. Israel was justified when she was released from her bondage and restored to her inheritance.[1011]

To sum up, that the "perfection" of which our author speaks is bound up with the new covenant is made plain by his repetition of the words of Jer 31:33 and his application of them to the effect of the sacrifice of Christ in Heb 9:10. The new covenant, according to Jeremiah's prophecy, not only involved the implanting of God's laws in the hearts of his people—together with the will and power to carry them out—it also conveyed the assurance that their past sins and iniquities would be eternally blotted out from God's record, never to

---

[1007] Rom 4:25; 5:1,18; 8:30.

[1008] Isa 32:1; 42:6; 51:5; 54:14; 58.8; 62:1–2.

[1009] Holland, *Contours*, 209.

[1010] Ibid., 176. According to Holland, in Acts 15 at the Council of Jerusalem, Peter's argument was that the Jews themselves had not been able to bear it. It was therefore, not right to demand that the Gentiles achieve what the Jews had failed to achieve. This reference to keeping the law cannot possibly be a reference to circumcision. It would have been inconceivable for a Jew not to be circumcised, so it would have been meaningless to say that the Jews had not been able to bear it. The same would be true of the other boundary markers, dietary laws and Sabbath keeping. There is no evidence of failure to fulfill these regulations. The yoke of the law in this context must be more than a reference to national boundaries or boundary markers. It surely refers to the moral obligations that the law made on those who were members of the old covenant community, obligations which they had failed to keep.

[1011] F. F. Bruce, *The Epistle of Paul to the Romans: An Introduction and Commentary* (London: Tyndale, 1967), 102–3.

be brought up as evidence against them. Here is something far beyond what the sacrificial law of Old Testament could provide: in that law there was an annual "remembrance of sins" whereas in the new covenant there is no more remembrance of them. Repeated remembrance of sins and repeated sin-offerings went inevitably together; therefore, the irrevocable erasing of sins from the divine record implies that no further sin-offering is called for. The finality of the sacrifice of Christ is thus confirmed.

Therefore, we may link justification with perfection because both are related to salvation. Those who believed in Jesus can be justified; they have access to God through his Son. In other words, Christ makes perfect those who draw near to worship. "Perfection" is in Christ.

Chapter 6: The Priestly King Theme

Introduction

Heb 5:1 states what a priest does: he acts for man in things relating to God, and he brings both gifts and sacrifices for sins δῶρά τε καὶ θυσίας ὑπὲρ ἁμαρτιῶν.[1012] Here we have two separate parts of the function of a priest, namely, the bringing of gifts, and the offering of sacrifices for sin.

Eichrodt understood the priest to have been an adviser on the ritual and ethical requirements for a right worship of Yahweh, on the means of obtaining God's favour, and on the methods of propitiating an angry God for offences against the law.[1013] Mowinckel claimed that the concept of sacral kingship was rooted in the "Yahweh cult."[1014] He understood Israel's king as a parallel of the kings of surrounding nations, that is, one who acted in the dual role of king and priest.[1015] Käsemann pointed out that the origin of the Melchizedek tradition was of partly Jewish, partly Christian-Gnostic.[1016] He saw that Jewish tradition identified the high priest with figures related to the beginning and to the end of time—figures such as Shem, the Archangel Michael, the Original Man, Adam, or Metatron.[1017] Cullmann supported Käsemann's claims in saying that at the time of Jesus there must have been speculations in Judaism which identified Melchizedek himself, if not with the Messiah, at least with other eschatological figures.[1018]

However, the author of Hebrews seems to link the function of high priest with the Old Testament priests.[1019] It has been pointed out that priests nearing the altar or entering the most holy place show that the purpose in view was that of

---

[1012] Cf. Some manuscripts omit the (τε) in this verse; if the (τε) be omitted, then the word sins (ἁμαρτιῶν) must be regarded as going with both the nouns, gifts (δῶρά) and sacrifices (θυσίας).

[1013] W. Eichrodt, *Theology of the Old Testament*, Vol. 1, trans. J. A. Baker (London: SCM, 1969), 396.

[1014] S. Mowinckel, *The Sacral Kingship* (Leiden: Brill, 1959), 34.

[1015] S. Mowinckel, *The Psalms in Israel's Worship*, Vol. 1 (New York: Abingdon, 1963), 114–25.

[1016] E. Käsemann, *The Wandering People of God* (Minneapolis: Augsburg, 1984), 203.

[1017] Ibid., 203. Käsemann points out that the figures change but the scheme remains.

[1018] O. Cullmann, *The Christology of the New Testament* (London: SCM, 1963), 85.

[1019] P. E. Hughes, *A Commentary on the Epistle to the Hebrews* (Grand Rapids: Eerdmans, 1977), 176; G. Vos, *Redemptive History and Biblical Interpretation*: The Shorter Writings of Geerhardus Vos, ed. R. B. Gaffin Jr. (Phillipsburg, NJ: Presbyterian and Reformed Publishing Co, 1980), 137–8.

making purification for the sins of the people. He concluded that Christ, as priest, draws us after himself to salvation in the light of the Day of Atonement.[1020] However, the author of Hebrews identified Christ's high priestly office as "a priest forever according to the order of Melchizedek,"[1021] who was the "king of Salem and priest of the Most High God." In Heb 7:1 Abraham honoured him by paying tithes and he blessed Abraham (Heb 7:6). It could be said that Levi himself (and hence Aaron, a descendant of Levi) offered homage to Melchizedek inasmuch as Abraham was the ancestor of Levi and of all Levitical priests (Heb 7:4–10). Thus, Merrill notes that the Old Testament prototype of the messianic high priest is not Aaron, founder of the priestly institution of Israel, but rather an individual who stood completely outside the narrow compass of the theocratic cultic community, namely, Melchizedek.[1022] However, he denies that Israel's king acted in the dual role of king and priest.

Anderson says that the Epistle to the Hebrews delineates the present ministry of Christ with the theme of high priesthood.[1023] He goes on to say that the use of Ps 110 in Hebrews determines whether Christ is confessed and presented as a currently functioning messianic figure who bestows promised blessings.[1024] According to Attridge, the author of Hebrews argues that Melchizedek, as the type of Jesus as high priest, rests fundamentally not only on the Genesis narrative of the Abraham-Melchizedek episode but also on the use of that episode in Ps 110.[1025]

It is possible, therefore, that there was widespread expectation of a Messiah who would be both king and priest, namely, a priestly king. This is the unique expectation which lurks behind the priest imagery. Thus I will first attempt to

---

[1020] Ibid., 137–143. The priest actually brings men to God. Other elements must be added to the idea. Therefore, the representative element must be included in the practice.

[1021] Heb 5:6; cf. 5:10; 6:20.

[1022] E. H. Merrill, "Royal Priesthood: An Old Testament Messianic Motif," *BibSac* 150 (January–March, 1993), 60. Cf. A. P. Telford, "An Interpretation of the Enthronement Psalm," (Unpublished Th.M. thesis, Dallas Theological Seminary, 1969), 2–46.

[1023] D. R. Anderson, *The King-Priest of Psalm 110 in Hebrews* (Oxford: Peter Lang, 2001), 3–4.

[1024] Ibid., 4. According to Anderson, in order to make such a determination the use of Psalm 110 must be studied independently from Ps 110.4. The former could deal with his ministry as a king, a priest, or a king-priest, while the latter emphasizes his ministry as a priest. It must also be decided if there is a relationship between the two verses as used in Hebrews.

[1025] H. W. Attridge, *The Epistle to the Hebrews*, Hermeneia (Philadelphia: Fortress, 1989), 145; Bruce, *Hebrews*, lii; G. W. Buchanan, *To the Hebrews*, The Anchor Bible (Garden City, NY: Doubleday, 1972), xxvii.

find out where this expectation came from. Then I will examine the role and function of the priestly king as portrayed in various sources: the Old Testament, Rabbinic Works, Qumran and the New Testament. I shall observe that Hebrews most probably constructs its argument for the priestly king on the basis of the form and function of the priestly king in the Old Testament. Then I shall explore several passages in Hebrews in regard to the priestly king's relationship to deliverance.

Some Views of the Priestly King Theme

The ministry of the priesthood in the matter of sins and redemption has been much investigated. Some scholars understood the role of priesthood to be rooted in Hellenism, and others saw it in Jewish categories. Among the latter, some claim that it is based on the Pentateuch, while others see that it is from the Pentateuch and the writings of the prophets in the eighth century BCE. Therefore, I will summarize some of these understandings of priesthood.

Philo's Understanding of the Priesthood

For Philo, the high priest symbolizes the Logos, and Philo speaks of him as great and sinless.[1026] He even speaks of the Logos as having the twofold office of representing sinful man to God and of being God's messenger to man. According to Philo, the priest and high priest are characterized by the Old Testament Levitical legislation having to do with sacrifices, ritual purity, and cultic festivals.

Philo asserts that the sanctuary of the Logos (high priest) is the cosmos of the soul. That is, he regards the Logos as standing metaphysically between God and the world, bringing order into the cosmos and reason to what was chaotic; he is the herald of peace from God to man. Thus the Logos represents not humanity alone, but the physical world and its elements, for which he makes prayers and offers thanksgiving.

Following Philo's understanding, Holtzmann said that the entire world-view of the New Testament authors moves with the metaphysical antithesis that was

---

[1026] See *De spec. leg.* I.66–298 and II.39–222; also, *De vit.* M. II.66–186.

established in dualism; between idea and phenomenon, eternal and finite.[1027] Goppelt challenged Holtzmann's assertion by saying that the contrasting of upper and lower worlds is found in Hebrews only in relation to the concept of the heavenly sanctuary.[1028] He pointed out that this idea, which can be traced to Exod 25:40, is not unique in Philo; it was already widespread in Judaism from an early date.[1029] Sowers points out that Philo's conception of high priest is different from that of the Epistle to the Hebrews, for the former is characterized by a total absence of soteriological elements; in it the Logos plays no expiatory part.[1030]

Daly understood Philo to be associating his understanding of the universal priesthood with the Passover.[1031] The Passover festival is the one occasion when the people of Israel are explicitly characterized as functioning priests, but the significance of the literal festival is transcended by the allegorical symbolism attached to such priestly representation. At the Passover the "entire nation acts as priests" and God bestows on them the honour and dignity of the priesthood. According to Scholer, it is conditional upon its presence in the Old Testament narrative and the major point that Philo desires to make is allegorical, not literal.[1032]

Thus, it is true that Philo speaks of the reconciling of man with God as a function of the Logos. But even for this no real expiation is required. From the ritual sacrifices Philo does not suggest a truly expiatory sacrifice of a higher order, but simply the spiritual sacrifice of the heart. Thus what Philo

---

[1027] J. Holtzmann, *Lehrbuch der Neutestamentlichen Theologie*, Vol. 2, 2d ed. (Tübingen: Mohr Siebeck, 1911), 331.

[1028] L. Goppelt, *Typos: The Typological Interpretation of the Old Testament in the New*, trans. D. H. Madvig (Grand Rapids: Eerdmans, 1982), 167.

[1029] Ibid., According to Goppelt, Hebrews does not introduce this idea as a self-evident metaphysical fact, but bases it on Exod 25:40, which is scarcely more than is done in Acts 7:44, Gal 4:26, Heb 12:22 and other similar passages, particularly in Revelation (e.g. 15:5).

[1030] S. Sowers, *The Hermeneutics of Philo and Hebrews: A Comparison of the Interpretation of the Old Testament in Philo Judaeus and the Epistle to the Hebrews Basel Studies of Theology* I (Richmond, VA: John Knox, 1965), 97.

[1031] R. J. Daly, *Christian Sacrifice: The Judaeo-Christian Background before Origen*, Catholic University of America Studies in Christian Antiquity 18 (Washington: Catholic University of America Press, 1978), 395 n. 102. Philo deals with the Passover at *De vit. M.* II.224; *De spec. leg.* II.145; *Qu. in Exod* I.4; *De dec.* 159. The single other context, in which the Jewish nation also is priest, is at the sheaf festival: *De spec. Leg.* II.163.

[1032] Scholer, *Proleptic Priests*, 68–9.

understood about the high priest does not fit well with the understanding of the author to the Hebrews.

The Levitical Priesthood

The title "high priest" הַכֹּהֵן הַגָּדוֹל occurs rarely in the Old Testament;[1033] however, the noun כֹּהֵן appears 740 times.[1034] Scholer points out that these terms are used indiscriminately.[1035] According to Vos, Christ is contrasted both with Melchizedek and with Aaron. Where a comparison with Aaron is expressed or implied, Christ is called high priest.[1036] When the comparison is between Christ and the Levitical order, he is called priest.[1037] In this text the term "priest" is expanded by the accompanying adjective "great", the expression "great priest" being equivalent to "high priest".[1038] Furthermore, De Vaux points out that the term "priest" is variously translated as "the priest", "priest" and even "high priest" by English translators, and that it is presumably on the basis of what they think the context demands.[1039] The Biblical authors appear to be quite conscious of the distinction between them.

In fact, it is possible to research the function of the priests in the Pentateuch; the priestly ministry is primarily an altar ministry. The priest's real role begins with the blood, which he sprinkles around the burnt offering or pours out at the foot of the altar (Lev 1–7). Thus, Dommershausen understands that, together with this priestly office of reconciliation and atonement, special rituals of purgation became of great importance.[1040]

Scholer defines priests as those men who were holy, who had separated themselves or have been separated from things profane, and this separation permitted them to approach to do divine service within the sacred realm and with the holy objects.[1041] Scholer points out that the prominent interest of the

---

[1033] Lev 21:10; Num 35:25, 28, 32; 2 Chr 34:9; Neh 3:1, 20; 13:28; Hag 1:1, 12, 14; 2:2, 4; Zech 3:1, 8; 6:11.

[1034] Dommershausen, "כֹּהֵן" in *TDOT* VII, 66. It is the only term used for priests of Yahweh.

[1035] Scholer, *Proleptic Priests*, 66.

[1036] Vos, *Redemptive History*, 132. Cf. Heb 2:17; 4:14; 5:1; 7:26, 28; 8.13; 9:11, 12.

[1037] Ibid., There is one passage where we would expect the term high priest, where the term priest occurs in Heb 10:21. According to Vos, the Authorized Version incorrectly translated priest into high priest.

[1038] Heb 9:6, 7 show clearly that the terms priest and high priest are not indiscriminately used.

[1039] R. de Vaux, *Ancient Israel: Its Life and Institutions* (London: Darton, Longman & Todd, 1965), 397–9.

[1040] Dommershausen, "כֹּהֵן" 70.

[1041] Scholer, *Proleptic Priests*, 16.

priests in sacrifice and the cult of the Old Testament is particularly the special access they enjoyed as mediators.[1042] The service and function of a priest was linked to his attachment to a particular sanctuary. This was not only obvious at the time of the centralized cultus in the temple at Jerusalem, but from the earliest traditions.[1043] He concludes that this basis of the form and function of priesthood penetrates Jewish literature, even the New Testament.

Lindars argues that the Day of Atonement provides the essential requirements for an atoning sacrifice.[1044] He says that the real priesthood of the Messiah qualifies him to perform the sacrifice which is required for atonement for sins.[1045] It is shown that these are fulfilled in the sacrificial death of Jesus, so the objection cannot be made that there is no remedy available for sinners in their troubled state of consciousness of sin.

6.2.3 The Priesthood in Qumran

The intertestamental literature shows the predominant function of the priest to be in the realm of sacrifice. Cross claimed sacrifice actually occurred at Qumran because of the celebrated cache of bones found stored in jars.[1046] However, Burrows challenged Cross's argument, saying that sacrifice was not practised by the sectarians; rather priests exercised functions of prayer and worship in the community.[1047] Scholer supports Burrows's thought, saying that Qumran has apparently replaced the active cultic ritual, performed in a

---

[1042] Ibid., 9–23.

[1043] At Judg 17, Micah installs his own son as priest of his sanctuary but later employs the sojourning Levite as attendant priest. This same Levite eventually became the sanctuary attendant at Dan (Judg 18:30). The wilderness account in the Pentateuch shows the close connection the priestly personnel had to the tent of meeting and its accoutrements. Priests were always in the nearest proximity to the tent, and were responsible for the transporting of it and the Ark (Num 1:50–53; 3:9, 21–26, 31, 32, 38; 4:5–15, 22–23; Deut 10:8; 31:9, 25–26. See also in Josh 3:3, 14; 4:10–14; 8:33; 1 Chr 15:2; 16:4, 41; 13:25–32; 2 Chr 5:4–5; Ezek 45:4.). In fact, it appears that the presence of the ark or tent implied a priestly attendant. Such was the case at Shiloh (1 Sam 1–2), at Kiriath-Jearim (1 Sam 7:1), and at Jerusalem (2 Sam 15:24–29; 1 Kgs 2:26–27, 35; 4:1; 12:31). See de Vaux, AI, 2.348–49.

[1044] B. Lindars, *New Testament Theology, The Theology of The Letter to the Hebrews* (Cambridge: Cambridge University Press, 1991), 72.

[1045] Ibid.

[1046] F. M. Cross, *The Ancient Library of Qumran and Modern Biblical Studies* (Garden City, NY: Doubleday, 1958), 102. Cf. CD 11.17–12.2 may speak of a sacrificial cult, but it appears to suggest the presence of an altar at Qumran, is best seen as dealing with purification regulations for prayer worship.

[1047] M. Burrows, *More Light on the Dead Sea Scrolls* (New York: Viking, 1958), 363. J. M. Baumgarten, "Sacrifice and Worship among the Jewish Sectarians of the Dead Sea (Qumran) Scrolls," *HTR* 46 (1953), 158–59.

polluted manner at Jerusalem, with its own sacrificial substitute, that is, the practice of offering praise and living correctly.[1048] Gartner concludes that the absence of sacrificial ritual activity at Qumran was merely a temporary feature; at the end of the evil age the temple and its pure cultus would again be established.[1049] In the literature from Qumran there is no evidence for active sacrificial ritual being practised by the community.[1050]

Concerning why the community did not practice sacrifice, Gartner argued that the Qumran sectarians accused the present temple workers of profaning the temple and of failing to keep the law and its regulations for service in the temple.[1051] McNamara points out that "the Qumran Community regarded their community as the Temple and themselves in some way as priests."[1052] This is suggested by the widespread concern for holiness among the sectarians. According to Scholer, CD 3.21–4.4 has ignored the original meaning of Ezek 44:15 and has reinterpreted it in terms of the situation in the Qumran community.[1053]

The spiritualized sacrifice offered by priests at Qumran effected atonement in the time of defilement at the temple. Furthermore, the priest expected that the community would possess Zion and the sanctuary in the eschatological age.[1054] In other words, they looked forward to the day when the priestly task of cultic sacrifice would again be the Zadokite function. According to the adherents of the Dead Sea Sect, however, the priestly (Aaronic) personage was bound up with the royal (Davidic) personage.[1055] This hope did not envisage the union of priesthood and kingship. It maintained a distinction between the anointed

---

[1048] Scholer, *Proleptic Priests*, 44.

[1049] B. Gartner, *The Temple and the Community in Qumran and the New Testament: A Comparative Study in the Temple Symbolism of the Qumran Texts and the New Testament*, SNTSMS 1 (Cambridge: Cambridge University Press, 1965), 21.

[1050] The apparent cessation of cultic sacrifices at Qumran is seen in 1QS 9.4–5; CD 9.14–16; 16.13–16, and is also attested to by Josephus (Ant. XVIII. 1.5) and Philo (Quod omn. prob. 75).

[1051] CD 5.5; 5.12–7.6: Gartner, *Temple*, 19. E. S. Fiorenza, "Cultic Language in Qumran and in the NT," *CBQ* 38 (1976), 159–77.

[1052] M. McNamara, *Palestinian Judaism and the New Testament*, Good News Studies 4 (Wilmington, DE: Glazier, 1983), 142. CD 3.21–4.4 shows the community depicted as a priest.

[1053] Scholer, *Proleptic Priests*, 51.

[1054] 1QM 2, 1–6, 7, 11; 4QpPs 37.2, 10–13. 4QpPs (abbreviated: 4QCommPs) means Commentary on Psalms.

[1055] 1QS ('Community Rules') 9, 10–11; 1QSa ('Rules of the Congregation') 2, 11–16, 18–21. R. E. Brown, "The Messianism of Qumran" *CBQ* 19 (1957), 57–82.

priest and the anointed king of the new age. Kuhn points out that the two-messiah concept was not created ex nihilo by the Qumran sectarians. He goes on to say that the Testament of the Twelve Patriarchs presented the concept of a higher-ranking priestly messiah.[1056] That is, the Qumran community favours the notion of two messiahs, with the priestly one possessing a superior dignity. According to Wright, some Jews thought that the time was around that of the death of Herod and the birth of Jesus of Nazareth.[1057] On the other hand, the biblical basis of the picture of the royal messiah is also clear.[1058] It is filled out in the "Blessings" Scroll.[1059] Horsley and Hanson make an extraordinary claim about this passage because the future king will destroy the nations with "the word of mouth."[1060] What is important here are the differences between the Qumran literature, the Old Testament, and the intertestamental literature in terms of the role of the two messiahs concerning the priesthood.

The Priestly King Resulting in Deliverance

The unique reference to the king's role as "priest," "כֹּהֵן", raises the controversial issue of Israelite sacral or priestly kingship. Horton attempts to interpret "priest" as primarily referring to a secular office of chieftain or administrative official.[1061] Koolhaas has pointed out that there is insufficient evidence for the king-priest complex in Israel.[1062] M. J. Paul, arguing that Israel did not have a king who was also a priest, points out that Ps 110 cannot address one of the kings of Israel, but speaks of a priest-king.[1063]

Armerding positively evaluated that a priestly role was given to David and his sons.[1064] De Vaux carefully evaluated the evidence for the sacerdotal activity of

---

[1056] K. G. Kuhn, "The Two Messiahs of Aaron and Israel," in *The Scrolls and the New Testament*, ed. K. Stendahl (New York: Harper and Row, 1957), 58.

[1057] N. T. Wright, *The New Testament and the People of God*, 311.

[1058] Cf. Ps 61:2; Isa 11:1–5; Mic 4:13.

[1059] 1QSb 5, 23–9. 1QSb (=1Q28b) means 'the Rule of Blessing'.

[1060] R. A. Horsley and J. S. Hanson, *Bandits, Prophets and Messiahs: Popular Movements at the Time of Jesus* (Edinburgh: T&T Clark, 1985), 130. Wright sees that "the word of his mouth" as a quotation from Isa 11:4: Wright, *The New Testament and the People of God*, 311.

[1061] F. L. Horton, *The Melchizedek Tradition: A Critical Examination of the Sources to the Fifth Century A.D. and in the Epistle to the Hebrews*, SNTSMS 30 (Cambridge: Cambridge University Press, 1976), 45–48, 50–52.

[1062] A. A. Koolhaas, *Theocratie en Monarchie in Israel* (Wageningen: Veenman, 1957), 137.

[1063] M. J. Paul, "The Order of Melchizedek (Ps 110:4 and Heb 7:3)," *WTJ* 49 (1987), 200.

[1064] C. E. Armerding, "Were David's Sons Really Priests?" in *Current Issues in Biblical and Patristic Interpretation*, ed. G. F. Hawthorne (Grand Rapids: Eerdmans, 1975),75–86.

the Judean kings.[1065] Bowker pointed out that the king seems to have acted as priest only on special occasions or in exceptional circumstances.[1066] Anderson concludes that the history of pre-exilic Israel is begging for clear evidence that any of the Israelite kings were also king-priests.[1067] Therefore, in the course of time, during the monarchy, the Levitical priests came to have a special relationship to another leader, the king.

Cody discussed the priesthood of kings in the Davidic line.[1068] According to him, the Israelite kings were bound up with the Assyrian kings who were chief administrators of the functionaries beneath them.[1069] These functionaries of the kings were the כהן. Thus, these kings were responsible for the organization and administration of the state worship of Yahweh, which did not include the performance of actual services in the temple.[1070] Cody seems to take a category from Assyria and impose it on Israel, which leaves us with the difficulty of why the Hebrew king was not called a priest, especially in the light of Gen 14:18 where Melchizedek is styled a king and כהן, and the king of Ps 110 is called a כהן after the same order as Melchizedek.

Dommershausen interprets passages relating to priests and kings differently, saying that the interaction between the kings and the priesthood was one of the outstanding features of Israel's history.[1071] 2 Sam 6 (cf. 1 Chr 15) shows a Davidic royal priesthood by recounting the procession of the ark into Jerusalem from Kiriath-Jearim, where it had been housed for a century or more.[1072] The entire enterprise was the initiative of David and though the regular Aaronic

---

[1065] De Vaux, *Ancient Israel*, 113-14. De Vaux pointed out that Israel's cult is not based on myth, but history. The king in Israel was not regarded as divine.

[1066] J. W. Bowker, "Psalm cx," *VT* 17(1967), 35-6.

[1067] Anderson, *King-Priest*, 27.

[1068] A. Cody, *A History of Old Testament Priesthood*, Analecta Biblica, no. 35 (Rome: Pontifical Biblical Institute, 1969), 65.

[1069] Ibid.

[1070] The functionary was responsible for service at a sanctuary, which included the giving of oracular responses or the Torah.

[1071] Dommershausen, in *TDOT* VII, 73. King David brings in the ark, dances before it, and appoints priests (2 Sam 6:12; 8:17). Solomon builds the temple and offers sacrifice; he blesses the people and incorporates the priests into his bureaucracy (1 Kgs 4:2, 8). The temple belongs to the king and its treasures are his to use as he wills. The king has "his" priests (2 Kgs 10:11). Joash orders the priests to repair damage to the temple (2 Kgs 12:5-17). Ahaz commissions the priest Uriah to build an altar and establishes cultic ordinances to be observed by the priests (2 Kgs 16:10-18).

[1072] E. H. Merrill, *Kingdom of Priests: A History of Old Testament Israel* (Grand Rapids: Eerdmans, 1975), 85-6.

order of priests and Levites were involved, David himself was in charge—leading the entourage, clothed in priestly attire, offering sacrifices, and issuing priestly benedictions.[1073] To maintain that David merely supervised the occasion and did not actually participate as priest goes against the clear intention of the text.[1074] David's ministry shows the marks of a high priest. Solomon also had that kind of ministry. He as a king went to Gibeon, the site of the Mosaic tabernacle, to offer sacrifice (1 Kgs 3:1–9; cf. 2 Chr 1:1–6). That is, the high priest presupposed other kinds of priests, namely, the royal priesthood itself. However, the priestly role of the kings of Israel and Judah is not well documented after Solomon's early years.[1075]

Therefore, Armerding suggests that David and his sons were priests.[1076] He goes on to say that the priestly functions that David, Hezekiah, and Josiah fulfilled were because they were priests after the order of Melchizedek. In other words, in capturing Zion (Salem) David became the inheritor of the priesthood that had been established there by Melchizedek the king of Salem. De Vaux supports Armerding's view, in arguing that David and his sons did not personally function as priests.[1077] Albeit he acknowledges that they had a kind of priestly function, and that this was according to the order of Melchizedek.[1078]

With the exile and the collapse of the house of David, the ruling royal family in Jerusalem, came the suspension of the order of Melchizedek. Therefore, the Israelites expected that another Davidic king would be returned to the throne

---

[1073] A. R. Johnson, "Hebrew Conceptions of Kingship," in *Myth, Ritual, and Kingship*, ed. S. H. Hooke (Oxford: Clarendon, 1958), 211–13.

[1074] Cf. David exercised authority over priests—2 Sam 6. It has never been denied that the Israelite king was ultimately the head of the cult, but this does not make him the high priest or any kind of priest, for that matter, but he is a high priest after the order of Melchizedek.

[1075] In 2 Chr 26:16–23, the king of Judah, Uzziah, burnt incense to the Lord. That is for the priests, the descendants of Aaron, who have been consecrated to burn incense (v. 18). The infraction was not that of a king functioning cultically, but of a king undertaking a cultic ministry limited to another order of priests (Num 16:40).

[1076] C. E. Armerding, "Were David's Sons really priests?" in *Current Issues in Biblical and Patristic Interpretation: Studies in Honour of C. T. Merrill Presented by his Former Students*, ed. G. F. Hawthorne (Grand Rapids: Eerdmans, 1975), 75–86.

[1077] De Vaux, "Ancient Israel," 114.

[1078] Ibid. Cf. Bruce, *Thoughts*, 89, points out that after David's capture of Jerusalem, all of the Davidic offering would have been under the Levitical priesthood, and would have functioned alongside the Levitical priesthood.

in Jerusalem. Such an understanding certainly held at Qumran, for they saw the Messiah as the descendant of David who would purge his people in the eschatological temple.

The king, anointed by a priest, is not only a sacral person but also himself a mediator empowered by Yahweh. The faithful kings bring blessings upon their people. Probably the king also depended on the priesthood in his role as supreme judge. According to Ezek 40–48, the main function of the king (prince) is to provide a sacrifice for the sins of the covenant community.[1079]

To sum up, Judaism knew of an ideal priest, the one true priest, who would fulfil in the last days all the elements of the Jewish priestly office. The kings also shared a priestly status but not with the same function as those of Levi. Thus, the priest theme naturally led to the theme of the priestly ministry of the king. The Jewish concept of a king-priest was bound sooner or later to lead to a king-priest messianic expectation. Thus the ministry of the priestly king was seen to bring blessing and salvation to the entire nation. There was widespread expectation of a Messiah who would be both a king and a priest. I will explore, therefore, how this expectation lurked in the Old Testament and penetrated the New Testament.

The Priestly King Theme in the Old Testament

Genesis

We have noted that the Old Testament prototype of the messianic high priest is not Aaron, but Melchizedek. In Gen 14:18, Abraham paid tithes to Melchizedek (מַלְכִּי־צֶדֶק), whose name means "King of Righteousness."[1080] Melchizedek is also described as a priest of "El Elyon" (אֵל עֶלְיוֹן).

According to von Rad, the combination of offices (priest and king) in one person was not unusual in the ancient Near East.[1081] Appeal is made to the mysterious figure of Melchizedek as the ancient priest of Yahweh rather than

---

[1079] Cf. Ezekiel saw the importance of the raising up of a Davidic prince. Especially, Ezek 45:25 tells us how the prince will offer an abundance of sacrifices for the sins of the people.

[1080] M. C. Astour, "Melchizedek," in *The Anchor Bible Dictionary*, Vol. 4, ed. D. N. Freedman (London: Doubleday, 1992), 684; G. J. Wenham, *Genesis 1–15*, 1, WBC (Dallas: Word, 1987), 316.

[1081] G. Von. Rad, *Genesis*, Old Testament Library (London: SCM Press, 1987), 179; Wenham, *Genesis* 1–15, 316; Westermann, *Genesis* 12–36, 204–05.

of a pagan Canaanite god.¹⁰⁸² Astour points out that Melchizedek's being the priest of God Most High (אֵל עֶלְיוֹן) does not necessarily point to the pre-Israelite, Canaanite character of the priest and his cultus.¹⁰⁸³ According to Wenham, "El Elyon" is one of the titles of the God worshipped by the patriarchs.¹⁰⁸⁴ Thus, his god is equated with Yahweh in the form of an epithet אֵל עֶלְיוֹן, now in the sense "God Most High."

Melchizedek blessed Abram in Gen 14:20, saying that "blessed be God Most High, who delivered your enemies into your hand." The verb ("deliver") מִגֵּן occurs in only two other passages, both times in parallel with נתן ("to give").¹⁰⁸⁵ Here too, "giving" is mentioned immediately afterwards (vv. 20–21). The cognate term מָגֵן ("shield") used in 15:1, seems to look back to this passage. צר ("oppressor") is a common word for enemies (cf. צר/צרה "narrow"/"distress") and this usage makes it particularly apt where enemy aggression has caused suffering, as in this case. Thus, these words are linked to the title Melchizedek as in the exodus theme. Similarly, in Gen 14 Abraham's submission to Melchizedek was probably intended to encourage Israel's submission to a new Melchizedek ruling from Jerusalem in the person of David.¹⁰⁸⁶

Psalms

The subject of Ps 110 is a matter of intense debate. Many scholars favour the view that the Psalm is strictly messianic. Merrill points out that, even if Davidic authorship is maintained, אדני is still appropriate, for the term no doubt became so formulaic that a king could use it even of himself.¹⁰⁸⁷ That is, the title אדני, given to the king in v. 1, is the usual polite formula of addressing the Hebrew monarch. Furthermore, as Mckenzie¹⁰⁸⁸ points out, the Israelite king is viewed as a religious figure who incorporates in himself the kingdom of Israel and its hope for a future in which the kingship of Yahweh will become universally effective. In this sense, this Psalm is messianic.

---

¹⁰⁸² Astour, "Melchizedek," *ABD*, Vol. 4, 683.
¹⁰⁸³ Ibid., 684.
¹⁰⁸⁴ Wenham, *Genesis* 1–15, 316.
¹⁰⁸⁵ Hos 11:8; Prov 4:9.
¹⁰⁸⁶ J. A. Emerton, "The Riddle of Genesis," *VT* 21 (1971) 421–26, 437–38
¹⁰⁸⁷ Merrill, "Royal Priesthood," 55.
¹⁰⁸⁸ J. L. Mckenzie, "Royal Messianism" *CBQ* Vol. 19 (1957), 36.

The term in Ps 110:4 for priest is כהן. Horton makes an argument for different types of כהנים.[1089] He makes way for an administrative official who did not descend from Aaron or Zadok. This is how he explains the "sons of David" who were priests (2 Sam 8:18). He finds support for this view in the LXX rendering of כהנים, which was αυλαρχαι.[1090] Horton compares the English word "minister" to כהן, suggesting that it may have had a dual meaning—inasmuch as it could apply to either the cultic or political life. But he ignores completely the requirements for Aaronic priesthood and the punitive measures taken against Uzziah for not respecting certain lines drawn between the secular and the spiritual. If this is a historical king in Ps 110, it would be the only time a king of Israel was called a כהן.

However, Anderson points out that there was not a separate term for the high priest or for the king as high priest.[1091] In Israel the sacral character of the king was rather suppressed.[1092] The priesthood as an institution in general was limited to the tribe of Levi and specifically to the descendants of Aaron.[1093] David's commission in the psalm is to a priesthood that operated outside the parameters of the normal cultic sphere, one that is said to be of a totally different order.

What the psalm is concerned with is not sacrifice, but empire. Mettinger observed that the psalm stresses the closeness between Yahweh and the king by using אדי ("lord") both in v. 1 and v. 5.[1094] Allen points out that אדי as the divine subject in v. 1 is supported by v. 2 where Yahweh is the subject, by אפו ("his anger") with divine reference in Ps 2:5, 8, and by יום אפו ("his day of

---

[1089] F. L. Horton, Jr., *The Melchizedek Tradition* (Cambridge: Cambridge University Press, 1976), 45–48, 50.

[1090] According to H. G. Liddell and R. Scott, revised and augmented by H. S. Jones and R. McKenzie, *A Greek-English Lexicon* (LSJ), reprint ed. (New York: Harper, 1883): "αυνλαρχης," 276a, this official was a mayor of the palace or a chief of the court.

[1091] Anderson, *King-Priest*, 55.

[1092] H. Ringgren, *Religions of the Ancient Near East* (Philadelphia: Westminster, 1973), 36–38, 105–5. According to Ringgren, the notion of royal priesthood is pervasive in the ancient Near East. From Egypt to lower Mesopotamia the rulers of various states were very active in their respective cults, functioning sometimes as the clergy and at other times alongside an order of priests. In Egypt the king, in fact, was believed to be divine, and so it followed that he not only functioned cultically but was himself an object of reverence. This was inevitable in that there was no bifurcation of life between the secular and sacred.

[1093] Merrill, "Royal Priesthood," 59.

[1094] T. N. D. Mettinger, *King and Messiah: The Civil and Sacral Legitimation of the Israelite Kings*, ConBOT Series 8 (Lund: Gleerup, 1976), 264.

anger") with reference to Yahweh in Isa 13:13.[1095] Anderson has suggested that this may be the prototype for the later concept of the Day of Yahweh.[1096]

Chronicles

The episode of 2 Chr 26 may reflect a dispute over the interpretation and application of the special royal priesthood rather than constituting an utter denial: Uzziah trespassed upon the territory of the Aaronic priesthood, בני אהרן ("the sons of Aaron" in 2 Chr 26:18). It is possible that the general import of the promise is simply that David was the founder of a new, permanent dynasty that was the legitimate heir to the priestly king rule of the previous dynasty associated with Melchizedek.[1097]

Ezekiel

In Ezek 45:18–25, there is no mention of atonement in the ritual itself, but the blood clearly had the power to remove sins. Here two points have to be dealt with: one is how the ritual of the Day of Atonement was absorbed into the Passover, and the other is what the role of the king was. Engnell saw the sacrifice's atoning significance in the text.[1098] Allen points out that the ceremony described in Ezek 45:18–27 is close to part of the Day of Atonement rites.[1099] Zimmerli understood that the sacrifice of the Day of Atonement was taken on the first day of the first month, that is, the beginning of the year.[1100] Cody saw the merger of the two feasts; furthermore,[1101] Fairbairn notes that the Day of Atonement sacrifices were adopted for the Passover.[1102] However, they do not realize how important the merger of the two feasts was in ritual. Holland concludes that Ezekiel merged atonement with redemption.[1103] That

---

[1095] Allen, *Psalm 101–150*, 117.

[1096] G. W. Anderson, "Israel's Creed: Sung, Not Signed," *SJT* 16 (1963), 277; G. Von. Rad, *Old Testament Theology*, Vol. 2, trans. D. M. G. Stalker (New York: Harper, 1965), 119–25). Cf. Isa 13:9; Zeph 2:3.

[1097] P. J. Nel, "Psalm 110 and the Melchizedek Tradition," *JNSL* 22 (1996), 6.

[1098] I. Engnell, *A Rigid Scrutiny: Critical Essays on the Old Testament,* trans. J. T. Willis (London: SPCK, 1970), 186. Engnell's theory of a common pattern in the ancient Near Eastern New Year festivals appears most clearly on "New Year Festivals," "Passover," and "The Exodus from Egypt."

[1099] L. C. Allen, *Ezekiel* 20–48, WBC, 258–59. J. Milgrom, "Sin-Offering or Purification-Offering?" *VT* 21 (1971), 237–39. G. Wenham, *Leviticus*, NICOT (Grand Rapids: Eerdmans, 1979), 88–89.

[1100] W. Zimmerli, *Ezekiel: A Commentary on the Book of Ezekiel* Vol. 2 (Philadelphia: Fortress, 1983), 482.

[1101] A. Cody, *Ezekiel, Old Testament Message* 11 (Wilmington, DE: Michael Glazier, 1984), 240.

[1102] P. Fairbairn, *An Exposition of Ezekiel* (Grand Rapids: Sovereign Grace, 1971), 237.

[1103] Holland, *Contours*, 160–61.

is, Ezekiel pulled the sacrifices of the Day of Atonement into the orbit of Passover celebration. What he says is that these offerings are not made on the Day of Atonement, but offered during the Passover. He is emphasizing the importance of the Passover for dealing with the sins of the people.

Block sees that the נשיא plays a leading role.[1104] Ezekiel charged the national head of state with responsibility for the celebration. According to Engnell, on the basis of a reference to the "prince" in Ezek 45:21, the king played a central role in the original Passover ceremony and that the figure of Moses was "modelled after the figure of the sacral king throughout".[1105] However, neither pointed out that Ezekiel saw the importance of the raising up of a Davidic prince. According to Holland, Ezekiel saw this prince's main function as offering sacrifices for the sins of the covenant community in Ezek 45:25.[1106] In other words, the prince, as a Davidic son, provides the paschal atoning sacrifices. As royal patron of the Passover, Hezekiah had also initiated the celebration, resolved problems of timing, issued the decree for national participation and spiritual renewal, interceded on behalf of the people, encouraged the Levites, and provided the animals.[1107] Josiah's similar role appeared decades later.[1108]

The Priestly King Theme in the Intertestamental Literature

The priestly king theme also occurs in the Testaments of the Twelve Patriarchs.[1109] Opinion is divided on the origins of the present Testaments. According to Pfeiffer, the Testaments of the Patriarchs were written in Hebrew

---

[1104] D. I. Block, *The Book of Ezekiel Chapter 25-48*, The New International Commentary on the Old Testament (Grand Rapids: Eerdmans, 1998), 665. The following passages mention about the Davidic prince; Ezek 34:23-4; 37:24-5; 44:3; 45:7,22.

[1105] Engnell, *A Rigid Scrutiny*, 191.

[1106] According to Holland, it is the son of David who was to bring deliverance about. In regard with Ezek 45:25, the fact that Jesus had died with the inscription 'the King of the Jews' above his head at Passover spoke of the Davidic prince offering paschal sacrifice: Holland, *Contours*, 29, 161.

[1107] 2 Chr 30

[1108] 2 Chr 35:1–19

[1109] R. F. Surburg, *Introduction to the Intertestamental Period* (St. Louis: Concordia, 1975), 129. The pattern for this work was given by Gen 49, where Jacob faced by death called his sons to the bedside and foretold the future of each; possibly also by Deut 33, where Moses blesses the 12 tribes, one by one, and assures them of ultimate triumph.

about 140–110 BCE, probably in the days of John Hyrcanus (135–104 BCE).[1110] Thomson disagrees with Pfeiffer and Charles and argues for the dependence of the book on the New Testament and not vice versa.[1111] That is, some believe that the work was composed by a Jew or Jewish Christian in the first or second century CE, whilst others maintain that they are of pre-Christian and Jewish, possibly Essene origin.

What is important is that certain sections of the Testaments seem closely related to the New Testament. They contain a prediction about a new priest, who is at the same time also to be a king. Various acts are ascribed to him, mostly eschatological in character, in T. Levi 18:1–4.[1112]

> And after their punishment shall have come from the Lord, the priesthood shall fail. Then shall the Lord rise up a new priest. And to him all the words of the Lord shall be revealed; and he shall execute a righteous judgment upon the earth for a multitude of days. And his star shall arise in heaven as of a king. Lighting up the light of knowledge as the sun the day. And he shall be magnified in the world. He shall shine forth as the sun on the earth. And shall remove all darkness from under heaven. And there shall be peace in all the earth.

He is also connected to Abraham in T. Levi 18:6.[1113] The passage is based on Ps 110.[1114] It is said of him, in T. Levi 18:8–9 that he shall have no successor in eternity, for sin shall disappear.

> For he shall give the majesty of the Lord to His sons in truth for evermore. And there shall none succeed him for all generations forever, And in his priesthood the Gentiles shall be multiplied in knowledge upon the earth, And enlightened through the grace of the

---

[1110] R. H. Pfeiffer, *The Literature and Religion of the Pseudepigrapha* (Nashville, TN: Abingdon, 1952), 421; R. H. Charles, *Religious Development between the Old and New Testaments* (London: Oxford University Press, 1956), 228. Charles believes the author to have been a Pharisee who wrote in the early part of the reign of John Hyrcanus.

[1111] J. E. H. Thomson. "Apocalyptic Literature," in *International Standard Bible Encyclopedia* I, 176.

[1112] M. McNamara, *Intertestamental Literature* (Wilmington, DE: Michael Glazier, 1983), 100.

[1113] "The heavens shall be opened. And from the temple of glory shall come upon him sanctification. With the Father's voice as from Abraham to Isaac."

[1114] G. Vos, *The Teaching of the Epistle to the Hebrews* (Phillipsburg, NJ: The Presbyterian & Reformed Publishing Company, 1975), 92.

Lord: In his priesthood shall sin come to an end, And the lawless shall cease to do evil. [And the just shall rest in him.].

In a midrash on Exod 3:1 preserved in the Tanhuma collection, both offices are associated with the wilderness period at the time of Moses. Moses longed for the wilderness because he saw that he was to receive greatness from the wilderness. The gifts to come were the Torah, the commandments, the Tabernacle, the Shekinah, kingship and priesthood, the well, the manna, and the clouds of glory.[1115] It is also shown that both offices are implicit in Moses's reply to God's call at the burning bush. "Here I am" for Moses (in Exod 3:4), as for Abraham (Gen 22:11), meant "Here am I for priesthood. Here am I for kingship."[1116] Meeks points out that the form of the tradition is that preserved in Tanhuma, in which Moses, like Abraham, was both king and priest.[1117]

The Priestly King Theme in the Gospels and Acts and the Epistles

There is no explicit mention of Christ as high priest in the New Testament outside of Hebrews.[1118] According to Vos, the reason was that the sacrificial character of Christ's work was universally recognized.[1119] This idea is not presented in Hebrews as if it were a novelty, but rather as a well-known idea, as is evident from the manner in which it is introduced throughout the New Testament. Dunn points out, therefore, that the language of the New Testament stems directly from such Old Testament usage, and it is well appreciated.[1120]

[1115] *Midrash Tanhuma*: מדרש תנחומא על חמשה חומשי תורה, ed. S. Buber (Wilna: Verlag Wittwe & Gebruder Romm, 1985), II–7.

[1116] *Midrash Tanhuma*: מדרש תנחומא על חמשה חומשי תורה, ed. S. Buber (Wilna: Verlag Wittwe & Gebruder Romm, 1985), II–9.

[1117] W. A. Meeks, *The Prophetic-King: Moses Traditions and the Johannine Christology* (Leiden: Brill, 1967), 182. The parallel between Moses and Abraham, both seen as kings and prophets, has turned up before, in Philo. The assimilation of the Moses and Abraham legends to each other is very frequent. However, Meeks sees that the prophetic and royal elements are to be understood in their combination and mutual interpretation, especially in the Johannine Christology.

[1118] Christ Himself never calls Himself priest, but he does represent Himself as the sacrifice in the establishment of the new covenant (Matt 26:28; Mark 14:24).

[1119] Vos, *Hebrews*, 92

[1120] J. D. G. Dunn, *The Theology of Paul the Apostle* (Cambridge: Eerdmans, 1998), 345; S. K. Williams, "The 'Righteousness of God' in Romans," *JBL* 99 (1980), 260–63.

The Synoptic Gospels

The priestly king status of Jesus is hinted at in the Synoptics. The passages involved in the Synoptics highlight three points.[1121] Although there are differences in contextual settings and slight variations in the use of the LXX, all three Synoptic writers appear to be in agreement on these three points. They will be examined together: Matthew serving as the point of reference with the variations in Mark and Luke noted along the way.

Jesus himself, in Mark 12:35–40, placed the significance of Ps 110 before his accusers.[1122] However, some scholars doubt the authenticity of this pericope because this idea does not follow the usual pattern of Jesus.[1123] Bultmann saw Mark 12:35–37 as "a community product."[1124] Funk supports Bultmann's view, in saying that when Jesus begins with a dialogue or debate, the dialogue or debate is a secondary composition.[1125] However, Cranfield[1126] and Evans[1127] challenge Bultmann, by saying that this saying is not the creation of the early church because the church believed that the Messiah did descend from David.[1128] Hay remarks that "this pericope may be the only one in the entire synoptic tradition which can be regarded as directly expressing Jesus's understanding of messiahship."[1129] Anderson supports Hay's thought, pointing

---

[1121] Matt 22:41–46; Mark 12:35–37; and Luke 20:41–44. Three points are as follows: (1) Jesus believed David spoke Ps 110 through the superintendence of the Holy Spirit; (2) Jesus thought of himself as the Messiah; and (3) Jesus's opponents did not object to his use of the psalm as a messianic proof text.

[1122] Cf. Matt 22:41–46; Luke 20:41–44. Matthew is unique in stating it was the Pharisees whom Jesus interrogated in this pericope. In Mark it is not clear. Only a "great crowd" is specified, which could have included the Pharisees and Herodians (Mark 12:13), the Sadducees (Mark 12:18), and the scribes (Mark 12:28). Luke says even less than Mark, although he does suggest that the scribes have just been silenced (Luke 20:39–40).

[1123] C. A. Evans, *Mark 8.27–16:20*, 34B, Word Biblical Commentary (Nashville, TN: Thomas Nelson, 2001), 270. In Jesus's usual pattern, he is first asked and then he responds with a counter question.

[1124] R. Bultmann, *The History of the Synoptic Tradition* (Oxford: Blackwell, 1972), 136–7. Bultmann points out that the proof that Messiah could not be David's son could hardly have had any meaning for Jesus.

[1125] R. W. Funk, *Mark*, 187–88.

[1126] C. E. B. Cranfield, *The Gospel according to Saint Mark*, CGTC (Cambridge: Cambridge University Press, 1963), 381.

[1127] Evans, *Mark 8.27–16:20*, 270–71.

[1128] Jer 23:5; 33:15; Isa 9:2; 11.1; Ezek 34:23–24; 37:24; Zech 3:8; 6:12. "Son of David" as a messianic reference is also commonplace in the Second Temple period (Pss. Sol 17.21; Test Sol 1.7. This is also seen in the genealogies of the Matthaen and Lukan Gospels and in Paul (Rom 1:3–4; 2 Tim 2:8).

[1129] D. M, Hay, *Glory At the Right Hand: Psalm 110 in Early Christianity*, Society of Biblical Literature Monograph Series, no. 18, ed. R. A. Kraft (New York: Abingdon, 1973), 111.

out that Jesus believed τωκυριωμου was a messianic reference.[1130] Ps 110:4 points out that the same "son" of David was to be a priest forever after the order of Melchizedek. Holland appreciates that the discourse was in the setting of the temple where the priests ministered in Mark 12:35.[1131] Christ himself interpreted the 110th Psalm messianically, thus clearly implying the priestly king function.

The writers of the Synoptics use the reference to the Son of David in its messianic overtones.[1132] All three are related to Ps 110, though Matthew and Mark are more explicit. In Mark 14:61, Jesus was questioned by the high priest Σὺ εἶ ὁ χριστὸς ὁ υἱὸς τοῦ εὐλογητοῦ ("Are you the Christ, the son of the Blessed?") In Matthew and Mark, the quotes are virtually the same with only a word order change in the Ps 110:1 reference. Cullmann thinks that there is significance in that the only place where Jesus publicly affirmed his identity is when challenged by the high priest to say if he was the son of the Blessed One.[1133] Cullmann sees this statement, Jesus's only public confession made before the high priest, as indicating a priestly status for Jesus.[1134]

This question is particularly interesting in light of the Pharisaic response to the "Son of David" question. If the Pharisees lacked the concept of a divine Messiah, how is it that the high priest would be expecting a Messiah who would be the "Son of God"? Gundry notes that divine sonship was attributed to the Davidic kings in 2 Sam 7:14 and Ps 2:7, and the Samuel passage was given a pre-Christian Jewish messianic interpretation in 4QFlor 1.10–12.[1135] Also, according to Hengel, the Jewish view of the "Son of God" only signified divine appointment, not divine nature.[1136] It is important to recognize Messiahship as the key point at issue, for Jesus's reference and identification with Ps 110:1 further underscores the fact that he interpreted the psalm messianically and viewed himself as the Messiah.

[1130] Anderson, *King-Priest*, 90.

[1131] Holland, *Paschal*, 153.

[1132] Matt 26:62–65; Mark 14: 62–64a; Luke 22:66–71.

[1133] Cf. Mark 14:62; "I am, and you will see the Son of Man sitting at the right hand of the Mighty One and coming in the clouds of heaven."

[1134] Cullmann, *Christology*, 89.

[1135] R. H. Gundry, *Mark* (Grand Rapids: Eerdmans, 1993), 908. He also notes that "the Son of God" as used in 4Q243 may also be a pre-Christian reference to the Messiah.

[1136] M. Hengel, *The Son of God* (Philadelphia: Fortress, 1976), 21–56.

Acts

What Luke is trying to say in Acts 5:31–32 (which pertains to the significance of Ps 110 for the present ministry of Christ) is that God raised[1137] the crucified Jesus from the dead and exalted him to his own right hand, and that the exalted Jesus had two titles: ἀρχηγὸν and σωτῆρα. The former is usually used for a military or political leader.[1138] The latter speaks of his present function. That is, salvation is derived from the intercessory ministry of Christ in heaven as our priest.[1139] Stauffer supports Hodges, saying that "from now on Christ is our Advocate at the right hand of God, our high priest who has passed into the heavenly places intercedes for us before God's face."[1140]

Anderson points out that the role of Christ as Savior is further explained by the two functions ascribed to him: giving repentance for Israel and forgiveness of sins.[1141] Clearly these are salvific blessings. He goes on to say that a key verb here is δουναι, which speaks of prerogatives belonging to the new monarch, that is, the right to give or grant repentance and forgiveness of sins to Israel.[1142] However, he does not see that Jesus as savior is in the order of Melchizedek.

John

John points out that Christ's sacrificial death forms part of his priestly function as expressed in the idea of the Paraclete, a term which should be understood as meaning not merely a comforter but also an advocate. In John 17 the high priestly prayer is an example of priestly understanding. Furthermore, attention ought to be paid to the chapter which speaks of Jesus's messianic kingship to gain a full appreciation of John's theology in this regard because priesthood

---

[1137] The verb ὑψόωις used to emphasize the direct line between resurrection and exaltation. In fact, this passage would appear to see no distinction between the resurrection and the exaltation, but rather views them as one act or complex. The ascension appears to be a necessary corollary of the resurrection.

[1138] Anderson, *King-Priest*, 100. Cf. C. K. Barrett, *The Act of the Apostles, The International Critical Commentary* (Edinburgh: T&T Clark, 1994), 290.

[1139] Z. C. Hodges, "A Dispensational Understanding of Acts 2" in *Issues in Dispensationalism*, eds. W. R. Willis and J. R. Master (Chicago, IL: Moody, 1994), 177.

[1140] E. Stauffer, *New Testament Theology*, 5th ed. trans. J. Marsh (London: SCM, 1955), 139.

[1141] Anderson, *King-Priest*, 100.

[1142] Ibid.

and kingship are inseparably linked in the Messiah.[1143] In the Book of Revelation, believers are represented as being made kings and priests unto God (1:6); and in order to do this, he must be a king and priest himself (5:10; 20:6).

Romans

Paul does not call Christ a priest, but he uses various expressions which imply the idea of a priest as a redeemer.[1144] In Rom 8:34-35a, there is nothing explicit to prove a priestly ministry, unless it is the verb ενντυγχανω which, according to Bauernfeind, is the term used for "intercession" in a variety of contexts.[1145] The term speaks of his ministry as high priest linked to Ps 110.[1146] However, some scholars point out that the setting here would appear to be a court room.[1147] So, according to Anderson, the real emphasis in this passage is on his power and authority, using the imagery of a court room.[1148] However, Anderson does not relate the court imagery to the priesthood. This is a merger in which the ministry of priest is absorbed into that of prince.[1149]

Timothy

In 1 Tim 2:5 we find the clearest echo of the priestly theme:[1150] "For there is one God, one mediator also between God and men, himself man, Christ Jesus." Verse 6 continues, "who gave himself a ransom for all." Kelly sees that this verse is based on Jesus's saying in Mark 10:45, but it is not Paul's theory of the atonement.[1151] His insistence is only that the important words were "for all"; it is the fact that Christ died for all men, without any kind of favouritism.[1152]

[1143] Holland, *Paschal*, 158.

[1144] In Romans, even though Paul does not call Christ priest, he speaks of Christ as the sacrifice, the mercy-seat, as giving himself up for us, as an offering and sacrifice to God.

[1145] O. Bauernfeind, "ενντυγχανω," in *TDNT* VIII, 1972 ed., 242-43.

[1146] Ibid.

[1147] C. E. B. Cranfield, *The Epistle to the Romans*, The International Critical Commentary, ed. J. A. Emerton and C. E. B. Cranfield (Edinburgh: T&T Clark, 1975), 438. He suggests that Satan as the accuser of the brethren may have been in Paul's mind. See also W. Schneider, "Judgment," in *NIDNTT* II, 1971 ed., 365-66, for a similar conclusion.

[1148] Anderson, *King-Priest*, 103; W. Sanday and A. C. Headlam, *The Epistle to the Romans*, 5th ed., The International Critical Commentary (Edinburgh: T&T Clark, 1975), 221; J. Murray, *The Epistle to the Romans*, NICNT, ed. F. F. Bruce (Grand Rapids: Eerdmans, 1980), 329.

[1149] The high priest functioned as a judge—so Caiaphas examined Jesus in the Synoptics.

[1150] Holland, *Paschal*, 159.

[1151] J. N. D. Kelly, *The Pastoral Epistles; I & II Timothy, Titus* (London: Adam & Charles Black, 1963), 63.

[1152] Ibid., 64.

Fairbairn argued that Christ gave himself as mediator.[1153] Mounce points out that vv. 5–6 has two stanzas: the first asserts the uniqueness of the one God and the one mediator; the second asserts the nature of the mediator and that of his work.[1154] Verse 6 could not be understood in the light of the imagery of the Levitical priesthood in verse 5, because the term αvντιλυτρον means "a ransom-price", which the Levitical priest did not mean. In fact, the Levites were a ransom-price for the firstborn. This needs another imagery, namely the priestly king imagery.

Peter

Vos considered that Peter's epistles did not stress the uniqueness of Christ's priestly office because they speak of that which believers share in common with Christ.[1155] Anderson notes that the allusion to Ps 110 is introduced in 1 Pet 3:21–22.[1156] Peter's mention of baptism in v. 21 reminds Anderson of the resurrection of Christ. Thinking of the resurrection also brings to mind the present location of Christ at the right hand of God. Hay thinks that the connection between baptism and Ps 110:1 is a link that suggests the intercessory ministry of Christ.[1157] According to him, it makes much more sense to understand the tie between Ps 110:1 and the ascension as implying that forgiveness is a regal, not priestly, prerogative.[1158] As occurs so often in Paul, the installation of Christ at God's right hand is somehow related to the defeat of supernatural powers.

In fact, the significance of 1 Pet 3:22, as it relates to the present reign of Christ, centers on the two participles, "having gone" (πορευθεὶς) and "being subjected" (ὑποταγέντων). According to Wallace,[1159] because both of these participles are aorist passive, any action inherent in the verbs is antecedent to the action/state of the main verb, which is in the present tense. In other words, Christ is presently at the right hand of God. But before his present sitting at the right hand began, two prior events took place: (1) ὕψωσεν—he had to go to the right

---

[1153] P. Fairbairn, *Pastoral Epistles* (Minneapolis: James Klock, 1976), 117.

[1154] W. D. Mounce, *Pastoral Epistle*, 46, WBC (Nashville, TN: Thomas Nelson, 2000), 87.

[1155] Vos, *Hebrews*, 93

[1156] Anderson, *King-Priest*, 111.

[1157] D. M. Hay, *Glory*, 312–16.

[1158] Ibid.

[1159] D. B. Wallace, *Greek Grammar Beyond the Basics* (Grand Rapids: Zondervan Publishing House, 1996), 174.

hand of God before he could sit or be there; and (2) ὑποταγέντων—the angels, authorities, and powers were subjected to him. This means that Christ has fulfilled the ministry of the priest-king, having the ministry of priest and that of king.

The Priestly King Theme in Hebrews

We have found that the priestly king, who is in the order of Melchizedek, was linked to the ideas of sin and redemption. The messianic high priest is an individual who stood completely outside the narrow compass of the theocratic cultic community. Thus, the author of Hebrews, following this idea of the priestly king, proves that the priestly kingship of Jesus is not in the order of Aaron and his descendants, but of Melchizedek.

Here the author of Hebrews identifies these two eschatological personages, priest and king, in such a way as to provide the fulfillment of the divine oracle in Ps 110:4.[1160] That is, the promised prince of the house of David is, by the same divine right, perpetually a priest after Melchizedek's order. Thus, there was a soteriological significance in the title "high priest" and it was linked with his status in the new creation, which he was instrumental in bringing about. The author of Hebrews made the final step of combining the title with Christ's role as the paschal victim. We will see that the implications of this are unfolded in detail throughout the Epistle to the Hebrews.

Priestly King Relating to Deliverance

Heb 7:25 shows that Christ, like Melchizedek, is able to save completely those who come to God through him because he always lives to intercede for them. With regard to this verse Bruce points out that the way of approach to God through him is a way that is always open, because in the presence of God he represents his people as a priest forever.[1161] Bruce sees Christ as the unique Mediator between God and humanity because he combines Godhead and humanity perfectly in his own person.[1162] Hughes also, without mentioning

---

[1160] T. Levi 8:14. "a king shall arise out of Judah and shall establish a new priesthood...for all Gentiles."
[1161] Bruce, *Hebrews*, 153.
[1162] Ibid., 153-4. In Christ God draws near to men and in him men may draw near to God, with the assurance of constant and immediate access. In Heb 2:17 we find that he became high priest to make propitiation for his people's sins and strengthen them in temptation; in Heb 4:15 we discover that he sympathizes with their

salvation in relation to Melchizedek, saw Christ as our intercessor, supporting people by his strength and surrounding people with his love.[1163] Both Bruce and Hughes fail to see the role of Melchizedek as a priestly king, and instead understand this verse in the light of the Old Testament priesthood. Lane sees that the scope of Christ's priestly ministry is suggested by the infinitives σῴζειν ("to save") and ἐντυγχάνω ("to intercede")."[1164] According to him, in relation to the present tense of σῴζειν, the community has already begun to participate in salvation as a result of the obedience and sacrificial death of Christ and his subsequent exaltation.[1165] Lane concludes that the perfection and eternity of the salvation he mediates is guaranteed by the unassailable character of his priesthood. Lane sees deliverance to be forgiveness of sin, and he thinks that sin could be forgiven on the Day of Atonement.[1166]

The Aaronic priesthood, which was instituted by Moses, was impotent to achieve salvation. It is clear from 7:19, 25 and 10:1 that "perfect" (τελειόω) in this context has to do with approaching God, with coming into fellowship with him.[1167] The Aaronic priesthood did not have and could not procure this salvation, because its ceremonies could not purify the conscience of the worshipper (9:9), in contrast to what the faithful could obtain through Christ's sacrifice (10:4; 11:40; 12:23).

Wright points out that Jesus's actions in the temple were royal.[1168] It was the king who had ultimate authority over the temple. According to him, Ps 110 refers to the enthronement of the Messiah, to his successful battle against the kings of the earth, and to his being "a priest for ever after the order of

---

weakness and supplies the mercy and grace to help them in time of need. Here his high-priestly function is summed up in terms of intercession: "he is always living to plead on their behalf." Thus the intercessory work of Christ at the right hand of God is not a doctrine peculiar to our author.

[1163] Hughes, *Hebrews*, 270.
[1164] Lane, *Hebrews 1–8*, 189.
[1165] Ibid., cf. 2:3–4; 6:4–5, 9.
[1166] Ibid., 190.
[1167] G. Schrenk, "ἱεροσυλέω," in *TDNT* III, 275.
[1168] Wright, *Victory*, 491. Among those who have repeatedly urged this point we may note particularly O. Betz, *What Do We Know About Jesus?* trans. M. Kohl (London: SCM, 1968), 87–93; B. F. Meyer, *The Aims of Jesus* (London: SCM, 1979), 197–202. According to Meyer, "the entry into Jerusalem and the cleansing of the temple constituted a messianic demonstration, a messianic critique, a messianic fulfilment event, and a sign of the messianic restoration of Israel."

Melchizedek."[1169] Wright applies the phrase "priest forever" in Heb 7:17 to Simon Maccabaeus in 1 Macc 14:41.[1170] Wright sees Jesus's temple-action as a claim to royal status, similar to what Simon Maccabaeus and his brothers had done. Yet Wright remains silent over Jesus's action as a priest. Similarly, Collins, discussing 4Q491, suggests that the one who is enthroned may have been "the eschatological priest/teacher".[1171] He continues by saying that "the claim that he has a throne in heaven is a validation of his authority, and serves the purpose of exhortation in the face of the tribulation of the eschatological battle."[1172] He also did not see the absorption of the priesthood into the kingship.

In Heb 7:1-2, however, the author of Hebrews reminds his hearers of a story of Gen 14, in which the designation of Melchizedek as king of Salem and priest of the Most High God first occurs. The entire narrative is about deliverance. As we argued before, deliverance involves forgiveness of sins and restoration. Therefore, the author of Hebrews, after mentioning Melchizedek in Gen 14, introduces the Levitical priesthood to explain forgiveness of sins in Heb 7:10-13. Thus we should examine two texts, Gen 14 and Ps 110, relating to Melchizedek to enquire how the priestly king is related to salvation and how he is equated with Jesus.[1173]

The event in Gen 14 happened after Abram went up from Egypt (Gen 13). It shows the account of a military campaign with various kings named. The story falls into two main parts: three accounts of battle, and the subsequent confrontation between Abram, the king of Sodom and Melchizedek.[1174] The

---

[1169] Wright, *Victory*, 492.

[1170] Ibid., 508.

[1171] J. J. Collins, *The Scepter and the Star: The Messiahs of the Dead Sea Scrolls and Other Ancient Literature* (Garden City, NY: Doubleday, 1995), 148.

[1172] Ibid. Cf. M. Hengel, *Studies in Early Christology* (Edinburgh: T&T Clark, 1995), 201-3.

[1173] J. A. Fitzmyer, *The Semitic Background of the New Testament: Essays on the Semitic Background of the New Testament* (Grand Rapids: Eerdmans, 1997), 223. According to Fitzmyer, the theological conception used in Hebrews is related much more to controllable Jewish apocalyptic writers with their expectations of a messianic priesthood rooted in Genesis 14.

[1174] G. J. Wenham, *Genesis 1-15*, WBC (Dallas: Word, 1987), 304. According to Wenham, the arrangement is as follows:
1-16 Three battle reports:
1-4 Eastern kings vs Westerners: round 1
5-12 Eastern kings vs Westerners: round 2

three battle reports conform to a regular convention in Hebrew narrative of telling a story in three scenes, and they serve to heighten Abram's final victory. Abram's victory forms the backdrop to the centerpiece of the story, the three-way discussion between Abram, the King of Sodom, and Melchizedek. Wenham thinks that it is probably by virtue of his priesthood that Abram gave him the tithe.[1175]

Melchizedek the king of Salem "brought out bread and wine" in Gen 14:18. The precise significance of this gesture is uncertain, but is possibly no more than a token of goodwill.[1176] Vawter has suggested that this action shows that Melchizedek and Abram had a covenant meal together.[1177] This suggestion seems to be going beyond the evidence. Westermann pointed out that Gen 14:20a corresponds to the "deliverance formula" of the war of Yahweh and it is very like Exod 18:10.[1178] The verb מגן ("deliver") here occurs in only two other

---

13-16 Abram vs Eastern kings
17-24 Confrontation between Abram, the king of Sodom, and Melchizedek:
17 King of Sodom meets Abram
18-20 Melchizedek blesses Abram
21 King of Sodom's demand
22-24 Abram's reply

In the first battle, Chedorlaomer and his allies defeat the king of Sodom and his allies. In the second campaign, Chedorlaomer defeats various inhabitants of Canaan and the Dead Sea kings. This double victory underlines the invincibility of Chedorlaomer and his allies. But in the third battle, Abram defeats the all-conquering Easterners and rescues the captives. Abram's military prowess is shown to be superior, not simply to that of the King of Sodom, twice defeated by Chedorlaomer, but also to that of Chedorlaomer.

The grudging attitude of the king of Sodom toward his great benefactor Abram (v. 21) stands in sharp contrast both to Melchizedek's open acknowledgment of divine blessing on Abram (vv. 18—20) and also to Abram's generosity to those he had saved (vv. 22-24).

[1175] Ibid., 316. For as Abram has received a priestly blessing from Melchizedek, it is fitting that he should respond in the customary fashion. Here Abram (cf. Jacob 28.22), father of the nation, sets an example for all his descendants to follow (cf. later legislation on tithing: Num 18; Lev 27:30-33). "Everything" in context must refer to all the booty captured from the fleeing kings, since it was on his way home that Abram met Melchizedek.

[1176] Wenham, *Genesis 1-15*, 316. It is noteworthy that a king of Jerusalem mentioned in Josh 10:1 is called Adonizedek ("my lord is Sedeq"), and David's high priest was called Zadok. According to Wenham, this seems to corroborate the narrator's assumption that Melchizedek was king of Jerusalem. Ps 110 associates the king in Zion with Melchizedek, and Ps 76:3 [2] puts Zion and Salem in parallel.

The name "Melchizedek" may be understood in three different ways: "My king is Sedek," "Milku is righteous" or "my king is righteous [i.e. legitimate]:" The first two interpretations presuppose that either Melek or Sedeq is the name of a god. The third does not: if it were correct, it would be the equivalent of Akkadian Sarru ken (Sargon). Since theophoric names are frequent in the ancient orient, the first or second explanation is to be preferred. The Genesis Apocryphon (22:13) and Josephus (Ant. 1.10.2 [1:180]) also affirm the identity of Salem with Jerusalem.

[1177] B. Vawter, *On Genesis: A New Reading* (Garden City, NY: Doubleday, 1977), 157.

[1178] C. Westerman, *Genesis 12-36: A Commentary* (Minneapolis: Augsburg, 1981), 206

passages (Hos 11:8; Isa 64:6); in the Qal it means "to give."[1179] Here too, giving is mentioned immediately afterwards (vv. 20–21). The cognate term מגן ("shield"), used in 15:1, seems to look back to this passage. "He gave him a tenth of everything." Tithing given to both sanctuaries and kings was an old and widespread custom in the ancient orient.[1180] Melchizedek qualifies on both counts. Thus, Westermann sees the event portrayed in Gen 14 as the narratives of liberation; however, he understands that the narrative in Gen 14:12–24 originated in the period of the judges and comes from a cycle of savior narratives.[1181] What is important for our study is that Gen 14 is an event about salvation, that Abram defeats the Eastern kings, and on the way home Melchizedek as king and priest performs a royal banquet for Abram. Bread and wine is royal fare (1 Sam 16:20) and regularly accompanied animal sacrifice (Num 15:2–10; 1 Sam 1:24; 10:3). Melchizedek, who in traditional Near Eastern fashion combined the offices of king and priest, should have had ample supplies of bread and wine. Here he is portrayed as laying on a royal banquet for Abram the returning liberator.

The author of Hebrews also cites Ps 110 in his use of the Melchizedek tradition in Heb 1:13 and 5:5–10, which is also linked to victory. Eaton related Ps 110:4 to the concluding phase of the enthronement ceremony, looking back in vv. 5–6 to a dramatic enactment of the defeat of the king's enemies.[1182] Del Medico associated the psalm with a pre-battle ritual as a promise of victory.[1183] Dahood judged that it celebrates a victory already won.[1184] Horton considered the psalm to be a song of victory sung on David's return to Jerusalem after defeating

---

[1179] Ibid., According to Westermann, God is also the subject who delivers.

[1180] Wenham, *Genesis 1–15*, 317.

[1181] Westermann, *Genesis 12–36*, 191.

[1182] J. H. Eaton, *Kingship and the Psalm*, SBT 2.32 (Naperville, IL: Allenson, 1976), 124. Cf. W. van der. Meer, "Psalm 110: A Psalm of Rehabilitation?" In *The Structural Analysis of Biblical and Canaanite Poetry*, ed. W. van der Meer and J. C. de Moor, JSOTSup 74 (Sheffield: JSOT Press, 1988), 222–23. Meer observes that a reference to swearing (v. 4) is frequently used to refer back to a past utterance, for example in Josh 14:9; Judg 21:1; 1 Kgs 1:17, and that two other royal psalms, Pss 89 and 132, look back to earlier oracles.

[1183] H. E. del. Medico, "Melchisedech" *ZAW* 69 (1957), 169. Cf. A Bentzen, *King and Messiah* (London: Lutterworth, 1955), 23–25; A. R. Johnson, *Sacral Kingship in Ancient Israel*, 2nd ed. (Cardiff: University of Wales Press, 1979), 130. Bentzen and Johnson associated the Psalm with an annual New Year festival.

[1184] M. Dahood, *Psalms III: 101–150*, AB (Garden City, NY: Doubleday, 1970), 112.

Ammon.[1185] What is important is that the psalm is thought to relate to a victorious conflict by some scholars.

In regard to the question of the background of the psalm, Rowley reconstructed the psalm's setting as a cultic ceremony of recognition after the capture of Jerusalem.[1186] He claimed that in Ps 110 Zadok, whom he held to be the pre-Israelite priest of the Jebusite sanctuary, addressed David in vv. 1–3, while David confirmed Zadok in his priesthood in v. 4 and Zadok blessed David in vv. 5–7.[1187] He interpreted the Psalm in a priestly context.

However, some have argued that Melchizedek's role in Ps 110 was to be a priestly king. Bowker argued that Ps 110:4 agrees with the evidence that the king seems to have acted as priest only on special occasions or in exceptional circumstances; it emphasizes that the king's priesthood is not the normal one but of a strange and different sort.[1188] Nel points out that David was the founder of a new, permanent dynasty that was the legitimate heir to the priest-kingly rule of the previous dynasty associated with Melchizedek.[1189] Allen understands Ps 110:4 as a solemn pledge of the king's sacred role in Yahweh's purposes.[1190] A divine oath is especially associated with the Davidic covenant, in Pss 89:4, 35–36 (3, 34–35); 132:11 (cf. 2 Sam 3:9). There was now a divinely appointed successor to the dynastic line of Jebusite priest-kings, but his rule was destined not to be superseded as theirs had been. From his Jebusite predecessors the king inherited the title of priest to Yahweh the Most High God, as sacred mediator between God and his people. Allen links the Psalm to Gen 14:17–24 concerning the priest-king.[1191] Thus Ps 110 presents the king as the heir of Melchizedek, succeeding him as a priest forever.

Turning to Heb 7:25, the author of Hebrews specifies that the benefit of Christ's priestly kingship is that he is able to save those who come to God

---

[1185] F. L. Horton, *The Melchizedek Tradition: A Critical Examination of the Sources to the Fifth Century A.D. and in the Epistle to the Hebrews*, SNTSMS 30 (Cambridge: Cambridge University Press, 1976), 34.

[1186] H. H. Rowley, "Melchizedek and Zadok," in *Festschrift für A. Bertholet*. ed. W. Baumgartner et al. (Tubingen: Mohr, 1950), 461–72.

[1187] Ibid.

[1188] J. W. Bowker, "Psalm cx," *VT* 17(1967), 35–6.

[1189] P. J. Nel, "Psalm 110 and the Melchizedek Tradition." *JSNL* 22(1996), 6.

[1190] L. C. Allen, *Psalm* 101–150, 116.

[1191] Ibid.

completely (εἰς τὸ παντελὲς). In Hebrews "deliverance" is presented as a future eschatological inheritance (1:14; 5:9; 9:28), including both forgiveness of sins and restoration. There is, nevertheless, a definite sense in which the community has already begun to participate in deliverance as a result of the obedience and sacrificial death of Christ and his subsequent exaltation (cf. Heb 2:3–4; 6:4–5, 9). The present tense of σῴζειν reflects the current experience of the community and suggests that Jesus's support is available at each critical moment. He has a sustained interest in the welfare of his people. The perfection and eternity of the salvation he performs is guaranteed by the unassailable character of his priestly king.

Melchizedek is not even mentioned when quoting Ps 110:4,[1192] but his status as a priestly king is seen in Heb 7:26–28. According to Ellingworth, the exposition of Ps 110:4 is gathered up into a summary which fuses the major themes of Christ's priesthood in Heb 7:11–25. There the writer has argued on the basis of Ps 110:4 that the promised exalted priest supersedes the old priesthood and that he is effective where the Levitical priests were not.[1193] The exposition is brought to a conclusion in vv. 26–28 with a majestic statement concerning Jesus's character, achievement, and status as high priest. Clearly, the theme of his living forever is repeated over and over by the author of Hebrews to prove the superiority of the priestly kingship of Christ. And in connection with the priestly king, this truth is unique to Ps 110:4 and its use in Hebrews.

Such a definition of the priestly king may be seen in Heb 1:2.[1194] Westcott argues that here the Son is represented as becoming heir of all things because all things were made through him, not as a result of sin and redemption, but because of his work at the creation.[1195] However, according to Hughes, the statement that the Son was appointed the heir of all things is a statement concerning the mediatorial office of Christ.[1196] In this connection, it is worth

---

[1192] P. Ellingworth, *The Epistle to the Hebrews*, New International Greek Commentary, eds. I. H. Marshall and W. W. Gasque (Grand Rapids: Eerdmans, 1993), 392.

[1193] Anderson, *King-Priest*, 230–1.

[1194] "his Son, whom he appointed heir of all things, through whom also he made the worlds."

[1195] Westcott, *Hebrews*, 6–8.

[1196] Hughes, *Hebrews*, 38–9.

noting that some scholars associated the statement with the words of Ps 2:8;[1197] words which come immediately after and belong to the declaration of Ps 2:7,[1198] a text which in the teaching of the apostles was seen as bearing a particular relationship to the mediatorial work of Christ. The heirship of Christ, then, is established within the perspective of redemption: his inheritance is the innumerable company of the redeemed and the universe renewed by virtue of his triumphant work of reconciliation. "The name 'heir' is attributed to Christ as manifest in the flesh," says Calvin; "for in being made man and putting on the same nature as us, he took on himself this heirship, in order to restore to us what we had lost in Adam."[1199] Although Hughes and Calvin understand that the term "Son" includes the function of both priest and king, nevertheless, they tried to interpret the Epistle to the Hebrews in the light of the Levitical priesthood.

If the "Son" in Heb 1:2 is associated with the words of Ps 2:7–8 then, as Hughes points out, then the author of Hebrews says that this role is fulfilled in Christ, adapting "Son" to be a messianic title.[1200] In other words, while Jesus is a high priest, he as a king provides redemption. Thus we may interpret the verse, on this basis, as follows: God made him redemptive heir of all things, as he had also created all things through him. Because he was the Creator of all things, Christ is also the redeemer who is heir of all.

Westcott held that the bringing of gifts in Heb 5:1 was independent of sin because of the two separate functions of a priest.[1201] He argues that, apart from sin and redemption, Christ's incarnation would have been necessary to enable him to realize the creative goal of the human race.[1202] It seems that Westcott's

---

[1197] Ps 2:8 "Ask of me, and I will make the nations your heritage, and the ends of the earth your possession."

[1198] "You are my son, today I have begotten you,"

[1199] J. Calvin, The *Epistle of Paul The Apostle to the Hebrews and The first and Second Epistle of St Peter*, trans. W. B. Johnstan (Grand Rapids: Eerdmans, 1979), 6–7.

[1200] Holland, *Paschal*, 151. Cf. P. Ellingworth, *The Epistle to the Hebrews: A Commentary on the Greek Text* (Carlisle: Paternoster, 1993), 150; D. A. Carson, "Christological Ambiguities in the Gospel of Matthews" in *Christ the Lord*, Studies presented to Donald Guthrie, ed. H. H. Rowden (Leicester: IVP, 1982), 97–114. They have argued that the Psalm is being used to show nothing more than that Jesus is a human being and therefore able to act as high priest.

[1201] Westcott, *Hebrews*, 118–19. In Heb 5:1 we have here two separate parts of the function of a priest because of the τε, namely, the bringing of gifts, and the offering of sacrifices for sin. In that case, the bringing of gifts is independent of sin.

[1202] Ibid.

interpretation fails to understand the author of Hebrews concerning sin and redemption. However, the author applies Ps 110:4 to Jesus in Heb 5, undoubtedly understanding it as messianic (although he does not expressly state this link).[1203] Having first introduced Ps 2:7 to establish the risen Jesus as the possessor of regal inheritance, he adds Ps 110:4 to present this kingly Son of God as one appointed also to an eternal priesthood.

The author of Hebrews links the term "high priest" to eternal redemption in Heb 9:11–14. If Heb 9 is interpreted in the light of the Day of Atonement,[1204] it is difficult to explain why the theme of redemption should be associated with the ritual. Holland proposes that there is only one cultic event in which redemption is celebrated, and that is Passover.[1205] Passover controlled Israel's self-consciousness, it controlled her existence. She could not define herself apart from the fact that Yahweh had redeemed her. Therefore, Heb 9:11–14 is understood on the basis of Ezekiel's vision that the ritual of the Day of Atonement was to be absorbed into the Passover (Ezek 45:21–25). The main function of the king in the united ritual is to provide a sacrifice for the sins of the community. Then the king provides redemption with forgiveness for the restoration for the community.

Christ's Priestly Kingship in Eschatology

The expression "forever" is one of the major themes in Heb 7, comparing Aaron with Melchizedek. The author of Hebrews sets forth two orders of priesthood, namely the order of Aaron and the order of Melchizedek. Concerning the priest's function, Holland points out that while the order is different it does not mean that their functions are different.[1206] There would seem to be parallel functions between the two orders. However, Melchizedek is far greater than Aaron. In the matter of attribute, Bruce pointed out that the order of Aaron would then be the earthly priesthood, and that of Melchizedek would be the heavenly priesthood.[1207] On the Day of Atonement the former

---

[1203] It is apparently part of the author's own theology to apply Ps 110:4 to Christ as the messianic priest. No rabbi is attested as having applied Ps 110.4 to the Messiah before the second half of the 3rd century A.D.

[1204] Koester, *Hebrews*, 401.

[1205] Holland, *Contours*, 169.

[1206] Holland, *Paschal*, 167.

[1207] A. B. Bruce, *Humiliation of Christ* (New York: Welford & Armstrong, 1876), 201.

had to perform the act of slaying the sacrificial animal in the court before the sanctuary. That is, he had his business only in the most holy place under the old covenant. But the latter seemed to be a higher person than Abram in Gen 14, and he acted like both a priest and a king in Ps 110. Melchizedek seems to be a divine person according to the two Old Testament passages. Thus, it has been argued that the Aaronic priesthood lacked the dimension of eternity. In the matter of eternity, Vos viewed that Melchizedek was a historical person and not eternal, but was regarded as eternal because he was without a recorded father or mother or genealogy, and had no recorded beginning of days nor end of life.[1208] In these respects Melchizedek is like the Son of God, who is stripped of all earthly attachments. Vos saw that Melchizedek is a type of the Christ to come.

The author of Hebrews links the fact that Christ's priestly kingship is eternal to his sinlessness,[1209] as the fact of Christ's sinlessness is brought into connection with his priesthood in Heb 7:26.[1210] The word ἄκακος ("guileless, pure, innocent") is used in the LXX predominantly with a passive and moral significance. It was an appropriate term for denoting the moral qualification of Jesus to be high priest.[1211] It signifies not only that Jesus was guileless in his relationship with other people, but that he was not touched by evil.[1212] The term ἀμίαντος ("undefiled") denotes cultic purity.[1213] It is mostly applied to things, not to a person, but in two passages in Philo he applies the term directly to the high priest, as in Heb 7:26.[1214] Taken together, the Levitical high priest demanded only ritual purity and bodily completeness, but the high priest appropriate to the new community qualified by spiritual and moral purification.

[1208] Vos, *Hebrews*, 106. Cf. Heb 7:3. According to Vos, although the Greek word αιωνιος has a double meaning, Heb 7:15 has the connotation of power, of having the energy or the dynamic of the eternal world.

[1209] Heb 4:15; 7:26, 27–28; 9:14.

[1210] F. Hauck, "μιαινω, μιάσματα, μιασμοῦ, ἀμίαντος" in *TDNT* IV, 647. J. Moffat, *A Critical and Exegetical Commentary on the Epistle to the Hebrews*, ICC (Edinburgh: Clark, 1924), 101.

[1211] Lane, *Hebrews*, 191.

[1212] W. Grundmann, "κακός"[kakos] in *TDNT* III, 482; Bruce, *Hebrews*, 156.

[1213] 2 Macc 14:26; 15:34

[1214] On Flight and Finding, 118; On the Special Laws, 1.113

Heb 7:27–28 also shows that Christ's sinlessness is stressed in connection with his priesthood.[1215] It is striking that when the writer speaks of Jesus's qualification for his priestly/kingly ministry he adds the proviso that he was without sin. In Heb 7:28 the comparison is between Christ and the Old Testament high priests; Jesus's entire separateness from sin and sinners is emphasized as essential to his priesthood, while the Old Testament priests had sinful infirmities.[1216] The contrast is twofold: the law appoints men, the word of the oath swearing appoints a son; the men appointed are men having infirmity, the son appointed is a son made perfect forevermore. This second contrast creates some difficulty.

Christ's sinlessness is also expressed in Heb 4:15, with the words: κατὰ πάντα καθ' ὁμοιότητα χωρὶς ἁμαρτίας ("in all points tempted like as we are, yet without sin"). Christ as a high priest can sympathize with the feeling of our infirmities because he was tempted. In Heb 5:2, sinfulness is mentioned as virtually a necessary qualification of the Old Testament priesthood, but in the New Testament Christ as a high priest was necessarily sinless. In the Old Testament type experience of sin served as a help to the priestly office, in the New Testament antitype it would be a hindrance. So the author applies μετριοπαθεῖν ("be gentle") to the Old Testament high priest; in the matter of the fact of Christ's sinlessness, on the other hand, he uses συμπαθῆσαι ("sympathize" in 4:15).[1217] Therefore, Melchizedek as the high priest seems to be a divine person.

According to Cullmann, Heb 7:24 describes Christ's priesthood as ἀπαράβατον ("permanent").[1218] He argued that the expression ἐκ δευτέρου ("a second time")

[1215] Koester, *Hebrews*, 368.

[1216] "For the law appointed as high priests men who are weak; but the oath, which came after the law, appointed the Son, who has been made perfect forever."

[1217] Cf. The term μετριοπαθεῖν has been variously interpreted. Calvin and the Authorized Version confuse it with συμπαθῆσαιin Heb 4:15— "Who can have compassion with the ignorant and erring": J. Calvin, *The Epistle of Paul The Apostle to the Hebrews and The First and Second Epistle of St. Peter*, trans. W. B. Johnston (Grand Rapids: Eerdmans, 1979), 59–60. Beza and the Dutch version have a better rendering: Die behoorlijk medelijden kan hebhen—"no lack of sympathetic emotion"—that is to say, Christ is not like a Stoic, who is ανπαθειν (devoid of emotion). G. Vos (*Hebrews*, 100) points out that the expression used in 5:2, however, is even stronger than this, and is accurately translated in the Revised Version: "who can bear gently with the ignorant and erring"—that is, who has no excess of indignation. Thus, Vos says that the term μετριοπαθεῖν cannot be used of Christ.

[1218] Cullmann, *Christology*, 101–02. Cf. Vos, *Hebrews*, 107, also pointed out that Christ's eternity is shown in the sphere of life in Heb 7:23–25.

in 9:28[1219] describes the eschatological work of the high priest, just as the expression ἐφάπαξ ("once for all") in 7:27 describes his earthly work and διηνεκές ("in perpetuity") in 7:3 describes his present work. He went on to say that "after the order of Melchizedek" is synonymous with "forever" as a description of the priest. Cullmann links eternity to Christ's priesthood in saying that Hebrews emphasizes that the high priest remains in the holy place and there continues his work in the present.

Hughes points out that Ps 110 provides a link in the chain of the argument which demonstrates the superiority of the order of Melchizedek to that of Levi. He sees that Jesus as the "priest forever" is the fulfillment of the priesthood of Melchizedek in his person.[1220] Bruce points out that the Lord's indissoluble life makes it possible for him to fulfill the words "You are a priest forever."[1221] If these words were applied to a dynasty of priests, according to him, "forever" could be understood only of an inherited succession of indefinite duration.[1222]

What is affirmed of Melchizedek in Heb 7, then, is affirmed of him in his typical appearance. In this purely typical sense his eternity could well be affirmed in both directions, past as well as future. This would be equally true of Melchizedek as the type and of Christ himself.

Moffatt points out that the author defines the meaning of the oracle of Ps 110:4 from v. 11, showing that the whole Levitical system of approach to God is ineffective and that the law that regulated its priesthood has been superseded.[1223] The oracle in Heb 7:15 has reference to a priest whose quality would be like Melchizedek as he is described in Gen 14:18–20 and in Ps 110:4.

[1219] Ibid., 103. According to Cullmann, the expression ἐκ δευτέρου, a second time, points clearly to the return of Christ. He goes on to say that Heb 9:28 contains not only the idea but also a literal reference to the second coming of Jesus.

[1220] Hughes, *Hebrews*, 266. Cf. When quoting Ps 110:4 in Heb 7, but the common thread of εἰς τὸν αἰῶνα is found in all three of the subdivisions (Heb 7:20–22; 23–25; 26–28).

[1221] Bruce, *Hebrews*, 152.

[1222] Ibid., Cf. as in Exod 40:15; Num 25:13.

[1223] J. Moffatt, *A Critical and Exegetical Commentary on the Epistle to the Hebrews*, ICC (Edinburgh: Clark, 1924), 164. Cf. G. L. Cockerill, *The Melchizedek Christology in Heb 7:1–28* (Ann Arbor: University Microfilms International, 1979), 99–101.

The promise was fulfilled in Christ who is actually what Melchizedek was typologically, an eternal priestly king who exercises his kingly prerogatives.[1224]

The word ὅς ("who") in Heb 7:16, refers to the closet antecedent in v. 15b, ἱερεὺς ἕτερος ("a different priest") who is the promised priest like Melchizedek. The description ἀλλὰ κατὰ δύναμιν ζωῆς ἀκαταλύτου ("but by virtue of the power of an indestructible life") in Heb 7:16 also defines the corresponding expression in v. 11, κατὰ τὴν ὁμοιότητα Μελχισέδεκ ("like Melchizedek"). Peterson understands that the phrase δύναμιν ζωῆς ἀκαταλύτου ("the power of an indestructible life") describes the new quality of life with which Jesus was endowed by virtue of his resurrection and exaltation to the heavenly world, where he was formally installed in his office as high priest.[1225] Here in v. 16 the characterization of δύναμινby the qualitative genitive ζωῆς ἀκαταλύτου offers a striking definition of the meaning of the phrase εἰς τὸν αἰῶνα ("forever") in Ps 110:4, which is cited in v. 17. Williamson holds that the central place of Ps 110 in the argument of Hebrews results from the writer's firm conviction that the resurrection provided absolute proof of Jesus's imperishable life.[1226] It designates the eternity of the new priest, the priestly king, from the perspective of his post-resurrection existence. That is, to be a priest like Melchizedek is to be a priestly king by virtue of the power of an indestructible life.

In Heb 7:23–25, furthermore, the superiority of Jesus's priestly kingship is demonstrated by its permanence. In vv. 23–24 the main emphasis appears to rest on the contrast between the "many" and the "one": οἱ μὲν πλείονές ...ὁ δὲ ("on the one hand these many... but on the other hand that one"). That is, there were many priests under the Levitical arrangement.[1227] In v. 23 the

---

[1224] Cf. There are many scholars who see that Christ fulfilled what Melchizedek was symbolically, an eternal priest who exercises his priestly rights, e.g. W. Lane, *Hebrews*, 47A, 183; P. Ellingworth, "Just like Melchizedek," *BT* 28 (1977), 236–39.

[1225] D. G. Peterson, *An Examination of the Concept of 'Perfection' in the Epistle to the Hebrews* (PhD diss., University of Manchester, 1978), 185–86. Cf. W. Manson, *The Epistle to the Hebrews: An Historical and Theological Reconsideration* (London: Hodder & Stoughton, 1951), 116; R. Williamson, *Philo and the Epistle to the Hebrews*, 82. They thought that the acknowledgement that Jesus is a priest "like Melchizedek" implies that he is priest by virtue of his resurrection.

[1226] R. Williamson, *Hebrews*, 447.

[1227] *Ant.* 20.227. According to Josephus, a total of eighty-three high priests was installed from the inception of the Aaronic priesthood to the cessation of temple worship in 70 CE. Cf. J. W. Thompson, *The Letter to the Hebrews* (Austin, TX: Sweet, 1971), 200. In Hebrews multiplicity signifies incompleteness, imperfection, and inconclusiveness. Vos, *Hebrews*, 107–8.

direction of the author's thought is indicated more precisely by the causal clause in v. 23b: the reason there were many priests is that every one of them was prevented from continuing in office by the simple fact of death. Consequently, the continuity of the Levitical priesthood was repeatedly disrupted.[1228]

By way of contrast, Jesus has been invested with an eternal and final priesthood because of a causal clause in v. 24a: διὰ τὸ μένειν αὐτὸν εἰς τὸν αἰῶνα ("because he continues forever"). When quoting Ps 110:4 in Heb 7,[1229] the common thread of εἰς τὸν αἰῶνα is found in all three of the subdivisions. The choice of the infinitive μένειν ("to continue") appears to be theologically significant. In the LXX the term μένειν signifies God's continuing life in contrast to limited human existence.[1230] Lane sees that μενειν, together with εἰς τὸν αἰῶνα ("forever") recalls the striking declaration concerning Melchizedek in 7:3.[1231]

Juxtaposing the two causal clauses (v. 23 and v. 24d) in the chiastic structure of vv. 23–24 emphasizes the temporal character of the many priests and the permanence of the one. What is true of Melchizedek in a literary and symbolic way attains its definitive realization in the priestly king of the new covenant. The predication "he continues forever" implies Christ's participation in the life of God.

In Heb 7:25, the author of Hebrews specifies the benefit of Christ's priestly kingship that he is able to save εἰς τὸ παντελὲς. The expression is at the same time a resumption and an amplification of the εἰς τὸν αἰῶνα of Ps 110:4.[1232] It is enriched by its ambivalence, combining the notions of perpetuity on the one hand—thus "for all time" (RSV)— and of completeness on the other—thus "absolutely" (NEB), "fully and completely" (Phillips). Thus, we may take the

---

[1228] Cf. According to Exod 40:15 LXX, Aaron and his sons had been appointed to the priesthood εἰς τὸν αἰῶνα ("forever"), but this unlimited expression is immediately qualified by the phrase εινςταςγενεαςαυντων, ("in their respective generations"). The Levitical priesthood was perpetuated only because provision had been made for a succession of priests to exercise the ministry.

[1229] Heb 7:20–22; 23–25; 26–28.

[1230] F. Hauck, "μένω" [meno] in *TDNT* IV, 575–76, e.g. Dan 6:27 LXX: εστινθεος ζωνκαι μενων εις τους αιωνας ("God continuing and living from generation to generation forever").

[1231] Lane, *Hebrews 1–8*, 189. "He continues as priest without interruption."

[1232] Hughes, *Hebrews*, 269. n. 35.

words in such a comprehensive sense as to include the meaning of both these interpretations.

Thompson pointed out that the expression showed an awareness of the finality and duration of Christ's priestly ministry on behalf of his people.[1233] Lane sees the expression εἰς τὸ παντελὲς as "absolutely," and argues that it is a benefit of Christ's eternal priesthood.[1234] However, the expression εἰς τὸ παντελὲς, which means either "for all time" or "absolutely", indicating completeness of salvation, is not performed by the Levitical priests but by Melchizedek.[1235] The former disappeared through death and succeeded to one another in great numbers (7:23); a circumstance which shows how restricted was their accomplishment. However, clearly, the theme of his living forever is repeated over and over by the author of Hebrews to prove the superiority of the priestly kingship of Christ. And in connection with the priestly king, this truth is unique to Ps 110:4 and its use in Hebrews.

The Old Testament priests were many in number, because death continually took them away, but Christ abides forever. Therefore, Christ is able to save to the uttermost—not only in degree, but also in point of time—those that draw near to God through him.

If the ministry of the priestly king is eschatological, then, our question now is where he fulfills his ministry. Where is the sanctuary which continues after the resurrection? This may be indicated in Heb 8:4 where the author declares that the priesthood of Jesus is not an earthly priesthood, but a priesthood in the heavenly realm. According to Vos, this verse is not related to ordinary geographical conceptions, but those of a ritual geography.[1236] Lane points out that Christ who has taken his seat at God's right hand is understood in the light of the theme of heavenly sanctuary.[1237] In fact, the earthly order is the order of Levi, as required by the old covenant. Therefore, Christ's priestly kingship belongs to a sphere that is not on earth. This consideration in no way

---

[1233] J. W. Thompson, "The Conceptual Background and Purpose of the Midrash in Hebrews VII," *NovT* 19 (1977), 221.

[1234] Lane, *Hebrews 1–8*, 189.

[1235] L. Sabourin, *Priesthood: A Comparative Study* (Leiden: Brill, 1973), 184.

[1236] Vos, *Hebrews*, 113. Vos thought that the author compares the ministry of Christ with the ministry of the Old Testament high priest.

[1237] Lane, *Hebrews 1–8*, 204–11.

detracts from the point that Christ's priestly kingship involved his offering his humanity as a sacrifice on earth. Yet his resurrection brings the restoration of our humanity and its exaltation with himself to the glory which is now his. He who has gone to heaven is the one who first came from heaven, the true sanctuary. The abiding sphere of his priestly kingship is heavenly and eschatological, not earthly and temporal.

In Heb 9:24 Christ is represented as entering into heaven as high priest.[1238] On the basis of this it seems natural to argue that he must have been such before entering heaven, but it is also possible that it was the entrance into heaven that made him high priest.[1239] He is present "on our behalf". Christ as our representative received for us the eternal blessing which his atoning death has procured. So believers may experience daily the benediction of his sovereign redemption in their lives. The efficacy of the priestly kingship of Christ is available to the covenant people of God. Leonard says that Christ is able to save in perpetuity all who come through him to God, always living to intercede for them.[1240]

Identification of the priestly kingship with his people

Heb 5:1–10 sets forth the characteristics of a high priest. This is expressed by the words: "Every high priest is appointed on behalf of men in things pertaining to God" (τὰ πρὸς τὸν θεόν). A high priest is one who stands at the head of others and thus mediates their approach unto God. Thus, priesthood is distinctly leadership based on and involving identification of nature and experience.

The term καθίσταται in Heb 5:1 is to be construed as a passive.[1241] It interacted with the phrase, τὰ πρὸς τὸν θεόν in the form of an adverbial phrase, "every high priest ordains the things which pertain to God." Therefore, the author's meaning is that the high priest is a representative to God for men.

[1238] Heweit, *Hebrews*, 152. According to Heweit, Christ entered the heavenly Holy of holies through his final, complete and all-sufficient sacrifice. It had already been done when he offered himself to God on the cross.

[1239] Vos, *Hebrews*, 110.

[1240] W. Leonard, *The Authorship of the Epistle to the Hebrews: Critical Problem and Use of the Old Testament* (London: Burns Oates and Washbourne, 1939), 73.

[1241] Bruce, *Hebrews*, 88; Hughes, *Hebrews*, 175. Those who take it as passive, render it as follows, 'He is appointed for these things,' thus understanding the preposition which governs the noun things.

Characteristic of the high priest in the order of Melchizedek is his ability to sympathize with those whose cause he maintains.

Furthermore, the priestly leadership is such that it cannot be performed by the one who stands outside of the circle in whose interest he serves, according to the old covenant. The author accordingly emphasizes in the definition of 5:1 that a high priest must be λαμβανόμενος ὑπὲρ ἀνθρώπων ("taken from among men"). The force of the present participle should be noticed: "one who is constantly, in each case, taken from among men," the permanent force of the requirement thus being brought out, as Westcott strikingly observed.[1242] Since a high priest is "chosen" and "appointed" as a representative in v. 1, he is expounded by the assertion that he is called by God in v. 4. The appointment is dependent on the calling of God. Thus, the author cites these two messianic passages in 5:5–6, namely Ps 2:7 and Ps 110:4.

Many scholars have thought that Ps 2 is cited in Ps 110 by the Lord's Anointed as the ground of his confidence in the face of the plotting of his enemies.[1243] Johnson finds in the original intention of Ps 2 "the thought of the eventual fulfillment of this promise [that David would be made supreme over the kings of the earth] in the person of his descendant and ideal successor upon the throne, the true Messiah of the House of David".[1244] That is, with regard to the Davidic dynasty, it was believed that this psalm would be most fully realized in the Messiah of David's line who would be raised up for his people in the time of fulfillment.[1245]

[1242] Westcott, *Hebrews*, 118.

[1243] Bruce, *Hebrews*, 94; J. Calvin, *The Epistle of Paul the Apostle to the Hebrews and The First and Second Epistles of St Peter*, 59.

[1244] Johnson, *Sacral Kingship*, 128–9.

[1245] Ibid. For example, about the middle of the first century BCE, Ps 2:7 is quoted in the Psalms of Solomon with reference to the Davidic Messiah whose advent is ardently prayed for (Pss. Sol. 17:26). An allusion to it may be found in Gabriel's annunciation to Mary about her coming child (Luke 1:32). More important still is the fact that the heavenly voice which greeted Jesus at his baptism hailed him in the opening words of the decree of Ps 2:7. The "Western" text of Luke 3:22 represents the heavenly voice as addressing to Jesus the fuller wording from Ps 2:7 which is quoted here by the author of Hebrews: "Thou art my Son, this day have I begotten thee". The words were evidently in widespread use as a testimonium in the apostolic age, as Acts 13:33 bears witness; and not only these words but the other parts of the psalm were given a messianic interpretation, as may be seen from the quotation and explanation of its first two verses in Acts 4:25.

The author also applies Ps 110:4 to Jesus in Heb 5:6; but this was, in a way, an unprecedented move within the early church because a distinction was made between the lay Messiah (the Messiah of Israel or prince of the house of David) and the priestly Messiah (the Messiah of Aaron) in some strands of Jewish expectation.[1246] Thus some have argued that the people to whom this epistle was addressed were related to those groups which held a twofold messianic hope of this kind.[1247] If indeed our author has the Qumran teaching in mind, they were wrong in two important respects: first, because for the author there is only one messianic personage, who is both king and priest, and, second, because his priestly category is that of Melchizedek, not Aaron.

But here Jesus is acclaimed by God as the Davidic Messiah in Ps 2:7, while he was also acclaimed by God as high priest in Ps 110:4. Lindars challenged Yadin's interpretation in saying that the Messiah is both king and priest, not two messiahs.[1248] But Lindars thinks that the author bases his argument on the Day of Atonement ceremony, which is performed by the high priest alone.

If the messiah of David's line is high priest as well as king, he cannot be a "Messiah of Aaron"; Aaron belonged to the tribe of Levi, whereas David and his house belonged to the tribe of Judah, "as to which tribe Moses spoke nothing concerning priests" (Heb 7:14). No appeal can be made to those scriptures which establish the Levitical and Aaronic priesthood to support the claim that Jesus the son of David exercises a high-priestly ministry on his people's behalf.[1249] Therefore, the Davidic king as another priestly order was designated as priest of this order.

[1246] This distinction appears most clearly in the Qumran literature (e.g. 1QS ix, 11); K. G. Kuhn, "The Two Messiahs of Aaron and Israel", in *The Scrolls and the New Testament*, ed. K. Stendahl (New York: Harper, 1957), 54; Bruce, *Biblical Exegesis*, 41.

[1247] Y. Yadin, "The Dead Sea Scrolls and the Epistle to the Hebrews", *Scripta Hierosolymitana* iv (1958), 36

[1248] B. Lindars, *New Testament Apologetics: The Doctrinal Significance of the Old Testament Quotations* (Philadelphia: Westminster, 1961), 142. According to Lindars, there is no fundamental distinction between priest and high priest, the author of Hebrews prefers to call Jesus high priest.

[1249] Ibid. Hippolytus was first to see that Jesus was descended from Levi as well as from Judah (an inference apparently drawn from Testament of Simeon 7:2). He also interprets Moses's blessing of Levi (Deut 33:8) with reference to Jesus. And then Luke established a Levitical relationship for Jesus through his mother's kinswoman Elizabeth, who was "of the daughters of Aaron" (Luke 1:5). Cf. J. L. Teicher, "The Damascus fragments and the Origin of the Jewish-Christian Sect," in *Journal of Jewish Studies* 2 (1950), 134. He attempted to establish a similar argument.

In the matter of citing two messianic Psalms, however, Westcott believed that Melchizedek "represented a non-Jewish, a universal priesthood," and that "in relation to the priesthood he occupies the position which Abraham occupies in relation to the Covenant."[1250] According to Hughes,[1251] the immediate purpose of the two quotations given here from the Psalms is to corroborate the doctrine that Christ's high-priestly office was not from himself but from God for people. However, both Westcott and Hughes did not explore why in the one category of Melchizedek, who was both king of Salem and priest of God Most High, there is a union of the royal and priestly functions.

The collocation of these two messianic affirmations, namely, "Thou art my Son, today I have begotten thee," and "Thou art a priest forever, after the order of Melchizedek," shows how closely within the perspective of the history of redemption the Sonship and the Priesthood of Christ belong together, corresponding to the combination of deity and humanity in the anthropic person of the Mediator. This union of sonship and priesthood was indeed implied in the opening paragraph of the epistle, where (Heb 1:2) it is precisely the Son who is spoken of as having, like a priest, "made purification for sins."

According to Hughes, the thought of Heb 2:10 is recapitulated, for the description of Christ here as αἴτιος σωτηρίας αἰωνίου in Heb 5:9 corresponds to his designation there as τὸν ἀρχηγὸν τῆς σωτηρίας.[1252] However, Vos sees that the rendering of the term ἀρχηγὸν in 2:10 and 12:2 of either "author" or "captain" is inadequate precisely because it leaves the element of identification in experience unexpressed. While ἀρχηγὸν etymologically and according to usage may mean both "author" and "captain," the writer in the two passages cited attaches to it a more specific sense. The ἀρχηγὸν τῆς σωτηρίας is one who leads others unto salvation by himself treading the path of salvation before (cf. 5:1); the πίστεως ἀρχηγὸν καὶ τελειωτὴν is one who leads others to faith by himself exercising faith in an ideal manner.[1253] Furthermore, the word πρόδρομος in 6:20 shares with ἀρχηγὸν this reference to identification in

---

[1250] Westcott, *Hebrews*, 279–92.

[1251] Hughes, *Hebrews*, 181.

[1252] Hughes, *Hebrews*, 188.

[1253] Similarly, the ἀρχηγὸν τῆς ζωῆς in Peter's speech in Acts 3:15 is not merely the Ruler of life, but the one who first entered into life for his own person and now dispenses life unto others.

experience, the "forerunner" being one who not merely leads and opens access, but also anticipates in himself the enjoyment of the access he mediates to others.[1254] What is important is that the priestly king's leadership is distinctly based on identification with the experience with his people.

The salvation which Jesus has procured, moreover, is granted "unto all them that obey him". There is something appropriate in the fact that the salvation which was procured by the obedience of the Redeemer should be made available to the obedience of the redeemed. Once again the readers are encouraged to persevere in their loyalty to Christ, in whom alone eternal salvation is to be found—in whom also they have a high priest designated for them by God himself, "after the order of Melchizedek". The author reverts to Melchizedek at the end of this section of his argument in Heb 5:10, because he intends to go on now and elaborate the significance of his high-priestly order.

In Heb 2:16–18, the high priestly identification with the people is also marked. The author of Hebrews emphasizes the Lord's solidarity with his brothers by saying that he helps Abraham's descendants in Heb 2:16.[1255] But now in v. 17 he introduces that particular aspect of his solidarity with them which he is especially concerned to expound—his high priestly ministry on their behalf.

The priestly king must be one with those whom he represents before God, and this is equally so with Christ as his people's high priest.[1256] In order to serve them in this capacity, he was obliged to become completely like them—apart from sin, of course, as is pointed out in Heb 4.15. He as a representative suffered with them and for them, and through his sufferings was made perfect—qualified in every way to be their high priest.

[1254] Vos, *Redemption History*, 133.

[1255] The term ἐπιλαμβάνεται ("help") in v. 16 is the same as that used in Heb 8:9, where God recalls how he "took hold" of his people Israel to bring them out of Egypt, in both places the term carries with it the idea of deliverance.

[1256] Our author views the mission of the high priest in terms of his redemptive work. Many scholars see that his redemptive work is the antitypical fulfilment of the sacrificial ritual of the Day of Atonement, where the high priest in person was required to officiate.

Conclusion

The Old Testament prototype of the messianic high priest is Melchizedek. He is not only the human archetype of the ideal priestly king of Jerusalem, but according to the author of the Epistle to the Hebrews, the eternal priest of Yahweh, a supernatural being engendered by Yahweh. The psalmist links Melchizedek to David, who was the founder of a new, permanent dynasty that was the legitimate heir to the priestly king rule of the previous dynasty associated with Melchizedek. David's role as prototypical founder of a line of kings that finds ultimate and perfect expression in Jesus, his greater Son, takes on enhanced meaning and the relationship of the Sinaitic and Davidic covenants becomes more understandable.

The idea of a priestly king in Hebrews, therefore, as in the prophets of the Old Testament and the celebrations of the Passover, is linked to the role of Melchizedek who foreshadows the one who brings forgiveness of sin and restoration as both high priest and king. This forms part of the development of Hebrews at this point, where Jesus as a king is shown to have all the qualities of the perfected high priest. His characteristics are described in terms of his eschatological work as high priest in the order of Melchizedek. The implied unity between the priestly king and his people is examined throughout the epistle. The priestly king must be one with those whom he represents before God, and this is true of Christ as his people's high priest.

Chapter 7: The Holy Spirit Theme

Introduction

In Heb 9 the author points out that the Holy Spirit is related to the tabernacle. It has been argued that the doctrine of the Spirit has a significant position in the Old Testament.[1257] In the record of the tabernacle arrangements and the Levitical offerings, Bruce points out that the Holy Spirit has a teaching role, as seen in the prescriptions for the Day of Atonement.[1258]

Other scholars depend largely on the intertestamental literature to explain the background of the Spirit for the New Testament.[1259] Turner offers a survey of the literature of intertestamental Judaism, and he argues that the term "the Spirit of prophecy" is from the Targums.[1260] Menzies also says that the gift of the Spirit is needed for salvation in Wisdom of Solomon and 1QH.[1261]

For a backdrop of the Spirit, furthermore, Bultmann borrows from the Mandean Sect in a gnostic community. He defines the Spirit ($\pi\nu\epsilon\tilde{\upsilon}\mu\alpha$) as the miraculous divine power that stands in absolute contrast to all that is human.[1262] The manifestations of the Spirit are revealed in a person's conduct

---

[1257] F. A. Gosling, "An Unresolved Problem of Old Testament Theology," *ExpT*, 106:8 (1995), 237.

[1258] F. F. Bruce, *The Epistle to the Hebrews*, NICNT (Grand Rapids: Eerdmans, 1975), 194.

[1259] M. Turner, "Spiritual Gifts: Then and Now," *VoxEv* 15 (1985), 7–64. According to Turner, the Old Testament 'offered comparatively little help to the reader attempting to forge a "theology" of the Spirit'. C. K. Barrett, *The Holy Spirit and the Gospel Tradition* (London: SPCK, 1966), 10–14; G. D. Fee, *God's Empowering Presence: The Holy Spirit in the Letters of Paul* (Peabody, MA: Hendrickson, 1994), 914. Fee asserts that noticeably missing in the intertestamental literature . . . is the sense that the Spirit speaks through any contemporary "prophet". This is almost certainly the result of the growth of a tradition called "the quenched Spirit", which begins in the later books of the Old Testament and is found variously during the Second Temple period. R. P. Menzies, *The Development of Early Christian Pneumatology with Special Reference to Luke-Acts* (Sheffield: JSOT Press, 1991), 112. Menzies argues that Luke consistently represents the Spirit as a prophetic endowment which enables its recipient to fulfill a mission from God.

[1260] M. Turner, *Power from on High: The Spirit in Israel's Restoration and Witness in Luke-Acts* (Sheffield: Sheffield Academic Press, 1996), 88. Turner sees that the Spirit of prophecy in Judaism is regarded as the source of power as well as the source of the potential for spiritual and ethical renewal (*Power*, 105–38). For him, there is no difference between the Spirit of prophecy and the Spirit of power in Judaism, and the prophetic Spirit and soteriological Spirit as well.

[1261] Menzies, *Development*, 61–63.

[1262] R. Bultmann, *Theology of the New Testament*, Vol. 1 (London: SCM Press, 1968), 153. Bultmann points out that this comes out in Paul when he denies that the Corinthians are "spiritual men" and asks them in view of their conduct, "are you not (ordinary) men?" (1 Cor 3:1–4). Or again Ignatius expresses it (Eph 5:1) when he describes his "fellowship" with the bishop of Ephesus as "not human, but spiritual." According to Bultmann, "in

in ways that are extraordinary, mysteriously mighty in contrast to merely human capabilities and powers. Thus Bultmann sees that the Spirit in regard to his role, which is to reveal certain truths, came from Yawar of the Mandean Sect.[1263] Yawar was one of the revealers in heaven and his name means helper. Bultmann understands that this thinking has been absorbed by the New Testament writers. However, Dodd[1264] and Kim[1265] criticized those who emphasized the importance of Mandaean literature for New Testament studies, and opposed the idea that Mandaeism was one of the sources of the New Testament, arguing for a quite late date for the Mandaean tradition.

However, the Old Testament continually speaks of the ministry of the Holy Spirit in bringing salvation. The Spirit enables ordinary people to do great things. By the Spirit power, the Israelites were saved from their enemies.[1266] Kings were ritually anointed with oil, which publicly indicated that they were chosen (1 Sam 16:13). The ritual signified that they received holy authority and the Spirit had come upon them. The Old Testament prophecies predict that the Spirit will be poured out on people like rain that gives life to the ground (Isa 32:15), and as breath which enters bones that are dry when the Messiah comes (Ezek 37).

Barrett points out that when Haggai, Zechariah, and Malachi died, the Holy Spirit departed from Israel.[1267] Jeremias supports Barrett's understanding about

---

animistic thinking πνευμαis conceived as an independent agent, a personal power which like a demon can fall upon a man and take possession of him, enabling him or compelling him to perform manifestations of power. In dynamistic thinking, on the contrary, πνευμα appears as an impersonal force which fills a man like a fluid, so to say." (*Theology 1*, 155). He cites animistic conception (Rom 8:16; 1 Cor 2:10–16; 14:14) and dynamistic conception, the usual one, reflected in talk of the Spirit "given" or "poured out" (Theology 1.155–56).

[1263] H. Jonas, *The Gnostic Religion* (Beacon Hill: Beacon, 1958); R. Bultmann, *The Gospel of John: A Commentary*, trans. G. R. Beasley-Murray (Oxford: Blackwell, 1971); K. Rudolph, *Gnosis, the Nature and History of an Ancient Religion*, ed. R. M. Wilson, trans. P. W. Coxon and K. H. Kuhn (Edinburgh: T&T Clark, 1983). Also see E. M. Yamauchi, *Pre-Christian Gnosticism: A Survey of the Proposed Evidences* (London: Tyndale, 1973), 117–42.

[1264] C. H. Dodd, *The Interpretation of the Fourth Gospel* (Cambridge: Cambridge University Press, 1953), 115–30.

[1265] S. Kim, *Johannine Theology* (Seoul: Durano, 2001), 179. Kim says that Mandean writings date from after 50 CE, so they are not linked with the New Testament.

[1266] Judg 3:10; 11.29; 14:6; 1 Sam 11:6.

[1267] C. K. Barrett, *The Holy Spirit*, 108–9; G. W. H. Lampe, "Holy Spirit," in *The Interpreter's Dictionary of the Bible II*, ed. G. A. Buttick (Nashville, TN: Abingdon, 1962), 630. Lampe says that "in the main, the Spirit continues to be thought of as being, pre-eminently, the Spirit of prophecy, manifested in the distant past in such great figures as Elijah or Isaiah, but which was now no longer present in Israel."

the departure of the Holy Spirit from Israel, saying that the Spirit was quenched because of the sin of Israel.[1268] He goes on to say that after that time, God spoke only through the echo of his voice. Levison concludes that in Second Temple Judaism the Spirit had been withdrawn from Israel.[1269] Dunn also supports the view that Haggai, Zechariah, and Malachi were the last of the prophets and that thereafter the Spirit had been withdrawn.[1270] He sees the period of Second Temple Judaism as a drought of the Spirit.[1271] Later the first Christians saw that the Spirit had been poured out as promised. In eschatological terms, this experience of the Spirit was decisive for the Christians' self-understanding. So the question to be asked is, "what is the Spirit for?"

It has been argued that the Holy Spirit is related to "empowering for mission". Stronstad argues that the Spirit is related to "service."[1272] Menzies supports Stronstad's claim, arguing that the Spirit is shown as a prophetic endowment which enables recipients to perform a mission from God.[1273] However, Dunn points out that the Spirit is primarily the source of salvation.[1274] Turner seems to follow Dunn's idea about the nature of the Spirit, arguing that the promised Spirit is not only given for witness but he also is a gift to bring the salvation.

Therefore, if the Spirit is related to deliverance, then I will examine whether this point of view can be seen in connection with the Old Testament and the intertestamental literature. I will also examine whether the New Testament writers follow this interpretation or not. Then if so, I will show that the author of Hebrews accepts this.

[1268] J. Jeremias, *New Testament Theology* (New York: Charles Scribner's Sons, 1971), 81.

[1269] H. R. Levison, "Did the Spirit Withdraw from Israel? An Evaluation of the Earliest Jewish Data," *NTS* 43 (1997), 35-57. Cf. 1 Macc 9:27; 14:41; Bar 85:3. Cf. E. Sjoberg, "πνευμα, in *TDNT* VI, 385.

[1270] J. D. G. Dunn, *Christology in the Making: A New Testament Inquiry into the Origins of the Doctrine of the Incarnation* (Philadelphia: Westminster, 1980), 135.

[1271] J. D. G. Dunn, *Baptism in the Holy Spirit: A Re-examination of the New Testament Teaching on the Gift of the Spirit in Relation to Pentecostalism Today* (Philadelphia: Westminster, 1970), 27.

[1272] R. Stronstad, *The Charismatic Theology of St. Luke* (Peabody: Hendrickson, 1984), 13. He thinks that the thought of the New Testament writers about the Holy Spirit is rooted in the charismatic theology of the Old Testament,

[1273] Menzies, *Development*, 112. However, Menzies deals the fact that the gift of the Spirit is given for salvation in Wisdom of Solomon and 1QH with the only exception.

[1274] Dunn, *Baptism*, 32.

Some Views Relating to the Spirit

It is widely recognized that the Old Testament had a considerable influence on the understanding of the Spirit of the New Testament writers.[1275] However, there is a divergence of opinion among scholars on the frequency of the use of רוח for the divine Spirit because the meaning of רוח varies.[1276] Thus it has been argued that the exact meaning of רוח must depend on the context. Using this method, we will survey the writings of the Old Testament.

Therefore, my first task is to trace the Old Testament development of the concept of the Spirit of God. It is to discover in broad terms the evidence of Hebrew thought concerning the Spirit in the Old Testament.[1277] In doing this our interest is especially in the relationship between salvation and the Spirit.

[1275] N. H. Snaith, "The Spirit of God in Jewish Thought", in *The Doctrine of the Holy Spirit: Four Lectures* (London: Epworth, 1937), 11–37; H. B. Swete, 'Holy Spirit', *Dictionary of the Bible II*, ed. J Hastings (Edinburgh: T&T Clark, 1904), 402–404, 410–11; G. W. H. Lampe, "Holy Spirit," 626–29; L. Neve, *The Spirit of God in the Old Testament* (Tokyo: Seibunsha, 1972); L. J. Wood, *The Holy Spirit in the Old Testament* (Grand Rapids: Zondervan, 1976); G. T. Montague, *Holy Spirit: Growth of a Biblical Tradition* (Peabody, MA: Hendrickson, 1976), chs. 1–8; F. W. Horn, "Holy Spirit," in *The Anchor Bible Dictionary III*, ed. D. N. Freedman (Garden City, NY: Doubleday, 1992), 262–63.

[1276] F. Brown, S.R. Driver and C.A. Briggs, *A Hebrew and English Lexicon of the Old Testament* (BDB), 924–26; see also C. A. Briggs, "The Use of Ruach in the Old Testament," *JBL* 19 (1900), 132–45; W. R. Schoemaker, "The Use of Ruach in the Old Testament, and of πνευμα in the New Testament," *JBL* 23 (1904), 13–25. The Hebrew word רוח appears 378 times in the Masoretic Text; it sometimes denotes a storm or wind, sometimes "breath", sometimes "vitality" or "life", and so it was not always easy to be sure whether or not a particular instance of רוח referred to God's Spirit. For example, NIV reads "and the Spirit of God was hovering over the waters," while NRSV (like one of the oldest translations of the OT, the Aramaic Targum) renders, "while a wind from God swept over the face of the waters." Cf. W. Eichrodt, *Theology of the Old Testament*, Vol. 2 (London: SCM, 1967), 47. The term רוח in the Old Testament has retained at all times the meaning "wind", denoting the movement of air both outside humanity in nature, and inside him, his own breath (Ps 135:7; Job 9:18; 19:17). The term חיי נשמת (Gen 2:7; Job 33:4) plays the same part in J as the חיי רוח in P (Gen 7:22 with 6:17 and 7:15), and must be the older and more popular expression for the breath of life; hence the Job passage is justified in using both in synonymous parallelism. It is akin to the Greek πνευμα. G. E. Ladd, *A Theology of the New Testament* (London: Lutterworth, 1974), 287. According to Ladd, the ruach Yahweh in the Old Testament is not a separate, distinct entity; it is God's power—the personal activity in God's will achieving a moral and religious object. God's רוח is the source of all that is alive, of all physical life. The Spirit of God is the active principle that proceeds from God and gives life to the physical world (Gen 2:7). It is also the source of religious concerns, and the raising up charismatic leaders, whether judges, prophets, or kings. "The God's רוח is a term for the historical creative action of the one God which, though it defies logical analysis, is always God's action."

[1277] Fee, *God's Empowering Presence*, 905–906. Fee argues that Paul was not primarily influenced by the Old Testament in his understanding of the Spirit, but rather that Paul worked from his direct personal experience of the Spirit as the empowering presence of God back to the Old Testament.

Persian Influences

Some scholars ascribe the concept of the Spirit in later Judaism to the influence of corresponding religious ideas in Persian thought.[1278] In the earliest religious poems of the Persian reformer, the Gathas, a good deal is already said about the holy and divine Spirit, Spenta Mainyu, and functions are ascribed to him similar to those with which the Jews credited the רוח. According to Persian teaching, Spenta Mainyu is the mediator of God's own activity and as such is a part of the divine nature, co-operating both in the creation of the world and in its winding-up at the end of time. Moreover, by virtue of its opposition to the evil spirit, Spenta Mainyu is almost an ethical cosmic principle in accordance with which good men are empowered and rewarded, and the wicked are delivered up to judgment. Belief in this good spirit seems to be fundamentally associated with the Persian dualistic world-view as a whole.[1279]

The possibility that these ideas may have exercised some influence on Jewish belief in the Spirit certainly deserves serious consideration.[1280] It is conceivable that on the Jewish side, perhaps, in an effort to reach a mutual understanding with their Persian overlords, some may have spoken of the work of the Spirit with as much deliberation as they used in referring to Yahweh as the God of Heaven. However, Eichrodt points out that the Spirit-hypostasis does not become "naturalized" in popular thinking until the Hellenistic period, because, apart from the Babylonian Diaspora, there was no longer any great incentive for Judaism to accommodate itself to the ideas of Persian religion.[1281] Such caution commends itself all the more in that an internal motivation for the

---

[1278] M. Boyce, "Zoroaster, Zoroastrianism" in *The Anchor Bible Dictionary* Vol. 6, ed. D. N. Freedman (London: Doubleday, 1992), 1168, 1171–72. Mazdaism or Zoroastrianism was once the official religion of Sassanid Persia, and played an important role in Archaemenid times. The foundation of the religion is ascribed to the prophet Zarathushtra, who is commonly known in the west as Zoroaster, the Greek version of his name. The modern Persian form of the prophet's name is Zartosht. "Doctrines of Zoroastrianism appear in the Jewish intertestamental writings which, in Pharisaic Judaism and Christianity, form an eschatological system markedly similar to the Zoroasyrian one."

[1279] Cf. Isa 45:7 seem indeed to be direct polemic against such an idea: "I form the light and create darkness, I bring prosperity and create disaster; I, the LORD, do all these things."

[1280] E. Langton, *Essentials of Demonology: A Study of Jewish and Christian Doctrine* (London: Epworth, 1949), 61.

[1281] Eichrodt, *Theology*, 68.

growth of the Jewish view of the Spirit of God is clearly discernible, and that therefore it is possible that its development was exclusive to Judaism.[1282]

Philo

Philo thinks of πνεῦμα as a term for the higher element of the air, which remains God's property.[1283] He distinguishes πνεῦμα from ψυχή ascribing the former to the heavenly man and the latter to the earthly man.[1284] This distinction, which is based on Gen 1:2 and 2:7, enables Philo to explain the quantitatively different endowments of the heavenly and the earthly man with the divine spirit.[1285] According to Philo, the use πνεῦμα and ψυχή is different because Gen 1:2 (πνεῦμα) and 2:7 (ψυχή). That is, the πνεῦμα which represents the rational soul is an impress of the divine power, but the πνεῦμα which man receives as a morally striving rational being is an emanation of the divine nature.

Philo also utilizes the concept of "wisdom" for expounding his understanding of the Spirit. He gives the examples of Bezalel, Moses and the seventy elders. "God called up Bezalel", he says, and "filled him with the divine spirit, with wisdom, understanding, and knowledge to devise in every work" (Exod 31:2). In these words, we have suggested to us a definition of what the spirit of God is. Such a divine spirit is that of Moses, which is given to the seventy elders that they may excel others (Num 11). For Philo the Spirit of God here is clearly related to wisdom, understanding, and knowledge.[1286]

For Philo the concept of the Spirit was expanded to a world-controlling moral force, which as a cosmic element of pantheistic type helps to maintain the fabric of the universe. It clearly betrays Stoic influences, paving the way for a rationalistic and idealist interpretation of the cosmos. For him, therefore,

---

[1282] Ibid.

[1283] W. Bieder, "πνεῦμα in Hellenistic Judaism" in *TDNT* VI, 372. Philo never equates πνεῦμα with God; he maintains the divine transcendence.

[1284] Op. Mund, 135: F. H. Colson and G. H. Whitaker, *Philo with an English Translation*, 10 Vols. (London: William Heinemann, 1919), 62.

[1285] Allegorical Interpretation I (Leg. All. I,) 36. By defining ψυχή as ανποφορα he makes it clear that for all the distinction between πνεῦμα and ψυχή he is not setting the two in antithesis, for ενεπνευσεν is used in interpretation of the נשמה of Gen 2:7.

[1286] M. H. Choi, *The Personality of the Holy Spirit in the New Testament with Special Reference to Luke-Acts* (PhD diss., University of Wales Lampeter, 1999), 83-4.

πνεῦμα is entangled with various ideas, amongst which are the formation of man, the power of reason, wisdom, prophetic experience, and ethical components.

The Holy Spirit Related to Redemption in the Passover

We need firstly to trace the Old Testament development of the concept of the Spirit of God because it will clarify the relationship between salvation and the Spirit. For the Old Testament writers, the Spirit seems to have been understood as God's presence related to salvation. God's רוח first appears in Gen 1:2, where the power of God's רוח emerges in creation. God's רוח is implied to be "a creative divine power" which brings life to the formless and empty earth.[1287] It is noteworthy that God's רוח is in relation to creation.[1288] God's רוח as the creative power and life-giver also appears in the creation of man. The Lord God breathed "the breath (נשמת) of life" and man became "a living (נפש) being" (Gen 2:7).[1289] The term נשמת is used as a synonym of רוח in other Old Testament passages.[1290] Thus the Spirit appears as the "principle of life", "life itself in the creation of man".[1291] Withdrawal of רוח and נשמת means death for man (cf. Job 34:14–15).[1292]

God's רוח was continuously recognized as an endowment on Moses (Num 11:17, 29) through which he liberated and led Israel at God's direction. Joshua was understood to have had a similar endowment (Num 27:18 and elsewhere). The same endowment was shared with the seventy elders (11:25–29), and gave them wisdom (with Moses) to judge Israel's disputes. God's wisdom and

---

[1287] Cf. This is further supported by other creation texts. In the context of creation Isa 40:13 says that none has directed or instructed the Spirit of God: all things were created by his own creative power (Cf. Ps 104:30; Isa 34:16).

[1288] G. F. Moore, *Judaism in the First Centuries of the Christian Era: The Age of the Tannaim*, I (Cambridge: Harvard University Press, 1927), 414–22.

[1289] R. G. Bratcher, "Biblical Words Describing Man: Breath, Life, Spirit," *BT* 34:2 (1983), 201. Bratcher points out that נפש, רוח and נשמת are not precise terms and can be used interchangeably. The phrase נשמת usually means "the breath of life" when the term is used in relation to man. Cf. TWOT, II, 605.

[1290] Cf. In Job 33:4 "God's רוח" is parallel to the "נשמת of the Almighty". Job 27:3 says, "as long as I have life (נשמת) within me, the breath (רוח) of God in my nostrils" (Cf. Job 33:14; Isa 42:5).

[1291] G. E. Whitloch, "The Structure of Personality in Hebrew Psychology: The Implications of the Hebrew View of Man for Psychology of Religion," *Int* 14:1 (1960), 4–5. Whitloch sees רוח as breath developed to mean the vital principle of life itself.

[1292] Bratcher, "Biblical Words Describing Man," 202–203.

enabling were also portrayed as given by God's Spirit to the craftsmen who made the cultic furniture (Exod 28:3; 31:3; 35:31).

In brief, God's רוח emerges in creation as the invisible creative divine power which brings life to nature and to man. God's רוח is given to God's chosen people for a special purpose. The most typical gifts anticipated from the Spirit were accordingly various types of charismatic revelation.[1293] The Spirit's revelatory roles were understood (in many quarters) as transformative, and thus as potentially soteriological (Num 27:18; Deut 34:9).

Therefore, Holland argues that the Spirit acted in the major redemptive event experienced by the community as salvation.[1294] Holland claims that the exodus of the Jews from Egypt is a type of salvation in the New Testament. Furthermore, he links the Spirit to a corporate baptism which is to form the one body. That is, in exodus the baptism into Moses is the type of the Spirit's baptism to form the one body in Christ.[1295] The Jews were baptized into Moses and drank of the water from the rock, likewise in the antitype the baptism is into Christ.[1296] According to Holland, it was baptism by the Spirit that brought the covenant community into existence.

The new exodus was the act of new creation, bringing the chosen race to a new birth out of chaos and slavery. At the inauguration of the old covenant, gifts were given to the Jews (Exod 12:36; 35:30–35), gifts that were essential for the building of the tabernacle and for the worship of Yahweh. These gifts were to typify spiritual gifts later to be given at the inauguration of the new covenant. Thus, God's רוח is a source of salvation at the exodus in the Old Testament.

[1293] M. Turner, *The Holy Spirit and Spiritual Gifts Then and Now* (Cumbria: Paternoster, 1996), 6–8. Turner understands that the Spirit of prophecy affords charismatic revelation and guidance, charismatic wisdom, invasively inspired prophetic speech, and invasively inspired charismatic praise or worship. Compared to charismatic revelation and guidance, according to Turner, charismatic wisdom means a lively enthusiasm and understanding of God's word that is characterized by doxological joy in God and enables the sage to become a charismatic teacher. It is quite similar to what is prayed for by Paul in Eph 1:17–20; 3:16–21, and what he commends to them 5:18b–20:18. For other examples see targums to Exod 31:3; Frg. Tg. Num 11:26–27; Tg. Onq. Deut 34:9; Wis. 7:7; 9:17–18; and cf. 1QH 12.11–13; 13.18–19; 14.12–13. However, charismatic revelation is similar to charismatic wisdom in so far as the unaided human mind could not achieve it; God must intervene by his Spirit and guide the mind in order to make such understanding possible (cf. 4 Ezra 14:22, 25, 40–41).

[1294] T. Holland, *Contours*, 142–3. Baptism is closely associated with the death of Christ.

[1295] Ibid., 144.

[1296] E. E. Ellis, "A note on 1 Cor. 10.4," *JBL* 76 (1957), 53–56.

Furthermore, God's רוח in the majority of these various Old Testament incidents seemed to act as the channel of communication between God and a human person.[1297] The Spirit was perceived to have made God's will and wisdom known to the charismatic leader, to the king, and even to the cult carpenter, especially (though not exclusively) through the phenomenon of oracular speech termed "prophecy" in which a message of the Lord was granted by the Spirit in a dream, vision, or word. Thus God's revelation was directly or indirectly traced to the Spirit in early prophecy (as in Num 11:25–29; 24:2; 1 Sam 10:10; 19:20) and later in classical prophecy.

The Spirit Theme in the Old Testament

The prophets of the eighth and seventh centuries BCE proclaimed the coming storm of annihilation hanging over a nation ripe for judgment, and the invasion of the divine in a new form. As a result of this new vision of God the traditional statements of faith about the divine order were applied to the present and filled with new content. The prophets preserve many of the older insights about the Spirit but for the first time begin to disclose the coming of a new era in the Spirit's ministry. God's people could look forward to restoration from exile and to a new covenant in which the Spirit will empower the covenant community in the creation of a new spiritual reality.[1298] A close knowledge of God lay at the heart of the hoped-for new covenant. In the new covenant each would "know the Lord" for himself or herself (Jer 31:34). The future was thus expected to be an epoch characterized by the abundant outpouring of God's Spirit (as in Isa 32:15; 44:3; Ezek 39:29) and the revelation of his glory and the power (Hab 2:14) of humankind in obedience.[1299] This pouring out of the Spirit on all God's people was anticipated as leading to the deep existential renewal of Israel.

[1297] Turner, *The Holy Spirit*, 4. According to Turner, this was "the Spirit of prophecy" as Judaism came to understand it.

[1298] C. L. Blomberg, "Holy Spirit," in *Evangelical Dictionary of Biblical Theology*, ed. W. A. Elwell (Grand Rapids: Baker, 1996), 345. Cf. Joel 2:28; C. K. Barrett, *John*, 148; cf. Num 11:29

[1299] Jer 31:31–40; Ezek 36:24–29; cf. Ps 51:10–14 for an analogous individual expression of such hope.

Isaiah

Isa 63:10–11 contains the only other Old Testament use of "Holy Spirit", harking back to God's guidance of Moses from Egypt and the wilderness wanderings.[1300] The operation is seen in the great saving acts of the people of God in the past; it is in the age of salvation to come that the Spirit is expected to consummate God's rule by the inner transformation of people's hearts. That is, it is the Spirit which, in the past, present, and future, is the true governor of Israel, and in which the transcendent God, dwelling in light unapproachable, in authentically draws near to his people.

In Isaiah, therefore, the Spirit is the key to Israel's eschatological future. The reconstituted people of God are characterized by the work and power of the Holy Spirit. The Spirit is usually expected to rest upon particular individuals who are to carry out specific tasks for Yahweh.[1301] This is now promised to be bestowed upon the entire eschatological community of the new era.[1302] That is, if there is to be a real renewal, then not only the one who leads the people to salvation, but also those who are led, must receive a share in God's spirit. With increasing certainty, the promise of an inner relationship with the Spirit of God is extended to the citizens of the messianic kingdom, in which it is to be poured out upon them.[1303]

Ezekiel

In Ezekiel the pouring out of the Spirit on God's people, which leads to the renewal of Israel, is shown in a future eschatological restoration of the nation in 36:25–27.[1304] This will take place in three stages. In the first stage such renewal will be accomplished by the ritual purification with water (Ezek 36:25).[1305] This is, in a sense, the purification of the body. In the second stage the Lord will give a new heart and a new spirit (Ezek 36:26). The Lord will

---

[1300] C. Westermann, *Isaiah* 40–66 (London: SCM, 1969), 388; E. J. Young, *The Book of Isaiah*, III (Grand Rapids: Eerdmans, 1972), 482. Young says that in this context it is difficult to deny the concept of the Spirit as a personal being. So J. B. Payne, *The Theology of the Older Testament* (Grand Rapids: Zondervan, 1962), 173.

[1301] G. Vos, *Redemptive History*, 96. Cf. Isa 11:1–3; 42:1 and 61:1, in which the Spirit similarly anoints the suffering servant: Fee, *God's Empowering Presence*, 910.

[1302] Cf. Isa 44:3; 59:21 and 63:14.

[1303] Isa 32:15; 44:3.

[1304] It becomes characteristic of the eschatological state itself.

[1305] W. Zimmerli, *Ezekiel* 2 (Philadelphia: Fortress, 1983), 249. Zimmerli argues that in Exod 36:25 "we should see behind this the image of a ritual act of sprinkling with water for the purpose of cultic purification."

remove a heart of stone and give a heart of flesh. This describes the renewal of the heart. In the third stage an act of renewal will take place in the outpouring of the Spirit by the Lord (Ezek 36:27). As a result, the renewed Israel will follow the Lord's command and keep his laws. Thus the Spirit of the Lord is a gift which will be given after the renewal of the heart (and of the body).

Therefore, these passages directly link the Spirit to salvation.[1306] Ezekiel shows this by Israel's revival from the dead (Ezek 37:1–14). This is not about the restoration of the individual, but the whole nation.[1307] The Lord will "pour out" his Spirit on the house of Israel (Ezek 39:29). The verb in this passage is probably used to highlight an implicit contrast which describes the outpouring of the wrath of the Lord in the destruction of the temple and exile of Israel (Ezek 36:18).[1308] Therefore, the kingdom will be established by the ideal king who will be anointed by the eschatological Spirit, and in the last days the Spirit will be poured out on all people.

Joel

Perhaps the most important prophetic text on the Spirit is Joel 2:28–32, which Peter quotes at Pentecost (Acts 2:17–21). Here the prophet envisages a day in which God will pour out his Spirit on all people, irrespective of gender, age, social status, or ethnicity, particularly bestowing the gift of prophecy on many of his choice.[1309]

Thus it can be seen that the prophets anticipated a new era in which the Spirit would work among a greater number of people and different kinds of people to create a new faithful community of men and women serving God.[1310] In fact, we have seen increasingly that the Israelites were full of the eschatological expectation of the outpouring of the Spirit. We have also seen that the Spirit emerges as the direct source of salvation in the Old Testament.

[1306] G. Fredrick, "Rethinking the Role of the Holy Spirit in the Lives of Old Testament Believers," *TrinJ* 9 (1988), 86; L. J. Wood, *The Holy Spirit in the Old Testament*, 65–66. However, Choi argues in that the Spirit is associated with regeneration resultantly in the Old Testament. He claims that it is hard to find any direct reference to the Spirit as an agent of salvation in the Old Testament: M. H. Choi, *The Personality of the Holy Spirit*, 77–8

[1307] Cf. Ezek 37. We see a corporate presence of the Spirit not previously encountered (cf. 37:14; 39:29).

[1308] L. C. Allen, *Ezekiel* 20–48 (Dallas: Word, 1990), 209.

[1309] Cf. Mic 3:8 affirms the prophecy's origination in the Spirit.

[1310] G. Fredricks, "Rethinking," 86.

The Spirit Theme in the Intertestamental Literature

A major strand of Judaism anticipated a community enjoying the beginnings of eschatological salvation, and then attributed this principally to the Spirit.[1311] The revelatory Spirit has itself become at the same time the soteriological Spirit, the very basis of the transformed "life" and the sanctifying Spirit, enables the restored community.[1312]

In the Qumran Scrolls, there is an association between the Spirit and salvation. According to 1 QS 3.6 all sins of the members of the community shall be expiated through the Spirit of true counsel. 1 QS 3.7–8 says that "He shall be cleansed from all his sins by the spirit of holiness uniting him to his truth, and his iniquity shall be expiated by the spirit of uprightness and humility."[1313] These references imply the Spirit as the source of salvation. Furthermore, there is another statement. According to 1 QH 16.1–12 God has already bestowed his "spirit of mercy" on a Qumran covenanter. Despite this fact, he asked God for "further purification" by the Holy Spirit so as to draw near to him. This suggests that in the Qumran community there was a role of the Spirit: as the source of salvation and as the source of its maintenance.[1314] In the Qumran literature, the Spirit is associated with salvation. Thus, it is natural that the Spirit was closely linked to eschatology.

In Wisdom of Solomon[1315] the concept of πνεῦμα emerges in relation to God's creation of man. Wis 15:11b says that God breathed into man "an active soul". The writer of Wisdom was probably influenced by Gen 2:7. According to Wis 15:11c God inspired "a living Spirit" (πνεῦμα ζωτικόν) into man. This suggests πνεῦμα to be the "principle of life" in man. This claim is supported by other references. The Spirit in man is to be borrowed from God (Wis 15:16). The

---

[1311] It is rare to find out the most noticeable development of the concept of the רוח of God during the Second Temple period. Its concept reflects continuations of Old Testament motifs. Cf. Menzies, *Development*, 52.

[1312] J. Breck, *The Origins of Johannine Pneumatology* (Crestwood: St. Valdimir's Seminary Press, 1991), 161; Turner, *The Holy Spirit*, 16.

[1313] 1QH 17.25–26 (echoing Ezek 36:26–27), "to wipe out in my midst, for a spirit of fle[sh] ... is Thy servant ... Thou didst sprinkle [Thy] Holy Spirit upon Thy servant ... his heart."; similarly, 4Q 504.5 and 1QS 4.20–23.

[1314] Cf. G. T. Montague, *Holy Spirit: Growth of a Biblical Tradition* (Peabody, MA: Hendrickson, 1976), 122. According to Montague, in the Qumran community there were two different roles of the Spirit: as the source of salvation and as the source of its maintenance.

[1315] L. L. Grabbe, *Wisdom of Solomon* (Sheffield: Sheffield Academic Press, 1997), 87–90. According to Grabbe, the date of composition of the Wisdom of Solomon is generally assigned to the last half of the first century BCE.

departure of the Spirit means death for man (cf. Wis 16.14). Such an understanding of the Spirit is similar to that of the Old Testament. The Spirit is also in relation to salvation. Men cannot know the will of God without the help of the Holy Spirit (Wis 9:17). This passage implies that the Spirit is associated with salvation.

The Spirit Theme in the Gospels, Acts and the Epistles

In the Gospels the eschatological aspect of the Spirit is not much in evidence. According to Vos, it is because the Spirit in general remains in the background.[1316] The Synoptic writers focused on the supernatural character of Jesus's person, without referring to the pneumatic equipping of Jesus.

In this section I will examine briefly how the Spirit was understood in the writings of New Testament authors. Largely focusing on the character of the Spirit, I will be concerned with how the Spirit is related to salvation in the New Testament and whether he acts in salvation corporately or not.

The Gospels and Acts
Matthew

Matthew has few references to the Spirit.[1317] Taylor points out that Matthew was faithful to the tradition that he had received.[1318] In Matt 28:19, the Spirit is mentioned along with the Father and the Son. This Trinitarian baptismal formula is mentioned only by Matthew among the New Testament writers. So Lake argues that Matt 28:19 are not the very words of Jesus.[1319] However, the manuscript authority of Matt 28:19 is strong because most MSS and versions have the Trinitarian formula. It also occurs twice in the Didache along with the shortened formula, with only Christ. It is probably safer, with Barrett, to accept the present text of Matthew.[1320] If this is right, Matt 28:19 clearly

---

[1316] Vos, *Redemptive History*, 99. In Mark the representation that the Spirit is equipment for Jesus's activity, receives very little prominence.

[1317] E.g. Matt 1:18; 3:16; 4:1; 10:20; 12:28, 31–32; 28:19.

[1318] V. Taylor, "The Spirit in the New Testament", in *The Doctrine of the Holy Spirit* (London: Epworth, 1937), 51. See also Barrett, *The Holy Spirit*, 140–62.

[1319] K. Lake, "Baptism," in *Encyclopaedia of Religion and Ethics*, ed. J. Hastings, II, 379–81. However, Lake adds that there is little persuasive evidence, at any rate in his textual argument.

[1320] C. K. Barrett, *The Holy Spirit*, 103; Schweizer, "πνεῦμα",401. He notes that Paul sometimes used triadic formulae. G. T. Montague, *Holy Spirit: Growth of a Biblical Tradition* (Peabody, MA: Hendrickson, 1976), 310.

suggests that the Spirit has a status corresponding to the Father and the Son. In short, Matt 28:19 probably implies that the Spirit has a divine status comparable to the Father and Jesus for salvation, as in the prophets.

Mark

In Mark 1:10 after the opening of heavens, the Spirit descended on Jesus. Buse sees Isa 63:19 MT as the background to this Markan passage.[1321] Guelich also points out that Mark's σχίζω in Mark 1:10 may suggest a statement of Yahweh's coming.[1322] In the text the Baptism is linked with the descent of the Spirit described by καταβαῖνον. Furthermore, Schneck points out that in Isa 63 LXX this verb καταβαίνω is associated with both the exodus—a theme central to Mark's opening citation—and the descent of the Spirit.[1323] Watts concludes that both Mark and Isaiah link the "descent" (καταβαίνω) of the רוח with "coming up" out of water imagery.

The appeal to Yahweh "to rend the heavens and come down" in 63:19 MT must surely be understood in the light of the preceding context of the exodus remembrance, which remembrance not only forms the very basis of that appeal but is filled with רוח language. In other words, if the memory of Yahweh's great redemptive act from Isa 63 is characterized by his placing of his רוח presence in the midst of his people, then it is hardly surprising if the long-awaited repetition of the saving event should also be so characterized.[1324]

From this perspective, if Mark thinks in terms of the new exodus, his appeal to imagery from this text is eminently suitable. The passage is itself part of the last great lament in Isaiah over the delay of the new exodus, but Mark's

---

Montague says that the three-fold formula "shows an incipient realization of the personhood and equality of the Holy Spirit in a way that no other New Testament text does."

[1321] I. Buse, "The Markan Account of the Baptism of Jesus and Isaiah LXIII," *JTS* 7 (1956), 74; R. H. Gundry, *The Use of the Old Testament in St. Matthew's Gospel*, NovTSup 18 (Leiden: Brill, 1967), 28; C. Maurer, in *TDNT* VII, 962.

[1322] R. A. Guelich, *Mark 1-8.26*, 34A, WBC (Dallas: Word, 1989), 32. Cf. Gen 7:11; Ps 77:23 LXX. Cf. R. Bultmann, *Theology of the New Testament* (London: SCM, 1952), 155-6, sees the use of "the Spirit" as betrayed from a Hellenistic influence and setting.

[1323] K. Schneck, *Isaiah in the Gospel of Mark*, I-VII BDS 1 (Vallejo, CA: BIBAL, 1994), 45. Schneck also notes that in 1 Cor 10:1-4 Paul compares Christian baptism to Israel's passing through the sea.

[1324] Some have recognized that Isa 56-66 reflects post-exilic disappointment with the reality of the return. Cf. G. Fohrer, *Introduction to the Old Testament*, trans. D. Green (London: SPCK, 1970), 386; N. Gottwald, *The Hebrew Bible: A Socio-Literary Introduction* (Philadelphia: Fortress, 1985), 507.

description of the baptism closely echoes that which the petitioners long for: the descent of Yahweh through the rent heavens.

Thus, the nature of the Spirit in Mark goes beyond the Spirit of power, not as Schweizer said. The Spirit appears as a person linked with new exodus. It can be said that the pneumatology of Mark is similar to that of the prophets regarding Yahweh's great redemptive act.

Luke and Acts

In Luke 3:16, Dunn interprets "a baptism in the Holy Spirit and fire" as "one purgative act of messianic judgment which both repentant and unrepentant would experience".[1325] Through immersion in the fiery πνεῦμα of judgment the repentant will be refined and purged of all sin, as a result, it brings "salvation" and the "qualification" to enter the messianic kingdom. And through the same fiery Spirit the unrepentant will be totally destroyed. That is, according to Dunn, the repentant come to salvation through the fiery πνευμα of judgment.

In contrast, Fitzmyer argues that John the Baptist probably viewed water baptism in a positive way, as a sign of repentance, not in a negative sense, as a sign of judgment or wrath, because John's emphasis falls on "water" and the "coming" of the mightier one.[1326] That is, John emphasized that he baptizes "only" in water, and the coming mightier one (John is subordinate to him) will baptize in the "Holy Spirit and fire". If John's water baptism brings repentance (positively), the coming one's Spirit-fire baptism makes readers expect something more positive, not negative (judgment, tribulation or the like).[1327] According to Marshall and Fitzmyer, the repentant will be immersed in the gracious Spirit (Luke 3:16), not in the fiery breath of the judgment of God, and the unrepentant will be burned with unquenchable fire by his winnowing fork

---

[1325] J. D. G. Dunn, *Baptism; Jesus and the Spirit: A Study of the Religious and Charismatic Experience of Jesus and the First Christians as Reflected in the New Testament* (London: SCM, 1975), 11. Cf. C. K. Barrett, The Holy Spirit, 125-6. Barrett interprets the baptism of Spirit and fire simply as "a baptism of judgment".

[1326] J.A. Fitzmyer, *The Gospel According to Luke*, 468; I. H. Marshall, *The Gospel of Luke: A Commentary on the Greek Text* (Exeter: Paternoster, 1978), 136. According to Marshall, the Baptist John's baptism is "a way of escape from the coming wrath."

[1327] Fitzmyer, *The Gospel According to Luke*, 474. He thinks that "if John's own water-baptism were intended to produce 'repentance', it might at least be thought that a baptism involving God's Spirit and fire would be expected to accomplish something positive too". Also see J. Giblet, "Baptism in the Spirit in the Acts of the Apostles," *OC*, 164.

(Luke 3:17). However, there is no difference between the former and the latter except in a positive and negative sense. The context is still the same.

Dunn points out that Luke understood the descent of the Spirit at Jordan as both Jesus's own entry into the new age and covenant and his anointing with the Spirit as Messiah, servant and representative of his people.[1328] According to him, therefore, the gift of the Spirit was almost understood as the gift of the matrix of Christian life. Holland suggests that baptism by the Spirit refers to the major redemptive event.[1329] Dunn concludes that the baptism in the Spirit is part of the event (or process) of becoming a Christian.[1330]

Then the definitive statement of the work of the Holy Spirit in Jesus is given in Luke 4:18 with the citation of Isa 61:1: Πνεῦμα κυρίου ἐπ' ἐμέ. Luke has now established the basic function of the Holy Spirit in the narrative. The relationship between Jesus and Spirit is that the Spirit as a person is crucial for Jesus's work of salvation.[1331] Thus, the essential character of the Spirit which Jesus experienced is implied to be one who is a person related to salvation. According to Shepherd, because Luke omits further mention of the Spirit during most of the rest of the Gospel, it is equally important to point out that the narrative of the Spirit continues in Acts.[1332] Therefore, Luke 4 should be interpreted together with the narrative of Acts.

In Acts 2:17 Luke links the outpouring of the Spirit to the arrival of the eschatological age by the insertion of the phrase "in the last days" (ἐν ταῖς ἐσχάταις ἡμέραις) cited from Joel.[1333] The outpouring of the Spirit at Pentecost

---

[1328] J. D. G. Dunn, Baptism in the Holy Spirit: A Re-examination of the New Testament Teaching on the Gift of the Spirit in Relation to Pentecostalism Today (London: SCM, 1970), 23–37. According to Dunn, Jesus himself is not related to the new age until the Spirit descends upon him (41) and Jesus' supernatural birth belongs entirely to the epoch of Israel (31).

[1329] Holland, *Contours*, 143.

[1330] Dunn, *Baptism*, 4.

[1331] D. L. Bock, *Proclamation from Prophecy and Pattern: Lucan Old Testament Christology* (Sheffield: JSOT Press, 1987), 109. Bock says that "the synagogue speech is a statement about Jesus and the Spirit made in close connection with the baptismal event".

[1332] W. H. Shepherd Jr., *The Narrative Function of the Holy Spirit as a Character in Luke-Acts*, SBLDS 43 (Atlanta, GA: Scholars Press, 1994), 137.

[1333] Cf. Isa 2:2.

is a decisive sign of the eschatological events which proceed the day of the Lord.[1334]

Acts 3:19–21 shows how the Holy Spirit is related to the restoration of Israel. Lane points out that the word ἀναψύξεως in Acts 3:20 appears in Symmachus's translation of Isa 32:15, where it makes reference to the outpouring of the Spirit.[1335] There the outpouring of the Spirit is understood as the arrival of ἀναψύξεως. Lane goes on to say that there is parallel between Acts 2:38 and 3:19–20 in terms of the outpouring of the Spirit.[1336] This parallel launches the identity of the "times of refreshing" as the outpouring of the Spirit in Acts 2. Pao supports Lane's idea, saying that the "times of refreshing" is also tied to the programme of restoration."[1337] Furthermore, the phrase "these days" (τὰς ἡμέρας ταύτας) in Acts 3:24 clearly refers to a time contemporaneous with the early Christian community. The "times of refreshing" and "these days" are times that the people of God had long anticipated and are now becoming a reality.

Taken together, Luke linked the Spirit to the restoration of Israel. This relationship is established by Isa 32:15, where the passage plays an important role in the restoration programmes of both Isaiah and Acts. God's plan is related to the salvation of human beings in Luke-Acts.[1338] This salvation history is clearly associated with the Holy Spirit in Luke-Acts.[1339]

[1334] Cf. Menzies, *Development*, 244. Menzies rejects the interpretation of Pentecost as "a new Sinai". The gift of Pentecost is prophetic inspiration and the Spirit of mission. According to Menzies, Luke is influenced by a Jewish view which emphasizes the Spirit as the Spirit of prophecy, that is, the pre-Pauline concept of the Spirit.

[1335] W. Lane, *Times of Refreshment: A Study of Eschatological Periodization in Judaism and Christianity* (Th.D. diss., Harvard Divinity School, 1962), 163.

[1336] Lane, "Times of Refreshment," 171. According to Lane, the coming and presence of the Holy Spirit is what is meant by "times of refreshment".

[1337] Pao, *Acts and the Isaianic New Exodus*, 133. Pao says that this is not a surprising fact in light of the Isaianic programme of the restoration of Israel depicted in Isa 32. Moreover, the connection of the Spirit with the programme of restoration can already be found in the quotation of Joel 2:28-32, where it depicts the hope of restoration, in Acts 2:17-21.

[1338] H.J. Cadbury, *The Making of Luke-Acts* (New York: Macmillan, 1927), 303–6; H. Conzelmann, *The Theology of St. Luke* (London: Faber, 1960),149–57; F. Bovon, *Luke the Theologian: Thirty-three Years of Research: 1950–1983* (Allison Park: Pickwick, 1987), 76. According to Bovon, Luke's perspective is that God's plan of salvation unfolds throughout human history. This is commonly known as "salvation history". J. T. Squires, *The Plan of God in Luke-Acts* (Cambridge: Cambridge University Press, 1993), passim. Cf. L. S. Thornton, *Confirmation: Its Place in the Baptismal Mystery* (Westminster: Dacre, 1950). Thornton sees that Jesus's dual relationship to the Spirit—through conception and the Jordan event—prefigures Christian baptismal regeneration and subsequent

John

In the conversation between Jesus and Nicodemus in John 3, the Spirit is related closely to salvation. Jesus tells Nicodemus that no one can see the kingdom of God unless he was born again (ἄνωθεν) in John 3:3. The term ἄνωθεν can be rendered either "again" or "from above." Buchsel points out that the expression "to be born *from above*" is expounded as being born of water and Spirit in John 3:5.[1340] That is, this birth from above is the same as birth by water and the Spirit. Although the relation of "water" and "Spirit" is disputable, it is evident from what Jesus said that spiritual birth is only possible by the Spirit. Beasley-Murray understands that the conjunction of water and Spirit in eschatological hope is deeply rooted in the Jewish consciousness, as attested by Ezek 36:25–27 and various apocalyptic writings (e.g. Jub. 1:23; Pss. Sol. 18:6; Test. Jud. 24:3).[1341]

This is further supported by John 6:63: "It is the Spirit that gives life; the flesh is of no avail." The source of life is the Spirit not the flesh.[1342] That is, the Spirit is clearly the agent of salvation. However, the passage taken out of context could reflect a sort of Greek dualism of a realm of spirit over against a realm of flesh, with connotations that the realm of flesh is evil. This would mean that spiritual realities are to be sought in complete detachment from the fleshly realm. The point, however, here is that Jesus's death as a human being

---

confirmation. T. S. Smail, *Reflected Glory: The Spirit in Christ and Christians* (London: Hodder, 1975). Smail sees that Jesus's conception by the Spirit and subsequent baptismal anointing anticipate rather Christian birth by the Spirit and empowering respectively (though he does not think the latter two need be separate events). G. W. H. Lampe, *God as Spirit* (Oxford: Clarendon, 1976); "The Holy Spirit in the Writings of Saint Luke", in *Studies in the Gospels*, ed. D. E. Nineham (Oxford: Blackwell, 1957), 159–200; "The Holy Spirit and the Person of Christ", in *Christ Faith and History*, ed. S.W. Sykes and J.P. Clayton (Cambridge: Cambridge University Press, 1972), 111–130. Lampe interprets the parallel in terms of the Spirit of sonship and obedience given both to Jesus and to Christian disciples in their respective baptisms—though he is sometimes doubtful whether Luke thought this way.

[1339] Conzelmann, *The Theology of St. Luke*, 183–84; G. W. H. Lampe, "Holy Spirit," 167; W. B. Tatum, "The Epoch of Israel: Luke 1–2 and the Theological Plan of Luke-Acts," *NTS* 13 (1966–67), 184–95; H. Flender, *St Luke: Theologian of Redemptive History* (London: SPCK, 1967), 140–46; L. Goppelt, *Theology of the New Testament*, I (Grand Rapids: Eerdmans, 1981), 248; Bovon, *Luke the Theologian*, 219; J.A. Fitzmyer, *The Gospel According to Luke*, I–LX (Garden City, NY: Doubleday, 1981), 227–31.

[1340] F. Buchsel, in *TDNT* I, 378.

[1341] G. R. Beasley-Murray, *John* 36, WBC (Dallas: Word, 1987), 49.

[1342] R. E. Brown, *The Gospel According to John*, I (London: Geoffrey Chapman, 1966), 300. Brown says that "the Spirit is the divine principle from above which alone can give life."

and a mere historical event has no saving power. It is only when his death is interpreted and understood through the Holy Spirit that it becomes a saving event. This is the meaning of the next statement: "The words that I have spoken to you are Spirit and life" (6:63). However, some do not believe (6:64), for they have not responded to the Spirit's illumination.

However, here the more important thing is that the passage has to read in light of the Jewish Passover Feast in John 6:4. I have earlier discussed the meaning of the Jewish Passover relating to salvation. This chapter has also to be linked to the Passover for the Spirit. Thus, the Spirit comes from above—from God. The Spirit comes to inaugurate a new age of redemptive history in contrast to the old age of the Law. John does not consciously reflect on twofold dualism, but it clearly underlies the structure of his teaching about the Spirit. In John 7:37–39 Jesus speaks of the Spirit which believers should receive at future time for salvation, since the Holy Spirit was not yet given.

The Epistles
Romans

In Romans Paul clearly links the possession of the Spirit to the Old Testament eschatological promise.[1343] What is important in Rom 8:1-3 is that the Spirit has made the decisive difference in countering the law abused by sin to bring about death.[1344] That is, the Spirit is to be seen as the defining mark of the Christian. It is "having the Spirit" which defines and determines someone as being "of Christ." The implication is clear: in Paul's understanding, it was by receiving the Spirit that one became a Christian.

Rom 8:10–11 shows the statement which introduces the Spirit in an eschatological state.[1345] In verse 10, the body and the Spirit are distinguished. Vos points out that the former is dead on account of sin, the latter is life on

---

[1343] F. F. Bruce, "The Holy Spirit in the Acts of the Apostles," *Int* 27 (1973), 178; L. Goppelt, *Theology of the New Testament*, II (Grand Rapids: Eerdmans, 1981), 118–24; J. D. G. Dunn, Baptism *in the Holy Spirit: A Re-examination of the New Testament Teaching on the Gift of the Spirit in Relation to Pentecostalism Today* (London: SCM, 1970), 54. According to Dunn, "the phrase 'baptism in Spirit' is never directly associated with the promise of power, but is always associated with entry into the messianic age or the Body of Christ".

[1344] Holland, *Paschal*, 81. Holland sees that this part marks the relief of acquittal.

[1345] Here the Spirit and the resurrection go together: the resurrection as an act is derived from the Spirit, the resurrection-state is represented as in permanent dependence on the Spirit. Cf. Vos, *Redemptive History*, 101.

account of righteousness.[1346] God gave life to their mortal bodies in connection with Jesus being raised through the Spirit. The renewed spiritual life of the Christian is the immediate effect of the life-giving Spirit, now also the indwelling Spirit. That has begun a process which will reach its end in the resurrection of the body, the climactic saving act of the life-giving Spirit in 8:11.

8:14–16 is in close parallel to 8:9; membership in God's family is defined in terms of the Spirit: "as many as are led by the Spirit of God, they are sons of God" (8:14).[1347] Thus, you are sons of God, because "you have received the Spirit of adoption," the Spirit of the Son.[1348] Paul the apostle identifies the Christian as one who has received the Spirit and lives in accordance with it. Membership in God's family is no longer defined as being a *bar mitzvah* ("son of the commandment"), but as one who has been adopted by God and shares the Spirit of God's Son. The adoption is made real by the presence and witness of the Spirit in Rom 8:16.

Corinthians

In 1 Cor 6:11 Paul reminds the Corinthians of their new identity in the name of Christ and by the Spirit of our God using three particular verbs, ἀπελούσασθε in the middle voice, ἡγιάσθητε and ἐδικαιώθητε in the passive voice. Some point out that Paul lays particular emphasis on the Christian rite of baptism.[1349] Moreover, according to Lee, these three verbs are exactly parallel to the words

---

[1346] Vos, *Redemptive History*, 101. Vos sees that the term πνευμα in Rom 8:10 is not the human spirit; it is the divine pneuma in its close identification with the believer's person.

[1347] Fee, *Empowering Presence*, 564: "These ['and no others' is implied] are God's children. As in Gal 3:1–5, the Spirit alone identifies the people of God under the new covenant."

[1348] It is important to translate υἱοί here as "sons" (8:14), since it is the Spirit of the Son which is in view (as the parallel, Gal 4:6, confirms). It is notable, however, that having implied the son/Son correlation, Paul at once switches to the gender neutral τέκνα "children" (8:16–17).

[1349] C. K. Barrett, *The First Epistle to the Corinthians*, BNTC (London: A&C Black, 1971), 141–42; Lightfoot, *Notes on the Epistles of St. Paul* (Peabody, MA: Hendrickson, 1995), 213; A. Robertson, and A. Plummer, *A Critical and Exegetical Commentary on the First Epistle of St Paul to the Corinthians*, ICC (Edinburgh: T&T Clark, 1963), 119. According to them, the middle ανπελουσασθε is closely related to baptism in Acts 22:16, which is the only other occurrence in the NT, many regard it as referring to the rite of baptism. However, J. D. G. Dunn, *Baptism in the Holy Spirit: A Re-examination of the New Testament Teaching on the Gift of the Spirit in Relation to Pentecostalism Today* (London: SCM, 1970), 121, understands it as denoting spiritual cleansing. M. Newton, *The Concept of Purity at Qumran and in the Letters of Paul*, SNTSMN 53 (Cambridge: Cambridge University Press, 1985), 81–84.

redemption (ἀπολύτρωσις), sanctification (ἁγιασμός) and righteousness (δικαιοσύνη) recorded in 1:30, where Paul underlines Christ to be the source of the new life of God's chosen people, that is, the source of their corporate entity.[1350] He continues to say that the expressions ἐν τῷ ὀνόματι τοῦ κυρίου Ἰησοῦ καὶ ἐν τῷ πνεύματι τοῦ θεοῦ ἡμῶν in 1 Cor 6:11, point to Paul's emphasis on the Christians' new corporate identity in Christ. That is, Paul presses the Corinthians to think of their new corporate identity in Christ effected by the Spirit. His saying in v. 11 therefore implies that litigation against fellow believers "is fundamentally inconsistent with their true identity in Christ." To Paul, they have been transferred into a new reality and given a new identity under the Lordship of Jesus Christ and the Spirit, and thus conduct such as suing one another is inconsistent with new corporate identity.[1351]

Peter

The Spirit in 1 Pet is associated with salvation. The Spirit sanctified the people who were chosen by God (1 Pet 1:2).[1352] That is, the sanctifying activity of the Spirit is related to the foreknowledge of God.[1353] 1 Pet 1:2 suggests the divine status of the Spirit. The Spirit in this passage is parallel to ῥαντισμὸν αἵματος Ἰησοῦ Χριστοῦ.[1354] In other words, the Spirit participates in God's work of redemption with God the Father and Jesus Christ. This implies partly that the Spirit has a status comparable to God the Father and the Son.[1355]

[1350] K. Lee, *Paul's Corporate Perspective 1 Corinthians with Special Reference to Εκκλησια as the New Covenant Community of God's Holy People: Towards a Corporate Interpretation* (PhD diss., University of Wales, 2004), 129.

[1351] R. B. Hays, *First Corinthians*, Interpretation (Louisville: John Knox, 1997), 96.

[1352] Cf. G. T. Montague, *Holy Spirit: Growth of a Biblical Tradition* (Peabody, MA: Hendrickson, 1976), 312–13.

[1353] J. R. Michaels, *1 Peter* (Waco, TX: Word, 1991), 11. Michaels sees in this passage not only a spiritual but also a moral connotation.

[1354] Schweizer, "πνευμα," 447. Schweizer notes that in this passage πνεύματος is used only as a subjective genitive. However, E. Schweizer, "The Spirit of Power: The Uniformity and Diversity of the Concept of the Holy Spirit in the New Testament", *Int* 6 (1952), 267. Schweizer argues that "in the Old Testament as in Judaism the Spirit is never regarded as necessary for salvation".

[1355] E. Best, *1 Peter* (Oliphants: Marshall, Morgan & Scott, 1971), 72. Best says that "we have here the beginnings of Trinitarian doctrine (cf. Matt 28:19; 1 Cor 12:4–6; 2 Cor 13:14; Eph 4:4–6; 2 Thess 2:13–14). The present formulation was not created in order to bring Father, Son and Spirit into parallel egalitarianism but has emerged from the description of the readers' Christian existence; this is true of the other expressions of Trinitarian doctrine in the New Testament (Matt 28:19, which gives the baptismal formula of Matthew's community, may be an exception). Thus both the order, Father, Spirit, Christ, and the description of the Second Person as Christ and not Son, arise from the context and are not indicative of pre-eminence or dignity".

The Spirit Theme in Hebrews

It has been noted that Hebrews has only a few references to the Spirit and the usage is complex. However, these references are significant despite the diverse use of the term. Like other New Testament writings, the Spirit in Hebrews is closely related to salvation based on the new exodus.

We have earlier pointed out that deliverance involves atonement and redemption. The phrase αἰωνίαν λύτρωσιν in Heb 9:12 is linked to the term πνεύματος αἰωνίου in Heb 9:14.[1356] Therefore, although the premise of the Day of Atonement can be seen in Heb 9:1–10, Heb 9 should be understood in the light of the Passover.

Therefore, I will examine how the Spirit is related to deliverance. And I will show what the main characteristic of the Spirit is. Then I will explore how the Spirit witnesses to his people to enable them to create unity and fellowship out of former enemies. We shall deal with these issues in turn.

The Spirit and Deliverance

In Hebrews the Holy Spirit is related to deliverance.[1357] In regard with deliverance, Heb 6:4–6 has been disputed among scholars. Some scholars have looked on Heb 6:4–6 as proof enough that one can lose one's deliverance.[1358] They say little more about the passage because it clearly says that those who fall away cannot be renewed "again unto repentance." However, in practice, they are found urging repentance on those who have "fallen away." This literally flies in the face of Heb 6:6.

Others argue that among the readers of the epistle, one group had to all appearances been incorporated into the church of Christ based on Heb 6:4–6, the other had failed to a degree.[1359] The latter made an external profession of

---

[1356] Koester, *Hebrews*, 410.

[1357] Heb 6:4; 9:14; 10:29–30.

[1358] R. Shank, *Life in the Son* (Springfield, MI: Westcott, 1961), 229–34; H. O. Wiley, *The Epistle to the Hebrews* (Kansas City, MO: Beacon Hill, 1959), 210; I. H. Marshall. *Kept by the Power: A Study of Perseverance and Falling Away* (Minneapolis: Bethany, 1975), 137–53; G. Osborne, "Soteriology in the Epistle to the Hebrews," in *Unlimited Grace*, ed. C. H. Pinnock (Minneapolis: Bethany, 1975), 144–66.

[1359] Hughes, *Hebrews*, 217; D. Mathewson, "Reading Heb 6:4–6 in Light of the Old Testament," *WTJ* 61 (1999), 224; S McKnight, "The Warning Passages of Hebrews: A Formal Analysis and Theological Conclusions," *Trinity Journal* 13 (1992), 48. McKnight says that the warnings in Heb 6:4–6 address the sin of apostasy, and that

acceptance after a thorough exposure to the gospel and consequently shared in the blessings of God's people through their fellowship with them. But later, because of persecution, they renounced their profession and returned to their former manner of life. Mathewson points out that they are not genuine believers or true members of the new covenant community.[1360] They had only become acquainted with certain blessings as corporate members of the community. However, the phrase "renew them again to repentance" (v. 6) suggests that these readers had at once time repented from their sins, which clearly implies they were believers.

Some think that the warning in Heb 6:4-6 relates to an apostasy that is impossible to commit.[1361] Hewitt believed those described in Heb 6:4-6 were obviously saved but the situation posed was hypothetical.[1362] Unfortunately, Hewitt was unaware that there is no "if" in the Greek at all. As a matter of fact, those described in Heb 6:4-6 had already fallen away. The term παραπεσόντας is an aorist participle, which is to be translated either as those who "fell away" or those "having fallen away". Their fall was a fact.

Others view that those described in 6:4-5 are genuine believers who became "dull of hearing" (5:11) and lapsed back into spiritual babyhood (5:13).[1363] They were warned not to "fall away" into a state of spiritual retrogression and

---

although believers experience the reality of salvation in the present, a failure to persevere to the end can result in the cessation of that reality. J. MacArthur Jr., *Hebrews* (Chicago, IL: Moody, 1983.), 136; S. D. Toussaint, "The Eschatology of the Warning Passages in the Book of Hebrews," *Grace Theological Journal* 3 (Spring 1982), 68. Cf. J. Owen looks at Heb 6:4-6 as a description of unregenerated people.

[1360] Mathewson, "Heb 6:4-6," 224.

[1361] D. Guthrie, *Hebrews* (Grand Rapids: Eerdmans. 1983), 145-47; Hewitt, *Hebrews*, 108, 111; H. A. Kent Jr., *The Epistle to the Hebrews* (Grand Rapids: Baker, 1972), 113; B. F. Westcott, *Hebrews*, 165; K. S. Wuest, "Hebrews Six in the Greek New Testament," *BibSac* 119 (January-March 1962): 52. Cf. Its main weakness is that if falling away is impossible then the warning is pointless.

[1362] Hewitt, *Hebrews*, 106-107. As therefore in v. 1 links 6:1-3 with v. 11-14 so for links verses 4-8 with these two former passages. The change of pronoun from "we" to "those", they and them suggests that these persons are different from the readers, and the phrase if they shall fall away is in favour of this being a hypothetical case.

[1363] J. C. Dillow, *The Reign of the Servant Kings: A Study of Eternal Security and the Finally Significance of Man* (Miami Springs, FL: Schoettle, 1992), 433-66; M. A. Eaton, *The Theology of Encouragement* (Carlisle: Paternoster, 1995), 212-17; R. G. Gromacki, *Stand Bold in Grace* (Grand Rapids: Baker, 1984), 112; R. T. Kendall, *Once Saved, Always Saved* (London: Hodder and Stoughton, 1983), 133-4; G. H. Lang, *The Epistle to the Hebrews* (London: Paternoster, 1951), 98-107; T. K. Oberholtzer. "The Thorn-Infested Ground in Hebrews 6:4-12," *BibSac* 145 (July-September, 1988), 319-28; J. D. Pentecost, *A Faith That Endures* (Grand Rapids: Discovery, 1992), 10-13, 20-22.

rebellion. Kendall points out that they were saved but had nothing to "accompany" their salvation—viz. no reward.[1364]

It seems that interpretation of the passage is not clear. Thus I will focus on the phrase "those who have shared (μετόχους) in the Holy Spirit." First, we need to know what the term μετόχους means. The derivative word of the term is introduced in two ways in the New Testament. It means either "very close participation" (attachment)[1365] or "a loose association with the other person".[1366] What is important is that someone is related to the other person. Secondly, it is important to know what we can share in the Holy Spirit. What is clear is that the phrase is related to the ministry of the Holy Spirit. We have earlier dealt with the Holy Spirit who relates deliverance. It means that a person partakes of saving benefit from the Spirit. Thus, "to share in the Holy Spirit" is to receive things that the Holy Spirit gives including deliverance.

With regard to "partakers of the Holy Spirit" in Heb 6:4, Bruce offers the opinion that they had not only been baptized and received the Eucharist, but had experienced the laying on of hands.[1367] Delitzsch argues that the partaking of the Holy Spirit is the same as the imposition of hands.[1368] Hughes points out that this kind of assumption must be treated with caution, by saying that there is no fixed pattern for the impartation of the Holy Spirit in Acts.[1369] Gleason points out that this corresponds to God's placing the Holy Spirit on the seventy elders to instruct the exodus generation concerning his power in Num

---

[1364] Kendall, *Once Saved*, 133.

[1365] R. C. Gleason, The Old Testament Background of the Warning in Hebrews 6:4-8," *BibSac* 155 (Jan–Mar, 1998), 77. For example, the cognate verb μετέσχεν in Heb 2:14 described how Jesus "partook" of flesh and blood in His incarnation. Regarding all other New Testament occurrences of μετεχω (1 Cor 9:10, 12; 10:17, 21, 30; Heb 5:13), Dunham observes, "In every case it refers to an actual participation, a real sharing, not a mere assent or acquiescence to something": D. A. Dunham, An Exegetical Examination of the Warnings in the Epistle to the Hebrews (Th.D. diss., Grace Theological Seminary, 1974), 163. Hewitt links Heb 6:4 with the forgiveness of sins and the gift of redemption: Hewitt, *Hebrews*, 106. Cf. Heb 3:14, where becoming partakers of Christ means sharing salvation which Christ brings.

[1366] Mathewson, "Heb 6:4-6," 224. Cf. In Luke 5:7, here μετόχοις are just people who were in the same job in the other boat. Also see Heb 1:9 quoted from Ps 45:7 and Eph 5:7.

[1367] Bruce, *Hebrews*, 121, cites Simon in Acts 8:9, 18. Simon believed when he heard the gospel, was baptized, attached himself to the evangelist whose preaching had convinced him, and presumably received the Spirit when apostolic hands were laid upon him.

[1368] F. J. Delitzsch, *Commentary on the Epistle to the Hebrews*, trans. T. L. Kingsbury (Edinburgh: T&T Clark, 1871), 381.

[1369] Hughes, *Hebrews*, 210.

11:16–30.[1370] It is also related to Israel's deliverance. Fishbane links the subjects of Heb 6:4–6 to the incident at the exodus.[1371] Holland links the Holy Spirit to the giving of the gifts to the Jews at the exodus in Exod 12:36, and later the gifts were essential for the building of the tabernacle and for the worship of Yahweh.[1372]

What is important is that "partakers of the Holy Spirit" refers to one of the principal benefits of God, which is deliverance. I have pointed out that the Holy Spirit is related to deliverance, and I dealt earlier with Heb 6:4–6 in relation to the new exodus motif. Thus the Spirit is the guide and protector of the eschatological exodus. That is, deliverance is experienced according to this passage by his people through the agency of the Holy Spirit.

Heb 9 begins with the tabernacle. Some scholars tried to understand this chapter in the light of the Day of Atonement. However, this chapter should be interpreted regarding the Holy Spirit in the light of deliverance. I earlier mentioned that the gifts given to the Israelites by the Egyptians are types of the gifts given by the Spirit to the church in her deliverance for the kingdom of darkness. These gifts are for the building of the spiritual temple, the church, so that Yahweh can be worshipped in Spirit and in truth. In Heb 9:14, furthermore, the Spirit is associated with the death of Jesus on the cross, where through the eternal Spirit (διὰ πνεύματος αἰωνίου), Christ offered himself without blemish to God.[1373] This passage speaks of the association of the Spirit with the death of Jesus. Thus the Spirit is seen by our writer as part of a whole redemptive movement initiated by the grace of God. The author appeals to a typological parallel between the Passover sacrifice and the Spirit.

Some commentators interpret the phrase as "through the eternal spirit," implying that Jesus offered himself to God by his own eternal spiritual nature.[1374] Westcott explains that "in virtue of His inseparable and unchangeable Divine Nature, Christ was Priest while He was victim also."[1375]

[1370] Gleason, "Hebrews 6:4–8," 77.
[1371] M. A. Fishbane, *Text and Texture: Close Readings of Selected Biblical Texts* (New York: Shocken, 1979), 121.
[1372] Holland, *Contours*, 145.
[1373] Cf. John 2:19–22. Jesus links the temple to himself.
[1374] B.F. Westcott, *Hebrews*, 263; T. Hewitt, *Hebrews*, 148; P. E. Hughes, *Hebrews*, 358–9.
[1375] Westcott, *Hebrews*, 264.

Hughes supports Westcott, saying that this interpretation accords well with the teaching earlier that Christ has become a priest "by the power of an indestructible life" (7:16) and that "he holds his priesthood permanently, because he continues for ever" (7:24).[1376] Hughes also understands that this teaching is related to the similitude of the priesthood of Melchizedek, who, as portrayed in Gen 14 and Ps 110, "has neither beginning of days nor end of life, but resembling the Son of God continues a priest forever" (Heb 7:3).[1377] In other words, one endowed with the eternal spirit could give to his sacrifice the character of eternal redemption. He concludes that a finite, temporal creature could never offer himself as a propitiation of eternal efficacy for the sins of the whole world. Denney identifies the "eternal spirit" of this passage with his very personality or his own power, of transcendental worth, which ensures for him eternal life and priesthood even by way of death.[1378]

Furthermore, Moffat points out that the phrase ζωῆς ἀκαταλύτου in 7:16 is replaced with πνεύματος αἰωνίου in 9:14.[1379] According to him, the term αἰωνίου closely describes πνεύματος (hence it has no article). He concludes that the sacrificial blood resulted in αἰωνίαν λύτρωσιν because it operated in an eternal order of spirit. The sacrifice of Jesus purified the inner personality (συνείδησιν) because it was the action of a personality, a sinless personality which belonged by nature to the order of the Spirit or eternity.[1380]

But others explain the expression as "through the eternal Spirit," suggesting Jesus gave himself to God by the help of the eternal Spirit.[1381] And this in fact is the reading found in the Vulgate, which doubtless reflects an early gloss and which inevitably fixed the "Catholic" understanding of the expression for centuries. It also coincides with the interpretation of numerous other

---

[1376] Hughes, *Hebrews*, 359.
[1377] Ibid.
[1378] J. Denney, *The Death of Christ* (London: Tyndale Press, 1951), 119.
[1379] J. Moffat, *A Critical and Exegetical Commentary on the Epistle to the Hebrews*, The International Commentary, ICC (Edinburgh: T&T Clark, 1924), 124.
[1380] Ibid. The implication (which underlies the entire epistle) is that even in his earthly life Jesus possessed eternal life. Hence what took place in time upon the cross, the writer means, took place really in the eternal, absolute order. Christ sacrificed himself ενφαπαξ, and the single sacrifice needed no repetition, since it possessed absolute, eternal value as the action of someone who belonged to the eternal order
[1381] D. A. Hagner, *Hebrews* (San Francisco, CA: Harper&Row, 1983), 117; D. Guthrie, *New Testament Theology* (Downers Grove, IL: Inter-Varsity, 1973), 568.

Protestant commentators; and, indeed, there is nothing inappropriate in the explanation that Christ, God's chosen one anointed with the Holy Spirit for the fulfillment of his mediatory high-priestly office (cf. Isa 42:1; 61:1; Mark 1:10; Luke 4:18), lived the perfect life and offered the perfect sacrifice in the power of that same Spirit.

Bruce asserts that "behind our author's thinking lies the portrayal of the Isaianic servant of the Lord" who "in the power of the Divine Spirit... accomplishes every phase of his ministry."[1382] When this servant is introduced for the first time, God says: "I have put my Spirit upon him" in Isa 42:1. It is in the power of the divine Spirit, accordingly, that the servant accomplishes every phase of his ministry, including the crowning phase in which he accepts death for the sin of his people, filling the paschal lamb's role. The Spirit again appeared at the climax of Jesus's earthly ministry, a very important moment in God's plan of salvation, and helped Jesus to offer himself as a perfect sacrifice to God.[1383] If this is the case, the meaning here is very significant. We earlier dealt with the Holy Spirit related to the Passover. That is, the Spirit has to be understood in the light of the Passover and he is related to deliverance in this passage.[1384] In Heb 10:29–30, furthermore, he who insults the Spirit of grace cannot avoid the judgment of God. Here it is also being hinted that the Spirit is linked to salvation.[1385]

The Spirit in Eschatology

Heb 3:7–11 quoted from Ps 95:7b–11 is introduced by the words Διό, καθὼς λέγει τὸ πνεῦμα τὸ ἅγιον ("Therefore, as the Holy Spirit is saying"). Some

---

[1382] F. F. Bruce, *Hebrews*, 205. However, Bruce understands Heb 9 in the light of the Day of Atonement.

[1383] G. F. Hawthorne, *The Presence & The Power: The Significance of the Holy Spirit in the Life and Ministry of Jesus* (Dallas: Word, 1991), 183–84. Hawthorne says that "it is thus possible to conclude that the Holy Spirit even now at the end of Jesus's life, as throughout the whole of it, was playing a tremendously vital part in his ministry. For the Spirit was the instrument, the agent, the enabler by whose power Jesus achieved his greatest work on earth, that of providing eternal redemption for all (Heb 9.12). Therefore, it is here in the passion of Jesus that one is struck full force with the overwhelming significance of the Holy Spirit in the life of Jesus".

[1384] Heb 9:14. "the blood of Christ related to the Holy Spirit cleanse our consciences from acts that lead to death, so that we may serve the living God. Therefore, salvation is cleansing our sins and restoration to his son."

[1385] A. Richardson, *An Introduction to the Theology of the New Testament* (London, SCM, 1958), 108; L. Goppelt, *Theology of the New Testament*, II (Grand Rapids: Eerdmans, 1981), 258. Both scholars point out that the context suggests that the Spirit is closely related to salvation. Cf. Schweizer, "πνευμα," 446. Schweizer says "10.29 is not to be construed as the cause of salvation; the Spirit here is a sign of the eschatological grace of God".

commentators have seen the καθὼς λέγει τὸ πνεῦμα τὸ ἅγιον as a reference to the Holy Spirit's authorship of the biblical text.[1386] The author of Hebrews clearly states, moreover, that the inspiration of the Old Testament was through the Holy Spirit. That is, the Spirit is the one who "speaks" in the Scriptures.[1387]

Emmrich also points out that the insertion of διό ("therefore") connects the forty years to εἶδον ("they saw") rather than to προσώχθισα ("I was angry") in 3:9b–10.[1388] Thomas supports Emmrich's note, saying that this use is obviously intentional.[1389] If Emmrich is right, the forty-year period is characterized by Israel experiencing God's gracious interventions on behalf of the nation: καὶ εἶδον τὰ ἔργα μου ("and they saw my works").[1390] That is, the length of Israel's opportunity of witnessing God's salvific activity heightened their responsibility to believe in God's promises and persevere on the trek to the holy land. In this case, then, the Holy Spirit's change of the wording has created a different meaning and so re-presents the speech of Ps 95 as a new oracle that transcends its original context. It is in this sense that we must understand the notion of "the Holy Spirit is saying."[1391]

To sum up, καθὼς λέγει τὸ πνεῦμα τὸ ἅγιον and the following citation from Ps 95 introduces the Holy Spirit as the voice of God. Here the Spirit as orator functions in decidedly eschatological terms. The Spirit exhorts the wandering people of God in an eschatological event.

In Heb 9:8 the Spirit "shows", concerning the regulations about the tabernacle, based upon Yahweh's directions for the manufacturing of the tent and its inventory recorded in Exod 25–26. At 9:6 the emphasis shifts to the priestly functions within the tabernacle, in particular to the high priest's entry into the

---

[1386] F. F. Bruce, *Hebrews*, 60; D. A. Hagner, *Hebrews*, 63; M. E. Isaacs, *The Concept of the Spirit: A Study of Pneuma in Hellenistic Judaism and Its Bearing on the New Testament* (London: Heythrop, 1976), 125.

[1387] M. Emmrich, "Pneuma in Hebrews: Prophet and Interpreter," *WTJ* 64 (2002), 57–8. Emmrich points out that the language of 3:7 more specifically bespeaks the role of πνεῦμα ἅγιον as orator with a powerful eschatological thrust.

[1388] Ibid., 58. Cf. In MT and LXX "forty years" belongs to the following clause ("Forty years long was I grieved with that generation"); but the author of Hebrews clearly attaches it to the words that precede by inserting διό ("Wherefore") before προσωχθισα ("I was displeased").

[1389] K. J. Thomas, "The Old Testament Citations in Hebrews," *NTS* 11 (1964–65), 307; cf. also H. J. B. Combrink, "Some Thoughts on the Old Testament Citations in the Epistle to the Hebrews," *Neot* 5 (1971), 30.

[1390] Emmrich, "Pneuma in Hebrews," 59.

[1391] Ibid.

inner sanctuary on the Day of Atonement (cf. Lev 16). Here πνεύματος τοῦ ἁγίου makes his appearance as the "revealer of secrets." The verb δηλόω (to show) is a suitable choice for conveying this notion of disclosure of something previously concealed.[1392] The use of δηλοῦντος in Heb 9:8 serves to bring out the character of the Spirit's exposition as a revelation to the audience. This disclosure of the deeper import of Scripture is an inherently eschatological one, inasmuch as it builds on the reality of the Christ event (cf. 9:11).

The author of the epistle also viewed πνεῦμα as the revealer of interpretative secrets in Heb 9:6–10. In other words, the author attributes a typological interpretative approach to the Spirit. Again, this use of Scripture is implicitly eschatological, since the impetus for this kind of pneumatic interpretation derives from the historical reality of Christ's advent. Thus the Spirit's agency is continuing interpretation of Scripture until the end of time.

Furthermore, the Spirit bears witness to us μαρτυρεῖ δὲ ἡμῖν καὶ τὸ πνεῦμα τὸ ἅγιον in Heb 10:15. It is of the new covenant which the Lord made in the last days. He also says: "I will put my laws on their hearts, and write them on their minds ... I will remember their sins and their lawless deeds no more." (Heb 10:16–17; cf. Jer 31:33–34).

In summary, the author's understanding of the Spirit is significant. For the author, the Spirit is associated with salvation, especially with the death of Jesus which was the culmination of his ministry. Also the author links the Spirit to the promise of eschatological salvation. Thus it is suggested that the author of Hebrews partly shares a common understanding of the Spirit with regard to eschatological salvation with the writer of other New Testament books.

The Spirit and His Corporative Presence

In 6:4–5, the readers are designated as those who "have been made partakers of the Holy Spirit." The key word here is μετόχους which Dunhan links to a sharing or an actual participation in something or with someone.[1393] Verbrugge pointed out that the reader's focus of attention is not on the individual Christian but upon the church as a corporate body, as a covenant

---

[1392] Ibid., 64. The verb (δηλόω) in Heb 9:8 has eschatological nuances. It is now that the full extent of the promised shaking has become clear. Cf. 1 Cor 3:13; 1 Pet 1:11–12; 2 Pet 1:14): Lane, Hebrews 9–13, 481–83.

[1393] D. A. Dunham, *Examination*, 163.

community.[1394] The Spirit addresses the community in Heb 6:4.[1395] The community consisted of those who experience πνεῦμα as the guiding power on their earthly pilgrimage by way of Spirit-inspired utterances and Spirit-induced wisdom.

Participation in the Spirit bespeaks a genuine experience of God's presence that his people have (and in fact need) on their journey of faith. It has been pointed out that the reader's focus of attention is upon the church as a corporate body, as a covenant community.[1396] Hanse showed that the word functions as a technical term for Christians who have responded to God's call of salvation.[1397] Emmrich points out that the phrase "partakers of the Holy Spirit" in Heb 6:4 corresponds to God's placing of Moses's spirit on the seventy elders to instruct their contemporaries during the wilderness trek (Num 11:16–30).[1398] This fits the force of the author's argument, for returning to Judaism would mean entering the realm of God's physical judgment.[1399]

In 6:4 "partakers of the Holy Spirit" speaks of a genuine experience of the Holy Spirit's presence that accompanies salvation. Gleason points out that this was just as important as the other spiritual benefits of the exodus as confirmed by its inclusion in other Old Testament accounts of Israel's deliverance (e.g. Neh 9:20; Isa 63:11, 14; Hag 2:5).

In Heb 9:14 the term ἡμῶν which is related with the Holy Spirit, is disputable. The textual evidence is rather evenly divided between ὑμῶν ("your") and ἡμῶν ("our"); the latter is the reading of ARV margin, RSV margin and NEB. The term ἡμῶν ("our") seems to be correct. Therefore, the author regards recipients of the epistle as one community.

[1394] V. D. Verbrugge, "Towards a New Interpretation of Hebrews 6: 4–6", *CTJ*, Vol. 15 (April, 1980), 72

[1395] P. Ellingworth, *The Epistle to the Hebrews*, The New International Greek Testament Commentary (Grand Rapids: Eerdmans, 1993), 512.

[1396] V. D. Verbrugge, "Interpretation", 72

[1397] H. Hanse, "μετέτω, μετοχῇ, μέτοχοι," in *TDNT* II, 830–32. Cf. Heb 3:1 ("partakers of a heavenly calling"), 3:14 ("partakers of Christ").

[1398] Emmrich, "Pneuma in Hebrews," 85. Like Israel during the exodus journey, according to Emmrich, the addressees of the Epistle to the Hebrews have experienced the Spirit's guiding agency in their midst.

[1399] F. D Pentecost, "The Apostles' Use of Jesus' Predictions of Judgment on Jerusalem in A.D. 70," in *Integrity of Heart, Skillfulness of Hands: Biblical and Leadership Studies in Honor of Donald K. Campbell*, ed. Charles H. Dyer and Roy B. Zuck (Grand Rapids: Baker, 1994), 140–41.

The phrase μαρτυρεῖ δὲ ἡμῖν καὶ τὸ πνεῦμα τὸ ἅγιον in 10:15 indicates that what is following is to be read as a direct address ἡμῶν ("to us"—a quotation involving the use of the first person) to the audience. The change from "the house of Israel" (LXX Jer 31:33) to "with them" (πρὸς αὐτοὺς) in 10:16 has clearly been governed by the author's concern to actualize the oracle: πρὸς αὐτοὺς parallels the ἡμῖν ("to us") in the quotation formula and allows for a more direct textual application to the readers than is the case in 8:8–12.[1400]

Conclusion

We have explored in this chapter what the role of the Holy Spirit is throughout the Bible in order to understand what the letter to the Hebrews depends on. The Spirit is associated with salvation. The Spirit participated in the event of the creation of God. The Spirit is implied to be a creative divine power that brings life to the formless and empty earth.

The Spirit is the eschatological Spirit. For all authors of the Bible the Spirit was the fulfillment of the eschatological promise. That is, the Spirit works among a greater number of people and different kinds of people to create a new faithful community of men serving God. The author of Hebrews shares in this tradition and clearly sees the work of the Spirit as fulfilling prophetic predictions and expectations to bring about the new exodus.

[1400] Emmrich, "Pneuma in Hebrews," 62.

Chapter 8: Conclusion

It has been claimed by some that the New Testament message was adapted to and influenced by Hellenism as the Christian community tried to win the Gentile world. However, we have seen that this understanding was established on a false presupposition as to the origin of the early Christian teaching and its development. Recent scholarship has shown how the New Testament writers preserved a primitive Jewish message and applied it to Christ. They interpreted the Old Testament in the light of the promised new exodus eschatological expectations that had been achieved in the person of Christ. This fulfillment in the New Testament was a major theme unifying the New Testament with the Old Testament. The imagery which the author of Hebrews uses explains access to, and entrance into, the holy of holies on the Day of Atonement. However, the ritual of the Day of Atonement is merged with that of the Passover. Hebrews speaks of Christ's sacrifice in terms of eternal redemption. Christ's sacrificial death offers all those who are called, the forgiveness of sin and restoration, that is, eternal redemption.

The primary goal of the incarnation was the Son's sharing in death, through which he nullified the devil's ability to enslave the children of God through the fear of death. In this instance death was not the consequence of rebellion. It was an expression of consecration to the will of God (Heb 10:5–7), with the result that Satan's ability to wield the power of death was rendered ineffective over the Christian community. The death of Christ was thus the appropriate and necessary means of delivering the people of God from the devil's tyranny and the fear of death. Christ Jesus has broken the power of death.

Deliverance in the Old Testament was introduced in the event of the exodus. In the exodus the main character was the paschal lamb that was killed on behalf of the firstborn. In the New Testament antitype, it speaks of Christ as the one whose death has brought about redemption. Christ's death was the act that identified him completely with his brothers and sisters in that there would be no aspect of human experience in which he had not shared. The redeemed appear as brothers of the Redeemer in Hebrews. In the same sense, Jesus is not ashamed to call them brothers. The expression ταπαιδια, "the children," contributed by the previous quotation stresses Christ's filial relationship. Thus, the corporate theme of the new exodus model exists in Hebrews.

Hebrews connects the term παρεπίδημοί ("sojourner") with the concept of a journey to a city to come as a pilgrimage. It emerges that there are six essential elements in Hebrews concerning the pilgrim motif: first, pilgrimage in Hebrews is linked to the Passover. It is based on Israel's memory of her deliverance from slavery in Egypt, her formation as the covenant people of Yahweh at Mount Sinai, Yahweh's gift of land to them by the dispossession of others. Thus, pilgrimage can be defined as a process based on Israel's memory of her deliverance from slavery in Egypt at Passover. Secondly, pilgrimage requires physical discipline. There are physical and spiritual perils. Sin gestures its pleasures of deceitful power to destroy faith. The way at times is a struggle. Thirdly, pilgrimage is to press on to maturity. Sin was committed by believers. Their immediate problem was a passive drifting away from the word of Christ, a persistent lethargy to press on to maturity. They faced the danger of falling into a permanent state of immaturity through a willful "once for all" refusal to trust God to deliver them from their present troubles. Thus the problem is the failure to grow and mature as a Christian. Fourthly, pilgrimage is corporate. The writer is not so much interested in each separate individual as he is in the congregation as a whole. Where he does address the individual, he addresses him, also in the Old Testament manner, as standing within the covenant community. Thus, the way the writer addressed them as "holy brethren, partakers of a heavenly calling," "partakers of Christ," and "dear friends," and his constant use of "we" and "us" indicates that they were a converted community. Fifthly, pilgrimage involves a journey to a sacred place. They have their eyes fixed on "the city which has foundations, whose builder and maker is God." This is the "real" city, for it is invisible. It is not merely a city: it is God's city, the place of the heavenly sanctuary where Jesus Christ is high priest at the right hand of the Majesty on high and where countless angels assemble in festal gathering.

The term διαθήκη was examined. The term customarily translates ברית, and means "covenant" rather than "testament." It is proposed that Hebrews followed the pattern of the prophecies of Ezekiel in pulling the sacrifices of the Day of Atonement into the orb of Passover celebration. Thus, it was a covenant inaugurated by the redemptive paschal sacrifice that atoned for the familiar sin. Hebrews tells us how Christ in the new covenant fulfils all the sacrificial requirements of the old covenant. The death of Christ was related to the sacrificial concept in the Passover. His blood is effective for redemption only by means of his sacrificial death which ratified or made legally valid the new covenant which was promised in Jer 31:31–34. That is, Christ is described as the mediator of the new covenant. The covenant of which Jesus speaks concerns the promise of the coming kingdom of God, the new covenant promised by Jeremiah. Jesus will give his own blood to affect the new covenant, the restoration of Israel, and the kingdom of God "having come in power."

It has been shown that in Hebrews there was a soteriological significance in the title "high priest." This concept of salvation can be shown in the order of Melchizedek, not the Aaronic priesthood. In the category of Melchizedek, we see that there is a union of the royal and priestly functions. Therefore, the scope of Christ's priestly ministry can be interchanged with that of the priestly king which is suggested by the term "intercede" and "save." The priestly king was instrumental in bringing about the new creation. The priestly king's uniqueness is that he is eternal and sinless. Because of these characteristics he is different from a Levitical priest. The fact that he is eternal carries the connotation of power, of having the dynamic of the eternal world and the factor of duration. With respect to those characteristics, the writer of Hebrews shows that the promised exalted priestly king supersedes the old priesthood. That is, Christ's priestly kingship belongs to a sphere that is eternal. His resurrection was a means to the restoration of our humanity and its exaltation with himself to the glory which is now his.

The leadership of the priestly king is such that it can be performed by the one who stands inside of the circle whose interest he serves. The author of Hebrews is acquainted with this uniqueness of the leadership of the priestly king. The implied unity between the priestly king and his people is examined throughout the epistle. The priestly king must be one with those whom he represents before God, and this is equally so with Christ as his people's high priest. In order to serve them in this capacity, he was obliged to become completely like his brethren—apart from sin. It is the priest/king who leads his people to their inheritance and is therefore part of the new exodus paradigm.

We have found that the Spirit participated in the event of Jesus's death on the cross, the climax of his earthly ministry. The new exodus is the act of new creation, bringing the chosen people to a new birth out of sin and slavery. As gifts were given to the Jews at the exodus, the Spirit was promised in the last days. He acts in the new creation. He is a source of salvation at the new exodus in the New Testament era. We have examined how for the author of Hebrews the Spirit is the key to Israel's eschatological future. The future was expected to be an epoch characterized by the abundant outpouring of God's Spirit. Therefore, the new kingdom will be established by the eschatological Spirit. Finally, the Spirit acts among believers corporately. The Spirit addresses the community. Participation in the Spirit implies a genuine experience of God's presence that his people have on their journey of faith. It has been pointed out that the reader's focus of attention is upon the church as a corporate body, as a covenant community. Thus, the way the writer addressed them as "partakers of the Holy Spirit" indicates that they were a converted community. As in the Old Testament, the Spirit acts as the believing communities' protector and guide during its new exodus pilgrimage.

Bibliography

Achtemeier, E. *Deuteronomy, Jeremiah, Proclamation Commentaries.* Philadelphia: Fortress, 1978.

Achtemeier, P. J., J. B. Green, and M. M. Thompson. *Introducing the New Testament: Its Literature and Theology.* Cambridge: Eerdmans, 2001.

Alexander, T. D. "The Passover Sacrifice." in *Sacrifice in the Bible.* Edited by R. T. Beckwith and M. J. Selman. Grand Rapids: Baker, 1995.

Allen, L. C. *Psalms 101–150.* World Biblical Commentary 21. Waco, TX: Word, 1983.

—————. *Ezekiel* 20–48. WBC 29. Waco, TX: Word, 1990.

Anderson, D. R. *The King-Priest of Psalm 110 in Hebrews.* Oxford: Peter Lang, 2001.

Anderson, G. W. "Israel's Creed: Sung, Not Signed." *Scottish Journal of Theology* 16 (1963): 277–85.

Anonymous. "A Lawyer Looks at Hebrews 9:15–17." *Evangelical Quarterly* Vol. XL (1968): 151–156.

Armerding, C. E. "Were David's Sons Really Priests?" Pages 75–86 in *Current Issues in Biblical and Patristic Interpretation.* Edited by G. F. Hawthorne. Grand Rapids: Eerdmans, 1975.

Attridge, H. W. *The Epistle to the Hebrews.* Philadelphia: Fortress, 1989.

Baker, D. W. *Nahum, Habakkuk and Zephaniah: Tyndale Old Testament Commentaries.* Leicester, IVP, 1988.

Baltzer, K. *The Covenant Formulary: In Old Testament, Jewish, and Early Christian Writings.* Translated by D. E. Green. Philadelphia: Fortress, 1971.

Balz, H. and G. Schneider, eds. *Exegetical Dictionary of the New Testament.* Vol. I. Edinburgh: T&T Clark, 1995.

Barrett, C. K. *A Commentary on the Epistle to the Romans.* London: SPCK, 1957.

—————. "The Background of Mark 10:45." Pages 1–18 in *New Testament Essays: Studies in Memory of T. W. Manson.* Edited by A. J. B. Higgins. Manchester: Manchester University Press, 1959.

—————. *The Holy Spirit and the Gospel Tradition.* London: SPCK, 1966.

—————. *The First Epistle to the Corinthians.* Black's New Testament Commentary. 2nd ed. London: A&C Black, 1971.

----------. *The Epistle to the Romans.* Black's New Testament Commentary. London: Black, 1991.

----------. *The Act of the Apostles.* International Critical Commentary. Edinburgh: T&T Clark, 1994.

Barth, K. *The Epistle to the Romans.* Translated by E. C. Hoskyns. London: Oxford University Press, 1965.

Bateman IV, H. W. *Early Jewish Hermeneutics and Hebrews 1:5–13.* New York: Peter Lang, 1997.

Bauer, W., W. F. Arndt, and F. W. Gingrich. *A Greek-English Lexicon of the New Testament and Other Early Christian Literature.* 2nd ed. Revised by F. W. Gingrich and F. W. Danker. Chicago: University of Chicago Press, 1979.

Baumgarten, J. M. "Sacrifice and Worship among the Jewish Sectarians of the Dead Sea (Qumran) Scrolls." *Harvard Theological Review* 46 (1953): 141–60.

Beasley-Murray, G. R. *John* 36. World Biblical Commentary. Dallas: Word, 1987.

Beckwith, R. T. "Cautionary Notes on the Use of Calendars and Astronomy to Determine the Chronology of the Passion." Pages 183–205 in *Chronos, Kairos, Christos.* Edited by J. Vardaman and E. M. Yamauchi. Winona Lake, IN: Eisenbrauns, 1989.

Bentzen, A. *King and Messiah.* London: Lutterworth, 1955.

Berkouwer, G. C. *Faith and Perseverance.* Translated by R. Knudsen. Grand Rapids: Eerdmans, 1958.

Best, E. "Discipleship in Mark: Mark 8:22–10:52." *Scottish Journal of Theology* 23 (1970): 323–37.

--------. *1 Peter.* London: Oliphants, 1971.

Betz, H. D. *Galatians: A Commentary on Paul's Letter to the Churches in Galatia.* Philadelphia: Fortress, 1979.

Betz, O. *What Do We Know About Jesus?* Translated by M. Kohl. London: SCM, 1968.

Black, M. *Romans.* The New Century Bible Commentary. London: Marshall, Morgan & Scott, 1973.

Block, D. I. *The Book of Ezekiel Chapter 25–48.* The New International Commentary on the Old Testament. Grand Rapids: Eerdmans, 1998.

----------. "My Servant David: Ancient Israel's Vision of the Messiah." Pages 17–56 in *Israel's Messiah in the Bible and The Dead Sea Scrolls*. Edited by R. S. Hess and R. M. D. Carroll. Grand Rapids: Baker, 2003.

Blomberg, C. L. *Matthew*. The New American Commentary. Nashville, TN: Broadman, 1992.

----------. "Holy Spirit." Page 345 in *Evangelical Dictionary of Biblical Theology*. Edited by W. A. Elwell. Grand Rapids: Baker, 1996.

Bock, D. L. *Proclamation from Prophecy and Pattern: Lucan Old Testament Christology*. Sheffield: Journal of the Study of the Old Testament Press, 1987.

Boismard, M. E. *Moses and Jesus: An Essay in Johannine Christology*. Minneapolis: Fortress, 1993.

Borsch, F. H. *The Son of Man in Myth and History*. Philadelphia: Westminster, 1967.

Bovon, F. *Luke the Theologian: Thirty-Three Years of Research 1950–1983*. Translated by K. McKinney. Alison Park, PA: Pickwick, 1987.

Bowker, J. W. "Psalm cx." *Vetus Testamentum* 17 (1967): 31–42.

Bowman, J. *The Gospel of Mark: The New Christian Jewish Passover Haggadah*. Leiden: Brill, 1965.

Boyce, M. "Zoroaster, Zoroastrianism." Page 1168–74 in *The Anchor Bible Dictionary* VI. Edited by D. N. Freedman. Garden City, NY: Doubleday, 1992.

Bratcher, R. G. "Biblical Words Describing Man: Breath, Life, Spirit." *The Banner of Truth* 34:2 (1983): 201–9.

Breck, J. *The Origins of Johannine Pneumatology*. Crestwood, IL: St. Valdimir's Seminary Press, 1991.

Briggs, C. A. "The Use of Ruach in the Old Testament." *Journal of Biblical Literature* 19 (1900): 132–45.

Bright, J. *The Kingdom of God*. Nashville, TN: Abingdon, 1953.

----------. "Isaiah." Pages 489–51 in *PCB*.

Brown, C. *The New International Dictionary of New Testament Theology*. Vol. l. Exeter: Paternoster, 1986.

Brown, F. S., R. Driver, and C. A. Briggs *A Hebrew and English Lexicon of the Old Testament*. Oxford: Clarendon, 1903.

Brown, R. *The Message of Hebrews.* BST. Leicester: IVP, 1982.

Brown, R. E. "The Messianism of Qumran." *Catholic Biblical Quarterly* 19 (1957): 57–82.

———. *The Gospel According to John.* Vol.1. Garden City, NY: Doubleday, 1970.

Brownlee, W. H. "Messianic Motifs of Qumran and the New Testament." *New Testament Studies* 3 (1956–57): 12–30.

Bruce, A. B. *Humiliation of Christ.* New York: Welford & Armstrong, 1876.

Bruce, F. F. *Commentary on the Epistles to the Ephesians and Colossians.* Grand Rapids: Eerdmans, 1957.

———. *Second Thoughts on the Dead Sea Scrolls.* Grand Rapids: Eerdmans, 1961.

———. *The Epistle to the Hebrews.* The New International Commentary on the New Testament. Grand Rapids: Eerdmans, 1964.

———. *The Epistle of Paul to the Romans: An Introduction and Commentary.* London: Tyndale, 1967.

———. "The Holy Spirit in the Acts of the Apostles." *Interpretation* 27 (1973): 166–83.

———. "The New Testament and Classical Studies." *New Testament Studies* 22 (1976): 229–242.

Brueggemann, W. *The Prophetic Imagination.* Philadelphia: Fortress, 1978.

Buchanan, G. W. *To the Hebrews,* Anchor Bible. Garden City, NY: Doubleday, 1972.

Bultmann, R. *The Theology of the New Testament.* Translated by K. Grobel. Vols. 1&2. London: SCM, 1968.

———. *The Gospel of John: A Commentary.* Translated by G. R. Beasley-Murray. Oxford: Blackwell, 1971.

———. *The History of the Synoptic Tradition.* Oxford: Blackwell, 1972.

Burney, F. C. "Christ as the ARCHE of Creation." *Journal of Theological Studies* 27 (1926): 160–77.

———. "The Book of Isaiah: A New Theory." *Church Quarterly Review* 75 (1912): 99–139.

Burrows, M. *More Light on the Dead Sea Scrolls.* New York: Viking, 1958.

Burton, E. de W. *A Critical and Exegetical Commentary on the Epistle to the Galatians.* International Critical Commentary. Edinburgh: T&T Clark, 1921.

Buse, I. "The Markan Account of the Baptism of Jesus and Isaiah LXIII." *Journal of Theological Studies* 7 (1956):74–5.

Buttenweiser, M. *The Psalms: Chronologically Treated with a New Translation.* New York: KTAV, 1969.

Buttick, G. A., ed. *The Interpreter's Dictionary of the Bible II.* Nashville, TN: Abingdon, 1962.

Cadbury, H. J. *The Making of Luke-Acts.* New York: Macmillan, 1927.

Callan, T. "Pauline Midrash: The Exegetical Background of Gal 3:19b." *Journal of Biblical Literature* 99 (1980): 549–67.

Calvin, J. *The Epistle of Paul The Apostle to the Hebrews and The First and Second Epistles of St Peter.* Translated by W. B. Johnston. Grand Rapids: Eerdmans, 1979.

Campbell, J. Y. "κοινωνια and its Cognates in the New Testament." *Journal of Biblical Literature* 51 (1932): 352–80.

Campbell, K. M. "Covenant or Testament: Heb 9:16–17 Reconsidered." Evangelical Quarterly 44 (1972): 107–111.

Carlston, C. E. "Eschatology and Repentance in the Epistle to the Hebrews." *Journal of Biblical Literature* 78 (1959): 296–302.

Carson, D. A. "Christological Ambiguities in the Gospel of Matthews." Pages 97–114 in *Christ the Lord.* Studies presented to Donald Guthrie. Edited by H. H. Rowden. Leicester: IVP, 1982.

Casey, J. "The Exodus Theme in the Book of Revelation against the Background of the New Testament." *Concilium* 189 (1987): 34–43.

Casey, J. M. "Eschatology in Heb 12:14–29." PhD. diss., Catholic University of Leuven, 1977.

Casey, M. *Aramaic Sources of Mark's Gospel.* Society for New Testament Studies Monograph. SNTSM 102. Cambridge: Cambridge University Press, 1998.

Casey, R. P. "The Earliest Christologies." *Journal of Theological Studies* 9 (1958): 253–77.

Charles, R. H. *Religious Development between the Old and New Testaments.* London: Oxford University Press, 1956.

Cheyne, T. K. *The Book of Psalms*. London: Kegan, Paul, Trench & Co., 1888.

Childs, B. S. *The Book of Exodus*. Louisville: Westminster, 1974.

Chilton, B. D. and P. Davies. "The Aqedah: A Revised Tradition History." *Catholic Biblical Quarterly* 40 (1978): 514–46.

Choi, M. H. "The Personality of the Holy Spirit in the New Testament with Special Reference to Luke-Acts." PhD diss., Lampeter University, 1999.

Clements, R. E. *Beyond Tradition-History: Deutero-Isaianic Development of First Isaiah's Themes*. Journal of the Study of the Old Testament 31. Sheffield: Journal of the Study of the Old Testament Press, 1985.

Cockerill, G. L. *The Melchizedek Christology in Heb 7:1–28*. Ann Arbor: University Microfilms International, 1979.

Cody, A. *A History of Old Testament Priesthood*. Rome: Pontifical Biblical Institute, 1969.

----------. *Ezekiel*. Old Testament Message 11. Wilmington, DE: Michael Glazier, 1984.

Cohn-Sherbok, D. *The Jewish Messiah*. Edinburgh: T&T Clark, 1997.

Collins, J. J. *The Scepter and the Star: The Messiahs of the Dead Sea Scrolls and Other Ancient Literature*. Garden City, NY: Doubleday, 1995.

Colson. F. H. and G. H. Whitaker. *Philo with an English Translation*. 10 Vols. London: Heinemann, 1919.

Combrink, H. J. B. "Some Thoughts on the Old Testament Citations in the Epistle to the Hebrews." *Neotestamentica* 5(1971): 22–36.

Conzelmann, H. *1 Corinthians*. Translated by J. W. Leitch. Hermeneia. Philadelphia: Fortress, 1975.

----------. *The Theology of St. Luke*. London: Faber, 1960.

Craigie, P. C. *The Book of Deuteronomy*. The New International Commentary on the Old Testament. Grand Rapids: Eerdmans, 1989.

Cranfield, C. E. B. *The Gospel According to St. Mark*. Cambridge Greek Testament Commentary. Cambridge: Cambridge University Press, 1959.

----------. *The Epistle to the Romans*. International Critical Commentary. Vols. 1&2. Edited by J. A. Emerton and C. E. B. Cranfield. Edinburgh: T&T Clark, 1975.

Cross, F. M. *The Ancient Library of Qumran and Modern Biblical Studies.* Garden City, NY: Doubleday, 1958.

---------------. *Canaanite Myth and Hebrew Epic: Essays in the History of the Religion of Israel.* Cambridge, MA: Harvard University Press, 1973.

Crossan, J. D. *The Historical Jesus: The Life of a Mediterranean Jewish Peasant.* Edinburgh: T&T Clark, 1991.

Cullmann, O. *The Christology of the New Testament.* London: SCM, 1963.

---------------. "Pauline Midrash." *Journal of Biblical Literature* 99 (1980): 555–67.

Dahood, M. *Psalms* III 101–150. Garden City, NY: Doubleday, 1970.

Daly, R. J. *The Origins of the Christian Doctrine of Sacrifice.* London: SCM, 1978.

---------------. *Christian Sacrifice: The Judaeo-Christian Background before Origen.* Catholic University of America Studies in Christian Antiquity 18. Washington: Catholic University of America Press, 1978.

Danby, H. *The Mishnah.* Oxford: Oxford University Press, 1933.

Davies, G. H. "Psalm 95." *Zeitschrift für die Alttestamentliche Wissenschaft* 85 (1973): 183–95.

Davies, W. D. *Paul and Rabbinic Judaism.* London: SPCK, 1955.

Dawsey, J. W. *Jesus' Pilgrimage to Jerusalem* (Auburn, AL: Auburn University Press, 1987).

De Jonge, M. "Jesus' Death for Others and the Death of the Maccabaean Martyrs." Pages 142–54 in *Text and Testimony.* Kampen: Kok, 1988.

---------------. *Jesus, the Servant-Messiah.* New Haven: Yale University Press, 1991.

De Lacy, D. R. "The Form of God in the Likeness of Men: A Study in Pauline Christology." Ph.D. diss., University of Cambridge 1974.

---------------. "Jesus as Mediator." *Journal of the Study of the New Testament* 29 (1987): 101–21.

De Vaux, R. *Ancient Israel: Its Life and Institutions.* 2 Vols. New York: McGraw-Hill, 1961.

Del Medico, H. E. "Melchisedech." *Zeitschrift für die Alttestamentliche Wissenschaft* 69 (1957): 160–70

Deissmann, G. A. *Light from the Ancient East.* Translated by L. R. M. Strachan. New York: Hodder & Stoughton, 1927.

Delitzsch, F. J. *Commentary on the Epistle to the Hebrews.* Translated by T. L. Kingsbury. Edinburgh: T&T Clark, 1871.

Denney, J. *The Death of Christ.* London: Tyndale Press, 1951.

Dennison, J. T. "The Exodus and the People of God." *The Banner of Truth* 171 (1977): 6–32.

Dey, L. K. K. *The Intermediary World and Patterns of Perfection in Philo and Hebrews.* Society of Biblical Literature Dissertation Series 25. Missoula, MT: Scholars, 1975.

Dibelius, M. *Jesus: A Study of Gospels.* Translated by C. B. Hedrick and F. C. Grant. London: SCM, 1963.

Dillow, J. C. *The Reign of the Servant Kings: A Study of Eternal Security and the Final Significance of Man.* Hayesville, NC: Schoettle, 1992.

Dodd, C. H. "Hilakesthai [Gr]: Its Cognates: Derivatives and Synonyms in the Septuagint." *Journal of Theological Studies* 32(1931): 352–360.

------------. *The Interpretation of the Fourth Gospel.* Cambridge: Cambridge University Press, 1953.

------------. *According to the Scriptures: The Sub-Structure of New Testament Theology.* New York, NY: Scribner's, 1953.

Droge, A. J., and J. D. Tabor. *A Noble Death: Suicide and Martyrdom among Christians and Jews in Antiquity.* San Francisco, CA: Harper, 1992.

Dumbrell, W. J. *Covenant & Creation.* Milton Keynes: Paternoster, 2013.

Dumm, D. R. "Passover and Eucharist." *Worship* 61 (2003): 199–208.

Dunn, J. D. G. *Baptism in the Holy Spirit: A Re-examination of the New Testament Teaching on the Gift of the Spirit in Relation to Pentecostalism Today.* London: SCM, 1970.

------------. *Baptism; Jesus and the Spirit: A Study of the Religious and Charismatic Experience of Jesus and the First Christians as Reflected in the New Testament.* London: SCM, 1975.

------------. *Christology in the Making: A New Testament Inquiry into the Origins of the Doctrine of the Incarnation.* Philadelphia: Westminster, 1980.

――――. "Some Reflections of Issues of Method: A Reply to Holladay and Segal." *Semeia* 30 (1984): 100–07.

――――. "Works of the Law and the Curse of the Law (Galatians 3:10–14)." *New Testament Studies* 31(1985): 523–42.

――――. *Romans 1–8*. World Biblical Commentary. Dallas: Word, 1988.

――――. *The Epistle to the Galatians*. London: A&C Black, 1993.

――――. *The Theology of Paul the Apostle*. Cambridge: Eerdmans, 1998.

Dunnill, J. *Covenant and Sacrifice in the Letter to the Hebrews*. Cambridge: Cambridge University Press, 1992.

Durham, J. I. *Exodus*. World Biblical Commentary 3. Waco, TX: Word, 1987.

Eaton, J. H. *Kingship and the Psalm*. London: SCM, 1975.

Eaton, M. A. *A Theology of Encouragement*. Carlisle: Paternoster, 1995.

Egelkraut, H. L. *Jesus' Mission to Jerusalem: A Redaction Critical Study of the Travel Narrative in the Gospel of Luke, Lk 9.51–19.48*. Frankfurt: Lang, 1976.

Eichrodt, W. *Theology of the Old Testament*. Vols. 1&2. Translated by J. A. Baker. London: SCM, 1969.

――――. *Ezekiel: A Commentary*. Translated by C. Quin. Philadelphia: Westminster, 1970.

Ellingworth, P. "Just like Melchizedek." *The Banner of Truth* 28 (1977): 236–39

――――. *The Epistle to the Hebrews*. New International Greek Commentary. Edited by I. H. Marshall and W. W. Gasque. Grand Rapids: Eerdmans, 1993.

Ellis, E. E. "A Note on 1 Cor. 10.4." *Journal of Biblical Literature* 76 (1957): 53–56.

Ellison, H. L. "The Prophecy of Jeremiah." *Evangelical Quarterly* XXXVII No. 1 (Jan-March, 1965): 25–35.

Elwell, W. A., ed. *Evangelical Dictionary of Biblical Theology*. Grand Rapids: Baker, 1996.

Emerton, J. A. "The Riddle of Genesis." *Vetus Testamentum* 21 (1971): 403–39.

Emmrich, M. "Pneuma in Hebrews: Prophet and Interpreter." *Westminster Theological Journal* 64 (2002): 55–71.

Engnell, I. *A Rigid Scrutiny: Critical Essays on the Old Testament.* Translated by J. T. Willis. London: SPCK, 1970.

Enns, P. E. "Creation and Re-creation: Psalm 95 and Its Interpretation in Hebrews 3:1–4.13." *Westminster Theological Journal* 55 (1993): 255–80.

Evans, C. A. *Mark 8.27–16.20.* World Biblical Commentary 34B. Nashville, TN: Thomas Nelson, 2001.

Evans, C. F. "The Central Section of Saint Luke's Gospel." in *Studies in the Gospels: Essays in Memory of R. H. Lightfoot.* Edited by D. E. Nineham. Oxford: Blackwell, 1955.

Fairbairn, P. *An Exposition of Ezekiel.* Grand Rapids: Sovereign Grace, 1971.

Fanning, B. M. "A Theology of Hebrews." Pages 369–415 in *A Biblical Theology of the New Testament.* Edited by R. B. Zuck. Chicago: Moody, 1994.

Farmer, W. R. *Maccabees, Zealots, and Josephus: An Inquiry into Jewish Nationalism in the Greco-Roman Period.* New York: Columbia University Press, 1956.

Fee, G. D. *The First Epistle to the Corinthians.* The New International Commentary on the New Testament. Grand Rapids: Eerdmans, 1987.

----------. *God's Empowering Presence: The Holy Spirit in the Letters of Paul.* Peabody, MA: Hendrickson, 1994.

Flender, H. *St Luke: Theologian of Redemptive History.* London: SPCK, 1967.

Filson, F. V. "The Journey Motif in Luke-Acts." Pages 68–77 in *Apostolic History and the Gospel: Biblical and Historical Essays Presented to F. F. Bruce on the 60th Birthday.* Edited by W. W. Gasque and R. P. Martin. Exeter: Paternoster, 1970.

Fiorenza, E. S. "Cultic Language in Qumran and in the NT." *Catholic Biblical Quarterly* 38 (1976): 159–77.

Fishbane, M. A. *Text and Texture: Close Readings of Selected Biblical Texts.* New York: Shocken, 1979.

----------. *Biblical Interpretation in Ancient Israel.* Oxford: Oxford University Press, 1985.

Fitzmyer, J. A. *The Gospel According to Luke* 1–9. Anchor Bible Vol. 28. Garden City, NY: Doubleday, 1981.

----------. *The Gospel According to Luke* 10–24. Anchor Bible Vol. 28a. Garden City, NY: Doubleday, 1985.

----------. *The Semitic Background of the New Testament.* Grand Rapids: Eerdmans, 1997.

Fohrer, G. *Introduction to the Old Testament.* Translated by D. Green. London: SPCK, 1970.

France, R. T. "Chronological Aspects of "Gospel Harmony." *Vox Evangelica* 16 (1986): 33–59.

Fredrick, G. "Rethinking the Role of the Holy Spirit in the Lives of Old Testament Believers." *Trinity Journal* 9 (1988): 81–104.

Freedman, D. N. ed. *The Anchor Bible Dictionary* I–VI. Garden City, NY: Doubleday, 1992.

Garrett, S. R. "Exodus from Bondage: Luke 9.31 and Acts 12:1–24." *Catholic Biblical Quarterly* 52 (1990): 656–80.

Gartner, B. *The Temple and the Community in Qumran and the New Testament: A Comparative Study in the Temple Symbolism of the Qumran Texts and the New Testament.* Society for New Testament Studies Monograph Series 1. Cambridge: Cambridge University Press, 1965.

Gehman, H. S. "The Covenant: Old Testament Foundation of the Church." *Theology Today*, 7 (1950–51): 26–41.

Gerlach, K. *The Ante Nicene Pascha: A Rhetorical History.* Leuven: Peeters, 1998.

Giblet, J. "Baptism in the Spirit in the Acts of the Apostles." *One in Christ* 10:2 (1974): 162–71.

Glasson, T. F. *Moses in the Fourth Gospel.* London: SCM, 1963.

----------. "What is Apocalyptic?" *New Testament Studies* 27 (1980): 98–105.

Gleason, R. C. "The Old Testament Background of the Warning in Hebrews 6.4–8." *Bibliotheca Sacra* 155 (Jan–Mar 1998): 62–91.

----------. "The Old Testament Background of Rest in Hebrews 3:7–4.11." *Bibliotheca Sacra* 157 (July–September, 2000): 281–303.

Golding, P. *Covenant Theology: The Key of Theology in Reformed Thought and Tradition.* Fearn: Christian Focus, 2004.

Goppelt, L. *Theology of the New Testament.* Vols. I&II. Grand Rapids: Eerdmans, 1981.

---------. Typos: *The Typological Interpretation of the Old Testament in the New.* Translated by D. H. Madvig. Grand Rapid, MI: Eerdmans, 1982.

Gosling, F. A. "An Unresolved Problem of Old Testament Theology." *Expository Times* 106:8 (1995): 234–7.

Gottwald, N. *The Hebrew Bible: A Socio-Literary Introduction.* Philadelphia: Fortress, 1985.

Gray, G. B. *Sacrifice in the Old Testament: Its Theory and Practice.* Oxford: Clarendon, 1925.

Grabbe, L. L. *Wisdom of Solomon.* Sheffield: Sheffield Academic Press, 1997.

Graham, C. "The Mediator of the Covenant." *Reformed Theological Journal* 11 (1995): 25–32.

Grech, P. "The 'Testimonia' and Modern Hermeneutics." *New Testament Studies* 19 (1972–73): 318–24.

Green, J. B. *The Gospel of Luke.* The New International Commentary on the New Testament. Cambridge: Eerdmans, 1997.

Greenberg, M. *Ezekiel* 1–20. Garden City, NY: Doubleday, 1983.

Grogan, G. W. "The New Testament and the Messianism of the Book of Isaiah." *Scottish Bulletin of Evangelical Theology* Vol. 3 (1985): 1–12.

Gromacki, R. G. *Stand Bold in Grace.* Grand Rapids: Baker, 1984.

Grudem, W. "Perseverance of the Saints: A Case Study from Hebrews 6:4–6 and the Other Warning Passages in Hebrews." Pages 133–82 in *The Grace of God, the Bondage of the Will.* Edited by T. R. Schreiner and B. A. Ware. Grand Rapids: Baker, 1995.

Guelich, R. A. *Mark* 1–8.26.34A. World Biblical Commentary. Dallas: Word, 1989.

Gundry, R. H. *The Use of the Old Testament in St. Matthew's Gospel.* Novum Testamentum, Supplement 18. Leiden: Brill, 1967.

---------. *Mark: A Commentary on His Apology for the Cross.* Grand Rapids: Eerdmans, 1993.

---------. *Matthew: A Commentary on His Handbook for a Mixed Church Under Persecution.* Grand Rapids: Eerdmans, 1994.

Guthrie, D. *New Testament Theology.* Downers Grove, IL: Inter-Varsity Press, 1973.

---------. *The Letter to the Hebrews.* Grand Rapids: Eerdmans, 1983.

Hafemann, S. J. *2 Corinthians*. The NIV Application Commentary. Grand Rapids: Zondervan, 2000.

Hagner, D. A. *Hebrews*. San Francisco: Harper & Row, 1983.

----------------. *Matthew 1–13, 33A*. World Biblical Commentary. Dallas: Word, 1993.

Haran, M. *The Passover Sacrifice: Studies in the Religion of Ancient Israel*. Vetus Testamentum Supplement 22. Leiden: Brill, 1972.

Hasel, G. F. *The Remnant: The History and Theology of the Remnant Idea from Genesis to Isaiah*.Berrien Springs, MI: Andrews University Press, 1972.

Hastings, J., ed. *Dictionary of the Bible II*. Edinburgh: T&T Clark, 1904.

Hatch, E. *Essays in Biblical Greek*. London: Oxford University Press, 1989.

Hay, D. M. *Glory At the Right Hand: Psalm 110 in Early Christianity*. Society of Biblical Literature Monograph Series 18. Edited by R. A. Kraft. New York: Abingdon, 1973.

Hays, R. B. *First Corinthians. Interpretation*. Louisville: John Knox, 1997.

-------------. *The Faith of Jesus Christ: The Narrative Substructure of Galatians 3:1–4.11*. Grand Rapids: Eerdmans, 2002.

Hawthorne, G. F. *The Presence &The Power: The Significance of the Holy Spirit in the Life and Ministry of Jesus*. Dallas: Word, 1991.

Head, P. M. "The Self-Offering and Death of Christ as a Sacrifice in the Gospels and the Acts of the Apostles." Pages 111–29 in *Sacrifice in the Bible*. Edited by R. T. Beckwith and M. J. Selman. Grand Rapids: Baker, 1995.

Heinemann, J. *Prayer in the Talmud*. New York: De Gruyter, 1977.

Helyer, L. R. "The Prototokos Title in Hebrews." Studies in Biblical Theology (1977): 16–22.

Hengel, M. *The Son of God*. Philadelphia: Fortress, 1976.

-------------. *Atonement: The Origins of the Doctrine in the New Testament*. London: SCM, 1981.

-------------. *Studies in Early Christology*. Edinburgh: T. & T. Clark, 1995.

Hewitt, T. *The Epistle to the Hebrews*. London: The Tyndale Press, 1973.

Hill, D. *Greek Words and Hebrew Meanings: Studies in the Semantics of Soteriological Terms*. London: Cambridge University, 1967.

Hodges, Z. C. "A Dispensational Understanding of Acts 2." Pages 167–82 in *Issues in Dispensationalism*. Edited by W. R. Wills and J. R. Master. Chicago: Moody Press, 1994.

Holladay, W. L. *Jeremiah 1: A Commentary on the Book of the Prophet Jeremiah*. Philadelphia: Fortress, 1986.

Holland, T. S. *The Paschal—New Exodus Motif in Paul's Letter to the Romans with Special Reference to its Christological Significance*. PhD diss., University of Wales, 1996.

----------------. *Contours of Pauline Theology: A Radical New Survey of the Influences on Paul's Biblical Writings*. Fearn: Christian Focus, 2004.

Holtzmann, J. *Lehrbuch der Neutestamentlichen Theologie*. Vol. 2. 2nd ed. Tubingen, 1911.

Hooker, M. D. *Jesus and the Servant: The Influence of the Servant Concept of Deutero-Isaiah in the New Testament*. London: SPCK, 1959.

Horsley R. A. and Hanson, J. S. *Prophets and Messiahs: Popular Movements at the Time of Jesus*. Edinburgh: T & T Clark, 1985.

Horsley, R. A. *The Liberation of Christmas*. New York: Crossroad, 1989.

Horton Jr, F. L. *The Melchizedek Tradition: A Critical Examination of the Sources to the Fifth Century A. D. and in the Epistle to the Hebrews*. Society for New Testament Studies Monograph Series 30. Cambridge: Cambridge University Press, 1976.

Howard, J. K. "Passover and Eucharist in the Fourth Gospel." Scottish Journal of Theology 20 (1967): 329–37.

----------------. "Christ our Passover: A Study of the Passover-Exodus Theme in 1 Cor." Evangelical Quarterly 41 (1969):97–108.

Hughes, J. J. "Hebrews 9.15ff and Galatians 3:15ff: A Study in Covenant Practice and Procedure." *Novum Testamentum* 21 (1979): 27–96.

Hughes, P. E. *A Commentary on the Epistle to the Hebrews*. Grand Rapids: Eerdmans, 1977.

Isaacs, M. E. *The Concept of the Spirit: A Study of Pneuma in Hellenistic Judaism and Its Bearing on the New Testament*. London: Heythrop, 1976.

----------------. *Sacred Space: An Approach to the Theology of the Epistle to the Hebrews*. Sheffield: Sheffield Academic Press, 1992.

Jenni, E. and Westermann, C., eds. *Theological Lexicon of the Old Testament.* Translated by M. E. Biddle. Peabody: Hendrickson, 1997.

Jeremias, J. *The Eucharistic Words of Jesus.* London: SCM, 1966.

----------. *New Testament Theology: The Proclamation of Jesus.* New York: Charles Scribner's Sons, 1971.

Jewett, R. *Letter to Pilgrims: A Commentary on the Epistle to the Hebrews.* New York: Pilgrim, 1981.

Johnson, A. R. *Sacral Kingship in Ancient Israel.* Cardiff: University of Wales, 1955.

----------. "Hebrew Conceptions of Kingship." Pages 204–35 in *Myth, Ritual, and Kingship.* Edited by S. H. Hooke. Oxford: Clarendon, 1958.

Johnsson, W. G. "Defilement and Purgation in the Book of Hebrews." PhD diss., Vanderbilt University, 1973.

----------. "The Pilgrimage Motif in the Book of Hebrews." *Journal of Biblical Literature* 97 (1978): 239–51.

Johnston, E. D. "The Old Testament Background of Matthew 2–4." *Mishkan* 6/7 (1987), 20–26.

Jonas, H. *The Gnostic Religion.* Beacon Hill: Beacon Press, 1958.

Jones, P. R. "The Figure of Moses as a Heuristic Device for Understanding the Pastoral Intent of Hebrews." *Review & Expositor* 76 (1979): 95–107.

Kaiser, O. *Isaiah* 13–39. Philadelphia: Westminster Press, 1974

Kaiser Jr., W. C. *Toward Rediscovering the Old Testament.* Grand Rapids: Zondervan, 1987.

Käsemann, E. *Essays on New Testament Themes.* London: SCM, 1964.

----------. *Romans.* Grand Rapids: Eerdmans, 1980.

----------. *The Wandering People of God: An Investigation of the Letter to the Hebrews.* Translated by R. A. Harrisville and I. L. Sandberg. Minneapolis: Augsburg Publishing House, 1984.

Kaufmann, Y. *The Religion of Israel, From Its Beginnings to the Babylonian exile,* trans. and abridged by Moshe Greenberg (Chicago: University of Chicago Press, 1960).

Keck, L. E. "What Makes Romans Tick." Pages x–x in *Pauline Theology.* Vol. 3. Edited by D. M. Hay and E. E. Johnson. Minneapolis: Fortress, 1995.

Keesmaat, S. C. "Exodus and The Intertextual Transformation of Tradition in Romans 8.14-30." *Journal of the Study of the New Testament* 54 (1994): 29-56.

Kelber, W. H. *The Kingdom in Mark*. Philadelphia: Fortress, 1974.

Kelly, J. N. D. *The Pastoral Epistles; I & II Timothy, Titus*. London: Adam & Charles Black, 1963.

Kendall, R. T. *Once Saved, Always Saved*. London: Hodder & Stoughton, 1983.

Kennedy, H. A. A. *Paul's Conception of the Last Things*. London: Hodder &Stoughton, 1904.

Kent Jr, H. A. *The Epistle to the Hebrews*. Grand Rapids: Baker, 1972.

Keown, G. L., Scalise, P. J. and Smothers, T. G. *Jeremiah 1-25*. World Biblical Commentary 26. Dallas: Word, 1991.

--------------. *Jeremiah 26-52*. World Biblical Commentary 27. Dallas: Word, 1995.

Kim, S. *Johannine Theology*. Seoul: Durano, 2001.

Kistemaker, S. J. *Hebrews*. New Testament Commentary. Welwyn: Evangelical Press, 1984.

Kittel, G., ed., *Theological Dictionary of the New Testament*. Translated by G. W. Bromiley and D. Litt. Vols. I-IX. Grand Rapids: Eerdmans, 1964.

Klijn, A. F. J. "The Study of Jewish Christianity." *New Testament Studies* 20 (1974): 419-31.

Kline, M. *Treaty of the Great King*. Grand Rapids: Eerdmans, 1963.

Knox, W. L. "The 'Divine Hero' Christology of the New Testament." Harvard Theological Review 41 (1948): 229-49.

Koehler, L. and Baumgartner, W. *The Hebrew and Aramaic Lexicon of the Old Testament 3*. Translated by M. E. J. Richardson. Leiden: Brill, 1996.

Koolhaas, A. A. *Theocratie en Monarchie in Israel*. Wageningen: Veenman, 1957.

Kramer, W. *Christ, Lord, Son of God*. London: SCM Press, 1966.

Kuhn, K. G. "The Two Messiahs of Aaron and Israel." Pages 54-64 in *The Scrolls and the New Testament*. Edited by K. Stendahl. New York: Harper and Row, 1957.

Lacocque, A. *The Book of Daniel*. London: SPCK, 1979.

Ladd, G. E. *A Theology of the New Testament*. London: Lutterworth Press, 1974.

Lake, K. "Baptism." Pages 379–390 in *Encyclopaedia of Religion and Ethics*. Edited by J. Hastings II. New York : Charles Scribner's Sons, 1915.

Lane, W. *Hebrews 1–8*. World Biblical Commentary. Dallas: Word, 1991.

----------. *Hebrews 9–13*. World Biblical Commentary. Dallas: Word, 1991.

Lang, F. "Abendmahl und Bundesgednke im NT." *Ev Th* 35(1975): 524–38.

Lang, G. H. *The Epistle to the Hebrews*. London: Paternoster, 1951.

Langton, E. *Essentials of Demonology: A Study of Jewish and Christian Doctrine*. London: Epworth Press, 1949.

Lee, K. "Paul's Corporate Perspective 1 Corinthians with Special Reference to Εκκλησια as the New Covenant Community of God's Holy People: Towards a Corporate Interpretation." PhD. diss., University of Wales, 2004.

Lehne, S. *The New Covenant in Hebrews*. Sheffield: Sheffield Academic Press, 1990.

Levenson, J. D. *The Death and Resurrection of the Beloved Son: The Transformation of Child Sacrifice in Judaism and Christianity*. New Haven: Yale University, 1993.

Levison, J. R. "Did the Spirit Withdraw from Israel? An Evaluation of the Earliest Jewish Data." *New Testament Studies* 43(1997): 35–57.

Liddell, H. G. and Scott, R. "αυλαρχης." in *A Greek-English Lexicon*. New York: Harper, 1883.

Lightfoot, J. B. *Saint Paul's Epistle to the Galatians*. 10th ed. 1890. Reprinted London: Macmillan, 1986.

Lincoln, A. T. "Pilgrimage and the New Testament." Pages 31–56 in *Explorations in a Christian Theology of Pilgrimage*. Edited by C. Bartholomew & F Hughes. Aldershot: Ashgate, 2004.

Lindars, B., *New Testament Apologetics: The Doctrinal Significance of the Old Testament Quotations*. Philadelphia: Westminster, 1961.

--------------. "Re-Enter the Apocalyptic Son of Man." *New Testament Studies* 22 (1975–76): 52–72.

--------------. *New Testament Theology, The Theology of The Letter to the Hebrews*. Cambridge: Cambridge University Press, 1991.

Longenecker, R. N. "The Melchizedek Argument of Hebrews: A Study in the Development and Circumstantial Expression of New Testament Thought." Pages 161–

85 in *Unity and Diversity in the New Testament Theology.* Grand Rapids: Eerdmans, 1978.

----------------------. *Galatians.* World Biblical Commentary 41. Dallas: Word Books, 1990.

Longman III, T. *How to Read the Psalms.* Leicester: Inter-Varsity Press, 1988.

Longman III, T. and Reid, D. G. *God is a Warrior, Studies in Old Testament Biblical Theology.* Grand Rapids: Zondervan, 1995.

MacArthur Jr., J. *Hebrews.* Chicago: Moody, 1983.

Manek, J. "The New Exodus in the Book of Luke." *Novum Testamentum* (1957): 8–23.

Manson, W. *The Epistle to the Hebrews: An Historical and Theological Reconsideration.* London: Hodder & Stoughton, 1951.

--------------. *The Epistle to the Hebrews: Christ's and Ours.* Richmond: John Knox, 1958.

Marcus, J. *The Way of the Lord: Christological Exegesis of the Old Testament in the Gospel of Mark.* Kentucky: Westminster John Knox, 1992.

Marshall. I. H. *The Gospel of Luke: A Commentary on the Greek Text.* Exeter: Paternoster, 1978.

------------------. *Kept by the Power of God.* Rev. ed. Carlisle: Paternoster, 1995.

Martyn, J. L. *Galatians: A New Translation with Introduction and Commentary.* London: The Anchor Bible, 1997.

Martin, R. P. "Some Reflections on New Testament Hymns." Pages 37–49 in *Christ the Lord: Studies Presented to D. Guthrie.* Edited by H. H. Rowden. Leicester: IVP, 1982.

Mathewson, D. "Reading Heb 6:4–6 in Light of the Old Testament." *Westminster Theological Journal* 61 (1999): 209–225.

McComiskey, T. E. *The Covenants of Promises.* Nottingham: IVP, 1985.

McConville, J. G. *Law and Theology in Deuteronomy.* Sheffield: Journal of the Study of the Old Testament Press, 1984.

--------------------. "Pilgrimage and 'Place': An Old Testament View." Pages 16–32 in *Explorations in a Christian Theology of Pilgrimage.* Edited by C. Bartholomew & F. Hughes. Cornwall: Ashgate, 2004.

McCown, W. G. "ΟΛΟΓΟΣΤΗΣΠΑΡΑΚΛΗΣΕΩΣ: The Nature and Function of the Hortatory Sections in the Epistle to the Hebrews." PhD diss., Union Theological Seminary, Richmond, 1970.

———. "Holiness in Hebrews." *WesThJ* 16 (1981): 58–78.

Mckay, C. "The Argument of Hebrews." *Church Quarterly Review* 168 (1967): 325–38.

Mckenzie, J. L. "Royal Messianism" *Catholic Biblical Quarterly* 19 (1957): 25–52.

McKnight, S. "The Warning Passages of Hebrews: A Formal Analysis and Theological Conclusions." *Trinity Journal* 13 (1992): 21–59.

McLean, B. H. *The Cursed Christ: Mediterranean Expulsion Rituals and Pauline Soteriology.* Journal of the Study of the New Testament Supplement 126. Sheffield: Sheffield Academic, 1996.

McNamara, M. *Intertestamental Literature.* Wilmington, DE: Michael Glazier, 1983.

———. *Palestinian Judaism and the New Testament.* Good News Studies 4. Wilmington, DE: M. Glazier, 1983.

Meeks, W. A. *The Prophetic-King: Moses traditions and the Johannine Christology.* Leiden: E. J. Brill, 1967.

———. *The First Urban Christian: The Social World of the Apostle Paul.* New Haven: Yale University Press, 1983.

Melugin, R. F. *The Formation of Isaiah 40–55.* New York: Walter de Gruyter, 1976.

Menzies, R. P. *The Development of Early Christian Pneumatology with Special Reference to Luke-Acts.* Journal of the Study of the New Testament Supplement 54. Sheffield: Journal of the Study of the Old Testament Press, 1991.

Merrill, A. L. "Pilgrimage in the Old Testament-A Study in Cult and Tradition." *Ecumenical Institute for Advanced Theological Studies* (1974): 45–62.

Merrill, E. H. *Kingdom of Priests: A History of Old Testament Israel.* Grand Rapids: Eerdmans, 1975.

———. "Pilgrimage and Procession: Motifs of Israel's Return." in *Israel's Apostasy and Restoration.* Edited by A. Gileadi. Grand Rapids: Baker, 1988.

———. "Royal Priesthood: An Old Testament Messianic Motif." *Bibliotheca Sacra* 150(Jan–Mar, 1993): 50–61.

Mettinger, T. N. D. *King and Messiah: The Civil and Sacral Legitimation of the Israelite Kings.* Lund: Gleerup, 1976.

Meyer, B. F. *The Aims of Jesus*. London: SCM, 1979.

──────────. "The Expiation Motif in the Eucharistic Words: A Key to the History of Jesus." *Gregorianum* 69 (1988): 61–87.

Michaels, J. R. *1 Peter*. Waco: Word, 1991.

Milgrom, J. "Sin-Offering or Purification-Offering?" *Vetus Testamentum* 21 (1971): 237–39.

Moessner, D. P. "Luke 9:1–50: Luke's Preview of the Journey of the Prophet Like Moses of Deuteronomy." *Journal of Biblical Literature* 102/4 (1983): 575–605.

Moffatt, J. *A Critical and Exegetical Commentary on the Epistle to the Hebrews*. International Critical Commentary. Edinburgh: Clark, 1924.

Montague, G. T. *Holy Spirit: Growth of a Biblical Tradition*. Peabody: Hendrickson, 1976.

Montgomery, J. A. *A Critical and Exegetical Commentary on the Book of Daniel*. International Critical Commentary. Edinburgh: T&T Clark, 1927.

Moo, D. J. *Romans 1–8*. The Wycliffe Exegetical Commentary. Chicago: Moody Press, 1991.

Moore, G. F. *Judaism in the First Centuries of the Christian Era*. Vols. I–III. Cambridge: Harvard University Press, 1927.

Morgenstern, J. "The Suffering Servant: A New Solution." *Vetus Testamentum* 11 (1961): 292–320.

Morris, L. *The Apostolic Preaching of the Cross: A Study of the Significance of Some New Testament Terms*. London: The Tyndale Press, 1972.

──────────. *The Atonement: Its meaning and Significance*. Leicester: IVP, 1983.

Motyer, A. *Look to the Rock*. London: IVP, 1996.

Moule, C. F. D. *An Idiom-Book of New Testament Greek*. 2nd ed. Cambridge: Cambridge University Press, 1959.

──────────. *The Gospel According to Mark*. Cambridge Bible Commentary on the New English Bible. Cambridge: Cambridge University Press, 1965.

Mounce, W. D. *Pastoral Epistle*. World Biblical Commentary 46. Nashville: Thomas Nelson, 2000.

Mowinckel, S. *The Sacral Kingship*. Leiden: Brill, 1959.

———————. *The Psalms in Israel's Worship.* Vol. 1. New York: Abingdon, 1963.

Muilenburg, J. *The Book of Isaiah: Chapters 40–66.* IB. New York: Abingdon, 1956.

Murray, J. *The Epistle to the Romans.* The New International Commentary on the New Testament. Grand Rapids: Eerdmans, 1980.

Nairne, A. *Epistle of Priesthood.* Edinburgh: Clark, 1913.

Nanos, M. *The Mystery of Romans.* Philadelphia: Fortress, 1997.

Nel, P. J. "Psalm 110 and the Melchizedek Tradition." *JNSL* 22 (1996): 1–14.

Neve, L. *The Spirit of God in the Old Testament.* Tokyo: Seibunsha, 1972.

Nicole, R. "C. H. Dodd and the Doctrine of Propitiation." *WThJ* 17 (1955): 117–57.

Nixon, R. E. *The Exodus in the New Testament.* London: SPCK, 1963.

Nolan, B. M. *The Royal Son of God: The Christology of Matthew 1–2 in the Setting of the Gospel.* Orbis biblicus et Orientalis 23. Gottingen: Vandenhoeck & Ruprecht, 1979.

North, C. R. *The Suffering Servant in Deutero-Isaiah: An Historical and Critical Study.* London: Oxford University Press, 1956.

Norton, F. O. *A Lexicographical and Historical Study of DIATHEKE.* Chicago: Chicago University Press, 1908.

Oberholtzer, T. K. "The Warning Passage in Hebrews Part 2: The Kingdom Rest in Hebrews 3:1–4:13." *Bibliotheca Sacra* (April 1988): 185–196.

———————. "The Warning Passage in Hebrews Part 3: The Thorn-Infested Ground in Hebrews 6:4–12." *Bibliotheca Sacra* 145 (July–Sep 1988): 319–28.

———————. "The Warning Passages in Hebrews Part 4: The Danger of Willful Sin in Hebrews 10:26–39." *Bibliotheca Sacra* 145 (October 1988): 410–419.

O'Collins, G. G. "Salvation." in The Anchor Bible Dictionary, Edited by D. N. Freedman. 6 Vols. (Garden City, NY: Doubleday, 1992).

Oesterley, W. O. E. *The Psalms.* Vol. 2. New York: Macmillan, 1939.

Ollenburger, B. C. *Zion, City of the Great King.* Journal of the Study of the Old Testament Supplement 41. Sheffield: Journal of the Study of the Old Testament Press, 1987.

O'Neill, J. C. *Paul's Letter to the Romans.* London: Penguin, 1975.

Osborne, G. "Soteriology in the Epistle to the Hebrews." Pages 144-66 in *Unlimited Grace.* Edited by C. H. Pinnock. Minneapolis: Bethany, 1975.

Packer, J. I. "Reviews and Notices." Evangelical Quarterly 31 (1959): 225-27.

——————. *Among God's Giants: The Puritan Vision of the Christian Life.* London: Kingsway, 1991.

Pao, D. W. *Acts and the Isaianic New Exodus.* Grand Rapids: Baker, 2000.

Paul. M. J. "The Order of Melchizedek (Ps 110.4 and Heb 7.3)." *Westminster Theological Journal* 49 (1987): 195-211.

Payne, J. B. *Theology of the Older Testament.* Grand Rapids: Eerdmans, 1962.

Pederson, D. J. "The Pilgrim Gospel: The Old Testament as a Theology of Journey." *TTJ* II (November 1990): 150-61.

Pentecost, J. D. *Things to Come: A Study in Biblical Eschatology.* Grand Rapids: Zondervan, 1965.

——————. *A Faith That Endures: The Book of Hebrews Applied to the Real Issues of Life.* Grand Rapids: Discovery, 1992.

——————. "Kadesh-Barnea in the Book of Hebrews." in *Basic Theology Applied: A Practical Application of Basic Theology in Honor of Charles C. Ryrie and His Work.* Edited by Wesley and Elaine Willis and John and Janet Master. Wheaton: Victor, 1995.

Pentecost, F. D. "The Apostles' Use of Jesus' Predictions of Judgment on Jerusalem in A.D. 70." Pages 139-56 in *Integrity of Heart, Skillfulness of Hands: Biblical and Leadership Studies in Honor of Donald K. Campbell.* Edited by Charles H. Dyer and Roy B. Zuck. Grand Rapids: Baker, 1994.

Perkins, P. *Gnosticism and the New Testament.* Minneapolis: Fortress, 1993.

Perrin, N. "The Literary Gattung 'Gospel'—Some Observations." *Expository Times* 82 (1970): 4-7.

Petersen, D. L. *Haggai and Zechariah 1-8.* Philadelphia: Westminster, 1984.

Peterson, D. G. "The Situation of the Hebrews 5.11-6.12." *Reformed Theological Review* 35 (1976): 14-21.

——————. "An Examination of the Concept of 'Perfection' in the Epistle to the Hebrews." PhD diss., University of Manchester, 1978.

——————. *Hebrews and Perfection: An Examination of the Concept of Perfection in the Epistle to the Hebrews.* Cambridge: Cambridge University Press, 1982.

Petrement, S. *A Separate God: The Christian Origins of Gnosticism.* Translated by C. Harrison. London: Longman and Todd, 1990.

Pfeiffer, C. F. *The Dead Sea Scrolls and the Bible.* Grand Rapids: Baker, 1969.

Pfeiffer. R. H. *The Literature and Religion of the Pseudepigrapha.* Nashville: Abingdon, 1952).

Piper, O. "Unchanging Promises: Exodus in the New Testament." *Interpretation* 11 (1957): 3–22.

Porteous, N. W. *Daniel: A Commentary.* London: SCM, 1965.

----------------. "The Theology of the Old Testament." Pages x–x in *Peake's Commentary on the Bible.* Edited by M. Black, H. H. Rowley, and A. S. Peake. London: Routledge, 2001.

Pursiful, D. J. *The Cultic Motif in the Spirituality of the Book of Hebrews.* Lampeter: Mellen Biblical Press, 1993.

Pusey, E. B. *The Minor Prophets.* Vol. VI. London: SPCK, 1907.

Rad, G. von. *Old Testament Theology.* Translated by D. M. G. Stalker. Vol. 2. New York: Harper, 1965.

-----------. "There Still Remains a Rest for the People of God: An Investigation of a Biblical Conception." Pages x–x in *The Problem of the Hexateuch and Other Essays.* New York: McGraw-Hill, 1966.

-----------. *Genesis. Old Testament Library.* London: SCM, 1987.

Rea, J. "The Personal Relationship of Old Testament Believers to the Holy Spirit." Pages x–x in *Essays on Apostolic Themes: Studies in Honor of Howard M. Ervin Presented to him by Colleagues and Friends on his Sixty-Fifth Birthday.* Edited by P. Elbert. Peabody: Hendrickson, 1985.

Reumann, J. "The Gospel of the Righteousness of God in Pauline Interpretation in Rom 3:21–31." *Interpretation* 20(1966): 42–52.

Rice, G. E. "Apostasy as a Motif and Its Effect on the Structure of Hebrews." *Andrews University Seminary Studies*, Vol. 23 (Spring 1985): 29–35.

Richardson, A. *An Introduction to the Theology of the New Testament.* London: SCM, 1958.

Ridderbos, H. *Paul: An Outline of His Theology.* Translated by J. R. de Witt. Grand Rapids: Eerdmans, 1975.

Ringgren, H. *Religions of the Ancient Near East.* Philadelphia: Westminster, 1973.

Robertson, O. P. *The Christ of the Covenant.*Phillipsburg, NJ: Presbyterian and Reformed Publishing Co, 1980.

Rogers Jr, C. L. and Rogers III, C. L., eds. *The New Linguistic and Exegetical Key to the Greek New Testament.* Grand Rapids: Zondervan, 1998.

Rose, W. H. *Zemah and Zerubbabel: Messianic Expectations in the Early Postexilic Period.* Journal of the Study of the Old Testament Supplement 304. Sheffield: Sheffield Academic Press, 2000.

Rowland, C. C. *The Open Heaven: A Study of Apocalyptic in Judaism and Early Christianity.* New York: Crossroad, 1982.

Rowley, H. H. "Melchizedek and Zadok." Pages 161–72 *in Festschrift für A. Bertholet.* Edited by W. Baumgartner et al. Tubingen: Mohr, 1950.

Rudolph, K. *Gnosis: The Nature and History of an Ancient Religion.* Edited by R. M. Wilson. Translated by P. W. Coxon and K. H. Kuhn. Edinburgh: T&T Clark, 1983.

Ryken, L., Wilhoit, J. C., and Longman III, T., eds. *Dictionary of Biblical Imagery.* Leicester: IVP, 1998.

Ryrie, C. C. *The Basis of the Premillennial Faith.* New York: Loizeaux, 1953.

Sabourin, L. *Priesthood: A Comparative Study.* Leiden: Brill, 1973.

―――――――. *The Psalms: Their Origin and Meaning.* New York: Alba House, 1974.

―――――――. *Christology: Basic Tools in Focus.* New York: Alba House, 1984.

Sanday, W., and Headlam, A. C. *The Epistle to the Romans.* 5th ed. International Critical Commentary. Edinburgh: T&T Clark, 1975.

Sanders, E. P. *Paul, the Law, and the Jewish People.* Minneapolis: Fortress, 1971.

―――――――. *Paul and Palestinian Judaism: A Comparison of Patterns of Religion.* London: SCM, 1977.

―――――――. *Jesus and Judaism.* Philadelphia: Fortress, 1985.

―――――――. *Judaism: Practice and Belief. 63 BCE–66 CE.* London: SCM, 1992.

―――――――. *Paul, Past Masters Series.* Oxford: Oxford University Press, 1996.

Sanders, J. A. "From Isaiah 61 to Luke 4" Pages 75–106 in *Christianity, Judaism and other Greco-Roman Cults.* Vol. 1. Edited by J. Neusner. Leiden: Brill, 1975.

Schmidt, W. H. *Old Testament Introduction.* Translated by Matthew J. O'Connell. New York: Crossroad, 1984.

Schneck, K. *Isaiah in the Gospel of Mark.* I–VII BDS 1. Vallejo, CA: BIBAL, 1994.

Schneider, B. "The Corporate Meaning and Background of 1 Cor 15, 45b—ὁ ἔσχατος Ἀδὰμ εἰς πνεῦμα ζῳοποιοῦν" *Catholic Biblical Quarterly* 29(1967): 144–161.

Schoemaker, W. R. "The Use of Ruach in the Old Testament, and of πνευμα in the New Testament." *Journal of Biblical Literature* 23 (1904): 13–25.

Scholer, J. M. *Proleptic Priests: Priesthood in the Epistle to the Hebrews.* Journal for the Study of the New Testament Supplement Series 49. Sheffield: Journal of the Study of the Old Testament Press, 1991.

Schoors, A. *I am God Your Savior.* SupVT 24. Leiden: Brill, 1973.

Schreiner, J. "Fuhrung-Theme der Heilsgeschichte im Alten Testament.' *BZ* 5 (1961): 2–18.

Schweizer, E. *The Letter to the Colossians.* Translated by A. Chester. London: SPCK, 1982.

———. "The Spirit of Power: The Uniformity and Diversity of the Concept of the Holy Spirit in the New Testament." *Interpretation* 6 (1952): 259–78.

Scott, J. M., ed. *Exile: Old Testament, Jewish and Christian Conceptions.* Leiden: Brill, 1997.

Selman, M. J. "Sacrifice in the Ancient Near East" Pages 88–104 in *Sacrifice in the Bible.* Edited by R. T. Beckwith and M. J. Selman. Grand Rapids: Paternoster, 1995.

Seters, J. V. "The Place of the Yahwist in the History of Passover and Massot." *Zeitschrift für die Alttestamentliche Wissenschaft* 95 (1983): 167–82.

Shank, R. *Life in the Son.* Springfield: Westcott, 1961.

Shedd, W. G. T. *A Critical and Doctrinal Commentary on the Epistle to the Romans.* Minneapolis: Fortress, 1978.

Shepherd Jr. W. H. *The Narrative Function of the Holy Spirit as a Character in Luke-Acts.* Society of Biblical Literature Dissertation Series 43. Atlanta: Scholars Press, 1994.

Shogren, G. S. "Presently Entering the Kingdom of Christ: The Background and Purpose of Col 1:12–14." *Journal of Evangelical Theological Society* 51 (1988): 173–80.

Silva, M. "Perfection and Eschatology in Hebrews." *Westminster Theological Journal* 39 (1976): 60–71.

Simpson, E. K. *Words Worth Weighing in the Greek New Testament.* London: Tyndale Press, 1946.

----------------. "The Vocabulary of The Epistle To The Hebrews, II." Evangelical Quarterly 18 (July 1946): 187–90.

Smalley, S. S. "The Atonement in the Epistle to the Hebrews." Evangelical Quarterly 33 (January–March 1961): 36–43.

----------------. *John: Evangelist and Interpreter.* Exeter: Paternoster, 1978.

Smith, R. L. *Micah–Malachi.* World Biblical Commentary. Waco, TX: Word, 1984.

Snaith, N. H. "The Spirit of God in Jewish Thought." Pages 11–37 in *The Doctrine of the Holy Spirit: Four Lectures.* London: Epworth Press, 1937.

Sowers, S. *The Hermeneutics of Philo and Hebrews: A Comparison of the Interpretation of the Old Testament in Philo Judaeus and the Epistle to the Hebrews.* Basel Studies of Theology I. Richmond, VA: John Knox, 1965.

Stalker, D. M. *Ezekiel, Introduction and Commentary.* London: SCM, 1968.

Stauffer, E. *New Testament Theology.* 5th ed. Translated by J. Marsh. London: SCM, 1955.

Stibbs, A. M. *The Meaning of the Word "Blood" in Scripture.* The Tyndale New Testament Lecture 1947. London: Tyndale Press, 1948.

Stott, J. *Only One Way: The Message of Galatians.* London: Inter-Varsity Press, 1968.

--------. *The Cross of Christ.* London: Inter-Varsity Press, 1986.

Strauss, M. L. *The Davidic Messiah in Luke-Acts: The Promise and its Fulfillment in Lukan Christology.* Sheffield: Sheffield Academic Press, 1995.

Stronstad, R. *The Charismatic Theology of St. Luke.* Peabody: Hendrickson, 1984.

Stuhlmacher, P. *Reconciliation Law and Righteousness.* Essays in Biblical Theology. Philadelphia: Fortress, 1986.

Stuhlmueller, C. *Creative Redemption in Deutero-Isaiah.* AnBib 43. Rome: Pontifical Biblical Institute, 1970.

Surburg, R. F. *Introduction to the Intertestamental Period.* St. Louis: Concordia, 1975.

Swartley, W. M. "The Structural Function of the Term "Way" (Hodos) in *Mark's Gospel.*" Pages 73–86 in *The New Way of Jesus: Essays Presented to Howard Charles.* Edited by W. Klassen. Kansas: Faith and Life Press, 1980.

Swetnam, J. "Sacrifice and Revelation in the Epistle to the Hebrews: Observations and Surmises on Hebrews 9:26." *Catholic Biblical Quarterly* (1968): 227–34.

―――――. *Jesus and Isaac: A Study of the Epistle to the Hebrews in the Light of the Aqedah.* Rome: Biblical Institute Press, 1981.

Talbert, C. H. "The Myth of the Descending-Ascending Redeemer in Mediterranean Antiquity." *New Testament Studies* 22 (1976): 418–40.

Tate, M. E. "The Comprehensive Nature of Salvation in Biblical Perspective." *Evangelical Review of Theology* 23 (1999): 205–21.

Tatum, W. B. "The Epoch of Israel: Luke 1-2 and the Theological Plan of Luke-Acts." *New Testament Studies* 13 (1966–67): 184–95.

Taylor, V. *Jesus and His Sacrifice: A Study of the Passion Sayings in the Gospels.* London: Macmillan, 1937.

―――――. "The Spirit in the New Testament." Pages 140–62 in *The Doctrine of the Holy Spirit.* London: Epworth, 1937.

―――――. *The Gospel According to Mark.* Grand Rapids: Baker, 1981.

Teicher, J. L. "The Damascus Fragments and the Origin of the Jewish-Christian Sect." *Journal of Jewish Studies* 2 (1950): 115–43.

Telford, A. P. "An Interpretation of the Enthronement Psalm." Th.M. diss. Dallas Theological Seminary, 1969.

Thomas, K. J. "The Old Testament Citations in Hebrews." *New Testament Studies* 11 (1964–65): 303–25.

Thompson, J. W. *The Letter to the Hebrews.* Austin: Sweet, 1971.

―――――. "That Which Cannot be Shaken: Some Metaphysical Assumptions in Hebrews 12:27." *Journal of Biblical Literature* 94 (1975): 580–87.

―――――. "The Conceptual Background and Purpose of the Midrash in Hebrews VII." *Novum Testamentum* 19 (1977): 209–23.

Thomson. J. E. H. "Apocalyptic Literature." Page 176 in *International Standard Bible Encyclopedia* I. Edited by G. W. Bromiley. Grand Rapids: Eerdmans, 1979.

Thornton, T. C. G. "The Meaning of αιματεκχυσια in Heb IX. 22." *Journal of Theological Studies* 15 (1964): 63–65.

Toussaint, S. D. "The Eschatology of the Warning Passages in the Book of Hebrews." *Grace Theological Journal* 3 (Spring 1982): 67–80.

Tromp, N. J. *Primitive Conceptions of Death and the Nether World in the Old Testament.* Rome: Pont. Bib. Inst., 1969.

Trumper, V. L. *The Mirror of Egypt in the Old Testament.* London: Marshall Morgan & Scott, 1911.

Turner, M. "Jesus and The Spirit in Lucan Perspective." *TB* 32 (1981): 3–42.

----------. "Spiritual Gifts: Then and Now." *VoxEv* 15 (1985): 7–64.

----------. *Power from on High: The Spirit in Israel's Restoration and Witness in Luke-Acts.* Sheffield: Sheffield Academic Press, 1996.

----------. *The Holy Spirit and Spiritual Gifts Then and Now.* Cumbria: Paternoster, 1996.

Ullmann, S. *The Principles of Semantics.* 2nd ed. New York: Philosophical Library, 1957.

Van der Meer, W. "Psalm 110: A Psalm of Rehabilitation?" In *The Structural Analysis of Biblical and Canaanite Poetry.* Edited by W. van der Meer and J. C. de Moor. Journal of the Study of the Old Testament Supplement 74. Sheffield: Journal of the Study of the Old Testament Press, 1988.

Vawter, B. *On Genesis: A New Reading.* Garden City, NY: Doubleday, 1977.

Verbrugge, V. D. "Towards a New Interpretation of Hebrews 6.4–6." Calvin Theological Journal 15 (April 1980): 61–73.

Vermes, G. "Redemption & Genesis xxii: The Binding of Isaac and the Sacrifice of Jesus." Pages 193–227 in *Scripture and Tradition in Judaism Haggadic Studies.* Leiden: Brill, 1961.

Verseput, D. J. "The Davidic Messiah and Matthew's Jewish Christianity." Society of Biblical Literature Abstracts and Seminar Papers 34 (1995): 102–16.

Vos, G. *The Teaching of the Epistle to the Hebrews.* Phillipsburg, NJ: The Presbyterian & Reformed Publishing Company, 1975.

----------. *Redemptive History and Biblical Interpretation: The Shorter Writings of Geerhardus Vos.* Phillipsburg, NJ: Presbyterian and Reformed Publishing, 1980.

Walker, P. W. L. *Jesus and the Holy City: New Testament Perspectives on Jerusalem.* Grand Rapids: Eerdmans, 1996.

Wallace, D. B. *Greek Grammar Beyond the Basics.* Grand Rapids: Zondervan, 1996.

Watts, J. D. W. *Isaiah* 1–33. World Biblical Commentary 24. Waco, TX: Word, 1985.

——————. *Isaiah 34–66*. World Biblical Commentary 25. Waco, TX: Word, 1987.

Watts, R. E. "Consolation or Confrontation? Isaiah 40–55 and the Delay of the New Exodus." *Tyndale Bulletin* 41 (1990): 31–59.

——————. *Isaiah's New Exodus in Mark*. Grand Rapids: Baker, 1997.

——————. "The New Exodus" Pages 37–53 in *What Does It Mean to be Saved?* Edited by J. G. Stackhouse Jr. Grand Rapids: Baker, 2002.

Webb, W. J. *Returning Home: New Covenant and Second Exodus as the Context for 2 Corinthians 6.14–7.1*. Sheffield: Journal of the Study of the Old Testament, 1993.

Weinfield, M. "Jeremiah and the Spiritual Metamorphosis of Israel." *Zeitschrift für die Alttestamentliche Wissenschaft* 88 (1976): 17–56.

Weiser, A. *The Psalms*. Philadelphia: Westminster, 1962.

Wellhausen, J. *Prolegomena to the History of Israel*. Edinburgh: A&C Black, 1985.

Wenham, G. J. *Leviticus*. The New International Commentary on the Old Testament. Grand Rapids: Eerdmans, 1979.

——————. *Genesis 1–15*. World Biblical Commentary. Dallas: Word, 1987.

Westcott, B. F. *The Epistle to the Hebrews: The Greek Text with Notes and Essays*. 3rd ed. London, Macmillan, 1903.

Westermann, C. *Isaiah 40–66*. London: SCM, 1969.

——————. *Genesis 12–36: A Commentary*. Minneapolis: Augsburg, 1981.

Whitloch, G. E. "The Structure of Personality in Hebrew Psychology: The Implications of the Hebrew View of Man for Psychology of Religion." *Interpretation* 14:1 (1960): 3–13.

Wiley, H. O. *The Epistle to the Hebrews*. Kansas City: Beacon Hill, 1959.

Williams, S. K. *Jesus' Death as Saving Event: The Background and Origin of a Concept*. HDR 2. Missoula: Scholars Press, 1975.

——————. "The 'Righteousness of God' in Romans." *Journal of Biblical Literature* 99 (1980): 241–90.

Williamson, H. G. M. "The Concept of Israel in Transition." Pages x–x in *The World of Ancient Israel*. Edited by R. E. Clements. Cambridge: Cambridge University Press, 1989.

Williamson, R. *The Epistle to the Hebrews*. London: Epworth, 1965.

----------. *Philo and the Epistle to the Hebrews.* Leiden: Brill, 1970.

----------. "Hebrews 4:15 and the Sinlessness of Jesus." *Expository Times* 86 (1974–75): 4–8.

Wilson, M. "The Promise of the 'Seed' in the New Testament and the Targums." *Journal of the Study of the New Testament* 5 (1979): 2–20.

Wink, W. *Naming the Powers: The Language of Power in the New Testament.* Vol. I. Philadelphia: Fortress, 1984.

Wisse, F. "Prolegomena to the Study of the New Testament and Gnosis." Pages 142–53 in *The New Testament and Gnosis:* Essays in Honour of Robert M. Wilson. Edited by A. H. B. Logan and A. J. M. Wedderburn. Edinburgh: T&T Clark, 1983.

Witherington III, B. *Grace in Galatia: A Commentary on St Paul's Letter to the Galatians.* Edinburgh: T&T Clark, 1998.

Wood, L. J. *The Holy Spirit in the Old Testament.* Grand Rapids: Zondervan, 1976.

Wright, N. T. "The Paul of History and the Apostle of Faith." *Tyndale Bulletin* 29 (1978): 61–88.

----------. "The Messiah and the People of God." PhD diss., Oxford University, 1980.

----------. "The Meaning of περιαμαρτιας in Romans 8:3." In *Studia Biblica* 1978 III. Edited by E. A. Livingstone. Journal of the Study of the New Testament Supplement 3. Sheffield: Journal of the Study of the Old Testament, 1980.

----------. "Justification: The Biblical Basis and its Relevance for Contemporary Evangelicalism." Pages 13–37 in *The Great Acquittal.* Edited by G. Reid. London: Fount, 1980.

----------. "Theology and Poetry in Colossians 1:15–20." *New Testament Studies* 36 (1990): 444–60.

----------. *The Climax of the Covenant.* Edinburgh: T&T Clark, 1991.

----------. *The New Testament and The People of God.* London: SPCK, 1992.

----------. *Jesus and the Victory of God.* London: SPCK, 1996.

----------. *The Way of the Lord: Christian Pilgrimage Today.* London: SPCK, 1999.

Wuest, K. S. "Hebrews Six in the Greek New Testament." *Bibliotheca Sacra* 119 (January–March 1962): 45–53.

Yadin, Y. "The Dead Sea Scrolls and the Epistle to the Hebrews." *Scripta Hurosolymitana* iv (1958): 36–55.

Yahuda, A. S. *The Accuracy of the Bible.* London: Heinemann, 1934.

Yamauchi, E. M. *Pre-Christian Gnosticism: A Survey of the Proposed Evidences.* London: Tyndale Press, 1973.

Young, E. J. *The Book of Isaiah.* Grand Rapids: Eerdmans, 1972.

Zimmerli, W. *A Commentary on the Book of the Prophet Ezekiel. Chapters 1–24.* Translated by J. D. Martin. Philadelphia: Fortress, 1979.

──────────. *A Commentary on the Book of The Prophet Ezekiel. Chapters 25–48.* Translated by J. D. Martin. Philadelphia: Fortress, 1983.

www.ingramcontent.com/pod-product-compliance
Lightning Source LLC
Chambersburg PA
CBHW070233230426
43664CB00014B/2284